Clean Energy Diplomacy

This book systematically constructs theories of clean energy diplomacy in the context of the changing international strategic landscape of energy and climate. It aims to explain the scientific connotations and innovative significance of clean energy diplomacy.

The book focuses on analyzing how the development of renewable energy, including wind, solar, and biomass, plays out in the evolution of the international power system. It also touches upon energy efficiency and complementary energy technologies. This book integrates the studies of traditional energy and environmental diplomacy and defines its connotations and extensions from the perspective of major country diplomatic strategy. Based on the latest developments of international clean energy diplomacy, the author also discusses China's strategic option of clean energy diplomacy in the broad context of the profound changes in global energy and climate governance.

As a new diplomatic model to enhance national competitive advantages, clean energy diplomacy has attracted the attention of many countries. This book will therefore be of great interest to students and scholars of sustainable energy and environmental management, environmental politics and policy, and those interested in the low-carbon economy in general.

Dr. Li Xinlei is Professor and Doctoral Supervisor at the School of Political Science and Public Administration, Shandong University, China. She is also Deputy Director of the Environmental Politics Research Institute at Shandong University. Dr. Li specializes in areas of energy and environmental policy, with a particular focus on reginal and global climate governance, renewable energy policy, clean energy diplomacy, international public security, and transnational river governance.

China Perspectives

The *China Perspectives* series focuses on translating and publishing works by leading Chinese scholars, writing about both global topics and China-related themes. It covers Humanities & Social Sciences, Education, Media and Psychology, as well as many interdisciplinary themes.

This is the first time any of these books have been published in English for international readers. The series aims to put forward a Chinese perspective, give insights into cutting-edge academic thinking in China, and inspire researchers globally.

To submit proposals, please contact the Taylor & Francis Publisher for the China Publishing Programme, Lian Sun (Lian.Sun@informa.com)

Recent titles in politics partly include:

Politics of Democratic Breakdown
Gangsheng Bao

Nationalisation, Peasantry and Rural Integration in China II
Xu Yong

Geostrategic Psychology and the Rise of Forbearance
JIANG Peng

China's Aid, Trade and Investment to Africa
Interaction and Coordination
Wang Xinying

Nationalisation, Peasantry and Rural Integration in China I
Xu Yong

Clean Energy Diplomacy
Global Trend and China's Path
Li Xinlei

For more information, please visit www.routledge.com/China-Perspectives/book-series/CPH

Clean Energy Diplomacy

Global Trend and China's Path

Li Xinlei

Routledge
Taylor & Francis Group
LONDON AND NEW YORK

中国社会科学出版社
CHINA SOCIAL SCIENCES PRESS

Sponsored by B&R Book Program.

First published 2024
by Routledge
4 Park Square, Milton Park, Abingdon, Oxon OX14 4RN

and by Routledge
605 Third Avenue, New York, NY 10158

Routledge is an imprint of the Taylor & Francis Group, an informa business

Translated by Xiang Na

British Library Cataloguing-in-Publication Data
A catalogue record for this book is available from the British Library

ISBN: 978-1-032-56103-5 (hbk)
ISBN: 978-1-032-56105-9 (pbk)
ISBN: 978-1-003-43390-3 (ebk)

DOI: 10.4324/9781003433903

Typeset in Times New Roman
by Apex CoVantage, LLC

Contents

Tables

Preface

The global energy sector is in an important period of transition in the new era. This has several features: (1) the global oil and gas market will see structural changes; (2) energy geopolitics and industrial technologies are going through profound shakeup; and (3) clean energy develops rapidly to meet the demand for a green ecological environment, and energy security is more closely interrelated with such issues as global economy, social security, climate change, and the environment. Humanity has experienced two energy revolutions, from the age of burning firewood to the age of burning coal, and then to the age of oil and gas. They prompted two rounds of industrialization and revolutionarily raised the energy efficiency, but also seriously aggravated the reliance on depletable resources. To comprehensively realize the sustainable development goal, the energy transition in the new era relates to whether the human society can make a thorough shift from fossil energy to clean energy.

The global energy transition will take place in two steps, first from high-carbon energy to low-carbon energy, and then to an optimized global energy mix focusing on new energies and renewable energies that are efficient and clean. There are two deep-seated reasons why China hasn't accomplished either step yet. The first reason is China's energy mix. In 2017, coal, oil and gas, and renewables made up 62%, 25%, and 13% of China's primary energy consumption respectively, vastly different from the global average of 28%, 57%, and 15%. At the end of 2017, the thermal power capacity in China reached 1,100GW, including more than 1,000GW coal-fired units that burned over five million tons of coal per day. The coal-dominated energy mix impeded China's efforts for emission reduction and transformation of the energy mix.

The other reason is the low energy efficiency. In 2017, China created 14% of the world's GDP with 23.2% of its energies, while the US created 22% of the world's GDP with 16.5% of energies and Japan 6% of GDP with 3.4% of energies. That was a wide gap in energy efficiency between China and developed countries. Faced with these pressures and challenges in the context of global energy transition, China urgently needs to produce more intellectual products in the field of clean energy, and the book *Clean Energy Diplomacy: Global Trend and China's Path* comes just in time.

Invited by Dr. Li Xinlei from Shandong University, I attended several of her lectures and symposiums and had discussions with her in the early stage of her creation of the book. These activities set me thinking deeply. At the 19th CPC National Congress, China announced to the world its plan to build the global ecological civilization and a community with a shared future for mankind, contributing Chinese wisdom and strength to global governance. It dawned on me that China in its efforts for energy transition and clean energy diplomacy needs a book like this one, which crystalizes the long years of research by Dr. Li on energy and climate change since the UN Copenhagen Climate Change Conference 2009, commonly known as COP15. Following the main lines of governance-driven and competition-driven clean energy diplomacy, this book gives a systematic and authoritative analysis of the global clean energy governance system and the clean energy game and diplomatic responses among major countries. I was deeply impressed. The book establishes the theories on clean energy diplomacy in great rigor and order, systematically compares the clean energy development and foreign policies of different countries, and offers suggestions on enhancing China's capability of clean energy diplomacy on that basis. With a broad vision and incisive analysis, the book provides references for a comparative study of the energy transition in different countries, sheds light on how China should go global on clean energy, and creatively initiates the analysis of clean energy diplomacy corresponding to different types of countries. An original academic achievement of great value, it closely follows the new characteristics of the era of global energy transition in terms of theory, research methodology, case study and policy analysis, displays the new representations of major-country energy diplomacy, and presents innovations and highlights of the new era.

In reference to the book, I would like to share my thoughts on energy transition and clean energy diplomacy in the following areas.

In the new era of global energy transition, the retreat of traditional energies, given the low oil price, has become the new normal, whereas clean energy and low-carbon energy technologies have developed by leaps and bounds. Let me be more specific. First, the world energy mix is getting increasingly diversified. As we move toward clean energy, traditional fossil fuels such as coal and petroleum will continue to play a part, while renewables will come from more sources and take a larger share in the global energy supply. Moreover, energy-related sectors, such as energy storage, transportation, and electric grid, are also seeing a greater diversity. Constant breakthroughs have been made in relevant technologies, including storage, hydrogen energy, and nuclear fusion, and new clean energy technologies emerge incessantly to join the arena, as represented by the rivalry between hydrogen fuel cars and lithium battery cars and that between micro grid and ultra-high-voltage (UHV) grid. Second, the global energy transition depends on the progress of energy technology. Every change and upgrade of the energy mix is driven by technological progress, and technological revolution still plays a vital role in the ongoing energy transition worldwide. It is the strongest driving force and catalyst in the transition from fossil energy to clean energy, and the speed of technological progress fundamentally decides the pace of this round of energy transition. Third, the global clean energy industry has entered a period of acceleration, the price war between renewable energy and oil and gas intensifies day by day, and energy efficiency and technological innovation are the new battlefields of major-country rivalry. Fourth, the global energy market becomes integrated at a faster pace, with energy interconnectivity and the construction of intercontinental oil and gas pipelines and grid networks making steady progress. As the Energy Internet becomes more popular, electricity security and electricity market connectivity will be new aspects of global energy security.

At present, the shift toward clean energy is perceptible throughout our efforts for ecological progress and socioeconomic development. Of all clean energy sources in China, wind power, photovoltaics (PV), hydropower, nuclear power, and natural gas are the main alternatives, but the process of substitution will be constrained by institution, mechanism, and quantity of resources. Therefore, we need to draw on foreign experience in this respect and make the energy shift an important goal when making energy strategies and plans so as to continuously optimize the energy mix. China's energy transition, or energy revolution, won't be achieved overnight. It will be a long process involving the game of interests.

The starting point of the global energy transition is the economic and social modernization in different countries. The transition toward clean energy and international cooperation in that area will involve many external factors, and we need to think about how to realize the allocation of resources by the market in the clean energy sector. Major developed countries have adopted a range of approaches, including technological innovation, market regulation, administrative measures, and formulation of laws to promote the development of clean energy. Where China will stand in this round of energy transition will also depend on its comprehensive reforms. Therefore, we must implement the strategic energy thought of "Four Revolutions" and "One Cooperation" put forth by General Secretary Xi Jinping and create an energy governance system. First, we need to promote the revolutions in energy consumption, supply, technology, and system and intensify international cooperation across the board so as to achieve energy security amid opening-up. Second, we need to implement the strategic guideline highlighting energy conservation, cleanness, and security; accelerate the establishment of a modern energy governance system that is clean, efficient, secure, and sustainable; and balance the market's "decisive" role in resource allocation with the better exertion of government functions. We should also speed up the market-oriented reform of the energy sector, change the current situation that energy conservation goals are divorced from macroeconomic regulation and energy conservation depends on industrial and technological measures, and foster an energy-saving lifestyle and consumption mode. The primary challenge to China's energy transition now is how to find more clean energy sources to replace coal and other high-pollution energies since it is hard to reduce the total volume of energy consumption.

Technological innovation is a strong driving force of energy transition and development, and it reflects a country's competitiveness. Major developed countries and emerging developing countries all attach great importance to the progress and innovation in energy technologies, and they have kept investing more in this field in order to seize the commanding height in new technologies. As the world's largest energy producer and consumer, China must catch up and overtake quickly. We must fully consider that there are both advanced and efficient technologies and equipment and backward and inefficient ones in the country, and leverage the vast domestic market to promote the innovation and revolution of clean energy.

At last, I wish to congratulate Dr. Li on the publication of this book. I look forward to her making greater achievements in the study of clean energy diplomacy and more contributions to academic research and development in this field.

Li Junfeng
Former Director of National Center for
Climate Change Strategy and International Cooperation
Zayed Future Energy Prize Lifetime Achievement Award Winner

Introduction

The historical evolution of global power shifting shows that the change in the energy power structure is the precondition for major structural change in the international system. Nowadays, energy innovation is at the core of the energy and climate game. Whether a country can lead the new energy industry chain and dominate in new-generation energy largely decides its position in the international system.[1] For instance, in the 16th century, the UK led the shift to coal as a fuel through the invention of steam engine and became a precursor of the first Industrial Revolution in Europe. The US with its institutional and technological superiority was the first to use petroleum in the industrial sector and pioneered the second Industrial Revolution characterized by the invention of internal combustion engine, standing as a superpower ever since WWII.

In the 21st century, clean energy, as the dominant factor in the next-generation energy system, plays an ever-bigger role in the contention to dominate the international system.[2] Clean energy has a broad definition. In the narrow sense, it refers to renewable energy that can be recovered and replenished after consumed and that generates zero or little pollution, such as solar energy (PV and solar-thermal), wind energy (onshore and offshore), biomass energy, hydropower, geothermal energy, and tidal energy. In the broad sense, clean energy also encompasses some non-renewable energies, which have minimal pollution to ecological environment when being produced or consumed, such as nuclear energy, low-pollution fossil energy (e.g., natural gas), and fossil energies processed with clean energy technology such as clean coal. Some secondary energies produced with other energy sources also count as clean energy, such as hydrogen energy. This book defines clean energy in the narrow sense. Therefore, it focuses on analyzing how the development of renewable energies, including wind energy, solar energy, and biomass energy, plays out in the evolution of international power system. It also touches upon energy efficiency and technologies of energy complementarity.

The evolution of global climate and energy landscape is facing tighter carbon constraints. A country's ability to cope with or break through the carbon constraint will to a large extent decide its position in the transformation of international order. Dominant in the next-generation energy system, clean energy offers a package solution to three problems at once – climate change, energy security, and low-carbon shift.[3] Therefore, all countries are striving to develop their clean energy industry

DOI: 10.4324/9781003433903-1

and keep it competitive, promote the progress of clean energy technologies, lead the future trend of clean energy development, and occupy the commanding height in the new round of energy revolution.[4] An important way to achieve those goals is advancing clean energy diplomacy beneficial for themselves in the international energy governance system and the competition for resources.

Since 2009, China has made the largest investment in clean energy and installed the largest capacity in the world, laying a solid foundation for implementing clean energy diplomacy. Especially after 2013, high-level reciprocal visits by state leaders have comprehensively deepened energy cooperation between China and EU, ASEAN, Latin America, Africa, the Middle East, and Central Asia, with remarkable progress in clean energy cooperation and assistance and the establishment of an international order of new energy. This book studies clean energy diplomacy and analyzes China's strategic option on that front. In this book, clean energy diplomacy refers to diplomatic policies and activities formulated and conducted around clean energy issues, such as the lines, principles, strategies, and activities of foreign exchanges concerning clean energy. These include conducting important intergovernmental visits, signing bilateral or multilateral cooperation agreements, handling trade frictions and conflicts endangering national interests, forming dialogue and coordination mechanisms and institutional cooperation platforms, and providing foreign assistance through clean energy development. Clean energy diplomacy is a new diplomatic mode that has captured close attention in domestic and foreign academic circles for its role in enhancing a nation's competitive advantages, achieving win-win green development, and uplifting its international image in the era of low-carbon economy.[5]

In terms of the history of the study on clean energy diplomacy as a subject, clean energy got a booster first in the early 1970s. At that time, the outbreak of the global oil crisis prompted the international community to begin looking for alternative energies to fossil fuels to ensure the security of energy supply so as to rely less on traditional fossil energy, which created an important opportunity for the development of clean energy.[6] For instance, it was in that period that Brazil rolled out the National Fuel Alcohol Program and Bio-diesel Program to promote the rapid development of its biomass energy.[7] However, after the mid-1980s, alternative energy lost steam as the international oil price stayed low for more than ten years, although European trendsetters like Germany and the Netherlands insisted on adopting policies and industrial measures in support of clean energy. In the 21st century, clean energy draws attention again in the backdrop of rising energy demand, mounting oil price, and alarming climate change and has enjoyed rapid development, a general trend that isn't even reversed by the new round of oil price ebb in recent years.

In addition to energy demand, the politicization of environmental topics, represented by "international climate negotiations" and "sustainable development narrative", and the general enhancement of public awareness of environmental protection are other important drivers of clean energy development. In the 1960s and 1970s, environmental hazard incidents kept emerging in Western countries owing to the use of industrial raw materials and fossil fuels in the process of industrialization, such as the smog in London, Britain, Minamata disease in Japan, chemical pollution in Seveso, Italy, pollution of the Rhine in Germany, and the incident of America's Amoco Cadiz oil tanker. These events intensified public appeal for using clean and safe energy. Studies in that period focused on technological progress. The *Air Pollution Control and Clean Energy*[8] edited by Charanjit Rai and Lloyd A. Spielman and the eight-volume series *Alternative Energy Sources* edited by T. Nejat Veziroglu systematically elaborated on the development of clean energy technologies.[9] Talks about clean energy then didn't enter the political arena yet.

After the 1980s, the environmental narrative gradually shifted from the "deep green" existential pessimism to "light green" ecological optimism represented by "sustainable development", and environmental topics began to appear on the table of world politics. Under the influence of the "ecological modernization" theory that pursued a win-win result between environmental protection and economic development, Western studies of energy diplomacy began to turn "greener". A main manifestation was that the Western academia redefined energy security, moving from emphasizing the "security of external energy supply" alone to also considering the "inherent safety of energy use" that accommodated environmental impacts.[10] As a result, clean energy represented by wind, solar, and biomass energies gained rising attention from international academia for their multifaceted advantages in productive sustainability, environmental friendliness, and inherent safety of use.[11]

By the end of the 1990s, there were more studies on domestic policies and international cooperation on clean energy for two reasons. First, the rapid development of clean energy – especially wind, solar, and biomass – in pioneering European and American countries laid the empirical foundation for the comparative study of their policies. Therefore, numerous research findings in relation to clean energy policies and the establishment of green energy system were published on influential international periodicals, such as *Energy Policy* and *Environmental Politics*. Second, international climate negotiations had been held by then, and the *Kyoto Protocol* in particular had flexible mechanisms that attached more importance to clean energy in developed and developing countries. Influenced by this, many European and American academics analyzed international cooperation on clean energy as part of environmental diplomacy to cope with climate change.[12] In the 21st century, policy networks, think tanks, and online partnerships, represented by the REN21 (Renewable Energy Policy Network for the 21st Century) and REEEP (Renewable Energy and Energy Efficiency Partnership), have emerged in large quantities. They have released many research reports and real-time news on global clean energy development and cooperation and provided a global vision for strategic studies in this field. Although the financial crisis in 2008 threw a wet blanket on clean energy investment, European and American countries launched the "Green New Deal" for recovery and took clean energy as the engine to power the new round of energy and economic revolution that will take them out of the decline.[13] As a result, clean energy has maintained growth rate despite the many external challenges and adverse factors. In 2015, the global new investment in renewable power and fuel exceeded USD 285.9 billion, a year-on-year increase of 5%, and beating the 2011 record of USD 278.5 billion. Among that, the investment in renewable power (USD 265.8 billion) was twice as much as in power generation from coal and natural gas (USD

130 billion).[14] Against such a background, the Western academia changed its focus from comparative studies of clean energy policy to how clean energy development will affect national diplomatic strategy in the post-crisis period. What's notable was that intergovernmental mechanisms and summits, such as the IRECs (International Renewable Energy Conferences), IRENA (International Renewable Energy Agency), CEM (Clean Energy Ministerial), and G20, have provided increasingly institutional platforms for clean energy diplomacy. International NGOs and partnerships such as the CESA (Clean Energy States Alliance) and GNESD (Global Network on Energy for Sustainable Development) have enriched the interactive mode of clean energy diplomacy. Clean energy diplomacy has evolved into a new type of diplomatic approach with its own attributes – it was more than just the combination of traditional energy diplomacy and environmental diplomacy. It must be noted that clean energy diplomacy means much more than international clean energy cooperation. It also includes how to prevent and cope with the passive competition and zero-sum game that might emerge in the development of and interactions around clean energy.[15]

The latest findings by foreign academics are concentrated in the following four areas. The first one is the important position and unique role of clean energy in global energy transition. Bruce D. Jones said energy reform symbolized by clean energy has pushed the reform of the entire world order. Maintaining a vantage point during the energy transition will enable a country to play a critical role in the establishment of the new order of global governance.[16] Michael Aklin and Johannes Urpelainen wrote in their book *Renewables: The Politics of a Global Energy Transition* that as the world is acting faster to respond to climate change and improve energy security, major developed countries have actively developed clean energy and made notable progress. On the supply side, accelerating the development of hydropower, wind power, and PV; promoting the utilization of nuclear energy; and expanding the application of natural gas and shale gas is the general trend as the world goes low-carbon. On the demand side, sharply raising the energy efficiency in buildings and cars, promoting mature and efficient energy-saving and low-carbon technologies at a faster pace, and boosting the R&D and innovation of intelligent information and energy-use technologies are the common pathways adopted by developed countries. On the policy level, low-carbon strategies and plans have been made, goals set, the cap-and-trade system established, economic means perfected, and auxiliary laws and policies formulated. Clean energy is playing a more important role in global energy governance and domestic energy transition.[17]

The second area is that the focus of clean energy studies is moving from developed countries to developing ones, with special attention to China's rise in the global clean energy landscape.[18] REN21's *2014 Renewables Global Status Report* pointed out that renewable energies increased faster in emerging economies than in developed countries. The Pew Research Center's *2014 Who's Winning the Clean Energy Race?* revealed fast increase in Asia, with China topping the list of investment and installed capacity, which would lead to a new energy situation.[19] The third area is the special role played by clean energy in cooperation between developing countries, particularly the cooperation between China and other BRICS countries. As emerging economies rise in the clean energy sector, some European and American academics have turned their eyes from the cooperation between developing countries and Western developed ones to the green cooperation among BRICS countries.[20] Zaman and Abdullah said BRICS countries, standing at an advantage in clean energy development, can lead developing countries to achieve green, low-carbon revolution and energy transition.[21] In her *The Green BRICS: How to Cooperate and Leverage Renewable Energy Strategies*, Renata Thiébaut said the cooperation within BRICS is undergoing a critical green change. The *Multilateral Agreement on Cooperation and Co-financing for Sustainable Development* reached at the Durban Summit 2011 signified the initial formation of the green BRICS financing mechanism, but it didn't go into the specific approach of cooperation or the deep-level institutional establishment.[22]

The fourth area is the importance of clean energy in national diplomatic strategy. Lana Dreyer said Germany's green energy transition strategy can improve the country's reputation and competitiveness and gain it more soft power on the diplomatic front.[23] Sybille Roehrkasten wrote in *IRENA and Germany's Foreign Renewable Energy Policy* that Germany founded IRENA in 2011 with the aim of fostering a new international order of energy governance through clean energy diplomacy.[24] She continued to compare the features and approaches of clean energy governance of Germany and Brazil, respectively the representative of developed countries and developing countries, and generalized two different patterns of clean energy diplomacy.[25] David Criekemans made a geopolitical analysis of why clean energy development is important for America's diplomatic strategy. It will free America from its reliance on petroleum and the constraint of energy geopolitics by switching to cleaner energies and, through low-carbon "energy independence", enables it to play a leading part in global climate negotiations and the establishment of a new energy order.[26]

Compared with their Western colleagues, Chinese academics started late in studying the clean energy strategy. Their main achievements came out after 2007 when the country issued the *Plan for Medium and Long-term Development of Renewable Energies* and *China's National Climate Change Programme*. Though their research drew extensively on the West, Chinese academics already turned their eyes to China's own development. Some of them proposed such concepts as "energy and environmental diplomacy", "low-carbon diplomacy", and "new energy diplomacy", but they didn't put forth the concept of "clean energy diplomacy", nor did they establish systematic theories around it. A recent review shows the research findings of domestic academia as follows. First, they present the international trend of and cooperation in clean energy development, especially the cooperation between China and European and American countries. In his book *International Comparative Study on Clean Energy Development in the Low Carbon Era*, Xu Qinhua compared major countries' policies and financing mechanisms on clean energy and suggested the strategic priorities for China-Europe and China-US cooperation.[27] Ma Jianying, Kang Xiao, and Li Yang separately analyzed the China-US and China-Europe clean energy cooperation. All of them pointed out that although China has built cooperation channels of various forms with developed countries, their cooperation is still hindered by the lack of bilateral strategic mutual trust, trade protectionism, and other factors, and institutional cooperation must be deepened.[28]

Second, they analyze China's clean energy strategy through a new outlook of energy security and/or climate diplomacy. Zhao Hongtu, Zhao Qingsi, Yang Yanqiang, et al. believed a nation's energy structure is closely linked with global energy security and climate change, and clean energy development is an important part of the chain.[29] Yan Shigang said in "China's Energy Diplomacy under the New Outlook on Energy Security" that uplifting clean energy development as a national strategy reflects a new outlook on energy security highlighting pluralistic, low-carbon, clean, green, and win-win development.[30] In *China's Grand Vision of Energy, Environment and Climate Diplomacy*, Xia Yishan and Chen Dezhao expounded from a global perspective on the goals, connotations, and policy measures of China's energy, environmental, and climate diplomacy. They all underscored the importance of clean energy for promoting energy transition and responding to climate change but failed to set up a systematic theoretical framework to dissect the proactive effect of clean energy diplomacy in the evolution of the strategic international landscape.[31]

Third, they delve into the connection between clean energy development and China's peaceful rise. Wang Jisi said countries are in fierce competition and constant conflict concerning traditional energies. The supply of clean energy largely depends on technological innovation, so cooperation in this field better serves their long-term interests.[32] In his motion titled "New Energy and Peaceful Diplomacy", Liu Hanyuan asserted that strongly developing clean energy will not only facilitate China's energy deployments and sustainable economic growth but also better demonstrate its sense of morality and duty as a responsible major country in creating the new order of global governance.[33] Yu Hongyuan also said in his *Environmental Changes and Power Shift: Institutions, Negotiations and Policies* that China's "peaceful rise" is a process in which it gradually improves its energy chain by developing clean energy to increase national interests without completely changing the current international energy mechanism.[34]

Fourth, they study the clean energy cooperation between developing countries from the perspective of economy, trade, finance, and investment, especially the policies in each BRICS member and their modes of clean energy production, consumption, and market prospects.[35] However, these studies didn't go deep into the long-term green cooperation and the diplomatic patterns and features among BRICS countries, much less their role in establishing the new order of global clean energy governance.

Current research findings on clean energy diplomacy have provided helpful insights and references for this book, but they need to be deeper and more systematic. The shortcomings of current research can be found in the following areas. Regarding research perspective, most research stops at describing the history of clean energy development and international cooperation. Some researchers noted the connection between clean energy development and China's peaceful rise, but discussions about clean energy diplomacy, a new diplomatic mode, in the context of diplomatic strategy with a global vision are rare. For depth of research, papers on clean energy strategy generally present sporadic views but rarely put forth the clear-cut concept of clean energy diplomacy, indicating an unsound theoretical system. Meanwhile, current research abounds in the analysis of Western countries' green energy diplomacy but lacks the systematic study of the trajectory, operation, and driving mechanism of China's clean energy diplomacy. In terms of viewpoint, most studies only talk about China's clean energy cooperation with Europe and the US. While both Chinese and foreign researchers have begun to pay attention to BRICS' green cooperation, they rarely note how China's international aid in clean energy has contributed to the institutional innovation of South-South cooperation. Furthermore, they never lucubrate into the important role that China plays in building the new order of global climate and energy governance or link clean energy diplomacy with China's overall diplomatic strategy.

Based on the latest developments of international clean energy diplomacy, this book discusses China's strategic option regarding clean energy diplomacy in the broad context of the profound changes in global energy and climate governance, in hopes of supplementing, deepening, expanding, and innovating existing studies. The subject of study herein is not the simple combination of energy diplomacy and environmental diplomacy. This book endeavors to systematically construct the theories of clean energy diplomacy in the context of the changing international strategic landscape of energy and climate. It strives to explain the scientific connotations and innovative significance of clean energy diplomacy and helps develop the subject of new-generation diplomacy. Explicitly putting forward the concept of clean energy diplomacy, this book integrates the studies of traditional energy diplomacy and environmental diplomacy and defines its connotations and extensions from the perspective of major-country diplomatic strategy. It also comprehensively discusses the basic characteristics, influence factors, internal motivation, and operating logic of clean energy diplomacy in the backdrop of the changing global strategic landscape energy and climate and the global comparison of low-carbon transition, striving to make theoretical breakthroughs.

In making a systematic study of clean energy diplomacy, this book tries to innovate in three ways. The first innovation is the research perspective. Going beyond the traditional energy diplomacy and unidimensional environmental diplomacy, it establishes the theories and conducts an empirical analysis of clean energy diplomacy in the international landscape of energy and climate in transition, focusing on its connotations, basic traits, and unique functions. In particular, the book classifies and compares the strategic positioning of clean energy diplomacy on two important dimensions – governance-driven and competition-driven. It makes a systematic comparison of five major clean energy developers – Germany, the US, Japan, India, and Brazil – regarding the characteristics of their energy transition, the evolution of clean energy policies, and the strategic positioning of clean energy diplomacy, with a view to drawing policy references and experience for China's clean energy diplomacy.

The second innovation is the content of research. For one thing, this book analyzes clean energy in a larger scope. It is not limited to the clean energy cooperation between China and Europe, America and BRICS countries. Rather, on the level of national diplomatic strategy, this book discusses how clean energy can assist in innovating the modes of "South-South cooperation" and "international aid" and transforming the global order of climate and energy governance. In light of the global trend of diversified and networked clean energy governance, the book especially analyzes public clean energy diplomacy involving multiple stakeholders and the creation of global clean energy partnerships. For another, the analysis herein is deeper, more targeted, and more original. Noting the many opportunities and challenges during the transition of international landscape, the book goes to great lengths to explain how to enhance China's capability of clean energy diplomacy and consequently improve its crisis responsiveness, leadership, executive capability, and moral appeal in the complex international environment.

The third innovation is the academic emphasis on three points. First, the book emphasizes problem-oriented diplomatic capability building. With its rapid economic development, China needs to go global not only economically but also diplomatically. How strong our clean energy diplomacy is depends on how competitive our clean energy is, but flexible strategic deployments are also necessary in view of new situations. We need to hone China's capability of negotiation, establishment of institution, public diplomacy, and its discourse power so as to ensure its leading position in setting topics, agenda, systems, and narrative.

Second, the book emphasizes the holistic study of diplomatic strategy. The key to the success of China's clean energy diplomacy is that it is fully integrated in the grand Belt and Road Initiative (BRI). Through overall and strategic planning, China should give full play to the advantage of clean energy diplomacy in gaining green resource power, structural power, and discourse power. In particular, by providing clean energy as a green public good, it has advanced the new type of major-country relationship based on "mutual benefits" and the BRI-centered neighborhood diplomacy and "South-South cooperation" characterized by the "correct concept of justice and benefit". As a result, China has promoted justice and gained benefits while protecting its fundamental interests, thus realizing green and peaceful development.

Third, the book emphasizes practical diplomatic strategies. Noting the multiple challenges posed by the changing international strategic landscape, the book points out that China should have a clear understanding of the establishment of a new international order of energy and climate governance. On the one hand, the new order, to a large extent, remains the result of political struggles among major countries. In the increasingly intense global competition in green energy, China needs to bear in mind that "strength" is still the password on the international stage. It must implement clean energy diplomacy in a flexible, practical, and rational manner, attach importance to creating a new type of green major-country relationship, and aim at long-term development through win-win cooperation. To secure its dominant position in international clean energy diplomacy, China should make good use of its economic, political, and moral resources and provide more green public goods to enhance its green influence in neighborhood diplomacy. It must seize the initiative in building new orders of regional governance such as "Green BRICS", "South-South cooperation", and BRI and setting new agendas and systems.

In terms of research methodology, this book uses historical review, empirical analysis, and comparative analysis. In particular, "laterally" and "vertically" empirical comparisons are performed to analyze the new dynamics of international clean energy diplomacy and the unique path and operating features of China's clean energy diplomacy. The book employs historical review and logical speculation to decipher and evaluate the governance-driven and competition-driven development of global clean energy diplomacy. Through a "lateral comparison" of the strategic position of clean energy in five countries – Germany, the US, Japan, India, and Brazil – it reveals the basic trend of global clean energy diplomacy. On that basis, it summarizes with reason the basic trajectory of clean energy diplomacy in developing countries in the context of the changing situation of global energy and climate strategies. Then the book continues to conduct a "vertical comparison" of China's path of clean energy diplomacy development through historical review and process tracing, from which it generalizes the characteristics of this path and digs into its driving mechanism.

The book uses both primary and secondary research methods. It organizes and analyzes data from authoritative reports, and conducts semi-structured interviews to collect and analyze firsthand materials, thus keeping the study pioneering,

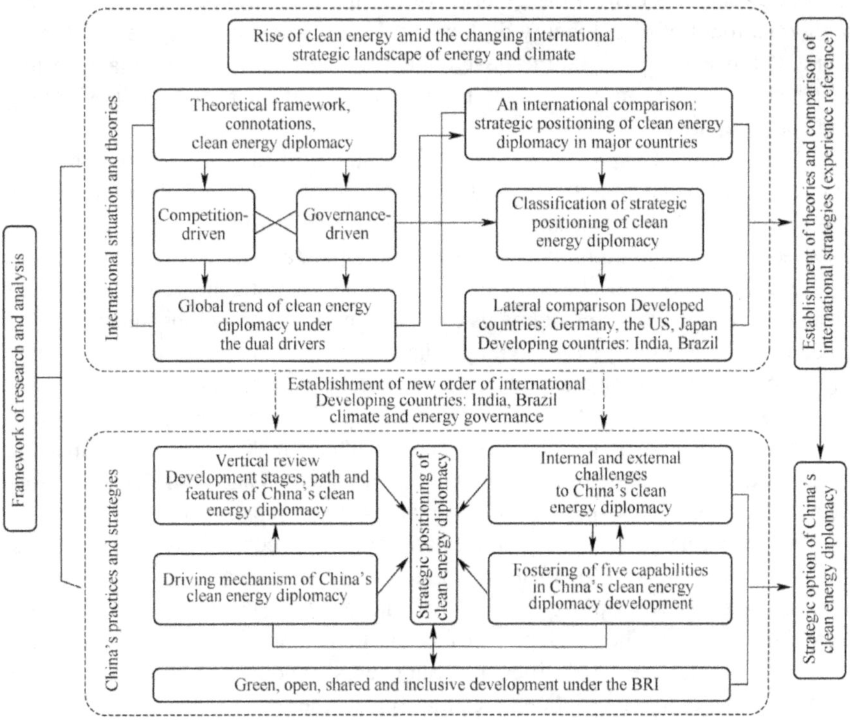

Figure 0.1 Logical framework of the book

Source: Originally created by the author.

in-depth, and authoritative. To be specific, the book obtains the latest data on clean energy development from the websites of established organizations such as IEA (www.iea.org/), IRENA (www.irena.org), REN21 (www.ren21.net/), and BloombergNEF (www.bloomberg.com), thus ensuring the authority and standardization of the data. Meanwhile, it conducts semi-structured interviews, including interviews in person, over the phone, or via email, to obtain firsthand materials. Questions are designed according to the goal of the study. Celebrated experts and academics, government officials, entrepreneurs engaged in clean energy, and NGO personnel both in China and overseas are interviewed so as to make the study scientific, open, and authoritative.

This book pays special attention to the new dynamics of global clean energy diplomacy when the international strategic landscape of energy and climate is in transition and to the strategic option of China's clean energy diplomacy. With this as the center, the book follows the basic line of thoughts as below: evolution of international landscape → establishment of theoretical framework → comparison of major countries' clean energy strategies → analysis of China's path of clean energy diplomacy → problem-oriented policies → the BRI diplomacy. Following this centerline, the book consists of two parts – international situation and theories, and China's practices and policies. The first part consists of four chapters. It aims to systematically establish the theories of clean energy diplomacy and analyzes the global trend of clean energy diplomacy within the existing theoretical framework. It especially presents the development of clean energy diplomacy in five major countries and makes a comparative analysis of their strategic positioning and characteristics.

To be specific, Chapter 1 analyzes the evolution of the international strategic landscape of energy and climate and the rapid rise of clean energy from the perspective of system transformation. It sets a macroscopic and scientific background for theoretical explorations into clean energy diplomacy later. Chapter 2, as the theoretical framework of the book, tries to build a systematic theoretical system for clean energy diplomacy and define its connotations, basic properties, functions, and categorization of strategic positioning. It lays the theoretical foundation for analyzing the clean energy diplomacy of China and foreign countries. Chapter 3 discusses the overall status and trend of global clean energy diplomacy on two dimensions – governance-driven and competition-driven. Chapter 4 makes a global comparison of the clean energy diplomacy of several major countries and their latest developments, referring to the experience of Germany, the US, Japan, India, and Brazil.

The second part – China's practices and policies – consists of three chapters. On the basis of theoretical construction and a comparative analysis on the global trend of clean energy diplomacy, this part analyzes China's practices of clean energy diplomacy and the challenges it faces at home and abroad. After discussing how to strengthen the capabilities of clean energy diplomacy, it also explores the strategic positioning and option of China's clean energy diplomacy in relation to the BRI. Specifically, Chapter 5 presents the green and low-carbon shift of China's energy security amid the changing international strategic landscape of energy and climate. Against that background, it traces the evolutionary stages of China's clean energy diplomacy, compares its features in each stage, and analyzes its driving mechanism.

In view of the internal and external challenges faced by China in the evolution of international strategic situation, Chapter 6 discusses how to enhance the country's strategic capabilities of clean energy diplomacy across the board, from fostering strengths, setting up institutions, and establishing a diplomatic network, to guiding green finance and building diplomatic discourse power. Noting China's grand diplomatic strategy, Chapter 7 points out that the BRI provides an important opportunity to implement the clean energy diplomacy. While acknowledging the special risks and challenges China encounters along the Belt and Road, it showcases how to exert the advantage of China's clean energy diplomacy in reinforcing the green resource power, structural power, and discourse power and how to blend clean energy development into China's overall diplomatic strategy by making provident and scientific choices. At last, the ending chapter condenses and summarizes the core viewpoints of the book and lists the directions in which further and deeper studies of clean energy diplomacy can be made.

Notes

1 Leading the new energy industry chain includes discovering new energies, exclusive possession of energy resources, revolutionary progress in energy application technology, popularization of energy technologies, improvement of energy utilization rate in economy and society, and national control over energy use.
2 Bruce D. Jones, David Steven, *The Risk Pivot: Great Powers, International Security, and the Energy Revolution*, Washington, DC: Brookings Institution Press, 2015.
3 Mihaela Papa, Nancy W. Gleason, "Major Emerging Powers in Sustainable Development Diplomacy: Assessing Their Leadership Potential", *Global Environmental Change*, No. 22, 2012, pp. 915–924.
4 Bruce D. Jones, David Steven, *The Risk Pivot*: *Great Powers, International Security, and the Energy Revolution*, Washington, DC: Brookings Institution Press, 2015.
5 Michael Aklin, Johannes Urpelainen, *Renewables*: *The Politics of a Global Energy Transition*, Cambridge, MA and London: The MIT Press, 2018, pp. 15–20.
6 Xu Hongfeng, *China and US: Clean Energy Cooperation in Response to Global Climate Change*, Beijing: Social Sciences Academic Press, 2017, pp. 26–27.
7 Morgan Brazilian, Benjamin F. Hobbs, Will Blyth, Iain MacGill, Mark Howells, "Interactions Between Energy Security and Climate Change: A Focus on Developing Countries", *Energy Policy*, No. 39, 2011, pp. 3750–3756.
8 C. Rai, L. A. Spielman, C. H. Amberg, *Air Pollution Control and Clean Energy*, New York: American Institute of Chemical Engineers, 1976.
9 T. Nejat Veziroglu, ed., *Alternative Energy Sources I–VIII*, Washington, DC: Hemisphere Pub. Corp., 1979–1989.
10 Dnaiel Yergin, "Energy Security in the 1990s", *Foreign Affairs*, Vol. 67, 1988, p. 111; Yang Zewei, "China's Energy Security: Challenges and Responses", *World Economics and Politics*, No. 8, 2008.
11 Michael Aklin, Johannes Urpelainen, *Renewables*: *The Politics of a Global Energy Transition*, Cambridge, MA and London: The MIT Press, 2018.
12 Pamela S. Chasek, *Earth Negotiations*: *Analyzing Thirty Years of Environmental Diplomacy*, Tokyo: United Nations University Press, 2001, pp. 61–67.
13 Janet H. Eldridge, *Global Clean Energy Cooperation*, New York: Nova Science Publishers, 2012, pp. 3–8.

14 REN21, *Renewables 2016 Global Status Report*, 2016, p. 14, https://www.ren21.net/wp-content/uploads/2019/05/REN21_GSR2016_FullReport_en_11.pdf.
15 Michael Aklin, Johannes Urpelainen, *Renewables*: *The Politics of a Global Energy Transition*, Cambridge, MA and London: The MIT Press, 2018, pp. 15–20.
16 Bruce D. Jones, David Steven, *The Risk Pivot*: *Great Powers*, *International Security*, *and the Energy Revolution*, Washington, DC: Brookings Institution Press, 2015.
17 Michael Aklin, Johannes Urpelainen, *Renewables: The Politics of a Global Energy Transition*, Cambridge, MA and London: The MIT Press, 2018.
18 UNEP, *South-South Trade in Renewable Energy – A Trade Flow Analysis of Selected Environmental Goods*, 2014, https://wedocs.unep.org/bitstream/handle/20.500.11822/9083/-South-South%20trade%20in%20renewable%20energy:%20a%20trade%20flow%20analysis%20of%20selected%20environmental%20goods-2014South-SouthTrade.pdf?sequence=3&amp%3BisAllowed=.
19 The Pew Charitable Trusts, *Who's Winning the Clean Energy Race*, Washington, DC: The Pw Centre, 2014.
20 Kenneth G. Lieberthal, *US-China Clean Energy Cooperation*: *The Road Ahead*, Washington, DC: Energy Security Initiative at Brookings, 2009; Janet H. Eldridge, *Global Clean Energy Cooperation*, New York: Nova Science Publishers, 2012.
21 K. Zaman, A. B. Abdullah, A. Khan, et al., "Dynamic linkages Among Energy Consumption, Environment, Health and Wealth in BRICS Countries: Green Growth Key to Sustainable Development", *Renewable & Sustainable Energy Reviews*, Vol. 56, 2016, pp. 1263–1271.
22 Renata Thiebaut, "The Green BRICS: How to Cooperate and Leverage Renewable Energy Strategies", *Conjuntura Internacional*, Vol. 10, 2013.
23 Lana Dreyer, "Renewables: Do They Matter for Foreign Policy?", *Brief Issue of European Union Institute for Security Studies*, No. 3, 2013.
24 Sybille Roehrkasten, Kirsten Westphal, "IRENA and Germany's Foreign Renewable Energy Policy Aiming at Multilevel Governance", *SWP Working Papers*, 2013, https://www.swp-berlin.org/publications/products/arbeitspapiere/Rks_Wep_FG08WorkingPaper_2013.pdf.
25 Sybille Roehrkasten, *Global Governance on Renewable Energy*: *Contrasting the Ideas of the German and the Brazilian Governments*, Berlin: Springer, 2015.
26 David Criekemans, "The Geopolitics of Renewable Energy: Different or Similar to the Geopolitics of Conventional Energy?", Canada: ISA Annual Convention, 2011, https://exploringgeopolitics.org/wp-content/uploads/2019/01/Criekemans_David_Geopolitics_Renewable_Energy.pdf.
27 Xu Qinhua, et al., *International Comparative Study on Clean Energy Development in the Low Carbon Era*, Guangzhou: Guangdong World Publishing Corporation, 2013; Chen Yue, Xu Qinhua, eds., *China International Energy Cooperation Report Towards Low Carbon Era's Global and Regional Energy Governance*, Beijing: Current Affairs Press, 2012.
28 Ma Jianying, "An Analysis of China-US Clean Energy Cooperation", *Contemporary International Relations*, No. 12, 2009; Kang Xiao, "Paths and Problems for China's International Cooperation on Renewable Energy", *Contemporary International Relations*, No. 6, 2009; Li Yang, "China-US Clean Energy Cooperation: Foundation, Mechanisms and Problems", *Contemporary International Relations*, No. 1, 2011; Yan Shigang, "China-EU New Energy Cooperation in the Low-carbon Era: Challenges and Solutions", *Economic Forum*, No. 3, 2011; Yan Shigang, "China's New Energy Cooperation with the US and Europe: Problems and Prospects", *Practice in Foreign Economic Relations and Trade*, No. 5, 2012.
29 Yang Yanqiang, *China's Energy Security in Low-carbon Economy*, Beijing: Guangming Daily Press, 2014; Zhao Qingsi, *International Cooperation and China's Energy Diplomacy: Concept, Mechanism and Path*, Beijing: Law Press China, 2012; Zhao Hongtu, "International Energy Transition: Current Status and Prospects", *Contemporary International Relations*, No. 6, 2009.

30 Yan Shigang, Liu Shuguang, "China's Energy Diplomacy Under the New Outlook on Energy Security", *China International Studies*, No. 2, 2014; Yan Shigang, "China's International New Energy Cooperation in Low-carbon Economy", *Foreign Affairs Review*, No. 5, 2012.

31 Xia Yishan, Chen Dezhao, *China's Diplomatic Vision: Energy, Environment and Climate*, Beijing: World Affairs Press, 2012.

32 Special Correspondent, "Climate Change and China's National Strategy – An Interview with Professor Wang Jisi", *The Journal of International Studies*, No. 4, 2009.

33 Special Correspondent, "New Energy and Peaceful Diplomacy – CPPCC Standing Committee Member Liu Hanyuan's Proposal at Two Sessions", *Sun Energy*, No. 2, 2011.

34 Yu Hongyuan, *Environmental Changes and Power Shift: Institutions, Negotiations and Policies*, Shanghai: Shanghai People's Publishing House, 2011; Yu Hongyuan, "China's Energy and Environmental Diplomacy Centered on Green, Win-win Development", *World Outlook*, No. 4, 2011.

35 Su Xing, Pang Jinfu, "Prospects of BRICS' Renewable Energy Market and Application of 'BRICS Plus' Mode", *Sino-Global Energy*, No. 3, 2018; Li Fan, Xu Xin, Dai Yongwei, "Comparative Study of Renewable Energy Policies in BRICS Countries", *Asia-pacific Economic Review*, No. 3, 2017; Li Zhiguo, Du Xiu'e, "Empirical Study of Clean Energy Utilization and Energy Consumption Structure in BRICS Countries", *Asia-pacific Economic Review*, No. 3, 2012.

Part I

International situation and theories

1 Rise of clean energy

Changing international strategic landscape of energy and climate

The transition of the global climate and energy situation is facing tighter carbon constraints. A country's ability to respond to or break the carbon restrictions will to a large extent determine its position in the transformation of international order. The transition of global climate and energy situation displays two features. One is that the international energy strategies and climate governance show a non-negligible trend of decarbonization. For instance, the energy sector is paying more attention to the development of clean energy and the continuous improvement of energy efficiency. The coming into force of the *Paris Agreement* signaled that at the negotiating table, low-carbon competition and cooperation were replacing mandatory reduction of greenhouse gas (GHG) emissions as the keyword of global climate governance. The other is that the international energy situation and climate governance situation are more closely interrelated. The fundamental solution to global GHG emissions is for all countries to decarbonize their energy mix and consequently make climate governance more effective.[1] In the meantime, the low-carbon shift in the energy sector is conducive to enhancing energy sustainability and security, with clean energy becoming the key factor in the interrelation.[2] In fact, the change of global climate and energy landscape has fundamentally driven the decarbonization of international order. The global economic domination is moving toward the low-carbon end, and the low-carbon economy is the new growth engine of the international economy. In this process, countries that are more successful in the low-carbon shift, backed by their clean energy competitiveness and innovativeness, will have a greater say and leverage in the future transformation of international order.[3] This chapter combs through the evolution and features of the international strategic landscape of climate and energy since the 1990s and analyzes the characteristics of the global rise of clean energy and its influence on energy and climate diplomacy. It presents the general international environment that has nurtured clean energy diplomacy and provides a macroscopically international background and a realistic basis for future studies.

Section 1 Evolution and features of international climate governance

The United Nations Framework Convention on Climate Change (UNFCCC) signed in 1992 laid the foundation for global climate governance.[4] Article 1 of the

DOI: 10.4324/9781003433903-3

Convention stated that scientists around the world agree that over 90% of global warming may be caused by humans themselves, especially by economic activities since the Industrial Revolution Clean – in the process of industrialization – that grow more and more reliant on fossil energies like coal and petroleum. The Intergovernmental Panel on Climate Change (IPCC) has released successively five assessment reports since 1990 and pointed out that many changes in the climate system observed since 1950 have never been seen in the past decades or nearly 1,000 years. Almost all regions on Earth have seen temperature rise, both on the Earth surface and the sea.[5] Global warming will cause the melting of the ice cap, glacier and frozen soil in Greenland and the Antarctic, which will raise the sea level and threaten the very survival of small island states. It will also affect the global climate system, distribution of precipitation and circulation of ocean currents, which will result in extreme climate events such as flooding, hurricane, earthquake, tsunami, drought, and extreme heat and cold. These will pose an immense threat to ecological balance, food, energy and water security, and even human survival. As a result, there will be massive ecological migration, huge amounts of environmental refugees, and an aggravated scramble for natural resources among regions. For instance, climate change causes drought and reduces surface water, which leads to tension between countries located in cross-border river basins, eventually drawing countries' growing attention to climate security. Climate issue thus becomes a security issue. On the very day that the 2017 UN Climate Change Conference kicked off in Bonn, the World Meteorological Organization (WMO) issued the Provisional Statement on the State of the Climate and warned that 2017 was set to be one of the three hottest years on record, with long-term indicators such as CO_2 concentration, sea level and ocean acidification still on the rise. Arctic sea ice coverage was lower than average, while the scope of Antarctic sea ice was at or approaching a record low. There was a notable increase in extreme weather events worldwide, and frequent climate disasters had caused severe losses around the world.[6]

The *Kyoto Protocol* signed in 1997 was the second milestone in global climate governance. After George Walker Bush pulled out of the protocol in 2001, the EU played a leading part in pushing the top-down mandatory distribution of GHG emission reductions. To ensure the effective implementation of this mode, the *Kyoto Protocol* set three flexible mechanisms – the Joint Implementation (JI) under Article 6, Clean Development Mechanism (CDM) under Article 12, and Emission Trade Mechanism (ET) under Article 17. After eight years of hard work, the *Kyoto Protocol* officially came into force in 2005, which was the first-ever legal document restricting the emission of GHG that aimed at pushing developed countries to meet their emission reduction targets through the top-down distribution of emission quota. However, this multilateral climate governance mode, with states as key climate negotiators, was hard to move forward due to the distribution of interests and calculations of benefits among different countries and gradually went into an impasse.[7] The dilemma of the Kyoto mode was reflected in two ways – divided perception and stagnant negotiations. With the shift of global power structure, the constant division of negotiating groups and the diplomatic struggle around Common but Differentiated Responsibilities (CBDR), the "Kyoto mode" of top-down distribution of emission reduction quota was hard to implement. As the gravity of the global economy moved from the West to the East, energy consumption and GHG emissions in developing countries increased rapidly. Especially after the 2008 financial crisis, the general economic decline in the West further set off the robust economic growth in emerging developing countries represented by China. After the United Nations Climate Change Conference 2009 in Copenhagen, the Western bloc of developed countries and the Eastern bloc of developing ones, which used to stand opposite each other, were regrouped driven by European and American countries and the Alliance of Small Island States (AOSIS). Their opposition was gradually replaced by the confrontation and opposition between major and minor GHG emission countries. Not motivated enough to participate in global climate governance in the first place, southern and northern countries had drastically opposed perceptions of the fundamental principles (their legitimacy) of the Kyoto mode – the compulsory distribution of emission reduction obligations. Seeing that developing countries, because of their rapid economic development, emitted a rising amount and proportion of GHG, developed countries were imposing pressure on them in various forms and demanded reshaping the CBDR principles. Their waning recognition of the CBDR principles made Annex I parties even less willing to fulfill their emission reduction obligations. Developing countries deemed such principles as "historical responsibilities" and "exemption for southern countries" as indisputably legitimate and just in global climate governance. However, small island states and least developed ones became increasingly dissatisfied with the immense emissions from major developing countries and the international responsibilities they bore. At the same time, the BASIC group comprising the four major developing countries of China, India, Brazil, and South Africa didn't see eye to eye either. For instance, Brazil has been promoting the emission reduction goals for developing countries. The divided perception of the Kyoto mode led to the constant division and fragmentation of the negotiating groups. The multilateral negotiations on the state level, being fatigued by ceaseless arguments over CBDR, eventually resulted in the inefficient operation of and stagnant negotiation about the Kyoto mode. This was keenly felt at the Copenhagen Climate Change Conference 2009, during which the EU's leadership was continuously weakened, and the "Denmark text" once put the negotiation in a stalemate. In the last stage of the conference, the EU was completely marginalized and reduced from a leader to an observer. African countries, small island states, ecologically fragile countries, and international environmental NGOs all found the Copenhagen Accord falling far short of their expectations. They thought the conference was a failure in reaching a legally binding agreement and in the second commitment period of the *Kyoto Protocol*. They also blamed China for hindering the progress despite it initiating the voluntary quantified target of carbon intensity reduction at the conference.

Because this top-down Kyoto mode based on multilateral negotiations became increasingly stagnant, the strategic layout of global climate governance experienced important changes. After the Copenhagen conference, multilateral climate diplomacy became more pragmatic and flexible. While the EU slid from the center, China and the US, with more aligned positions, played an important role in getting the *Paris Agreement* signed. In April 2013, the two countries reached the first *China-US Joint Announcement on Climate Change*; later that year, they decided to form the China-US Climate Change Working Group under the framework of the fifth round of the US-China Strategic and Economic Dialogue (S&ED) to decide how they would promote cooperation in such areas as technology, research, energy conservation, and clean energy. During the APEC Summit in 2014, they signed the second *China-US Joint Announcement on Climate Change*, indicating that the two countries would further align their actions in climate change and further power clean energy cooperation. When Chinese President Xi Jinping visited the US in 2015, the two countries issued the *China-U.S. Joint Presidential Statement on Climate Change*, declaring their commitment to reaching an ambitious agreement at the Paris Conference that reflects the principles of "common but differentiated responsibilities" and respective capabilities. The signing of the *Paris Agreement* in 2015 marked a major turning point in the global climate governance mode – from the EU-advocated, top-down, compulsory distribution of emission reduction quota to the China and US-advocated, bottom-up approach of nationally determined contributions respecting each country's capabilities. In March 2016, China and the US once again announced the *China-U.S. Joint Presidential Statement on Climate Change*, whereby they vowed to improve the institutional framework of bilateral climate and energy cooperation by implementing the Mission Innovation initiative announced at the Paris Conference and promoting the Clean Energy Ministerial (CEM). On November 4, 2016, the *Paris Agreement* was ratified and took effect one year after signing, and its position was not shaken even by Trump's withdrawal in 2017. This marked a new milestone in the transition of the global strategic landscape of climate governance, and the era it ushered in had the following characteristics.[8]

First, climate governance switched from the EU-advocated "top-down" approach[9] to the approach centered on the "Intended Nationally Determined Contribution (INDCs) + five-year assessment", and the focus of climate negotiations turned from emission reduction to low-carbon adaptation based on clean energy and efficiency improvement. Unlike the Kyoto mode that set legally binding reduction targets for developed countries, the Paris mode replaced the "asymmetric responsibilities" between southern and northern countries with participation by all contracting parties. The adjusting mechanisms committed by the parties, such as transparency and five-year stocktake, were legally binding, and they were updated dynamically to urge the countries to increase their nationally determined contributions step by step. This mode put more carbon emission restrictions on major developing countries and forced them to intensify decarbonization efforts at home.[10]

Second, the climate governance mechanism evolved from a unicentric mechanism with countries at the core to a polycentric compound of mechanisms.[11] This had twofold meanings. On the one hand, there were more intergovernmental governance agencies and their extensions under the UNFCCC framework. On the other hand, non-state and sub-state actors were more aligned on climate governance, which gave rise to various multinational cooperation initiatives or networks, such as the Partnership on Climate Change and Experimental Climate Governance.[12]

After the Lima Climate Change Conference (COP20) in 2014, public and private sectors had to take joint actions for greater synergy in climate change responses, given the distance between the countries' GHG emission reduction targets and the final goal of keeping global temperature rise within 2 Celsius degrees.[13] The *Paris Agreement* reached in 2015 explicitly supported non-party stakeholders (NPS) in taking an active part in climate actions and provided institutional channels to improve their capabilities and ensure their political participation.[14] The 2018 dialogue, known as the Talanoa Dialogue, called for all participants, including cities, businesses, and NGOs, to increase mutual trust and jointly search for solutions in an inclusive, participatory, and transparent manner. Especially, they were urged to explore how to mobilize countries, societies, and market forces to enhance climate actions and bridge the gap. During the Bonn Conference in 2017, the US didn't organize an official "American corner". But more than 600 state and city government officials, industrial and business leaders, NGOs, and think tank representatives, including the mayor of New York City Bloomberg and California governor Brown, set up the "US Climate Action Center" out of their own pocket and released the country's phase-1 emission reduction report, demonstrating the non-state and sub-state actors' resolve of emission cut.[15]

Third, the focus of climate negotiations turned from emission reduction to low-carbon adaptation based on clean energy and efficiency improvement, and setting clean energy goals was an important way for countries to respond to climate change and propose nationally determined contributions. The climate negotiations were essentially aimed at forcing a green change in the fossil-centered energy structure by controlling the GHG emissions in each country. Clean energy emerged as a practical option for enhancing the capability of climate mitigation and adaptation, making the current energy system more resilient, and ensuring a sustainable energy supply. As shown in Figure 1.1, with the 2°C goal, raising energy efficiency and developing renewable energy contributed to over 70% of emission reductions. After the Paris Conference, most countries committed to promoting renewable energies and improving energy efficiency by setting nationally determined contributions. Of the 189 countries that submitted their INDCs, 147 mentioned renewables and 167 energy efficiency.[16]

The low-carbon transformation based on clean energy is reflected in various international cooperation platforms, and it affects the development trend of many industries. In the 2030 Sustainable Development Goals (SDG) adopted at the UN General Assembly in 2015, the 7th goal was ensuring access to affordable, reliable, sustainable, and modern energy for all. The G20 Hangzhou Summit in 2016 committed to promoting renewable energies and improving energy efficiency and reached a broad consensus on gradually canceling the carbon subsidies in all countries and on other topics. Green energy was an important topic at the G20 Summit 2017 in Germany. The International Civil Aviation Organization (ICAO) adopted a global market-based measure scheme (GMBM) in 2016 to cut emissions in the civil aviation sector. China, the US, and Europe all promised to join the Carbon Offsetting and Reduction Scheme in the initial voluntary stage, with the aim to push the international aviation industry to control carbon emissions after 2020.[17]

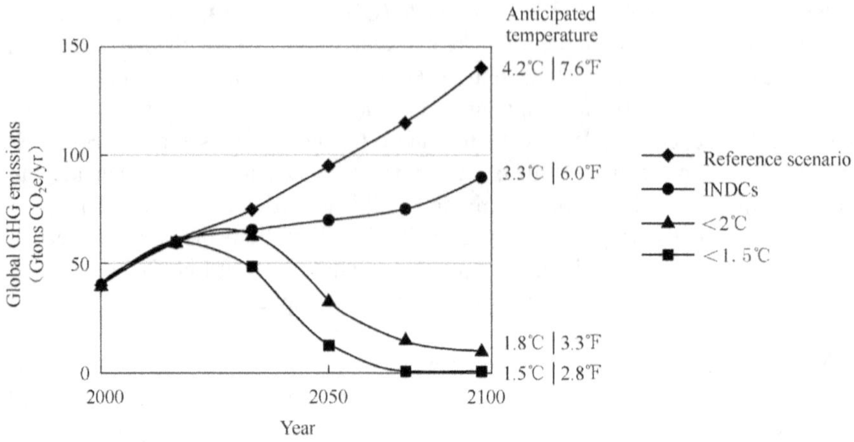

Figure 1.1 GHG emission forecast

Source: Climate Interactive, www.climateinteractive.org/pmgmm/scomboard/.

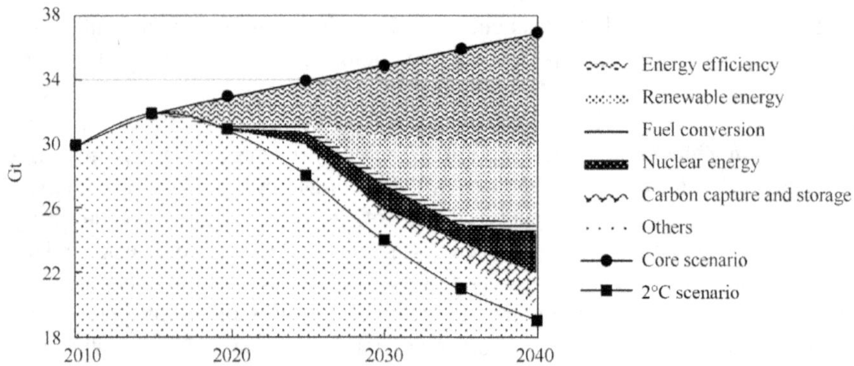

Figure 1.2 Technological categories of global CO_2 emission reduction under the 2°C goal

Source: IEA, World Energy Outlook 2017.

The 28th Meeting of the Parties to the *Montreal Protocol* at the end of 2016 also adopted an amendment on cutting hydrofluorocarbons (HFCs), an important step toward fulfilling the international commitment to the *Paris Agreement*. If a country wants to have the initiative and play a leading role in global climate governance, the key is to enhance its low-carbon strengths and the capability of coordinating and innovating climate and energy policies based on clean energy development.

If we look at the evolution of international climate negotiations and global climate governance, we'd find two key factors that affect the negotiations. One is the number of actors participating in global climate governance (including the number of negotiating groups and the number of regional governance platforms), and the other is the extent of decarbonization in the global economy. The following figure shows that climate negotiations have shifted from bloc-style diplomatic game under the "Kyoto mode" to the coexistence of multi-actor governance and diplomatic game under the "Paris mode".[18] First of all, the number of actors and platforms engaged in climate governance kept increasing. From 1997 when *Kyoto Protocol* was signed to 2005 when it came into force, the number of governance mechanisms revolving around the UNFCCC increased sharply, and climate topics appeared on the agenda of many international organizations. This involved two dimensions – lateral and vertical. Laterally, climate change made its way to other international organizations and became part of the political agenda at the World Bank, WTO, G7, G20, and other platforms, and the low-carbon principle was increasingly integrated into international trade systems, financial market rules, and intellectual property (IP) and investment rules. Vertically, more club-like blocs and regional bilateral/multilateral initiatives beyond the UNFCCC emerged, which in a way supplemented, without shaking, the UN governance framework. The US, for example, exited the protocol in 2001, but it formed a series of regional climate governance mechanisms, including the Asia-Pacific Partnership on Clean Development and Climate (APP) in 2005 and the Major Economies Meeting on Energy Security and Climate Change (MEM) in 2007, to maintain its discourse power on climate change. In the meantime, more non-state and sub-state actors took a more active part and played a bigger role in global climate governance after the 2009 Copenhagen Climate Change Conference, including NGOs, companies, investors, cities, and civil society organizations (CSOs).

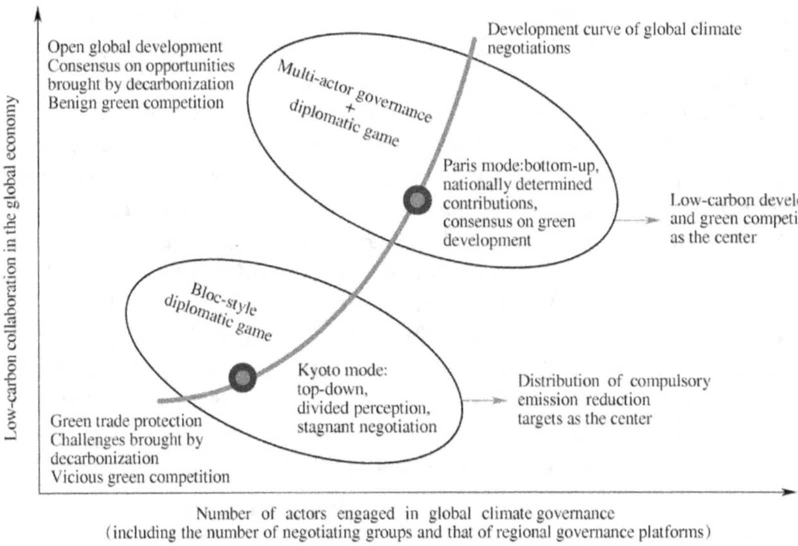

Figure 1.3 Development curve of global climate negotiations

Source: Original created by the author.

Second, as the global economy went low-carbon, green trade protection (the challenge theory) was gradually replaced by a green consensus (the opportunity theory). That led to the synergy effect of the changed perception of national interests, the development of the low-carbon market, and the rise of a green private sector. The rapid development of the global low-carbon and green economy and its growing inclusiveness created greater space for plural actors to play a part in global climate governance. When *Paris Agreement* took effect in 2016, ten petroleum giants, comprising China National Petroleum Corporation, Shell, Total, BP, Eni, Aramco, Statoil ASA, Repsol, Petroleos Mexicanos, and Reliance Industries Limited, announced to jointly establish the Clean Energy Development Foundation. The foundation would invest USD 100 million annually in the next ten years to develop GHG capture and storage technologies and raise energy efficiency. Apparently, market players were working with NGOs to advance the low-carbon transformation of the global supply chain and industry chain by setting green design and purchase standards, green trade rules, and green consumption concepts. At the same time, more countries tended to respond to climate change with market means and change the global economic rules, especially trade rules, by creating carbon markets.[19] The spreading decarbonization of the global economy resembled a kind of "race to the top balance", which meant that in economic competition, innovative environmental policies were rolled out, and environmental governance standards heightened to intensify green market access so countries that pioneered in innovation could realize "early mover's interests" by leading the market. Policy makers in other countries, to improve their overall national strength or encouraged by domestic companies to raise the environmental governance standards to adapt to the new changes in economic competition, learned from or imitated the policies of pioneering countries, thus achieving the coordination of low-carbon development policies worldwide. Adopting a bottom-up approach different from the Kyoto approach, *Paris Agreement* could help stimulate plural actors to engage in the low-carbon market and low-carbon governance actively and eventually accelerate the low-carbon shift of the economy. This green trend wouldn't be reversed even after Trump declared to quit the agreement and reduce input in renewable energies. About Trump's extremely passive attitude toward climate change, former US president Barack Obama published an article in *Science* shortly before he stepped down, in which he cited numerous data to prove that Trump couldn't reverse the momentum of clean energy either in the US or worldwide. During the eight years when Obama was in office (2008–2015), the US GDP grew by 10%, but carbon emission intensity and energy-sector CO_2 emission fell by 18% and 9.5%, respectively. Energy cost was slashed in the same period – down by 41% for wind power and 54% for rooftop PV.[20]

Section 2 Evolution and features of global landscape of energy governance

Austrian economist Joseph Alois Schumpeter wrote in his *The Theory of Economic Development* that "economic development is not a cyclical movement, it is spontaneous and discontinuous change in the channels of flow".[21] The alternation of energy in human history was usually accompanied by the adjustment of industrial structure. In the mid-18th century, Industrial Revolution spread to the whole world after a British man named James Watt improved the steam engine. The use of coal as the primary energy source during the first Industrial Revolution drove the development of heavy industries such as iron and steel, mining and metallurgy. Britain, by applying coal technologies and controlling the coal-based energy and industry chain, became the empire on which the sun never set. From the 1870s to the early 20th century, the arrival of the second Industrial Revolution brought humanity into the electric age, in which the widespread use of petroleum powered the high-speed development of energy-intensive industries such as electricity, transport, and communication. The US controlled the global petroleum industry chain by dominating the petroleum market (e.g., petro-dollar) and technologies and consequently became a global hegemon. Today, the shift from an energy-intensive industrial structure to a tech-intensive one is likely to trigger the third Industrial Revolution, which will put wings on clean energy industries such as solar, wind, and biomass. Whoever dominates the new energy chain, industry chain, and core technologies will occupy a vantage point in the new round of international competition.

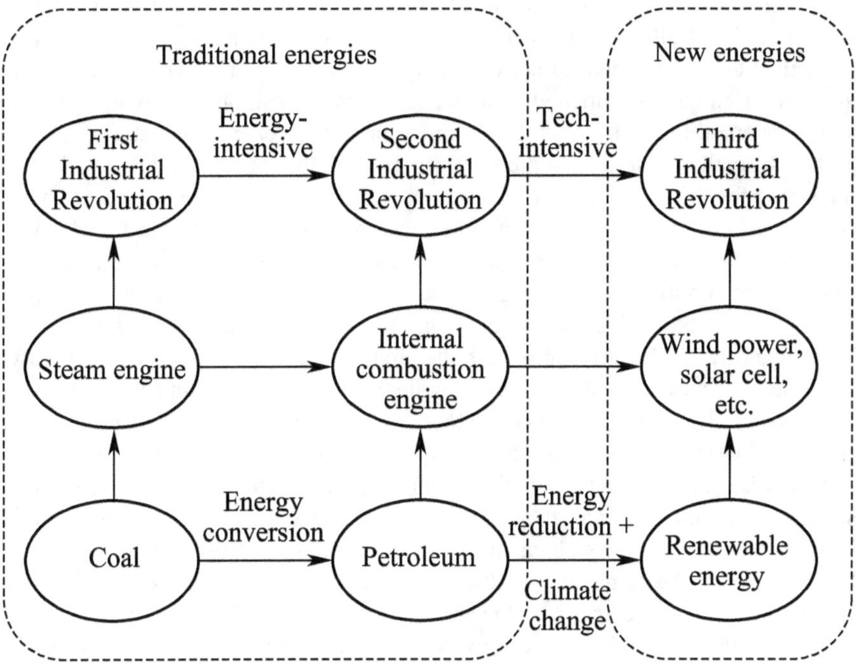

Figure 1.4 Trajectory of three industrial revolutions

Source: Peng Feng, "New development of and lessons from EU's green energy policy", Environmental Protection, No. 9, 2016.

The current global energy governance landscape is characterized by a changing industrial structure and improving energy mix. A range of factors, including the global power shifting, changes in energy supply and demand, and the rise of clean energy, have led to important changes in the global energy governance landscape, which display the following features.

First, the center of global energy supply is moving "westward" with growing diversity. As the output of conventional oil and natural gas has peaked and begun to fall in recent years, unconventional energy such as "shale oil" and "shale gas" has caught much attention. In particular, the output and prospect of three key unconventional oil and gas resources – Canada's oil sand, Brazil's deep-sea subsalt oil, and America's shale oil and gas – are so extraordinary that the gravity of the world energy landscape is moving from the Middle East to the Western Hemisphere. The shale oil and gas revolution in the US started with its pursuit of energy independence. Devoted to the development of relevant technologies since the 1980s, the country has dramatically lowered the development cost of shale oil and gas since the Obama administration thanks to mature exploitation and production technologies and sound pipeline facilities. Therefore, its shale oil and gas resources are in commercial exploitation on a large scale today at a cost slightly higher than that of traditional oil and gas, largely diversifying the energy mix. Meanwhile, by virtue of technological breakthroughs in the exploitation of unconventional natural gas, the US beat Russia to become the world's largest natural gas producer in 2009 with an output of 624 billion cubic meters, its unconventional natural gas reserve being more than eight times that of conventional natural gas reserve. The shale oil and gas revolution has fundamentally changed America's position in the world energy map. For one thing, it frees the US from its long-term reliance on natural gas imports, especially from the Middle East, which therefore is strategically much less important for the US. World oil production is seeing a tripod comprised of Saudi Arabia, Russia, and the US. For another, the shale gas revolution in the US will have notable influences on the international oil price. Around 2014, the cost of shale gas exploitation in the US was about USD 50. To protect its interests, the major oil exporter Saudi Arabia, leveraged on its low production cost, produced oil in large quantities in the attempt to slash the international oil price and consequently nip America's nascent shale gas revolution in the bud. The two countries, therefore, turned from oil supply allies to competitors in the international oil and gas market. Besides, the shale gas revolution has expedited the transformation of the world energy mix. Either to shake off the reliance on fossil energy import/export that sometimes put them over a barrel, or to reduce carbon emissions for environmental betterment, countries have all taken steps to raise their scientific and technological level and adjust the domestic industrial structure, which is conducive to ecological and environmental protection on the earth.

Second, the center of global energy demand is moving "eastward". As the gravity of global oil and gas production moves to the West, the consumption center is moving to the East. Oil and gas consumption in Asian countries represented by China and India is increasing fast, so is its proportion in global consumption. According to the *World Energy Outlook 2017: China* released by International

Energy Agency (IEA), China's oil consumption increased rapidly with an external reliance of 67%. The country is the world's second-largest oil consumer after the US and may become the largest in 2030. India's economic growth has also brought about a fast increase in oil consumption, and the country overtook Japan to be the world's third-largest oil consumer in 2015. The gravity of natural gas consumption is moving eastward too, with Asia taking an ever-larger share. To protect the environment and improve the energy consumption structure, the governments of Asian countries all support the development of natural gas, which has led to a rapid increase in natural gas consumption in recent years, with China's performance especially eye-catching. Its natural gas consumption grew 7.3 times between 2000 and 2016 and registered a year-on-year increase of about 15% in 2017, with about 40% import reliance. China is now the world's third-largest natural gas consumer and is expected to beat Russia and become the second largest by 2040, after the US.[22] In addition to China, India, Southeast Asia and other Asian countries and regions are also likely to see a fast increase in natural gas consumption. According to IEA's forecast, India's natural gas consumption will increase by 5.2% on an annual average between 2016 and 2040, higher than China's 4.6%. In the same period, natural gas consumption in Southeast Asia will increase by 1.9% on annual average, still higher than the world average though obviously lower than the growth rate in China and India.[23] As shown in Figure 1.5, IEA predicted that OECD countries, China and India, and other non-OECD countries would each consume 1/3 of world energy by 2040. The polycentric and diversified landscape of energy supply will diversify the energy pricing structure too. The regionally segmented pricing approach of oil and natural gas may be changed, and there is a clearer trend that energy finance will assume more importance in energy pricing. Meanwhile, the international energy market will turn from a "seller's market" to a "buyer's market", while Asian countries, including China and India, will have a greater say

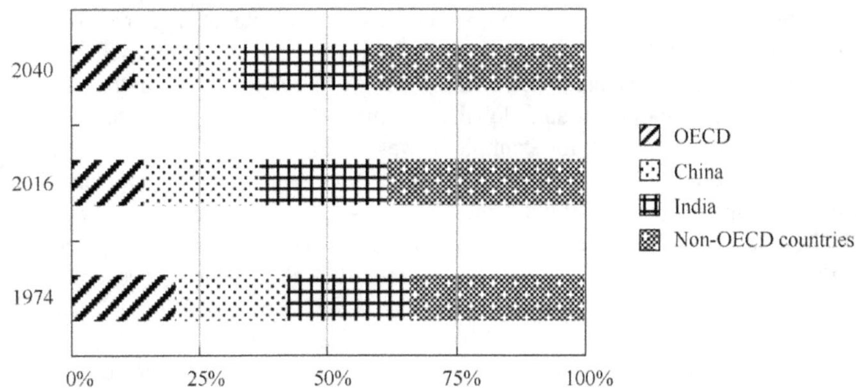

Figure 1.5 Global consumption of primary energy

Source: IEA, World Energy Outlook 2017: China, Petroleum Industry Press, 2017.

on the demand side. Organization of the Petroleum Exporting Countries (OPEC) is losing the crude pricing power, international trade rules on natural gas are changing profoundly, and emerging energy consumers in Asia are seeking more influence on the international pricing of natural gas.

Third, clean energy is considered an important engine that can lead the global economy into the next growth cycle. Both developed and developing countries put clean energy in an important position in their economic stimulus plan. Renewable energy has maintained growth despite the low oil price. Investment in renewable electricity after 2014 has exceeded the net investment in fossil energy power plants, and about 59% of the world's net new installed capacity came from renewable energy, reaching a record high of 161GW in 2016, up about 9% from 2015. Renewable energy accounts for 19.2% of end energy consumption worldwide, and its installed capacity is enough to meet 23.7% of the global power demand.[24] As the energy landscape changes, many countries choose to go low-carbon in a bottom-up approach through the market by bringing more stakeholders into the clean energy industry chain. Especially with the construction of the carbon market, although it's hard to form a global market yet, building regional ones has become the general trend, such as America's Regional Greenhouse Gas Initiative (RGGI) and the carbon trade markets in the EU, New Zealand, Mexico, ROK, and China. These regional carbon markets have given a strong impetus to the energy and power market reform and the development of a clean energy quota system at home and helped the private sector to get more involved in the pluralistic network of clean energy governance.

Section 3 Fast rise of clean energy and global impacts

Climate change is essentially an issue of the energy mix. According to a World Energy Council (WEC) report in 2016, the energy system dominated by fossil energy faces the trilemma of energy security, energy accessibility for the poor, and environmental sustainability, which makes the reform of the world energy system and transition of the energy mix both necessary and inevitable. The transition of energy mix means that the structure of energy production and consumption goes through fundamental changes and exerts deep-going effects on a country's social and economic development and global geopolitics. Take the EU, the precursor of clean energy development, for example. It was the first to take clean energy as the key to responding to climate change, improving energy accessibility, and ensuring energy security.[25] In March 2007, the EU passed the *2020 Climate and Energy Package* to cut 2020 GHG emissions to 80% of the 1990 level and accelerate the development of renewable energy to account for 20% of total energy consumption. In October 2014, it released the *2030 Framework for Climate and Energy Policies*, planning to cut GHG emissions in 2030 to 60% of the 1990 level and make renewable energy account for 27% of the energy supply. To meet the EU-wide targets on green energy, two reform measures were launched. One was the third liberal reform of the energy market initiated in 2009, for which the *Third Energy Market Package* was adopted; the other was *A Framework Strategy for a Resilient Energy Union with a Forward-looking Climate Change Policy* released under the Juncker Plan in February 2015, which kicked off the EU energy union strategy.[26] The release of the strategy created an opportunity for Europe, under the shadow of its debt crisis then, to build a low-carbon, secure and competitive economy. All in all, as the world is responding to climate change and promoting low-carbon development, the international energy system is going through profound changes. All countries are quickening their steps to eliminate fossil energy and increase the investment in clean energy in the endeavor to decarbonize their energy system. While European countries such as Germany and Britain put forth energy transition plans, many developing countries also set targets and rolled out measures for the same purpose, especially the emerging developing countries represented by the BRICS (China, India, Brazil, South Africa, and Russia), with renewable energy being an important direction of their energy shift. China, India, and South Africa need to switch from a coal-based energy mix to nonfossil energies; Russia is proactively implementing a renewable energy strategy despite its tremendous fossil energy reserve for the sake of economic sustainability; Brazil is moving from the reliance on hydropower to green diversification of its power supply by strongly developing wind power and solar power.[27] In 2016, the five BRICS countries accounted for 38% of the world's total renewable capacity, more than their percentage in the world's total GDP (22%). Among that, China accounted for 27% and Brazil and India each 5% or so. Clean energy development has got on a fast track in the 21st century with the following characteristics.

First, clean energy takes a larger percentage in energy consumption and attracts more investment. According to BP's statistics, the global consumption of renewable energy reached 1.33 billion tons of oil equivalent in 2015, accounting for 10.1% of total primary energy consumption. It increased at an annual rate of 5.7% from 2006 to 2015, much faster than fossil fuels' average annual growth rate of 1.5% in the same period. In terms of the increase of global energy demand, renewable energy accounted for 12% of the total increase between 2000 and 2010, after which measures to improve energy efficiency slowed down the increase of energy consumption. From 2010 to 2016, the percentage of renewable energy rose to 32% and that of natural gas from 23% to 31%, combining to make up nearly 2/3 of the increased demand. The *Renewables 2016 Global Status Report* (GSR) released by REN21 showed that renewables had surpassed fossil fuels for six consecutive years with respect to the net investment in newly installed capacity.[28] In 2015, more renewable capacity was installed than the combined new (net) capacity of fossil fuels worldwide. GSR2018 showed a record high in new PV capacity, driving the total PV capacity to 98GW in 2017, up 29% from 2016, and the increment was more than the combined net increase of coal, natural gas, and nuclear capacity.[29] The declining role for fossil fuels is offset by the rapid expansion of renewable energy. The increasing importance of renewable energy is supported by the continuing electrification of the energy system. The share of electricity in total final energy consumption increases from around 20% in 2019 to between 30% and 50% by 2050 in the three scenarios (New Momentum, Net Zero, Accelerated). In the meantime, the emergence of new energy vehicles (NEVs) has also sped up the change of the energy map. Several European countries have made plans to stop selling gas-fueled cars in the next 10 to 20 years, which will significantly boost the development of NEVs and electric vehicles (EVs). IEA expects EVs to make up 30% of world auto sales by 2030, while demand for gasoline and other fossil fuels will start falling after 2030.

From October 2008 to June 2013, the World Bank (WB) and other multilateral development banks invested nearly USD 8 billion through the Climate Investment Funds in 49 developing countries, which attracted close to USD 44 billion of joint financing for clean technology projects. In the fiscal year of 2012, WB invested a record USD 3.6 billion in renewable energy, which made up 44% of all its energy loans, and the percentage was as high as 84% regarding power generation. The UN launched the Sustainable Energy for All (SE4All) initiative in 2011, one of the goals of which was doubling the ratio of renewables in the global energy mix by 2030.[30] IEA's statistics showed that in 2015, global investment in renewable energy increased nine percentage points faster than that in fossil energy, and investment in new renewable power capacity was more than twice the combined investment in new fossil fuel and nuclear capacity. In 2017, renewable investment made up more than 2/3 of the power industry's total investment, and the percentage of renewable energy in the power industry will keep increasing. Investment in renewable energy was concentrated in several regions. In 2017, China, Europe, and the US accounted for nearly 3/4 of the global investment in renewable energy. It's worth noting that some developing countries, such as the Solomon Islands, Guinea-Bissau, and the Marshall Islands, left developed countries and emerging economies far behind regarding the ratio of their renewable investment per unit GDP. In January 2018, the International Renewable Energy Agency (IRENA) and Climate Policy Initiative (CPI) jointly issued the *Global Landscape of Renewable Energy Finance 2018*, which presented the trend of global financing for renewable energy from 2013 to 2016. Despite a slight fall in 2016, renewable capacity reached a record high. Policy changes affected investment greatly. Investment in offshore wind power increased fourfold in 2013–2016, and the trend was going on. The private sector

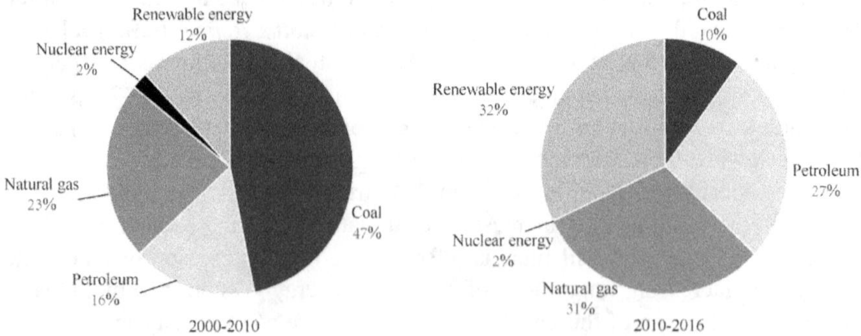

Figure 1.6 Percentage of energy growth in different periods (2000–2010, 2010–2016)
Source: IEA, World Energy Outlook 2017.

Table 1.1 Global development of renewable energy (Unit: GW)

		2010	2011	2012	2013	2014	2015	2016	2017	2018	2019	2020
Installed capacity (excluding hydropower)/GM		315	395	480	560	657	785	921	1,081	1,246	1,430	1,668
Installed capacity (including hydropower)/GM		1250	1355	1470	1560	1712	1849	2017	2,197	2,378	2,581	2,838
Hydropower capacity/GM		935	960	990	1000	1055	1064	1096	1,112	1,132	1,150	1,170
Biomass capacity/GM					88	93	106	112	121	130	137	145
Biomass power output/TWh		313	335	350	405	433	464	504	532	581	566	602
Geothermal capacity/GM					12.0	12.8	13.2	13.5	12.8	13.3	14.0	14.1
Synchronized PV capacity/GM		40	71	100	139	177	227	303	405	505	621	760
Solar thermal capacity/GM		1.1	1.6	2.5	3.4	4.4	4.4	4.8	4.9	5.5	6.1	6.2
Wind farm capacity/GM		198	238	283	318	370	433	487	540	591	650	743
Solar water heater capacity/GM		242	285	330	374	409	435	456	472	480	/	/
Transport fuel output	Fuel ethanol/100mln L	850	842	831	872	940	983	986	1040	1120	1150	1050
	Biodiesel/100mln L	185	224	225	263	297	301	308	395	410	475	465

provided most of the world's renewable energy investment (more than 90% in 2016), and traditional debt and equity were the most common financing tools.

Second, the trend of electrification is obvious in global energy consumption and power generation from clean energy increases continuously. Electric energy is clean and high-quality energy, and raising its ratio in the end-use energy is of great importance for optimizing the energy mix. With sci-tech progress, electric energy is playing a greater role in energy and economic development, pushing forward the industrialization process. BP's *Energy Outlook 2030* predicts that total electricity use in 2030 would be 61% more than in 2011; by then electricity would meet 33% of the world's non-transport energy demand. IEA forecasts electricity to account for 40% of end energy consumption by 2030. In this process, coal-based electricity will be replaced by electricity generated from gas, nuclear energy, and renewable energy, till an electricity-based green energy consumption layout is in place.

According to BP's statistics, 5,600TWh renewable electricity was used across the world in 2015, 23% of the total power consumption that year. In the decade from 2006 to 2015, consumption of wind and solar power increased 23% and 53% respectively on an annual average. In 2015, Germany and China registered the biggest increase in renewable electricity output – up 23.5% and 20.9% year-on-year each. Among that, Germany boasted the sharpest increase in wind power output of 53.4% year-on-year, while solar power output in China grew 32.6% year-on-year, making China the largest solar power generator in the world after Germany and the US. Renewable electricity output in the US increased 13.8% and accounted for 64% of the incremental power use in 2015, up 12% from the previous year's 52%. According to REN21's GSR2018, renewable electricity made up 70% of the net increase of global power output, the biggest jump for green electricity in history. According to IEA's statistics, the percentage of renewable electricity was 30% in 2000–2016, which the agency predicted would rise to 61% in the 2017–2030 period under the 2°C scenario. Half of the growth would come from wind power and solar power, and most renewable electricity would be highly competitive even without any subsidy. This proves false the inherent demand for "base load", which is usually met by fossil energy and nuclear energy. But even without it, a sufficiently flexible power system can synchronize a high percentage of intermittent renewable electricity through grid connectivity, sector coupling, and technological support such as ICT, energy storage, EV, and heat pump. Such flexibility not only balances intermittent power sources but also optimizes the power system and will undoubtedly help lower the overall cost of power generation. Therefore, a growing number of countries can now successfully handle the situation where renewable electricity reaches or exceeds 100% of the peak output. In 2016, Denmark and Germany respectively handled the situation where renewable electricity was 140% and 86.3% of the peak output. The *World Economic Outlook* released by International Monetary Fund (IMF) in January 2017 forecasts global economic growth of 3.4% and 3.6% for the current year and the next, obviously higher than the 3.1% forecast in 2016. The upbeat economic forecast will further push renewable energy into a period of high-speed development.[31]

Third, renewable energy is becoming the most cost-effective choice with its falling cost of use and rising competitiveness. Technological progress has led to the rapid decrease in the cost of clean energy, with which the cost of power generation is approaching that of fossil fuels. Negatively affected by the new normal and slowdown of the global economy, renewable energy investment in 2016 was down by 3% from five years earlier, but newly installed capacity still increased by more than 50% thanks to the reduced unit cost and the progress of PV and wind power technologies. Statistics from IRENA showed that the global investment cost of PV electricity fell to USD 1,810/kW and the levelized cost of energy (LCOE) to USD 0.13/kWh. The investment cost and LCOE of onshore wind power fell to USD 1,560/kW and USD 0.07/kWh, and those of offshore wind power down to USD 4,650/kW and USD 0.18/kWh. The US consulting company LAZARD issued a report in 2016 that listed the cost of power generation of various renewable energies in the US that year. As wind power is used on a larger scale and relevant technologies keep progressing, its development and utilization costs have fallen by about 30% in the past five years. In countries such as Brazil, South Africa, and Egypt, the bidding price for wind power is lower than the feed-in tariff of traditional fossil-fuel-based power; in the US, long-term agreement price for wind power has come down to the same level as that for fossil-fuel-based power. Wind power is displaying growing cost-effectiveness.

Bloomberg NEF predicted that the global renewable energy sector will attract USD 7.8 trillion investment from 2016 to 2040, which will reduce the LCOE of PV and onshore wind power by 41% and 60% respectively from 2015. By 2025, the average investment cost of ground PV stations larger than 1MW will be as low as 73 cents/W (compared with USD 1.14/W in 2016), and PV electricity will be more cost-effective than coal-based electricity. Technological progress in the renewable sector will directly reduce its cost of investment and use, with drastic reduction for solar power and wind power, in particular, making them more competitive than fossil energies. The *BP Statistical Review of World Energy 2016* said the energy mix

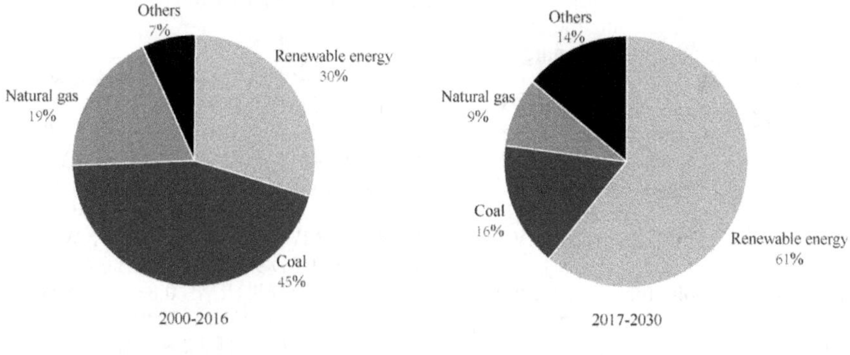

Figure 1.7 Percentage of different energy sources in civilian power output in different periods (2000–2016, 2017–2030)

Source: IEA, World Energy Outlook 2017.

was shifting towards low-carbon fuels thanks to the rapid development of clean energy in recent years.[32] IEA predicted that technological progress would continue to reduce the cost of developing and utilizing clean energy and consequently make it more competitive compared with traditional energies. By 2040, electricity generated from nonfossil energies is expected to account for 45% of total electricity output, and total consumption of nonfossil energies will be more than 4.6 billion tons of oil equivalent, basically on a par with petroleum consumption but more than coal consumption.[33]

Fourth, countries all roll out supportive policies for renewable energy. As the cost of producing renewable electricity and sending it to the grid remains high, countries need to formulate supportive policies to boost its development, including subsidies for R&D, verification, equipment, and sale of renewable electricity. By 2016, almost all countries had rolled out policies, either by national, sub-national, or local governments, to bolster the development and deployment of renewable energy. By setting a series of targets and releasing supportive policies, policy makers hoped to attract investment, promote deployment, push for technological innovation, and encourage greater flexibility in energy infrastructure. These policies and targets gave a strong impetus to the fast development of renewable energy. According to statistics from REN21, 173 countries and regions have set such targets, and 146 ones have issued supportive policies (e.g., feed-in tariffs and renewable portfolio standard), and 110 of them have adopted the feed-in tariffs (FIT) policy

Table 1.2 LCOE of various energy sources in the US, 2016 (excluding tax preferences)

Type of energy		*Cost of power generation*
Conventional energy	Coal-fired	USD 60–143/MWh (RMB 0.42–0.99/KWh)
	Natural gas combined cycle	USD 48–78/MWh (RMB 0.33–0.54/KWh)
	Natural gas variable load plant	USD 165–217/MWh (RMB 1.14–1.50/KWh)
	Nuclear power (excluding the cost of decommissioning)	USD 97–136/MWh (RMB 0.67–0.94/KWh)
	IGCC	USD 94–210/MWh (RMB 0.65–1.45/KWh)
Renewable energy	Residential rooftop PV	USD 138–222/MWh (RMB 0.95–1.54/KWh)
	Commercial rooftop PV	USD 88–193/MWh (RMB 0.61–1.33/KWh)
	Ground PV	USD 78–135/MWh (RMB 0.52–0.94/KWh)
	Polysilicon ground PV	USD 49–61/MWh (RMB 0.34–0.42/KWh) PV+storage: USD 92/MWh (RMB 0.64/KWh)
	Thin-film ground PV	USD 46–56/MWh (RMB 0.32–0.39/KWh) PV+storage: USD 92/MWh (RMB 0.64/KWh)
	Solar thermal with storage	USD 119–182/MWh (RMB 0.83–1.26/KWh)
	Onshore wind power	USD 32–62/MWh (RMB 0.22–0.43/KWh)
	Offshore wind power	USD 118/MWh (RMB 0.82/KWh)
	Biomass power	USD 77–110/MWh (RMB 0.54–0.76/KWh)
	Geothermal power	USD 79–117/MWh (RMB 0.55–0.81/KWh)

Source: Wang Bo, Li Chaoqian, "Global Status and Trend of Renewable Energy Development", *China Price*, No. 5, 2018.

aimed at guaranteeing the purchase and synchronization of all green electricity.[34] FIT is now considered a very important policy tool for promoting the application of renewable electricity.[35] Altogether 128 countries and regions have announced pro-renewable policies in the energy sector and 70 ones in the transport sector. For instance, Scotland vowed to increase the percentage of renewable energy in power consumption to around 100% by 2020; Germany said renewable energy will make up 30% of its energy consumption and 50% of electricity consumption by 2030. France aimed to have renewable energy account for 40% of its electricity consumption by 2030, while the US aimed at 20% and Brazil 23% (excluding hydropower) in the same period. China is set to have nonfossil energy make up 20% of its energy consumption by 2030, Vietnam strived to generate at least 7% of its electricity from renewable energy by 2020 and 10.7% by 2030, and India has vowed to have 100GW solar capacity and 60GW wind capacity by 2022. If these targets are met, renewable energy will make a big jump forward, and the installed capacity of wind power and solar power will grow by three to five times at least.[36]

There are two types of supportive policies for renewable energy – renewable portfolio standards (RPS), which is widely adopted in the US, Britain, Australia, ROK, and Japan, and FIT, which is adopted in Europe, represented by Germany, and Japan. This gives rise to two major support systems for renewable energy in the world – the US-led RPS system and the Germany-led FIT system. RPS stipulates the percentage of renewable electricity in total output, demands grid companies purchase all renewable output, and punishes responsible persons that

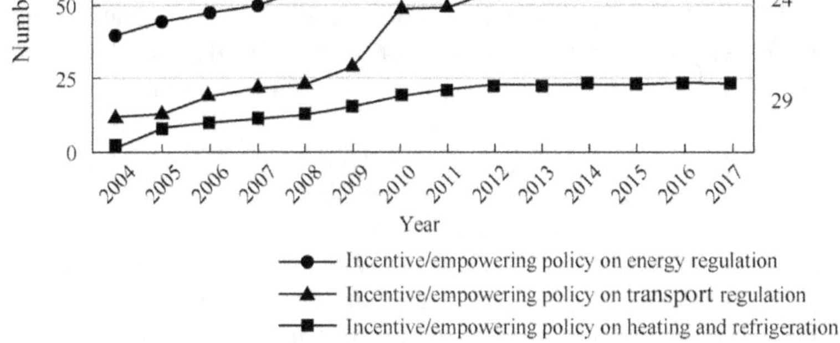

Figure 1.8 Number of countries that release supportive policies for renewable energy (by sector, 2004–2017)

Source: REN21, Renewables 2018 Global Status Report, p. 38.

Notes:

a. 29 Countries issued other heating and refrigeration policies.

b. Number of countries issuing different policies.

cannot meet the quota requirement, while factors such as price, suppliers, and supply conditions are decided by the market. The Renewable Energy Certificate (REC) system is a policy tool based on RPS, and they work together to create a mechanism for low-cost renewable electricity to enter the market. The Germany-led FIT system has eventually evolved into the Feed-in Premium (FIP) system. FIP scraps the obligation under FIT to purchase all renewable electricity. Instead, it asks the generators to sell their renewable electricity in the market with a subsidy determined through bidding and price discovery. FIP demands power generators to adapt to the market, join in the competition, and bear risks that hinge on their selling ability. In the meantime, the government sets rules to reward those generators whose selling price remains stable for a long time, thus ensuring long-term, steady profits for them.[37] Other countries, regions, and cities have launched carbon trade and carbon tax policies to support the development of clean energy. China's pilot carbon trade in seven provinces and municipalities (Beijing, Tianjin, Shanghai, Chongqing, Hubei, Guangdong, and Shenzhen) and carbon markets in Sichuan and Fujian have evolved into national markets. There is also the carbon market in the Tokyo Prefecture and Saitama Prefecture of Japan; the carbon market in California and the Regional Greenhouse Gas Initiative (RGGI) covering nine eastern states in America; and carbon markets in EU, New Zealand, Switzerland, ROK, and Canada's Quebec. Brazil, Chile, Mexico, Russia, Thailand, Turkey, Vietnam, Kazakhstan, and Ukraine are considering building carbon markets too (Table 1.3).

The *Paris Agreement* urges all countries to make united efforts to hold global average temperature increase to well below 2°C above pre-industrial levels and to pursue efforts to limit the temperature increase to 1.5°C above pre-industrial levels by the end of the 21st century. Under this overriding goal, a low-carbon future completely powered by renewable energy is getting clearer. Forty-eight Climate Vulnerable Forum (CVF) countries committed to 100% renewable energy powering by 2050 at the Marrakech Climate Change Conference. Renewable energy has grown at a robust momentum thanks to the massive reduction in the cost of PV and wind power. At the end of 2016, 1/4 of the world's electricity was generated from renewable energy, which IEA expected to rise to 40% by 2040. By February 2018, more than 100 cities worldwide had met at least 70% of their power demand with renewable energy.

In sum, the ambitious clean energy targets announced by countries have not only pushed their low-carbon transformation at home but also profoundly affected their diplomatic policy and strategic positioning. As the global strategic landscape of climate and energy is changing, the rapid development of clean energy combines energy diplomacy and climate diplomacy more closely, and gives a nation more initiative and flexibility in the latter. Take China for example. It combines clean energy development with its emission-reducing capability and South-South cooperation, which demonstrates its commitment to international responsibilities for climate governance. At the same time, clean energy is taking a more important position in energy diplomacy. Grasping the latest clean energy technology

Table 1.3 Targets and key areas of renewable energy development in main countries (regions)

Countries/ regions	*Targets*	*Key areas and measures*
EU	Renewable energy accounts for 20% of total energy consumption in 2020, 50% in 2050.	Promoting wind, solar, biomass, smart grid, and Emission Trade System (ETS).
Britain	Renewable energy accounts for 15% of total energy consumption in 2020, with 40% of electricity coming from green energy sources.	Actively developing onshore/offshore wind power and biomass power; promoting smart electric meter, demand-side power transmission technology; Contract For Difference (CFD).
Germany	In 2020, 2030, 2040, and 2050, the percentage of renewable energy in end energy consumption reaches 18%, 30%, 45%, and 60%; the percentage of renewable electricity in total power consumption 35%, 50%, 65%, and 80%.	Supporting wind, PV, and energy storage; expanding power transmission lines and facilities and energy storage capacity; FIT and FIP.
Denmark	Wind power accounts for 50% of total power consumption in 2020; zero consumption of fossil energy by 2050.	Supporting wind-power heating system, promoting the use of renewable energy in construction, industry, and transportation, advancing smart grid.
US	Reducing CO_2 emissions in the electric sector by 30% in 2030 from the 2005 level.	Promoting wind power, solar power, biofuel, and smart grid; implementing production tax credit (PTC) and investment tax credit (ITC); implementing RPS in 30 states.
China	Nonfossil energy accounts for 15% and 20% of primary energy in 2020 and 2030.	Supporting hydropower, wind power, solar power, and renewable-based thermal power and fuel; FIT for renewable electricity; subsidy for distributed PV electricity (per kWh).

Source: Originally created by the author.

means holding the key to developing a low-carbon economy and the initiative in international interactions. The reserve of clean energy, represented by wind, solar, and biomass energies, is unlimited, and the supply of it largely depends on technological progress and policy innovation. This is good for breaking away from the traditional concept of zero-sum competition and conservative policies. Inherently sustainable, inclusive, and pluralistic, clean energy diplomacy makes it easier for emerging developing countries to rise in the international energy governance system in a relatively moderate way instead of through cutthroat competition as with traditional energies.

Notes

1 Morgan Bazilian, Benjamin F. Hobbs, Will Blyth, Iain MacGill, Mark Howells, "Interactions Between Energy Security and Climate Change: A Focus on Developing Countries", *Energy Policy*, No. 39, 2011, pp. 3750–3756.
2 Harald Heubaum, Frank Biermann, "Integrating Global Energy and Climate Governance: The Changing Role of the International Energy Agency", *Energy Policy*, No. 87, 2015, pp. 229–239.
3 Li Huiming, "Global Climate Governance and Transition of International Order", *World Economics and Politics*, No. 3, 2017.
4 Climate change in the broad sense is reflected in three areas: global warming, acid deposition, and ozone depletion, the first one being most pressing.
5 Shen Yongping, Wang Guoya, "Latest Scientific Points about Global Climate Change in the Fifth Assessment Report by IPCC Working Group I", *Journal of Glaciology and Geocryology*, No. 5, 2013, pp. 1068–1076.
6 Chen Ying, "New Changes in International Climate Governance at Bonn Conference and China's Response", *Environmental Protection*, No. 1, 2018.
7 L. Groen, A. Niemann, "The European Union at the Copenhagen Climate Negotiations: A Case of Contested EU Actorness and Effectiveness", *International Relations*, No. 27, 2013, pp. 308–324.
8 Charles F. Sabel, David G. Victor, "Governing Global Problems under Uncertainty: Making Bottom-up Climate Policy Work", *Climatic Change*, No. 144, 2017, pp. 15–27.
9 The "top-down" approach is legally binding. It has a rigorous compliance mechanism, unified accounting rules, and strict measurement, reporting and verification rules to ensure transparency, but it's hard and slow to reach an action consensus under this approach.
10 Zhuang Guiyang, Zhou Weiduo, "Change of Global Climate Governance Mode and China's Contribution", *Contemporary World*, No. 1, 2016.
11 A. J. Jordan, D. Huitema, M. Hilden, et al., "Emergence of Polycentric Climate Governance and its Future Prospects", *Nature Climate Change*, Vol. 11, No. 5, 2015, pp. 977–982.
12 Matthew J. Hoffmann, *Climate Governance at the Crossroads*: *Experimenting with a Global Response after Kyoto*, New York: Oxford University Press, 2011.
13 Sander Chan, C. Brandi, S. Bauer, "Aligning Transnational Climate Action with International Climate Governance: The Road from Paris", *Review of European Comparative & International Environmental Law*, Vol. 25, No. 2, 2016, pp. 238–247; Thomas Hale, "'Al Hands on Deck': The Paris Agreement and Non-state Climate Action", *Global Environmental Politics,* Vol. 16, No. 3, 2016, pp. 12–22.
14 UNFCCC, *Adoption of the Paris Agreement*, Paris: Conference of the Parties (Twenty-first session), 2015, https://unfccc.int/documents/9064?gclid=EAIaIQobChMImofa lOj2_gIV06iWCh1Fdg36EAAYAiAAEgIQ5_D_BwE.
15 America's Pledge, *America's Pledge Phase 1 Report: States, Cities, and Businesses in the United States Are Stepping Up on Climate Action*. www.bbhub.io/dotorg/sites/28/2017/11/AmericasPledgePhaseOneReportWeb.pdf.
16 REN21, *Renewables 2016 Global Status Report*, 2016, p. 4, https://www.ren21.net/wp-content/uploads/2019/05/REN21_GSR2016_FullReport_en_11.pdf.
17 The International Air Transport Association (IATA) proposed a carbon neutrality target as early as 2009, but it was rejected at the global vote on carbon neutrality plans in 2013. Given this lesson, the GMBM will be implemented in two stages. In the first stage from 2021 to 2026, countries are encouraged to participate voluntarily; in the second stage from 2027 to 2035, the scheme will be enforced and those that don't participate will only have a tiny share in the international civil aviation sector.
18 Charles F. Sabel, David G. Victor, "Governing Global Problems under Uncertainty: Making Bottom-up Climate Policy Work", *Climatic Change*, No. 144, 2017, pp. 15–27.

19 Harald Heubaum, Frank Biermann, "Integrating Global Energy and Climate Governance: The Changing Role of the International Energy Agency", *Energy Policy*, No. 87, 2015, pp. 229–239.
20 Barack Obama, "The Irreversible Momentum of Clean Energy", *Science*, January 20, 2017, http://mahb.Stanford.edu/wp-content/uploads/2017/01/science.aam6284.full_.pdf.
21 Fan Liuyan, Qu Delin, Wang Haibo, et al., "Japan's New Energy Situation in the Post-Fukushima Era: Changes and Lessons", *Sino-Global Energy*, No. 8, 2011.
22 IEA, *World Energy Outlook 2017: China*, Beijing: Petroleum Industry Press, 2017.
23 Wang Haibin, "The Changing World Energy Landscape and China's Response", *Ziguangge*, No. 3, 2018.
24 REN21, *Renewables 2017 Global Status Report*, June 26, 2017, www.ren21.net/wp-content/uploads/2019/05/GSR2017_Full-Report_English.pdf.
25 Michael Aklin, Johannes Urpelainen, *Renewables: The Politics of a Global Energy Transition*, Cambridge, MA and London: The MIT Press, 2018, pp. 173–200.
26 Peng Feng, "New Development of and Lessons from EU's Green Energy Policy", *Environmental Protection*, No. 9, 2016.
27 Hydropower is the primary power source in Brazil, but the country has seen a serious shortage of power supply in recent years due to less precipitation in rain season and public objection to some hydropower projects that threaten the ecology. Therefore, Brazil has begun to promote the shift towards renewable energy.
28 REN21, *Renewables 2016 Global Status Report*, 2016, pp. 4–6, https://www.ren21.net/wp-content/uploads/2019/05/REN21_GSR2016_FullReport_en_11.pdf.
29 REN21, *Renewables 2018 Global Status Report*, 2018, www.ren21.net/wp-content/uploads/2019/08/Full-Report-2018.pdf.
30 Johannes Urpelainen, Thijs Van de Graaf, Lin Xuefei, "The International Renewable Energy Agency: A Successful Institutional Innovation?", *Foreign Theoretical Trends*, No. 2, 2017.
31 Wang Bo, Li Chaoqian, "Global Status and Trend of Renewable Energy Development", *China Prices*, No. 5, 2018.
32 BP, *BP Statistical Review of World Energy 2016*, pp. 5–12, http://oilproduction.net/files/especial-BP/bp-statistical-review-of-world-energy-2016-full-report.pdf.
33 IEA, *World Energy Outlook Special Report 2016: Energy ad Air Pollution*, 2016, pp. 5–6, https://iea.blob.core.windows.net/assets/6b75c4ae-e633-4fa0-9569-b28e226e6103/WorldEnergyOutlookSpecialReport2016EnergyandAirPollution.pdf.
34 FIT is one of the primary policy tools for promoting the development of renewable electricity. It sets a fixed purchase price at which the grid company buys renewable electricity from the power generator for a very long time (e.g., 20 years) to support renewable-based power generation. Karlynn Cory, Toby Couture, Claire Kreycik, "Feed-in Tariff Policy: Design, Implementation, and RPS Policy Interactions", *Technical Report*, NREL/TP-6A2-45549, 2009, pp. 2–6.
35 REN21, *Renewables 2016 Global Status Report*, 2016, pp. 4–6, https://www.ren21.net/wp-content/uploads/2019/05/REN21_GSR2016_FullReport_en_11.pdf.
36 Wang Bo, Li Chaoqian, "Global Status and Trend of Renewable Energy Development", *China Prices*, No. 5, 2018.
37 Luo Chengxian, "Supportive Policies for Renewable Energy: Changes and Trends", *Sino-Global Energy*, No. 9, 2016.

2 Clean energy diplomacy

Theoretical analysis

Traditionally, energy diplomacy refers to the international game revolving around petroleum, whereby major countries emphasize their power relation in the energy system, the resources they are interested in, and the competition for geopolitical power. Clean energy diplomacy represents a change in the rules of the inter-state energy game. Clean energy is gradually delinked from geography and resource reserve; technology, rules, and companies have obtained more influence than traditionally resource-rich countries and regions. In clean energy diplomacy, major countries are interested not only in the power relation but also in how to respond to global climate change through this approach. Unlike traditional energy diplomacy that focuses on resource-rich regions (e.g., the Middle East), clean energy diplomacy is pivoted on cooperation and competition of industrial standards, future lifestyle, and market rules. In traditional energy diplomacy, major countries are the main actors, and major-country struggle, even military competition, is the primary manifestation of energy politics. Now with clean energy diplomacy, there are major countries, international organizations, and other non-state actors. The International Solar Alliance jointly launched by India and IEA and the International Renewable Energy Agency (IRENA) formed by Germany and developing countries bypassing the US and Japan indicate the revolutionary changes in the main actors of clean energy diplomacy. Studies in this field will not only broaden the theoretical vision of research on traditional energy diplomacy but also deepen and enrich the theoretical dimensions of current studies of environmental diplomacy.

Section 1 Connotations of clean energy diplomacy

Traditionally, the state is often seen as the only actor of diplomacy. That is why diplomacy has long been defined as the

> official exchanges and communication between one sovereign state and another sovereign state or an international organization comprised of sovereign states through official representations, on the basis of observing international conventions, in customarily peaceful ways, and for the purpose of defending its own national interests, so as to effectively deal with inter-state relations, and participate in international affairs.[1]

DOI: 10.4324/9781003433903-4

This definition, which revolves around national interests, emphasizes the multiple functionalities of diplomacy in defending the state's core interests and the logic of the geopolitical game followed in the process of diplomatic interactions. This being said, clean energy diplomacy can be understood as the series of foreign exchanges, including international negotiation, consultation, and communication, conducted by a state to defend its clean energy development interests, ensure energy sustainability and security, and achieve its strategic goals in clean energy. To be specific, this includes the formulation of national roads, guidelines, and strategies for clean energy communication, with the purpose of guaranteeing energy security and enhancing the competitiveness of the green industry. It also includes specific activities of foreign exchange, such as important mutual visits between governments, signing bilateral or multilateral cooperation agreements, handling trade frictions and conflicts endangering national interests, and promoting the establishment of international rules and standards concerning clean energy development.

From the perspective of national interest game, Marjolein de Ridder and David S. Abraham, based on resource-driven geopolitics, held that the development of clean energy technologies and the manufacturing of clean energy equipment cannot do without 17 mineral resources represented by rare earth, such as NdFdB for wind turbine and NiMH and lithium-ion for electric vehicle (EV) battery. At present, all countries have set ambitious clean energy goals, so the development and sharing of as well as contention for rare mineral resources is an important aspect of clean energy diplomacy.[2] After the financial crisis in 2008, major emerging developing countries represented by China have progressed by leaps and bounds in clean energy. They have brought immense competitive pressure and anxiety to European and American countries and are increasingly regarded as important competitors in green development. Joel B. Eisen pointed out that competition in the field of clean energy is essentially a geopolitical scramble for new energies, and it will decide who will dominate the future international landscape.[3] With a passive mindset about the interest game, developed countries tend to curb major emerging developing countries in clean energy diplomacy by filing the anti-dumping lawsuit for trade protectionism, controlling industrial standards for clean energy, and contending in intellectual property (IP) application. For instance, China's PV and wind power products have been repeatedly subject to the anti-dumping and countervailing investigations launched by the US and EU since 2012. According to Yu Hongyuan, such a utilitarian approach is driven by the fact that China's clean energy development has affected developed countries' core development strategy and competitiveness. Moreover, it also reflects the increasingly heated inter-state competition for domination in clean energy development.[4]

There is no denying that with the global dispersion of power, IT development, and the demand for a professional response to complicated governance issues, actors of clean energy diplomacy have inevitably diversified.[5] Unlike with security cooperation, a kind of "high-level" political cooperation where resources are controlled by the states, resources are shared among supranational, national, and subnational entities when it comes to cooperation in clean energy, involving an array of stakeholders on all levels. Apart from states, many non-state actors, including

Table 2.1 Actors engaged in clean energy diplomacy

Type of actors	*Form of engagement*	*Main function/role*	*Typical representatives*
Sovereign state/ summit of head of states or ministerial meeting	Direct	States assign representatives to discuss clean energy cooperation, international assistance, and other topics.	International Renewable Energy Conferences (IRECs), Clean Energy Ministerial (CEM), G20
Intergovernmental organizations (IGOs)	Direct	They advise member states on clean energy policies, promote the establishment of information platforms, mediate divergences, release reports, draft plans, provide financial support, facilitate technology transfer, foster capacity building, etc.	International: International Renewable Energy Agency (IRENA), United Nations Development Programme (UNDP), International Energy Agency (IEA), World Bank (WB) Regional: Asia-Pacific Partnership on Clean Development & Climate (APP), Major Economies Forum on Energy and Climate (MEF)
Partnership networks	Direct/indirect	Partnership networks provide member states with best practices and project support in clean energy development and work with states to promote regional clean energy cooperation.	Renewable Energy and Energy Efficiency Partnership (REEEP), Johannesburg Renewable Energy Coalition (JREC), Mediterranean Renewable Energy Program (MEDREP), Clean Energy States Alliance (CESA)
Global policy networks and information exchange organizations	Direct/indirect	They promote renewable energy development and policy innovation worldwide by spreading specific information, promoting policies/best practices, and releasing professional reports.	Renewable Energy Policy Network for the 21st Century (REN21), Global Network on Energy for Sustainable Development (GNESD), International Science Panel on Renewable Energies (ISPRE)
Clean energy industrial associations	Direct/indirect	They represent the general interests of clean energy industry. They promote clean energy cooperation by participating in international conferences, developing industrial assessment reports, and holding training sessions and seminars.	International: Global Wind Energy Council (GWEC), International Solar Energy Society (ISES) National: American Council on Renewable Energy (ACORE), Chinese Renewable Energy Industries Association (CREIA)

International and national NGOs	Indirect	They work with industrial associations or government departments to release research reports, hold seminars, disseminate relevant knowledge and information, and supervise the implementation of agreements and legal documents in relation to clean energy.	Green Peace, World Wildlife Fund (WWF), Global Environmental Institute (GEI), Joint US-China Collaboration on Clean Energy (JUCCCE)
Multinationals	Direct/indirect	They lobby the government to influence its clean energy policies, invest in clean energy technologies, and engage in carbon trade.	Large international energy companies, clean energy multinationals, multinational environmental service providers, large grid companies, etc.
Research institutes in different countries	Direct/indirect	Scientific researchers directly engage in technological cooperation in clean energy, consultation on steps, and establishment of standards. They release evaluation and technical reports, spread relevant information, and provide intelligent and talent support for research.	Institutions and universities in different countries that study energy, environment and climate change, such as America's National Renewable Energy Laboratory (NREL), Lawrence Berkeley National Laboratory (LBNL), and China National Renewable Energy Centre (CNREC)
The media	Indirect	By reporting on clean energy, the media influences public opinions and government positions, and disseminates relevant knowledge and research information.	There are general media and specialized media, such as www.renewableenergyworld.com, www.energysources.cn/ and www.bjx.com.cn/
Individuals	Direct/indirect	They lobby the government to influence its clean energy policies by leveraging on their leadership and prestige.	UN Secretary-General, state leaders, representatives to conferences, and other environmental celebrities

Source: Originally created by the author.

intergovernmental organizations, multinational NGOs, research institutes and think tanks, industrial associations, policy or initiative alliances, partnership networks, civil societies and multinationals, become more active in international affairs. They operate on multiple levels (e.g., supranational, national, and sub-national) and exist in diverse forms (e.g., international government organizations, state actors, and sub-state actors). In the meantime, there is also a growing diversity of diplomatic approaches and practical forms. Approaches aimed at political and military security that focus on high-level politics used to be dominant, but attention is now paid to the interaction of economic, cultural, and technological factors in the arena of low-level politics. They take on a variety of diplomatic forms – regional and global, bilateral and multilateral, at home or abroad, official and private (public diplomacy, track-two diplomacy, and people-to-people diplomacy). To some extent, clean energy diplomacy is displaying more attributes of pluralistic governance on the premise of defending national interests. It can be defined as follows: an array of actors, including government departments of sovereign states, government officials, research institutes, NGOs, and clean energy industry associations, carry out diplomatic activities related to international clean energy collaboration on the political, economic, security, sci-tech, and cultural fronts. These activities, with the core of safeguarding national rights and interests in clean energy, and establishing the new international order of energy governance, aim to promote sound clean energy governance and advance the energy transition. From the perspective of multi-actor governance, clean energy diplomacy doesn't just mean the involvement of more actors. It puts more stress on the establishment of dialogue and coordination mechanisms and institutional interactive platforms of various levels and types so as to enhance the nation's agenda-setting power and discourse power through intensified institutional cooperation.

Integrating national interests with pluralistic governance, German researcher Dirk Messner and others said that Germany's clean-energy-based national transformation strategy (Energiewende) is not only committed to optimizing its energy mix but has also enhanced the country's green reputation and low-carbon competitiveness through low-carbon energy diplomacy. This has gained Germany more smart power in energy and climate diplomacy as the German mode promoting an energy transition spreads to other parts of the world.[6] Sybille Roehrkasten and others pointed out that Germany's clean energy diplomacy is aimed at a more systematic and professional global clean energy governance system. The International Renewable Energy Agency (IRENA) established under Germany's initiation in 2009 is an important international platform and diplomatic foothold to promote its clean energy development concept, best policy practices, and industrial standards of new energy. By strengthening its cooperation with such organizations as IEA, International Energy Forum (IEF) and International Energy Charter on the new platform, Germany aims to build a new type of international order of climate and energy governance.[7] Considering the competition for interests and pluralistic governance in international exchanges regarding clean energy, this book defines clean energy diplomacy as the action or process of formulating diplomatic roads, guidelines, and strategies concerning clean energy issues and carrying out concrete diplomatic activities. These include important visits between governments, signing bilateral or multilateral cooperation agreements, handling trade frictions and conflicts endangering national interests, building dialogue and coordination mechanisms and institutional cooperation platforms, and broadening the channels of providing development aid to foreign countries. The primary objective of clean energy diplomacy is ensuring the nation's green energy security, promoting comprehensive energy transition, realizing sound clean energy governance in the region, and creating the new international order of energy governance.

Section 2 Basic traits of clean energy diplomacy

Given the features of the production and use of clean energy, as well as international cooperation in it, the traits of clean energy diplomacy can be generalized into the following three points.

First, clean energy diplomacy is less geographically sensitive. Traditional fossil energies represented by petroleum, natural gas, and coal are all unsustainable with distinct geographical features. Their production chain (covering exploration, exploitation, production, transportation, processing, and sale) is closely related to specific geographical locations.[8] For geopolitical and geo-economic considerations, countries compete fiercely in the development of and investment in traditional energies, security of energy routes, and domination in international trade, which has led to incessant conflicts, even energy wars.[9] Unlike traditional energies, the supply of clean energies, which are sustainable, largely depends on the technological revolution in wind turbines, solar panels, and energy storage and synchronization. Therefore, clean energy cooperation is more likely to yield multi-win results and can be better in line with countries' long-term interests. German researcher Sebastian Oberthür and others held that international cooperation on the exploitation and utilization of renewable energy can contain potential conflicts and broaden the diplomatic space for most countries that seriously rely on energy import, although it will take a long time for them to basically or thoroughly shed the high reliance on mineral energy imports.[10] On the other hand, the development of clean energy technologies and manufacturing of relevant equipment need rare resources, but the number of mineral resources needed is much smaller compared with fossil energies that require large-scale exports and imports (e.g., coal, petroleum, and natural gas). Besides, thanks to technological progress, many rare earth resources and rare metals can now be recycled or replaced by alternatives.

Second, clean energy diplomacy is more dependent on technology. Clean energy development and cooperation are still somewhat related to local conditions such as wind, water resources, and solar illuminance, but large-scale development depends more on policy innovation, technological progress, and capital flow and technological support on a global scale. It's also affected by the "South-North gap". Clean energy development in the early stage requires a large sum of capital and policy guarantee due to the high cost and the difficulty in grid connection, but the falling cost driven by tech improvement will make it more competitive in both the domestic and international markets. For developing countries, clean energy can

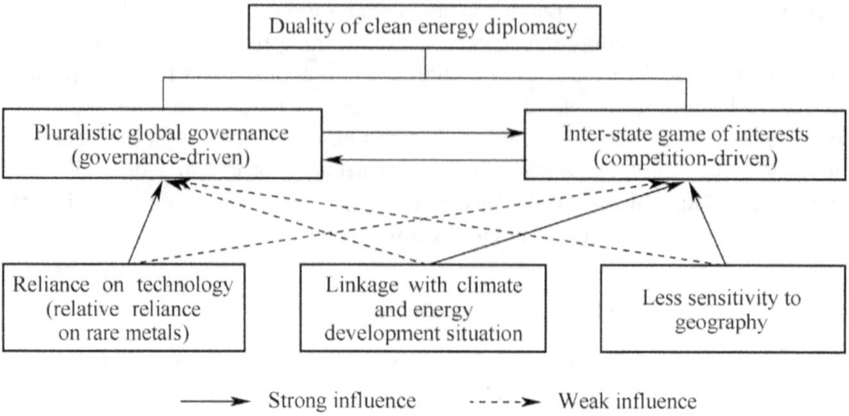

Figure 2.1 Connotations and traits of clean energy diplomacy

Source: Originally created by the author.

contribute hugely to poverty elimination. For instance, biomass, wind, and solar power stations can electrify poor regions. This will consequently eliminate the hazards of conflicts arising from poverty (e.g., poverty-driven migration) and make certain countries and regions more politically stable. Some international organizations, such as the United Nations Environment Programme (UNEP), World Bank, and Global Environment Fund (GEF), are committed to promoting clean energy in developing countries on a large scale, but their supportive measures are far from enough. Affected by the financial crisis, "Northern countries" have tightened their export of clean energy technology and cut government assistance projects, which has cast a shadow on international cooperation in this field. Insufficient capital and backward technology have prevented "Southern countries" from fully taking in the dividends of clean energy development. In addition, developed countries control the right of pricing and circulation in the global market of rare metals, so as to guarantee the supply of rare resources for their manufacturing of clean energy equipment. Even if certain rare metals are in unstable or reduced supply, developed countries are technologically well-positioned to seek alternatives or improve the recycling rate. Therefore, the development of clean energy technology may further widen the South-North disparity if the chasm in tech innovation is not bridged. At that time, there may be a new type of climatic divide between low-carbon developed countries and high-carbon developing ones, with the latter getting increasingly passive or even marginalized in clean energy diplomacy. Meanwhile, we cannot ignore the technological assistance between developing countries through South-South cooperation.

Third, clean energy diplomacy is linked with climate and energy development situations. Clean energy development is closely connected with the evolution of climate and energy development situations. This means that in addition to the financial and technological guarantee, political and strategic coordination is even more important for clean energy development. In particular, cutting subsidies for traditional energies, capping the total consumption of fossil energies, setting the peak of GHG emissions, and establishing a national or global carbon market can all expedite the rapid development of clean energies. To be more specific, in responding to climate change, what's essential is fundamentally optimizing a nation's energy consumption structure, especially controlling GHG emissions through climate negotiations, for the ultimate purpose of forcing the low-carbon, green transformation of the fossil-dominant energy mix.

Therefore, clean energy has received more attention for its important role in international climate and energy governance. On the one hand, it can be an alternative to fossil fuel and help countries improve their capability of mitigating and adapting to climate change through low or zero emission. On the other hand, it can fortify national energy security and make the current energy system more resilient. Given the ever-changing climate conditions, clean energy also gives poor regions a practical option to cope with the unavailability of modern energies and ensure sustainable and equitable energy supply. The constant changes in global climate governance mode have incessantly powered the development of clean energy and the expansion of global low-carbon cooperation. For example, in the post-Paris mode featuring "nationally determined contributions + five-year assessment", setting ambitious clean energy goals is an important path forward. At the same time, in global energy governance, while we emphasize the importance of keeping the price of global energy supply stable and ensuring sustained availability (demand security), we have also highlighted energy diversification and sustainability (energy security). This marks a green shift in our perception of energy security – clean energy topics are gradually embedded in traditional energy governance, although its weighting needs further enhancing. In September 2011, the UN Secretary-General launched the Sustainable Energy for All (SE4All) initiative with the aim of achieving three goals by 2030: ensuring universal access to modern energy services, doubling the global rate of improvement in energy efficiency, doubling the share of renewable energy in the global mix.[11] Against this background, developed and developing countries reached a consensus on the importance of developing clean energies, believing it to be a vital bond that integrated poverty elimination, balanced growth, and a healthy environment.[12] Yet we must beware of the downside of such integration. Once the climate and energy development situation regresses – for instance, the post-Paris mode of nationally determined contribution is no longer effective in restricting carbon emissions, or a nation in the middle of an economic or debt crisis decides to use more fossil energies regardless of environmental impacts – clean energy diplomacy will be negatively impacted in many ways.

As shown in Figure 2.1, in clean energy diplomacy, the inter-state competition for interests and the pluralistic international governance are two dimensions that usually exist in parallel – being repulsive of and dependent on each other at the same time. Countries have come to realize that their mid- to long-term international competitiveness is closely linked with the development of clean energy and environmental technologies.[13] In the future, a nation's competitiveness will depend on its capability in energy conservation, clean energy, and environmental technology.[14] The competition for national interests decides, in a very realistic way, that the starting point of clean energy diplomacy is protecting a nation's fundamental interests such as clean energy development and international competitiveness. That explains the geopolitical view of clean energy development and why stringent rules on trade, circulation, and technology transfer are set to limit the space of innovation for developing countries. The tech-dependence of clean energy diplomacy reinforces such competition. While developing countries need more capital and technological support to break through the bottleneck and obtain more modern energies, developed countries are generally more willing to maintain their vantage point by overlooking the governance-imposed restrictions.

Yet pluralistic international governance is indispensable for the realization of national interests. For example, although China, Germany, and the US have divergences in climate negotiations, all of them realize how important it is to stay competitive in green technology. Competition may lead to frictions, but there is greater potential for cooperation among them in the development and application of clean energy and environmental technology. On the one hand, because of the complexity and challenge of the energy transition, clean energy diplomacy, eyeing multi-party cooperation, needs to arrive at a pluralistic governance mode engaging multiple stakeholders. On the other hand, pluralistic governance provides a multilayered institutional platform to support clean energy diplomacy and an opportunity for countries to gain more rules-setting power, discourse power, and moral appeal in order to influence the clean energy agenda.[15] Therefore, the requirement for responsible sovereignty demands that major-country diplomacy takes on a bigger governance function. In particular, as clean energy diplomacy is less sensitive to geography, it can assuage the zero-sum geopolitical energy game among countries and proceed in the mindset of pluralistic governance.[16] But there is one thing that we need to bear in mind: While the linkage between clean energy diplomacy and climate and energy development situation is good for promoting pluralistic governance, the international countercurrent in climate governance and energy landscape has a direct bearing on the development of clean energy diplomacy. For instance, after Donald Trump was elected president in 2016, his denial of climate change and strong support for traditional energy exerted negative impacts on clean energy diplomacy on the global level.

Section 3 Functionality of clean energy diplomacy

During the transition of the global strategic landscape of climate and energy, clean energy has become the new green engine of climate diplomacy and energy diplomacy. It connects them more closely together and offers a package solution to climate change, energy security, and poverty reduction. Given the basic traits mentioned earlier, clean energy diplomacy mainly functions in the following four areas.

First, clean energy diplomacy, while promoting the sharing of green energy interests, intensifies a nation's friendly relations with its neighbors, particularly their affinity and trust. Energy is the vital "blood" that sustains economic development and prospers the people, but the current geopolitical game among various countries centered on fossil energies hasn't contributed to the economic development, industrial construction, and livelihood improvement in developing countries. Boasting abundant clean energies (e.g., PV, wind energy, tidal energy, and geothermal energy), developing countries urgently need to take advantage of them to develop their economy but are hindered by the lack of technology, investment, and technical personnel. To break through these bottlenecks, they need to continuously expand foreign exchange and cooperation in the development and utilization of clean energy. Therefore, practical actions aimed at boosting international clean energy interaction and cooperation can be an important entry point to innovate the mode of South-North cooperation and South-South cooperation. A nation can advance clean energy development and energy transition in developing countries through effective clean energy diplomacy. For instance, biogas, distributed wind energy, and PV projects can be developed to thoroughly address the power shortage and energy access in the poor regions of certain countries. Clean energy development can proceed side by side with poverty reduction, employment, environmental protection, and sustainable development to bring direct benefits to local people. With this, the nation can win the recognition and support of its neighbors and strengthen their affinity, cohesion, and friendly relations.

Second, clean energy diplomacy helps ease the grave geopolitical energy security situation in regions. Traditional fossil energies represented by petroleum and coal are key targets when countries are making geopolitical deployments because of their limited reserve and uneven distribution. The endless energy disputes usually end up triggering regional conflicts and even wars.[17] In comparison, clean energies are sustainable, and their supply to a large extent depends on technological progress in, for instance, wind turbines, solar panels, energy storage, and grid synchronization. Being geographically insensitive, they can free countries from the ideological shackle of "zero-sum competition" when pursuing energy security. Therefore, international cooperation in clean energy is more likely to yield multi-win results and suit the stakeholders' long-term interests, and the countries, realizing this, will be more willing to conduct clean energy diplomacy and cooperation for multi-win. While optimizing the regional energy mix and promoting sustainability, a nation can gradually improve its energy chain by developing clean energy and consequently achieve a peaceful rise. In the meantime, this trait of geographical insensitivity is good for decentralizing energy governance, meaning no country is solely dominant anymore like in traditional energy governance. This will cause twofold effects. For one, more stakeholders will engage in the governance; for another, the top-down, unidirectional, hierarchical governance switches to the multidirectional, networked governance, in which both top-down and bottom-up approaches are applied.

Third, clean energy diplomacy, while offering a way out of the dilemma in climate and energy diplomacy, demonstrates a major country's sense of responsibility and moral leadership. Take China for example. As a major developing country that emits 1/4 of the world's GHG, China must bear more responsibilities in international climate negotiations. In contrast, as the world's top energy consumer, China is quite marginalized in the global landscape of traditional energy governance, with its discourse power in need of enhancement. Clean energy diplomacy will not only give China more flexibility and initiative in world energy and climate governance but will also enhance its national image and, especially, offer a new path of carrying out South-South cooperation. In 2010–2012, China helped build 64 clean energy projects in 58 developing countries, including wind power, solar power, and biogas equipment. When Chinese President Xi Jinping visited the US in September 2015, he announced to earmark RMB 20 billion to build the China South-South Climate Cooperation Fund, under which clean energy projects have become a key means to helping other developing countries shift toward a green, low-carbon, and climate-adaptive economy. Therefore, conducting clean energy diplomacy in a more pragmatic, flexible, and comprehensive manner and seeking the opportunity to lead and build new platforms of diplomatic interaction leveraged on existing international mechanisms on the premise of defending core national interests will enhance a nation's discourse power and initiative in international climate and energy governance.[18]

Fourth, clean energy diplomacy helps heighten a nation's low-carbon influence and green competitiveness and reinforces its advantageous position in the future strategic layout amid the trend of the low-carbon transition. The governments of all countries have become more keenly aware that their mid- and long-term international competitiveness is closely related to the development of clean energies and environmental technologies. An international contest to lead or dominate this field is quietly on. China, Germany, Japan, and the US have adopted different approaches to developing and supporting clean energies and environmental technologies. Countries have increasingly realized how important green science and technology are for their economic competitiveness, and the contest to lead this field is also unfolding. For example, countries are racing to take a front row in clean energy technology, and governments are more actively seeking ways to help their companies. Years ago, Germany, Japan, and the US were dominant in the R&D of renewable energy technologies and manufacturing of equipment. But by 2010, although they still topped the world in clean technology patents, China had become the world leader in equipment manufacturing.

China has been increasing its investment in renewable energy and is already a world-leading manufacturer of wind turbines and PV panels. A Chatham House report on intellectual property and technology transfer released in 2009 showed that patent applications on clean energy technology (wind energy, solar battery, high-efficiency solar energy, biomass energy, clean coal, and carbon capture) increased drastically after the mid-20th century. While American, Japanese, and German companies control most of those patents, applications from multinationals in other countries, such as China, the UK, France, Canada, ROK, India, Italy, and Russia, have been on the rise.[19] This kind of competition and cooperation in green and low-carbon fields is continuously driving the standardized and well-regulated clean energy governance worldwide. On the other hand, without the guarantee of flexible and pragmatic clean energy diplomacy, a kind of resource nationalism may emerge in the field of green energy. This means countries would use resources, mainly energies, as diplomatic leverage and scramble for leadership in the resource system through geo-economic strategy in order to maintain their energy security and domination. Resource nationalism also refers to the phenomenon that developed countries employ "technology nationalism" (technology patents or blockade) and other means to control developing countries in the global economic chain and turn them into their resource suppliers. As anti-globalization and populism are gaining ground, technology blockade and control in clean energy have worsened with the rise of trade protectionism. Therefore, we need clean energy diplomacy to escort the development of the clean energy industry in all countries, reduce trade frictions and vicious competition, and facilitate the sound development and fast growth of green strength and competitiveness.

Section 4 Strategic positioning of clean energy diplomacy

Being counted as the hope to lead the rise of the new-generation energy industry chain, clean energy commands a more important position in the international strategic landscape of climate and energy. Under such circumstances, should we view clean energy diplomacy as an "inter-state game of interests", whether it's short-term competition in low-carbon technology, green trade protectionism or efforts to maintain the long-term advantages of national climate and energy strategy? Or should we view it as a diplomatic mode that transcends geopolitical competition and resembles "pluralistic international governance"? This question is even more thought-provoking now when right-wing conservatism is on the rise across the globe. On January 20, 2017, immediately after he was elected president, Donald Trump dropped Obama's Climate Action Plan[20] and Clean Power Plan and cut the subsidy for renewable energy. Trump's steps unavoidably brought negative impacts to global clean energy cooperation; it even gave a push to resource nationalism and its trend toward the zero-sum geopolitical game. As clean energy diplomacy gains traction, the academic circle is having more discussions about its strategic positioning.

Given the duality of clean energy diplomacy, this book defines its strategic positioning on two dimensions – governance-driven (institutional governance based on rules) and competition-driven (market competition based on interest game). On the governance-driven dimension, clean energy diplomacy refers to the institutional governance based on rules. It breaks away from the resource control in traditional energy diplomacy and realizes resource sharing and joint governance. This means that a variety of actors, including government departments of sovereign stages, government officials, research institutes, NGOs, and clean energy industry associations, all try to protect national rights and interests in clean energy and create a new international order of energy governance. With that as the core task, they strive to promote global clean energy cooperation by forming dialogue and coordination mechanisms and institutional interactive platforms of various types and on multiple levels, as reflected in the establishment of various clean energy governance mechanisms. For example, intergovernmental organizations and summits such as IRECs, IRENA, and CEM have set the institutional stage for global clean energy governance. At the same time, sub-state and non-state actors, such as cities, NGOs, social groups, enterprises, industrial associations, and research institutes, are getting more involved in global clean energy governance and turning it into a more pluralistic network. For example, the appearance of policy initiatives and partnership networks, including REN21 and CESA, has pushed clean energy diplomacy above the governmental level with great vitality and momentum.[21] On the competition-driven dimension, clean energy diplomacy refers to market competition based on the game of national interests, with the purpose of protecting a nation's fundamental interests, including its share in the clean energy market and international competitiveness. To be specific, it involves the geographical scramble for raw materials and resources (e.g., rare earth) of clean energy development and the international race in green technology and innovation investment amid the low-carbon transition. Developed countries tend to squeeze the space of innovation for developing countries by setting harsh trade and circulation rules and high technology transfer thresholds and hinder the clean energy development of emerging countries through clean energy trade protectionism (e.g., carbon tariff or clean energy anti-dumping policy).[22]

Based on these two dimensions, the strategic positioning of clean energy diplomacy can be further divided into four types according to the high standard and the low standard. They are respectively characterized by standard governance (high governance drive/low competition drive) as in Germany, green hegemony (high governance drive/high competition drive) as in the US during Obama's term, market competition (low governance drive/high competition drive) as in the US during Trump's term, and green economy (low governance drive/low competition drive) as in India and Brazil.

The first type of clean energy diplomacy is characterized by standard governance with high governance and drive and low competition drive. With this type, a nation tries to lead global clean energy governance by establishing international mechanisms and implementing international rules. It is mainly driven by governance rather than market competition, and the typical example is Germany. When the EU was filing an anti-dumping, countervailing suit against China on PV equipment, Germany, the founder of IRENA, insisted on taking a cautious position for

Table 2.2 Strategic positioning of clean energy diplomacy

		Governance-driven (institutional governance based on rules)	
		High	*Low*
Competition-driven (market competition based on the game of national interests)	High	Clean energy diplomacy characterized by green hegemony (e.g., America during Obama's term)	Clean energy diplomacy characterized by market competition (e.g., America during Trump's term)
	Low	Clean energy diplomacy characterized by standard governance (e.g., Germany)	Clean energy diplomacy characterized by green economy (e.g., India, Brazil)

Source: Originally created by the author.

fear that would lend a heavy blow to Europe's clean energy development. It also played an important role in persuading the EU to give up the suit in 2018.

The second type is characterized by green hegemony with high governance drive and high competition drive. Countries strong in clean energy development attach much importance to establishing the global clean energy governance mechanisms and norms through clean energy diplomacy so as to increase their rules-making power and discourse power. Meanwhile, these countries, with a high competition drive, tend to maintain their competitiveness and technological superiority in the clean energy market through protective trade and mandatory carbon tariffs. They also pay close attention to their share in the international clean energy market and the competition for the power of formulating industrial standards. The combination of high governance drive and high competition drive results in a tendency of green hegemony, with the US under Obama's reign being a typical example. On the one hand, the US initiated the CEM regime after the Copenhagen Climate Change Conference in 2009 to further institutionalize the global clean energy governance. On the other hand, it officially launched the anti-dumping and countervailing investigation against China's PV and wind power products in 2012.

The third type is characterized by market competition with low governance drive and high competition drive. Countries adopting this type of clean energy diplomacy don't care about global clean energy governance and only focus on market competition in clean energy. This means they, aiming solely at national economic interests, would implement conservative trade policies to protect the domestic clean energy market and set a high threshold of technology transfer to limit the space of innovation for developing countries. A typical example is the US under Trump's reign. As soon as he came into office, Trump made no secret of his inclination to withdraw from global governance, not only exiting the *Paris Agreement*, but also putting a stop to Obama's Clean Energy Plan and giving up America's leadership at CEM. At the same time, he was extremely conservative when it came to international trade. To maintain America's market share and competitive edge, he increased tariffs on Chinese PV and wind power products exported to the US by starting a trade war, putting yet another fetter on China after the anti-dumping and countervailing probe.

The fourth type is characterized by green economic development with low governance drive and low competition drive. This type is common among developing countries because they, neither strong in clean energy development nor capable in its governance, lay stress on international cooperation and technological assistance as the way to boost their green strengths. Usually playing second fiddle in global clean energy governance, these countries actively join various governance mechanisms to secure more international financial and technological support to promote the low-carbon transition of the domestic economy. With little power over establishing the systems and setting the narrative, they will hardly play the leading role, so they support free and fair trade in the international clean energy market and emphasize developed countries' obligation of providing financial support and transferring technologies to developing ones. Typical examples include India and Brazil, but their clean energy diplomacy is also undergoing new changes.

Given the four types of the strategic positioning of clean energy diplomacy, this book in Chapter 4 will make a comparative analysis of five major countries of clean energy development. Three of them are developed countries (Germany that pioneers clean energy development, the US that dominates low-carbon technology, and Japan that boasts high energy efficiency), and two are emerging countries (Brazil that's strong in bio-energy and India whose solar energy is rising quickly). It must be noted that there isn't a single country that adopts a purely competition-driven or governance-driven clean energy diplomacy – it's always the combination of both. Moreover, the strategic positioning of a country's clean energy diplomacy changes with time. As a country's policies of clean energy diplomacy are closely linked with its stance on climate governance and strategy of climate diplomacy, policy changes in climate diplomacy will affect its policies on clean energy diplomacy.

Notes

1 Jin Zhengkun, *Introduction to Modern Diplomacy*, Beijing: China Renmin University Press, 1999, p. 6.
2 Marjoleinde Ridder, "The Geopolitics of Mineral Resources for Renewable Energy Technologies", *The Report* of *Hague Center for Strategic Studies*, 2013, www.mmta.co.uk/wp-con-tent/uploads/2017/02/The-geopolitics-of-mineral-resources-Hague-2013.pdf; David S. Abraham, "The Battle for New Resources: Minor Minerals in Green Technologies", *RIETI Policy Discussion Paper Series 12-P-005*, March 2012, www.rieti.go.jp/jp/publications/pdp/12p005.pdf.
3 Joel B. Eisen, "New Energy Geopolitics: China, Renewable Energy, and the Greentech Race", *Chicago-Kent Law Review,* Vol. 86, 2011, pp. 9–58.
4 Yu Hongyuan, "Utilitarianism and Globalism in Global Energy Governance", *Journal of International Security Studies*, No. 5, 2013.
5 Charles F. Sabel, David G. Victor, "Governing Global Problems Under Uncertainty: Making Bottom-up Climate Policy Work", *Climatic Change*, No. 144, 2017, pp. 15–27.
6 Dirk Messner, Jennier Morgan, "Germany Needs an Energy Transformation Foreign Policy", *German Development Institute Report*, 2013, pp. 16–19.
7 Sybille Roehrkasten, Kirsten Westphal, "IRENA and Germany's Foreign Renewable Energy Policy Aiming at Multilevel Governance", *SWP Working Papers*, 2013, www.researchgate.net/publication/280921266_IRENA_and_Germany's_Foreign_Renewable–Energy_Policy; Lana Dreyer, "Renewables: Do They Matter for Foreign Policy?", *Brief Issue of European Union Institute for Security Studies*, No. 3, 2013, www.iss.europa.eu/publications/detail/article/renewables-do-they-matter-for-foreign-policy/.
8 Ann Florini, Benjamin K. Sovacool, "Who Governs Energy? The Challenges Facing Global Energy Governance", *Energy Policy*, No. 37, 2009, pp. 5239–5248.
9 David Criekemans, "The Geopolitics of Renewable Energy: Different or Similar to the Geopolitics of Conventional Energy?", Canada: ISA Annual Convention, 2011, pp. 6–9, https://exploringgeopolitics.org/wp-content/uploads/2019/01/Criekemans_David_Geopolitics_Renewable_Energy.pdf.
10 Sebastian Oberthür, Stephanie Pfahl, Dennis Tänzler, "Renewable Energy Needs International Cooperation", *World Economics and Politics*, No. 4, 2005.
11 United Nations, "Sustainable Energy for All", www.un.org/en/events/sustainableenergyforall/background,shtml.
12 The UNGA in 2012 announced that year as the "International Year of Sustainable Energy for All" through Resolution 65/151. The 2013 UNGA adopted a new resolution declaring 2014–2024 as the "Decade of Sustainable Energy for All" to promote the use and development of clean energy. In "Transforming Our World: the 2030 Agenda for

Sustainable Development" adopted by the UNGA in 2015, the 7th of the sustainable developed goals is "ensure access to affordable, reliable, sustainable and modern energy for all" (SDG7).

13 Benjamin Alter, Edward Fishman, "The Dark Side of Energy Independence?", *New York Times*, April 28, 2013.

14 Miranda Schreurs, Wang Congcong, "The Competition for Leadership in Clean Energy and Environmental Technology", *Green Leaf*, No. 3, 2012.

15 Mihaela Papa, Nancy W. Gleason, "Major Emerging Powers in Sustainable Development Diplomacy: Assessing Their Leadership Potential", *Global Environmental Change*, No. 22, 2012, pp. 915–924.

16 Charles F. Sabel, David G. Victor, "Governing Global Problems under Uncertainty: Making Bottom-up Climate Policy Work", *Climatic Change*, No. 144, 2017, pp. 15–27.

17 David Criekemans, *The Geopolitics of Renewable Energy: Different or Similar to the Geopolitics of Conventional Energy*?, Canada: ISA Annual Convention, 2011, pp. 1–17, https://exploringgeopolitics.org/wp-content/uploads/2019/01/Criekemans_David_Geopolitics_Renewable_Energy.pdf.

18 Mihaela Papa, Nancy W. Gleason, "Major Emerging Powers in Sustainable Development Diplomacy: Assessing Their Leadership Potential", *Global Environmental Change*, No. 22, 2012, pp. 915–924.

19 Bernice Lee, Ilian Iliev, Felix Preston, "Who Owns Our Low Carbon Future? Intellectual Property and Energy Technologies", in *A Chatham House Report*, London: Royal Institute of International Affairs, September 2009.

20 The Climate Action Plan was America's first national climate action plan. It was announced by Obama in 2013 with the key purpose of slashing carbon emissions from power plants, the main source of GHG emission, and promoting the development of renewable energy. The plan was implemented mainly with the president's administrative power without a congressional bill.

21 Mihaela Papa, Nancy W. Gleason, "Major Emerging Powers in Sustainable Development Diplomacy: Assessing Their Leadership Potential", *Global Environmental Change*, No. 22, 2012, pp. 915–924.

22 Michael T. Klare, *The Race far What's Left*: *The Global Scramble for the World's Last Resources*, New York: Metropolitan Books, 2012. Lucia Baldi, Massimo Peri, Daniela Vandone, "Clean Energy Industries and Rare Earth Materials: Economic and Financial Issues", *Energy Policy*, No. 66, 2014, pp. 53–61.

3 Global clean energy diplomacy

Overall development under dual drives

Clean energy diplomacy has been flourishing since the end of the 1990s, especially on the governance-driven dimension. Intergovernmental organizations such as CEM, IRENA, and IRECs as well as various summits, which get increasingly institutional, set the stage for global governance of clean energy. Compared with traditional energy governance, clean energy governance is apparently more pluralistic and networked. Sub-state and non-state actors, such as enterprises, industrial associations, research institutes, cities, NGOs, and social groups, are increasingly engaged in global clean energy governance. Their cross-border interactions and coordination have also intensified and given birth to a number of policy initiatives and partnership networks, with CESA, REN21, and GNESD being typical examples. This has expanded and enriched the global governance of clean energy. Besides, the green impetus from the private sector should not be neglected. The establishment of Bill Gates' one-billion-dollar Breakthrough Energy Ventures Fund in December 2016 and the flourishing carbon markets in various countries have injected sustained momentum to the development of clean energy diplomacy. In the meantime, the competition-driven clean energy diplomacy should not be underestimated either, as the competition ranges from raw materials and markets to green scientific and technological strengths amid the low-carbon transition. By encouraging and supporting clean energy, countries hope to foster new industry chains, nurture domestic markets, and adjust their economic structure. Eventually they hope to enhance their international competitiveness through the rise of the full industry chain of clean energy.[1] In addition to competition on the national level, more and more non-state actors have joined the green competition. This chapter will analyze the overall development of clean energy diplomacy worldwide on both the governance-driven dimension and the competition-driven dimension. It must be noted that the clean energy diplomacy of any country is a complex combination of both dimensions, which are coexistent and even interdependent sometimes. In a sense, competition is one of the key factors that drive the fast rise of clean energy. But to prevent vicious competition and regulate the development of clean energy, the governance-driven dimension has become more important and urgent.

DOI: 10.4324/9781003433903-5

Section 1 Governance-driven dimension of clean energy diplomacy

Governance-driven clean energy diplomacy is orientated toward rules-based, institutional governance. It emphasizes breaking away from the dimension of resource control in traditional energy diplomacy and realizes the sharing and joint governance of resources. In governance-driven clean energy diplomacy, different types of dialogue and coordination mechanisms, as well as institutional interactive platforms, have been established on various levels to enhance international cooperation in clean energy, and a variety of actors are introduced to diplomatic interactions. The development of governance-driven clean energy diplomacy has the following characteristics.

I. Major countries give a strong impetus to institutionalizing global clean energy governance in the early stage

Germany is a key pioneer in promoting global clean energy governance. As early as 2002, German chancellor Gerhard Schroder invited state leaders attending the World Summit on Sustainable Development in Johannesburg to participate in the global clean energy conference, putting clean energy on the official agenda of an international conference for the first time.[2] At the first International Conference for Renewable Energies held in Bonn, Germany, in June 2004, the ministers and government representatives from 154 countries passed the *Bonn Political Declaration* and decided to raise the share of renewables in total energy supply by a large margin while improving energy efficiency in parallel.[3] To make the conference sustainable, Germany handed over the convening power to REN21 (Renewable Energy Policy Network for the 21st Century) that was founded in 2005 in Copenhagen following the *Bonn Political Declaration*. REN21 has co-hosted several international renewable energy conferences with China, the US, India, and other countries since then.

What's most noteworthy is the founding of IRENA (International Renewable Energy Agency), the most influential international organization on clean energy so far, by Germany in Bonn in January 2009. An international platform dedicated to policy consulting, information exchange, mutually beneficial cooperation, and authoritative evaluation concerning clean energy, IRENA supports countries in shifting to an energy-sustainable future through the energy transition. Although the organization hasn't been in operation for long, it had surprisingly gathered 158 member states and 24 applicants by August 2018.[4] IRENA is the first major international organization expressly focused on the promotion of renewable energies. From a pragmatic point of view, it has strategically chosen to narrow down and focus on the deployment of renewables as well as collecting and disseminating information on relevant technologies and policies. IRENA attempts to maximize the effects of policies and investment with the aim of promoting renewable energies.[5]

IRENA's work includes collecting data about global and regional renewables development, providing suggestions on best practices and policy making, providing authoritative analysis on the financial mechanism and technological progress of clean energy, providing capability-building plans (resource sharing, project assistance, financial/technological support, etc.), advocating the learning network of clean energy,[6] and propelling other international organizations to jointly promote the development of renewables. It plays a leading and organizing role in the international governance of renewables. For one thing, IRENA helps forge greater political consensus within the renewables community and creates more normative standards for clean energy governance. For another, it largely lowers the information barriers for renewable energy investment through the exchange of information, thus stimulating private investment. For instance, IRENA's Global Atlas for Solar and Wind maps the technological and economic potential of wind and solar to stimulate investors' interests. For a third, by coordinating actions in the governance of renewables, IRENA enhances the influence and discourse power of this sector in the global landscape of climate and energy governance.

The US has played an important part in advancing CEM. This is another important international conference stemming from the Copenhagen Climate Change Conference in 2009 and a global clean energy summit founded by the US Department of Energy in 2010. Since its founding, CEM has held eight ministerial meetings in Washington of America, Abu Dhabi of UAE, London of Britain, New Delhi of India, Seoul of ROK, Mérida of Mexico, San Francisco of America, and Beijing of China. The meeting gathers main players in the clean energy market of 24 major countries and the EU.[7] They include prominent research institutes of clean energy technologies, leading equipment manufacturers, and main energy producers and consumers. Accounting for 90% of the world's clean energy investment and 75% of GHG emissions, these entities are vital for the transition of the world energy system. CEM aims to promote and deploy clean energy technologies more quickly by sharing best practices, experience, and lessons. It encourages the global transition toward a clean energy economy with three goals – strengthening the clean energy

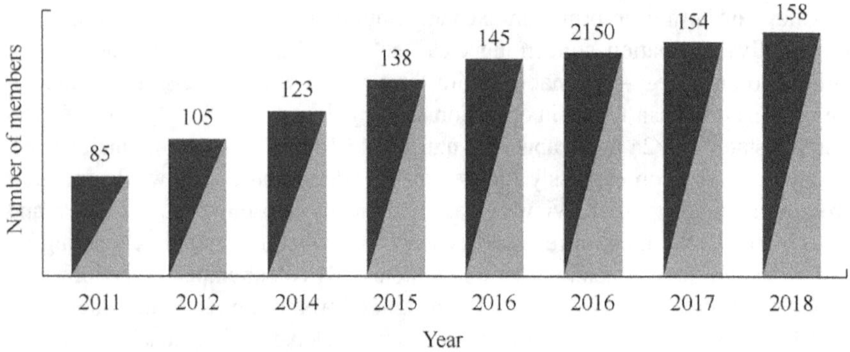

Figure 3.1 Growing membership in IRENA

Source: www.irena.org/irenamembership.

supply system, raising global energy efficiency, and enhancing the availability of clean energy. CEM's core values lie in perfecting policies, boosting the development and utilization of clean energy technologies, fostering competitive edges of clean energy more quickly, improving international dialogue mechanisms in the field, and impelling private partnerships. It has not only engaged state actors but also many other stakeholders.

After Trump took office, he abolished Obama's Clean Energy Plan and Climate Action Plan and refused to continue playing the leading role in CEM, but his actions didn't bring the mechanism to a deadlock. On the contrary, its actions were bolstered by IEA's newly formed multilateral secretariat at the 2017 CEM8 held in Beijing, which heralded a new stage of more vibrant multilateral cooperation. At the same time, CEM was combined with the Mission Innovation (MI) initiative jointly launched by 20 major countries in December 2015, when the *Paris Agreement* was being concluded.

The MI initiative pledged to double the public resources for energy R&D in participating countries within five years and carry out cooperation in research, capability building, and interaction with the industrial sector.[8] China, for instance, hosted the Eighth Clean Energy Ministerial (CEM8) and the Second Mission Innovation Ministerial (MI-2) – the CEM8 and MI-2 – in Beijing. Themed with "Tackling Challenges Through Innovation, Working Together for a Clean Energy Transition", the event invited representatives from a wide range of international organizations, including IEA, IRENA, International Partnership on Energy Efficiency Cooperation (IPEEC), SE4All, UN Environment Programme (UNEP), United Nations Industrial Development Organization (UNIDO), and World Energy Council (WEC). It also invited leaders and entrepreneurs from the private sector. In May 2018, Nordic countries (Denmark, Finland, Norway, and Sweden) and the EU co-hosted the CEM9/MI-3, at which the energy ministers of Sweden, Denmark, Finland, Iceland, and Norway issued a clean energy declaration in Lund, Sweden. The declaration contained three main points: (1) Nordic countries need to maintain their leading position in energy conservation, renewable energy, and smart energy sources and realize high-level competitiveness and supply security; (2) they should work more closely with other countries and international organizations and apply modern technologies to transform the global energy system in an economically and environmentally sustainable way; and (3) they must recognize the importance of the market for clean energy transition and support and encourage public-private cooperation in the field.

Also that year, the Technical University of Denmark released a series of international energy reports titled "Accelerating the clean energy revolution – perspectives on innovation challenges", which addressed seven innovation challenges – off-grid electricity, smart grid, sustainable bioenergy, carbon capture, clean energy materials, conversion of sunlight to fuels, and affordable heating and cooling. The reports urged accelerated innovation and the cost- and task-sharing of R&D activities. The MI secretariat could be set in the IEA together with the CEM secretariat, and it should support further development both within and across Innovation Challenges. Coalitions of interested countries should support joint projects on Innovation

Challenges that have already made progress in their strategic research programs and should create opportunities for cooperation with industry and co-financing.

II. A growing network of global clean energy governance

In terms of global energy governance, problem-oriented, significant energy, and climate events have to some extent pushed the development of international mechanisms. For instance, around the oil crisis in 1973, global/regional energy organizations began to emerge, represented by the Organization of the Petroleum Exporting Countries (OPEC), IEA, and Latin-American Energy Organization (OLADE). In the 21st century, more organizations appeared that are committed to developing clean and low-carbon energies, such as the Carbon Sequestration Leadership Forum (CSLF)[9] and Renewable Energy and Energy Efficiency Partnership (REEEP). Climate negotiations and global climate governance become important drivers of low-carbon energy. Especially after the *Kyoto Protocol* took effect in 2005, a lot of clean energy and low-carbon development mechanisms have been created, including REN21, IRENA, IPEEC, Global Bioenergy Partnership (GBEP), CEM, and SE4ALL. There are also comprehensive international organizations or governance mechanisms beyond mere energy governance, such as G20, Global Green Growth Institute (GGGI), and Global Green Grow Forum (3GF). They also take clean energy as a key factor for tackling climate change, improving energy security, increasing energy availability, and driving economic growth.

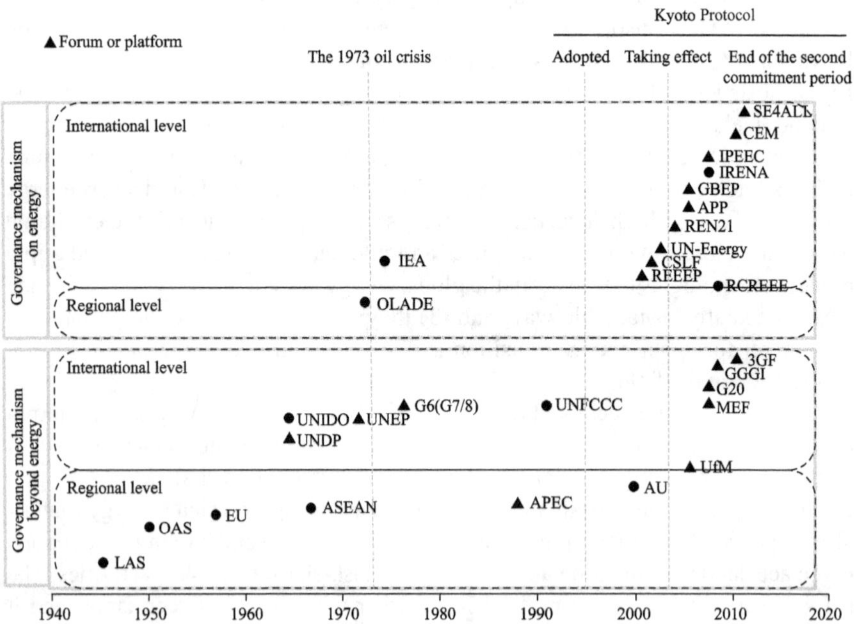

Figure 3.2 Development of (low-carbon) energy organizations

Source: IEA, World Energy Outlook 2017, p. 137.

While establishing global governance of clean energy, partnerships and policy initiatives and networks of various levels and types have come forth both on the global and regional level.[10] There are vertical supranational, international, national, and sub-national decision-making authorities, coalitions between parallel decision-making systems, and new types of cooperation like "public-private" and "private-private" partnerships.

Paul H. Suding and Philippe Lempp classified regional and global organizations of clean energy governance into five types. The first type is international conferences on clean energy, such as IRECs, CEM, and World Summit on Sustainable Development (e.g., Rio+20). The second type is intergovernmental organizations, such as IRENA, UN Commission on Sustainable Development (UN CSD), UNEP, and IEA. The third type refers to partnerships, such as GBEP, Johannesburg Renewable Energy Coalition (JREC), Mediterranean Renewable Energy Programme (MEDREP), Partnership for Clean Indoor Air (PCIA), and REEEP. The fourth type is policy networks based on information exchange and sharing, represented by REN21, Global Network on Energy for Sustainable Development (GNESD), International Science Panel on Renewable Energies (ISPRE), and Network of Expertise in Energy Technology (NEET). The fifth type refers to global clean energy councils and coalitions, such as Global Wind Energy Council (GWEC), International Solar Energy Society (ISES), and European Renewable Energy Council (EREC).[11] Of these five types, only the first two are governance networks among government departments, while the rest – global policy networks, partnerships, and international clean energy councils – are closely linked with the transnational community and global market while maintaining sound cooperation and interaction with governmental and sub-national actors like cities.[12] The five types of organizations are not

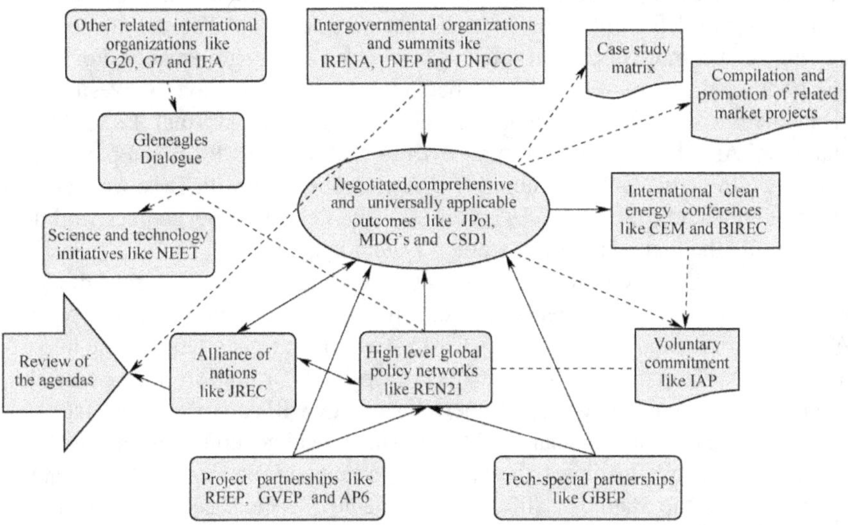

Figure 3.3 Global network of clean energy governance

Source: Based on Paul H. Suding and Philippe Lempp (2007), p. 8.

isolated from each other but are interrelated and coordinated to form a composite network of global clean energy governance. There is no denying that such a composite network makes global clean energy governance much more institutional and lures more stakeholders to join, thus invigorating the development of clean energy to the largest extent.

Clean energy is displaying a strong momentum worldwide, which hasn't even abated in face of such external challenges and headwinds as the financial crisis and counter-globalization. In 2015, the world's new investment in renewable electricity and fuel exceeded USD 285.9 billion, a year-on-year increase of 5%, of which the new investment in renewable electricity (USD 265.8 billion) was twice as much as that in coal- and natural gas–based electricity (USD 130 billion).[13] Such rapid development called for a corresponding global governance mechanism and system. The global governance of clean energy is spiraling up amid the diversifying and networking trend, during which it has developed a unique development path and specific features.

III. Closer cooperation among diverse actors, including government, market entities, and social groups in energy governance

The global energy landscape is undergoing profound changes. The centers of energy demand are quickly moving to emerging markets, and the restrictive goals put forth by *Paris Agreement* are forcing countries to expedite the switch to low-carbon energy sources. According to BP's estimate, the percentage of renewables in global energy demand will rise from 4% in 2018 to about 10% in 2035. World leaders attending the 2011 World Economic Forum in Davos launched a clean energy initiative. Connie Hedegaard, European Commissioner for Climate Action, said that when the government provided the right conditions for green growth, "solutions will definitely come from the business sector".[14] The private sector is playing an ever more important role in global clean energy governance. For example, traditional energy multinationals begin to pay close attention to investment in clean energies. Many international petroleum giants, such as Total, ExxonMobil, and Saudi Aramco, have turned their eyes to such areas as PV, wind power, and bioenergy. In particular, BP announced that its cooperation with Tesla was focused on breaking technical bottlenecks on the storage of clean energy sources, and they would build the first wind power storage system in the US.

Even in the US, a typical country of "regulatory degradation", the trend of closer cooperation among governments, market entities, and social groups is unstoppable. Although Trump abolished Obama's Clean Power Plan right after he came into office, he didn't stop the US Department of Energy (DoE) from strongly promoting technology R&D on renewables. Renewable energy will continue to be backed by the renewable portfolio standard (RPS), in which local governments, NGOs, businesses, and research institutes all play an important part. For instance, the State of New York and the State of California both planned to increase the percentage of renewable energy supply to 50% by 2030.[15] A hundred days through Trump's reign, the DoE approved the projects by 38 small and medium-sized American companies through bidding under the Small Business Certifications program, including eight solar and wind power projects. It granted the successful bidders, through public-private cooperation, access to the technological resources of US national laboratories, giving a strong boost to technological breakthroughs in clean energy.

Against such a background, more and more enterprises, social organizations, and research institutes begin to cooperate with government actors. They jointly engage in clean energy governance and try to perfect it by building networks of technology, information and partnership. On the one hand, this kind of networked cooperation facilitates the flow of information, experts, and capital; on the other hand, it can coordinate the work of most international organizations and experts, provide consulting services, spread technology, and set the framework for coordinating international law. Take REN21 for example. It is a global network on renewable energy policies with a variety of partners that aims at assisting in policy making by providing high-quality information, guiding discussions on relevant topics, promoting the exchange of expertise, and creating communication and coordination networks. It is an online platform connecting multiple stakeholders and key players, including governments, NGOs, research and academic institutes, international organizations, and industrial associations. The organization propels the stakeholders to promote the exchange of expertise, policy making, and the fast development of renewables worldwide. Building on the first International Conference for Renewable Energies in Bonn, REN21 has continued to organize and convene the IRECs and has held it five times so far in cooperation with different governments, including the 2005 BIREC in Beijing, 2008 WIREC in Washington, 2010 DIREC in Delhi, 2013 ADIREC in Abu Dhabi, and 2015 SAIREC in South Africa. It also held the first REN21 Academy in Bonn in 2014. These conferences have become important platforms for communication and exchange among governments, NGOs, research and academic institutes, international organizations, and industrial associations. REN21 also makes a point of connecting with other international organizations and clean energy governance networks. It has already launched several projects with IEA and IRENA. The Renewables Global Status Report (GSR) released by REN21 since 2005, with support from governments, enterprises, and NGOs, is the most-cited report when it comes to the market, industry, and policy concerning renewable energy. IRENA also pays close attention to cooperating with other intergovernmental organizations and NGOs on energy and the environment, viewing itself as a platform to promote the widespread use of renewables. The European Sustainable Energy Week launched by IRENA in June 2017 pooled together the public sector, private businesses, NGOs, and consumers to jointly advance the use of clean energies and create a clean, secure, and efficient energy future for Europe.

IV. More important role of developing countries in the global governance of clean energy

In recent years, clean energies have developed with a robust momentum in developing countries. As shown in Figure 3.4, in 2015, developing countries overtook developed ones for the first time in the combined investment in renewable electricity and fuel. The investment from them, including China, India, and Brazil, reached USD 156 billion (a year-on-year increase of 19%), China in the leading position with an investment of USD 102.9 billion (a year-on-year increase of 17%) that was 36% of the global total. Several other developing countries also invested more than USD 500 million in renewables that year, namely, Morocco, Uruguay, the Philippines, Pakistan, and Honduras.[16] Because of the sluggish economy, both developed and developing countries invested less in clean energy in 2016, but that didn't reverse the growing structural influence of developing countries in global clean energy development. China's investment in clean energy has grown notably since 2017, further widening the gap between developing and developed countries in this aspect – the gap narrowed from USD 32 billion in 2015 to USD 22 billion in 2016, but quickly widened to USD 74 billion in 2017.[17]

At present, developing countries are taking a more active part in global clean energy cooperation and demanding better governance. In international organizations of clean energy governance, not only are the governments of developing countries more deeply engaged, but there are also more enterprises and social organizations from developing countries, constituting the source of new power in the pluralistic and networked governance. For example, of the 150 member states of IRENA, more than 2/3 are from developing countries, and the 30 new applicants are almost all developing countries in Africa, Latin America, and Central and Eastern Europe.[18] Of the nearly 100 members of REN21, over 3/4 are intergovernmental organizations, social groups, NGOs, think tanks, multinationals, and industrial associations, with the percentage of members from developing countries continuously rising in recent years.[19]

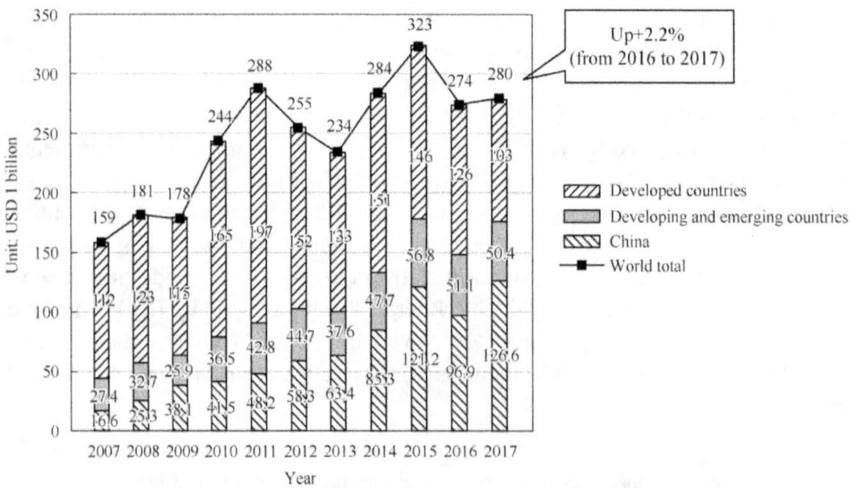

Figure 3.4 Investment in renewable energy: developed countries vs developing countries (2007–2017)

Source: REN21, Renewables 2018 Global Status Report.

It's worth special attention that the BRICS initiated by emerging developing countries including China, India, Brazil, and South Africa has exerted great influences on global clean energy cooperation and governance. As BRICS accounts for nearly 40% of the world's energy consumption and almost half of the incremental consumption, it is getting more structurally influential in global energy governance. Clean energy cooperation is now a critical part of BRICS cooperation. In 2016, the group accounted for 38% of renewable capacity in the world, larger than their percentage in the global GDP (22%). As shown in Table 3.1, the group produced 46.3% of the world's hydropower, 33.7% of wind power, 24.5% of solar power, and 25.1% of other renewable electricity in 2016, commanding an essential position in the global production of clean energy. China was absolutely dominant with 27% of the world's renewable capacity, while Brazil and India each accounted for 5% or so. These three countries were also among the top ten investors in renewable energy that year. Russia and South Africa were quite far behind but have seen fast renewable development in recent years.[20]

BRICS has also brought in more stakeholders through the New Development Bank (NDB). In 2011, leaders of BRICS countries released the *Sanya Declaration* at the 3rd BRICS Leaders Meeting, which supported the development and use of renewable energy sources and recognized its important role as a means to addressing climate change. The first Economic and Financial Forum of BRICS Countries was held in 2012. It sought to combine clean energy development with financial governance on existing cooperation mechanisms and platforms, so as to implement the strategy of green energy and low-carbon transformation with financial leverage. The NDB founded in 2015 is tasked with financing infrastructure construction and promoting sustainable development. It raises funds for the switch to green energy, low-carbon development, and climate change response in emerging countries. In April 2016, NDB announced the first batch of loans totaling USD 811 million, which went to four renewable energy projects respectively located in Brazil, China, India, and South Africa. This indicated how much importance BRICS attached to clean energy diplomacy and cooperation.

Table 3.1 BRICS' renewable electricity output and the global ranking, 2016

Country	*Solar*		*Wind*		*Hydro*		*Others*	
	Output/ (10^8kW·h)	*Ranking*	*Output/ (10^8kW·h)*	*Ranking*	*Output/ (10^8kW·h)*	*Ranking*	*Output/ (10^8kW·h)*	*Ranking*
China	662	1	2410	1	11628	1	734	2
India	119	7	448	5	1288	7	160	8
Brazil	1	44	329	7	3843	3	509	4
Russia	1	43	1	47	1866	5	5	41
South Africa	33	13	42	25	10	49	3	46
Combined	816		3230		18635		1412	
Global	3331		9595		40229		5617	
Percentage	24.5%		33.7%		46.3%		25.1%	

Source: BP Statistical Review of World Energy 2017.

Section 2 Competition-driven dimension of clean energy diplomacy

On the competition-driven dimension, global clean energy diplomacy means the competitive/cooperative relation among countries based on the game of interests. All countries are developing clean energies, raising energy efficiency, and adopting other technical measures to recover the economy and maintain their advantages in the future global economic competition. As far as national interests are concerned, clean energy diplomacy is aimed at protecting fundamental interests such as a nation's share and international competitiveness in the clean energy market. These include the geographical scramble for raw materials and resources and the international race in green science and technology and investment in innovation amid the low-carbon transition. To be specific, the development of competition-driven clean energy diplomacy has the following characteristics.

I. Geographical contention for raw materials for clean energy development

Worried about climate change, depletion of fossil fuel reserves, economic competitiveness, and innovation, the governments of all countries have set ambitious goals for renewable energy, an area that features a high concentration of high and new technologies as well as rare raw materials. For instance, solar panels, wind turbines, and electric vehicle (EV) batteries rely highly on a number of minerals. One of the key substances needed to develop renewable energy technology is rare earth, which is known as the "vitamin for new materials" for its unique optical, magnetic, and electric properties. It is listed by many countries as an essential element for developing high technologies and a strategic core resource indispensable for the development of green energy.[21]

Rare earth is vital for the development of green energy technologies. It is irreplaceable for new energy vehicles (NEV), wind power, a new type of electric light sources, and energy-saving motors, which explains why clean energy is considered dependent on rare earth. To be specific, wind power is taken by many countries as an important strategy for new energy development. The permanent magnet in wind turbine needs dysprosium (Dy) and neodymium (Nd), both of which are rare earth elements, so wind turbine is a pivot of the permanent magnet industry, and that

Table 3.2 Elements and rare materials needed to develop green technologies

Green technology	*Element*	*Materials*
Wind power	Engine/battery	Nd, Dy
Traffic vehicle	Engine	Nd, Dy
	EV battery	Li, Co, rare earth
PV battery	Thin-film PV component	Te, Ga, Ge, Im, Se, Cd
	CIGS thin film	Im, Ga
	CdTe thin film	Te, Cd
Luminous energy	Phosphor	Rare earth

Source: David Abraham, *The Battle for New Resources: Minor Minerals m Green Technologies*, RIETI Policy Discussion Paper Series 12-P-005, March 2012, p. 21.

drives the demand for high-performance rare earth elements like Nd, iron (Fe), and boron (B).[22] Permanent magnet motor is also the trend of NEVs, and rare earth–based permanent magnet synchronous motor represents the direction of auto motors. PV power generation needs thin-film battery, the production of which needs a series of rare earth minerals such as tellurium (Te), stannum (Sn), indium (Im), hafnium (Hf), and gallium (Ga). Europium (Eu), erbium (Er), and ytterbium (Yb)-based thin film can largely increase the conversion efficiency of solar batteries. Lithium (Li) and tungsten (W) are used in the charging battery for EV. Platinum (Pt) is used in anti-fouling devices and vehicles, and cobalt (Co) and magnesium (Mg) for bioenergy technology.[23] In recent years, renewable energies have enjoyed a growth rate of 30%–40%, and their global application is anticipated to grow threefold in the next decade, even six times in China and four times in India. The development of emerging clean energy technologies, such as battery, thin-layer PV, fuel cell, catalyst, and permanent magnet, will boost the international demand for an array of minerals. From a geopolitical perspective, many countries think their renewable energy goals may be threatened by the rarity of minerals, high import reliance, and potential supply risks.[24]

The geopolitics around mineral resources are shaped by the balance of power, conflict, and cooperation between major mineral producers and major importers. With rare earth, for instance, the major-country struggle is focused on trade disputes. In 2012, China issued a white paper titled *Situation and Policies of China's Rare Earth Industry*, which said that China's rare earth reserve accounts for 23% of the world total, and it has met most of the global demand at an unreasonably low price for a long time. Considering the environmental damages and rampant

Table 3.3 Demand for mineral resources driven by new clean energy technologies

Raw material	*Product 2006 (ton)*	*Demand driven by emerging technology 2006 (ton)*	*Demand driven by emerging technology 2030 (ton)*	*2006 index1*	*2030 index 1*
Ga	152	28	603	0.18	3.97
Im	581	234	1.911	0.40	3.29
Ge	100	28	220	0.28	2.20
Nd (rare earth)	16.800	4.000	27.900	0.23	1.66
Pt (platinum group metal)	255	Very small	345	0	1.35
Ta	1.384	551	1.410	0.40	1.02
Silver	19.051	5.342	15.823	0.28	0.83
Co	62.279	12.820	26.860	0.21	0.43
Pd (platinum group metal)	267	23	77	0.09	0.29
Ti	7.211.000[2]	15.397	58.148	0.08	0.29
Cu	15.093.000	1.410.000	3.696.070	0.09	0.24

Source: European Commission, "Critical Raw Materials for the EU: Report of the Ad-hoc Working Group on Defining Critical Raw Materials", p. 7.

smuggling in the course of rare earth exploitation, China vowed to better regulate the industry by limiting rare earth export, a policy that was strongly objected to by major importers. The US, EU, and Japan filed a suit to the WTO in March 2012 accusing China's restriction on rare earth export of violating WTO rules. In June that year, the three parties requested the WTO Dispute Settlement Body form an expert group to investigate the case, which was hence formed in July in spite of China's protest and rejection, putting China in a passive position. The dispute at WTO denoted the fiercer global competition for rare earth resources. Although China is a major producer of rare earth, it has no power to decide its international price or scale of export.[25]

Major countries have also issued mid- and long-term policies on mineral resource that are favorable for clean energy development. Statistics from the United States Geological Survey (USGS) indicated that America has the world's third-largest rare earth reserves. However, considering the environmental impacts and exploitation cost, the need for the strategic reserve of mineral resources, and the cheap export from China, the US closed all rare earth mines at the end of the 20th century and turned to import rare earth from China. After China launched a series of regulatory measures in the rare earth industry, the US had to quicken the adjustment of its rare earth strategy. It first established a global supply system covering various mineral resources to make sure the US has sustained, stable, and fairly priced supply worldwide. Second, it began to develop its own rare earth resources and tried to raise the utilization rate through technological upgrades. Third, it intensified international cooperation to reshape the international supply chain of rare earth. Fourth, it used new technologies to search for alternatives to rare earth in order to reduce the reliance on it.

Japan is a typical island country of scanty mineral resources, but its advanced high-tech industry has made it a major consumer of rare metals and nonferrous metals. In 2009, the Japanese Ministry of Economy, Trade, and Industry (METI) released the *Strategy of Ensuring the Stable Supply of Rare Metals*. The key message was guaranteeing the rare earth supply for Japan by all means so as to reduce the reliance on Chinese resources and protect Japan's core interests.[26] Its strategy included the following key points: (1) Strengthening the strategic reserve of rare earth resources by procurement by batches, import through entrepot trade, and building offshore plants; (2) encouraging investment in and development of resources overseas and assisting enterprises in prospecting overseas resource; (3) accelerating the development and use of undersea mineral resources – Japan began surveying rare earth and other mineral resources in its surrounding waters in 2010; (4) conducting studies of rare earth alternatives, rare metal recycling, and high-efficiency utilization, and (5) making rare earth part of its diplomatic agenda and working to get international support.[27]

With very little rare earth reserve, Europe needs to import from countries like China and India, and its advanced science and technology leads to especially pressing demand for the resource. The *Report on Critical Raw Materials for the EU* issued in 2010 stressed the significance of rare earth as a strategic reserve and recommended three ways to guarantee its supply. The first was tapping resources within the EU to promote the sustainable supply of raw materials and forming an expert group to monitor the supply of 49 essential raw materials. The second was eliminating restrictions imposed by third-party countries on raw materials trade to ensure EU's import. The third was increasing the efficiency and recycling of resources. Under this strategy, the EU, together with the US and Japan, filed a suit to WTO against China's limitation on the export of strategic raw materials, which laid bare the nonnegligible geopolitical struggle for strategic raw materials in the development of clean energy.

II. Competition in green science and technology and innovation input amid the low-carbon transition

Developing strategic emerging industries represented by clean energy is an important way of shifting the economic development mode, ensuring ecological sustainability, optimizing the energy structure, and realizing leapfrog development. In developing clean energy, only by grasping the core and key technologies in strategic emerging industries can we fundamentally ensure their healthy and sustained development. We should especially guarantee the sustained drive of innovation as well as the continuous growth of scientific and technological strength through systematic IP protection policies. Therefore, the green competition amid the low-carbon transition presents itself in the form of the countries' investment in clean energy technologies and the promotion of IP-related innovation.[28]

When the aftermaths of the 2008 financial crisis were still lingering, countries began to take developing strategic emerging industries represented by clean energy as an innovation "race" to seize the commanding height in future development, with the focus on IP deployments. After President Obama took office, he released the *American Recovery & Reinvestment Act 2009* and the *American Clean Energy and Security Act*, under which USD 21.8 billion was invested in energy conservation industries; USD 18.9 billion in energy transmission, distribution, and alternative energy studies; and USD 20 billion in the R&D and promotion of EV. Another USD 777 million would also be allocated to support the establishment of 46 frontier energy research centers. In March 2009, the European Commission announced to invest EUR 105 billion to support "green strategic industries" within the union, in a bid to maintain its leadership in innovative technologies as a normative green force. It continued to release an ambitious green economic plan in the *Energy 2020: A Strategy for Competitive, Sustainable and Secure Energy* published in November 2010. The German government put forth a "package plan for a green economy" in June 2009 to promote new energies and a low-carbon economy. In particular, it passed the second *German Renewable Energy Law Amendment* (EEG2009), which pledged to increase the percentage of renewable energy in power consumption to 30% by 2020, and approved a EUR 500-million budget for EV R&D. It also planned to realize mass production of lithium battery by 2011 as a way to stimulate the EV industry. Britain adopted in 2009 the *UK Low-carbon Transition Plan, UK Renewable Energy Strategy*, and *Low-carbon Industrial Strategy* as part of the "green recovery plan", hoping to recover from the economic decline with the help

Table 3.4 Key emerging industries in major developed economies and China after the financial crisis

Economy	*Time*	*Main plans and measures*	*Industry and technology*
US	February 2009	American Recovery and Reinvestment Act 2009	New energy, environmental protection, information and Internet, biology and medical care, space and marine industry
	June 2009	American Clean Energy and Security Act	Supporting the development of clean energy
EU	March 2009	Green economy plan	Investing EUR 105 billion to support green economy in the union and maintain its world leadership in green technology
	November 2010	Energy 2020: A Strategy for Competitive, Sustainable and Secure Energy	EU's new energy strategy for the next decade
Germany	June 2009	Package plan	New energy, low-carbon economy
	2009	German Renewable Energy Law Amendment (EEG2009)	Raising the targets for renewable power
Britain	June 2009	Digital Britain	Digital economy
	July 2009	UK Low-carbon Transition Plan, backed by UK Renewable Energy Strategy, Low-carbon Industrial Strategy and Low-carbon Transport Strategy	Low-carbon economy: energy-saving homes, nuclear energy, offshore wind energy, tidal energy, new energy vehicle (NEV)
	Jan.–Feb. 2010	GBP 325-million UK Innovation Investment Fund	GBP 125 million for clean energy technology, GBP 200 million for life sciences, digital industry, and advanced manufacturing
Japan	April 2009	Fourth Economic Stimulus Plan	Environment-friendly vehicle, electric vehicle (EV), low carbon emission, medical care, solar power, cultural tourism, etc.
	December 2009	New Economic Stimulus Plan	Energy conservation
China	September 2010	Decision on Accelerating the Fostering and Development of Strategic Emerging Industries	Emphasizing technological innovation capability in seven strategic emerging industries; enhancing their core competitiveness

Source: Originally developed by the author.

of the "low-carbon economic mode". Japan adopted the *Fourth Economic Stimulus Plan* and *New Economic Stimulus Plan* in 2009, putting its strategic focus on such industries as IT application, new types of automobiles, low-carbon industry, and new energy (solar energy).

In September 2010, the State Council of China adopted the *Decision on Accelerating the Fostering and Development of Strategic Emerging Industries*, which specified seven key directions of strategic emerging industries – energy conservation and environmental protection, new-generation information technology, biotech, high-end equipment manufacturing, new energy, new materials, and NEV. The Decision emphasized the importance of intensifying the studies of key and core technologies as well as frontier technologies and of strengthening the enterprises' capability of technological innovation.

Legal protection of intellectual property (IP) is an important guarantee for promoting innovation in clean energy technology. Especially the patent protection of high and new technology fundamentally preserves the technological vitality of emerging strategic industries. Green patent statistics are a key indicator that gauges a nation's scientific and technological innovation in clean energy.[29] The 2010 statistical report on patent applications issued by the European Patent Office (EPO) showed that there were 1,777 "environmental technology" patents closely related to clean energy development. A global ranking revealed the EU's unshakable leadership in the number of technology patent applications related to clean energy, which accounted for 43% of the annual applications. For single countries, the US left other countries far behind by making up 21% of patent applications in clean energy and low-carbon technology, followed by Germany (19%) and Japan (17%).

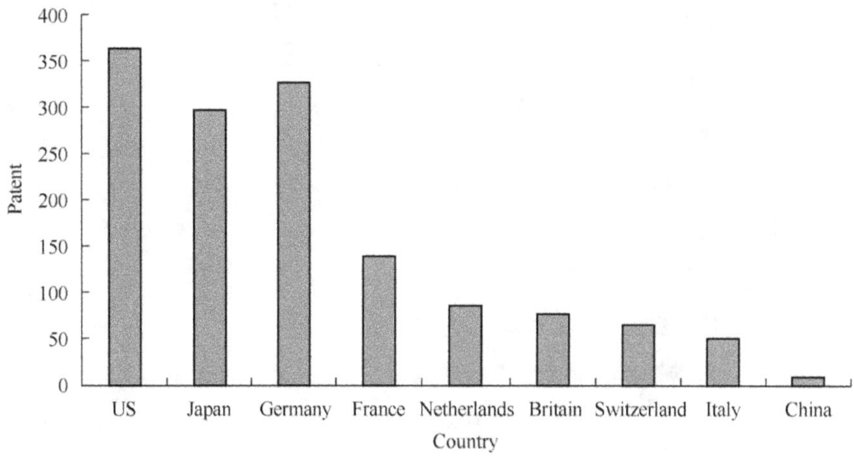

Figure 3.5 Top nine countries in the application for environmental technology patents at EPO in 2010

Source: Based on data from UNEP, EPO and ICTSD (2009).

China was the last of the top nine patent applicant states, with only 11 patents and a percentage of 0.6%.[30]

According to the latest statistics of national distribution of clean energy-related patents granted by the United States Patent and Trademark Office (USPTO), the US, Japan, Germany, and ROK were the top four countries in terms of cumulative patents in 2002–2015, each accounting for 47%, 24%, 8%, and 7%. Both the statistics from EPO and USPTO put the US on the top spot, which spoke for its absolute structural power and strong influence in the field of scientific and technological innovation. It's worth noting that emerging economies represented by China are doing better in the application for patents related to clean energy technologies. China (including the Taiwan region) applied to USPTO for 179 patents in 2002–2015, ranking fifth in the world even though it was only 1/10 of the US applications. It, therefore, had the most priority in clean energy technology among developing countries, ranking even higher than developed countries such as Denmark, France, Canada, and Spain. Other emerging countries such as India, Brazil, and Russia have also ramped up scientific and technological and financial input in clean energy technology. For instance, India is an active applicant for PV technology patents, and Brazil and Mexico rank first and second in the patent application for hydro/marine energy technology. Realizing their weakness in scientific and technological strength as well as R&D fund, developing countries call for more flexible terms on patent licensing with developed countries. For instance, a spate of measures can be taken, such as patent licensing, cooperative R&D, patent pool and cross-licensing, to break the patent bottlenecks on developing clean energy technology.

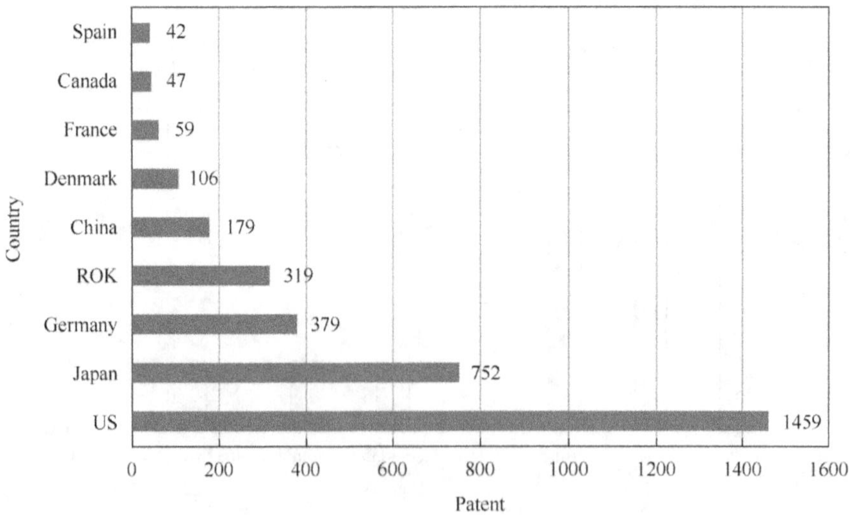

Figure 3.6 Top nine countries in the number of clean energy patents granted by USPTO in 2015

Source: Cleantech Group-Heslin Rothenberg Farley & Mesiti P. C., The Clean Energy Patent Growth Index (CEPGI) 2015, www.cleantechintellectualproperty.com.

In the registration of international patents, conglomerates in Europe, the US, Japan, and ROK are leaders in clean energy patents and key players in the international competition in clean energy technology. From 2002 to 2015, General Motors, an American company, maintained overall leadership in clean energy patent, followed by Japan's Honda Motor in the second place from 2002 to 2012 before it was overtaken by Toyota, also a Japanese company, in 2013. America's General Electric (GE) was in the fourth position for five years consecutively, while ROK's Samsung and Hyundai took the sixth and seventh position. Japan's Mitsubishi climbed to the ninth spot in 2002, followed by Denmark's Vestas in the tenth spot. According to the ranking in 2015, the top ten clean energy patent possessors were as follows: Toyota, GM, Hyundai, Honda, Ford, LG Electronics, Vestas, Siemens, GE, and Samsung. There was no company from developing countries on the list, implying that they needed to significantly enhance their innovative capability in the green industry.

Notably, international petroleum conglomerates have also begun to attach great importance to renewable energy technology, and their patents related to renewable energy accounted for 10.50% of all their patents in 2014, rising from less than 1%. These conglomerates have a myriad of patents on solar energy and biomass energy. Total and Shell are way ahead in the number of patent applications for clean energy technology, with the largest reserve of patented technologies on solar energy. BP and ExxonMobil are on the second rung with a brilliant performance on biomass energy. Shell and ExxonMobil have also reserved technologies in wind energy, fuel cell, hydrogen energy, and energy storage. They pay close attention to technological cooperation and joint patent application with other companies – that's how the top five petroleum conglomerates reduce the R&D cost and risks considering the vast diversity of renewable energies and related technologies as well as limited R&D funding. Established conglomerates have jointly applied for 181 basic patents with 116 enterprises, universities, and research institutes worldwide, including Centre national de la recherche scientifique (CNRS) of France, Power-light, Verenium, and Siemens, accounting for 15.67% of all renewable energy patents.[31]

III. Intensified competition in industrial standards and international market of clean energy

As far as global competition on clean energy is concerned, whether a country can upgrade its industrial structure and transform the energy mix will decide whether it will command a vantage point in the future low-carbon arena. Therefore, dominating clean energy standards, covering solar, wind, biomass, EV, smart grid, and energy storage and continuously expanding the international market are the main goals pursued by all countries and their major companies in the game of green economy. Tapping the clean energy industry and reshaping the global landscape of new energy – this is what world-leading companies are doing to remain invincible amid the transition of the international economic situation. High-tech companies or traditional energy firms are all important stakeholders that push the rapid

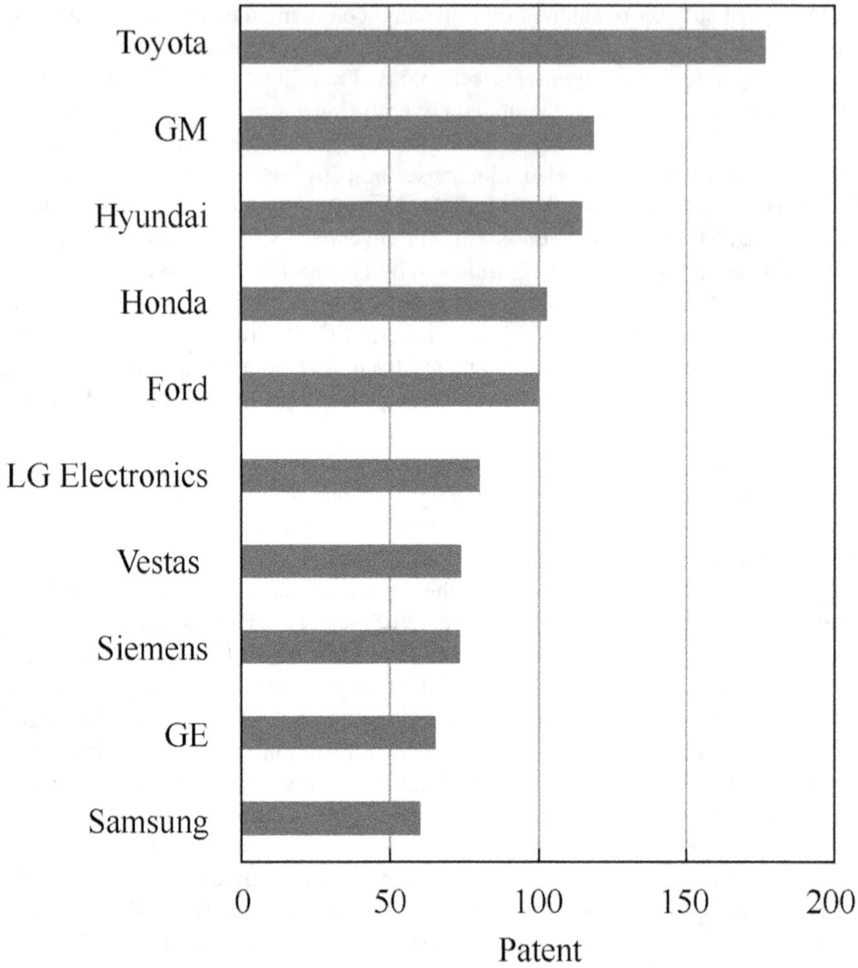

Figure 3.7 Top ten corporate applicants for clean energy technology patents in 2015

Source: Cleantech Group-Heslin Rothenberg Farley & Mesiti P. C., The Clean Energy Patent Growth Index (CEPGI) 2015, www.cleantechintellectualproperty.com.

development of clean energy worldwide and have continuously put forth new industrial standards on green technologies.

Studies by Boston University's Institute for Sustainable Energy showed 24 renowned multinationals that bought the most renewable energies, including Google, Amazon, Microsoft, Ikea, Equi-nix, Mars, Dow Chemical Company, Wal-Mart, Facebook, and China's Alibaba Group. As there are many administrative barriers with traditional energy, hi-tech companies prioritize the clean energy industry, represented by wind, solar, and biomass, as the entry point to the energy industry, with a view to securing a strong foothold in the new round of low-carbon development and seizing the opportunities of green development. In the meantime, to make advance deployments for the future competition in new energy and the transition to sustainable development order, and to adapt to the new trend of world energy development and the low-carbon shift in energy supply, international petroleum conglomerates such as Shell, BP, ExxonMobil, and Total all take developing and utilizing clean energy, especially influencing industrial standards for green energy, as the long-term strategic goal.[32]

While making asset investments in areas such as PV, wind, biomass, hydrogen energy, and fuel cell, international energy giants are also actively engaged in R&D of technologies and formulation of standards in renewables and busy applying for patents for technological "enclosure" and protection. They want to garner low-carbon technology innovations to lay the foundation for the establishment of clean energy industry standards. International petroleum giants have slightly adjusted their investment and technological reserve in renewable energy in terms of direction and priorities over recent years. As clean energy is receiving more attention, they have set up dedicated units to plan its overall development covering market investment, technology R&D, and formulation of standards. Besides, different giants have different focuses, ranging from wind, biomass, solar, to geothermal, hydrogen fuel, and energy storage. The British company BP, for example, reentered Europe's PV market in 2017 by acquiring 43% of the stakes in Europe's largest solar company, Lightsource, while making more investment in wind power projects in the US and biofuel projects in Brazil. Shell formed a new energy unit in 2016 and announced to invest USD 1 billion to 2 billion in clean energy annually through 2020. The money would mainly be spent on the R&D for EV charging stations and refueling stations for hydrogen fuel cell vehicles (HFCV).[33] After the *Paris Agreement* came into force in 2016, ten large petroleum companies in the world announced to form a Clean Energy Development Fund (CEDF) and planned to invest USD 100 million annually in the next decade to develop GHG capture and storage technologies while raising energy efficiency. The ten companies were Shell, Total, BP, PetroChina, Saudi Aramco, Statoil, Eni, Repsol, PEMEX, and Reliance Industries. Their executives said they will also work with venture capitals, private equity companies, and scientific research institutes to develop clean energy. Data from BloombergNEF showed large international oil and gas companies have invested a total of USD 6.2 billion in acquiring clean energy businesses in the past 15 years.[34]

The poor availability of modern energies is a serious problem facing African countries. The rate of electrification is less than 1/10 in many sub-Saharan countries. Africa needs huge amounts of energy investment for its development and sufficient electric power for its industries. Many experts in the academic and energy circles view Africa as an experimental zone for leapfrog energy transformation. This means it may skip the progression from firewood to fossil energy and realize energy transition and green development through foreign investment in clean energy, thus improving the availability of modern energies and environmental sustainability. Africa abounds in clean energy, but it is barely developed due to the lack of investment and technology. Kenya and Ethiopia are the only two African countries using geothermal energy to produce electricity, and less than 1/10 of the

Table 3.5 Clean energy cooperation by developed countries and emerging economies with Africa, 2010–2012

Country/ region	*Purpose of cooperation*	*Main areas*	*Main projects*
EU	Diversifying energy supply and energy structure, promoting regional stability and development, enlarging influence in Africa	Solar, wind, biomass	Desert Tech program, Africa-EU Renewable Energy Cooperation Programme
US	Pushing American companies to invest in clean energy projects in Africa through technological and financial assistance; seizing discourse power in US-African green cooperation	Solar, wind, biomass, nuclear	A series of clean power projects under the Africa Infrastructure Program (AIP) launched by the United States Agency for International Development (USAID); a series of projects between the United States Trade and Development Agency (USTDA) and African countries on clean energy development and utilization
Japan	Expanding diplomatic space, achieving energy interests	Solar, biomass	Low-carbon cooperation in the framework of Japan-Africa Science and Technology Minister's Meeting
India	Expanding influence in Africa, serving India's political, economic and diplomatic purposes with Africa	Solar, wind	ITEC and SCAAP training; clean energy cooperation agreements with Egypt and South Africa
Brazil	Promoting South-South cooperation, expanding international influence	Biomass, hydro	A series of biomass energy projects between Brazil and Portuguese-speaking African countries

Source: Zhang Yonghong, Liang Yijiang, Wang Tao, et al., "New Energy Cooperation Between China and Africa: Prospects, Challenges and Policies", *Journal of International Economic Cooperation*, No. 2, 2013.

region's hydro resources have been developed. Of the 15,000MW PV capacity around the globe, Africa has only 1/1000.

Wind power development in Africa has just started too, with wind farms under construction in Cape Verde, Kenya, Ethiopia, Morocco, and South Africa. The underdevelopment of new energy resources in Africa creates a vast stage for new energy companies. In March 2012, UNEP issued a report titled *Financing Renewable Energy in Developing Countries: Drivers and Barriers for Private Finance in sub-Saharan Africa*. According to the report, 7,000MW of new installed capacity is needed every year to meet the demand of economic growth in sub-Saharan Africa, which requires about USD 41 billion investment per year.[35] The African continent boasts plenty of untouched renewables, which should be able to meet most of its energy needs as long as there is a strong enough motivation for the energy transition. For instance, Mauritania's wind potential is almost four times its annual energy demand, while Sudan's wind potential can meet over 90% of its annual energy demand.

Africa's immense demand for energy and the broad prospects of clean energy development have drawn international attention to its energy transition and triggered an intense contention for the African market. Frost and Sullivan estimated the investment in renewable electricity in Africa will soar from USD 3.6 billion in 2011 to USD 57 billion in 2020. Main developed countries, such as the US, EU countries represented by Germany and France, and Japan, have stepped up efforts to implement their new energy strategy in Africa and have acquired outstanding comparative advantages for their mature concepts, established institutions, concrete policies and measures, strong finance, and advanced technology. Since 2012, the US has stationed troops in several African countries to implement military control, with the aim of tapping into the local clean energy market while controlling their traditional energies. It has also intensified new energy cooperation with Africa after 2012. The US provided South Africa with USD 250 million to develop solar energy, and Millennium Challenge Corporation provided new energy equipment for Tanzania. After the Africa-EU Energy Partnership (AEEP) was launched in 2010, main EU members entered the African clean energy market in big strides. In 2012, the EU provided Africa with a EUR 50-million initial fund for new energy development, which benefited Kenya, Ethiopia, Tanzania, Rwanda, Uganda, Djibouti, the Democratic Republic of the Congo, Malawi, and Zambia. In Morocco, Deutsche Bank granted a loan to a solar thermal power plant, and Siemens provided 44 sets of equipment for two wind farms.

In 2012, Japan, leveraging its technological advantages, began to support a joint solar research program between Nigeria and Algeria and a joint research program of Jatropha curcas-based biofuel in Mozambique. Emerging countries like India and Brazil also joined the competition using their geographical advantages and unique technologies. For instance, India planned to build 40 solar power stations and 40 biomass gas projects in Africa, along with a USD 5 billion loan and USD 700 million assistance for the development of small hydropower stations, rural electrification, and solar and wind power projects. Based on the South-South cooperation mechanism, Brazil, leveraged on its technological advantages in biomass and hydro energies, has implemented a series of bioenergy projects with Portuguese-speaking African countries.[36]

IV. Carbon tax restrictions and trade frictions in clean energy

Emerging industries such as energy conservation and environmental protection, new energy, IT, and bio-technology are regarded as important engines that will take the world economy out of the trough. All countries are developing strategic emerging industries as a new economic growth point. Based on their financial and technological advantages, they are also striving to occupy a vantage position in future industrial development and the moral highland in the green and sustainable transition. During the development of the clean energy industry, emerging developing countries are collectively on the rise, which has prompted European and American countries to limit access to their markets by employing trade protection measures, spreading protectionism from traditional industries to emerging ones. The rise of trade protectionism is undoubtedly one of the inevitable outcomes of a financial crisis. Meanwhile, trade friction in the emerging industry of clean energy is also closely related to the in-depth adjustment of global economic structure (change of international division of work), substantial changes in global economic and trade situation (rise of emerging economies), and global economic rebalancing (addressing global economic imbalance and inequity). Therefore, even if the global economy has recovered from the financial crisis, the rise of trade protectionism won't abate soon but will sustain for quite a while.[37] Especially in the face of China's fast rise in clean energy, European and American countries have kept creating trade frictions in the aspect of strategy, trade, and technical standards and have been squeezing the space of growth for developing countries by imposing carbon tax (including in the aviation sector) and carbon labeling.

After 2010, the US launched a series of prolonged investigations, such as the Section 301 investigation and anti-dumping and countervailing investigations, into Chinese clean energy products, including solar batteries (panels) and wind power products. In terms of China-US trade in clean energy products, the trade volume of PV products grew at the average annual rate of 28%, with China's export to America growing more than 10 percentage points faster than its import from America, and this exacerbated their trade deficit. As Chinese solar battery producers developed rapidly and their products took a growing share in the global market, the alliance of American solar companies felt so worried[38] that it demanded the US government impose anti-dumping and countervailing duties ranging from 49.88% to 249.96% on Chinese export. As to wind power, although China lagged behind developed American and European countries in science and technology, the high-speed development of its wind power products and its position as a major producer has drawn America's attention. Therefore, the US Wind Tower Trade Coalition filed a complaint against wind towers imported from China, accusing Chinese manufacturers of receiving government subsidies and dumping their products in the US at a lower-than-cost price, and demanded a higher-than-64% tariff on the towers. From November 2011 to January 2012, the US formally conducted "anti-dumping and countervailing" investigations into solar cells imported from China, followed by investigations into other China-originated clean energy products such as crystalline silicon PV cells and wind towers. In October 2012, the US Department of Commerce announced the final rate of anti-dumping (18.32%–249.96%) and countervailing duty (14.78%–15.97%) on Chinese PV products. As about 90% of Chinese PV products were exported, America's investigations lent a heavy blow to Chinese PV enterprises. In comparison, China-made wind power products were mostly sold domestically, so wind power companies were not seriously affected, but their steps of internationalization were hindered to some extent.

Compared with the US, the European PV market was vital for China as about 90% of its solar panels were exported there. As early as August 2009, two large solar energy companies in Germany requested the German government and the European Commission launched an anti-dumping investigation into China-made solar cells. In September that year, the alliance of the German PV industry prepared to collect evidence against Chinese companies and request the EU to start the investigation. In June 2012, the European Commission officially launched the anti-dumping investigation against Chinese PV cells and imposed in December 2013 an up to 64.9% anti-dumping duty and 11.5% countervailing duty on solar panels imported from China, which was extended at the end of 2015 after the two-year term.

During this round of trade frictions between China and the EU, Premier Li Keqiang, attaching great importance to the green industry, pushed for sound interactions in bilateral negotiations through proactive and fruitful clean energy diplomacy.[39] In the end, the EU exercised self-restraint and didn't follow in America's steps in imposing high anti-dumping duty on Chinese wind power products, and the frictions ended in a soft landing. In March 2017, the European Committee extended the anti-dumping and countervailing measures by 18 months rather than the usual five years.[40] On August 31, 2018, it released a notice announcing its decision to not extend the measures on Chinese solar panels after they expired on September 3. It explained that the decision, made in consideration for the interests of EU solar panel producers, users, and importers, was in the best interests of the union and conducive to meeting its new target on renewable energy.[41] This breathed new vigor into the Chinese PV industry that had met a wet blanket from the "531 new policy" (a policy issued by the National Development and Reform Commission, Ministry of Finance and National Energy Administration on May 31, 2018, to cut subsidies for PV). Now that the European solar market resumed free trade, Chinese enterprises could regain price advantages there and the overseas demand for PV products could be met steadily. The EU's termination of anti-dumping and countervailing measures against Chinese PV products was good for creating a more stable and predictable business environment for bilateral cooperation in clean energy, thus laying the foundation for the green development of both sides.[42]

While the EU realized that trade protection policies on clean energy would negatively affect the PV industry, some emerging countries began to follow suit. In July 2018, India decided to impose a two-year tariff on PV products imported from China and Malaysia, 25% in the first year, 20% in the first half of the second year and 15% in the second half. India explained that China's active engagement in the Indian market had caused the continuous fall in the market share of Indian PV products. However, solar panel manufacturers in India relied highly on Chinese equipment for its low cost. From January to September, India imported 1/3 of the USD 8 billion worth of Chinese shipments of solar panels, being the biggest importer of Chinese solar panels and modules. The Indian Prime Minister called for strongly boosting the domestic solar industry, but the country's heightened import duty on Chinese PV products had restricted its PV development.

In addition to trade protection concerning PV and wind power products, some developed countries, with advantages in environmental technology, had created such concepts as the low-carbon economy and green economy in the name of energy conservation and emission reduction. As a result, issues such as carbon tax,[43] carbon labeling, and carbon certification came into being and triggered the low-carbon trade war. Linking trade with the environment was a usual trick played by the US – it raised the environmental standards to stop China from exporting clean energy products with barriers of green trade. It also used technological protection and environmental barrier to hinder China's export of clean energy and consequently maintain its own leading position in the field. In June 2009, the US House of Representatives passed the *American Clean Energy and Security Act*, which authorized the US government to impose a carbon tax on certain products imported from countries that hadn't borne the mandatory carbon emission obligations (e.g., China and India) starting from 2020. Under such circumstances, developed countries may calculate the carbon emissions of imported goods with their existing domestic standards, which will expose high-carbon goods from developing countries to the risk of a high carbon tax and make them less competitive. Once carbon labeling becomes a passport for exported goods, it will seriously impede the export from developing countries. Once carbon certification is widely implemented in developed countries, their consumers will tend to buy domestic products that are geographically closer, which will contract the market share of imported products and help bring back manufacturing capacity. In response, developing countries can take the initiative to levy carbon tax or energy tax at home to offset the negative impacts from the international carbon tax.

Notes

1 Zha Daojiong, "Strategic Commanding Height in Clean Energy and National Competitiveness", in Wang Jisi, ed., *China International Strategy Review*, Beijing: World Affairs Press, 2010, pp. 293–301.
2 Sybille Roehrkasten, *Global Governance on Renewable Energy: Contrasting the Ideas of the German and the Brazilian Governments*, Wiesbaden: Springer VS, 2015, pp. 117–129.
3 "Bonn Political Declaration at the First International Conference for Renewable Energies", www.renewables2004.de/pdf/conference_report.pdf.
4 IRENA, www.irena.org/irenamembership.
5 Johannes Urpelainen, Thijs Van de Graaf, Lin Xuefei, "The International Renewable Energy Agency: A Successful Institutional Innovation?", *Foreign Theoretical Trends*, No. 2, 2017.
6 IRENA also trains renewable energy professionals, studies policies in different countries, and has a renewable energy patent pool. Its scope of work covers all key issues in the deployment and policy about renewable energy.
7 The 24 members of CEM are ministers and high-level representatives from Australia, Brazil, Canada, China, Chile, Denmark, Finland, France, Germany, India, Indonesia, Italy, Japan, Mexico, Norway, ROK, Russia, Saudi Arabia, South Africa, Sweden, UAE, Britain, the US, and the EU, as well as the observer state the Netherlands.
8 The MI is a standing high-level global forum and cooperative mechanism aimed at implementing the *Joint Member Statement on the Launch of Mission Innovation* issued by the heads of state and representatives of member states during the Paris Climate Change Conference 2015. It is committed to increasing input in technological R&D and innovation for clean energy, doubling the government or government-led investment in clean energy R&D in the next five years, and encouraging private investment in energy transition. The MI members include the EU and 22 countries – China, Australia, Brazil,

Canada, Chile, Denmark, Finland, France, Germany, India, Indonesia, Italy, Japan, Mexico, Norway, ROK, Saudi Arabia, Sweden, the Netherlands, UAE, Britain, and the US.

9 The Carbon Sequestration Leadership Forum (CSLF) is a multilateral ministerial-level mechanism aimed at promoting exchanges and cooperation in carbon capture, utilization and storage (CCUS) among the member states and in the international community. Founded in 2003, the forum is purported to promote the development and widespread application of more cost-effective technologies of CO_2 separation, capture, transmission, and long-term secure storage and identify and resolve issues related with carbon capture and storage, including fostering a favorable technological, political, and regulatory environment for technology development.

10 Emi Minghui Gui, Iain MacGill, "Typology of Future Clean Energy Communities: An Exploratory Structure, Opportunities, and Challenges", *Energy Research & Social Science*, No. 35, 2018, pp. 94–107.

11 Achim Steiner et al., "International Institutional Arrangements in Support of Renewable Energy", in Dirk Assmann et al., eds., *Renewable Energy, A Global Review of Technologies, Policies and Markets*, London: Sterling VA, 2006, p. 152.

12 Benjamin K. Sovacool, Thijs Van de Graaf, "Building or Stumbling Blocks? Assessing the Performance of Polycentric Energy and Climate Governance Networks", *Energy Policy*, No. 118, 2018, pp. 317–324.

13 REN21, *Renewables 2016 Global Status Report*, 2016, p. 14, https://www.ren21.net/wp-content/uploads/2019/05/REN21_GSR2016_FullReport_en_11.pdf.

14 Associated Press, "UN Climate Talks in Focus at Davos", *NPR*, January 27, 2011, https://phys.org/news/2011-01-climate-focus-davos-forum.html.

15 Charles F. Sabel, David G. Victor, "Governing Global Problems Under Uncertainty: Making Bottom-up Climate Policy Work", *Climatic Change*, No. 144, 2017, pp. 15–27.

16 REN21, *Renewables 2016 Global Status Report*, 2016, p. 14, https://www.ren21.net/wp-content/uploads/2019/05/REN21_GSR2016_FullReport_en_11.pdf.

17 REN21, *Renewables 2018 Global Status Report*, 2018, https://www.ren21.net/wp-content/uploads/2019/08/Full-Report-2018.pdf.

18 IRENA Membership, www.irena.org/menu/index,aspx?mnu=cat&PriMenuID=46&CatID=67.

19 Dries Lesage, Thijs Van de Graaf, eds., *Rising Powers and Multilateral Institutions*, New York: Palgrave Macmillan, 2015, pp. 220–223.

20 Su Xing, Pang Jinfu, "Prospects of BRICS Renewable Market and Application of 'BRICS Plus' Mode", *Sino-Global Energy*, No. 3, 2018.

21 Bai Ding, "Rare Earth – Essential Resource for Green Energy", *Rare Earth Information*, No. 9, 2014.

22 Michael T. Klare, *The Race far What's Left*: *The Global Scramble for the World's Last Resources*, New York: Metropolitan Books, 2012.

23 Jaakko Kooroshy, Rem Korteweg, Marjolein de Ridder, *Rare Earth Elements and Strategic Mineral Policy*, The Hague: The Hague Centre for Strategic Studies & TNO, 2010, http://static,hcss.nl/files/uploads/33.pdf.

24 Lucia Baldi, Massimo Peri, Daniela Vandone, "Clean Energy Industries and Rare Earth Materials: Economic and Financial Issues", *Energy Policy*, No. 66, 2014, pp. 53–61.

25 Li Jin, "Analysis of World Competition for Rare Earth Resources", *World Nonferrous Metals*, No. 4, 2013.

26 Lucia Baldi, Massimo Peri, Daniela Vandone, "Clean Energy Industries and Rare Earth Materials: Economic and Financial Issues", *Energy Policy*, No. 66, 2014, pp. 53–61.

27 Michael T. Klare, *The Race far What's Left*: *The Global Scramble for the World's Last Resources*, New York: Metropolitan Books, 2012.

28 Mao Jinsheng, Cheng Wenting, "An Initial Analysis of Intellectual Property Policy for Strategic Emerging Industries", *Intellectual Property*, No. 9, 2011.

29 Zuo Anlei, "Patent Protection in Clean Energy Technology and Industry – World Development and China's Response", *Science, Technology and Law*, No. 1, 2012.

30 The United Nations Environment Programme (UNEP), the European Patent Office (EPO) and the International Centre for Trade and Sustainable Development (ICTSD): *Patents and Clean Energy: the Gap Between Evidence and Policy (Final report*), 2009.
31 Bi Yantao, Wang Dan, Li Chunxin, et al., "Renewable Energy Development by International Petroleum Companies – Current Status and Lessons", *International Petroleum Economics*, No. 4, 2017.
32 Wang Bo, Li Chaoqian, "Current Status and Trend of Renewable Energy Development in the World", *China Prices*, No. 5, 2018.
33 "Global Energy Mix Changes, International Players Occupy Commanding Height in Renewable Energy", published on *Economic Daily*, April 27, 2018, http://shupeidian.bjx.com.cn/news/20180427/894568.shtml.
34 Michael Aklin, Johannes Urpelainen, *Renewables: The Politics of a Global Energy Transition*, Cambridge, MA and London: The MIT Press, 2018.
35 UNEP, *Financing Renewable Energy in Developing Countries*: *Drivers and Barriers for Private Finance in sub-Saharan Africa*, Report, 2012, www.unepfi.org/fileadmin/documents/Financing_Renewable_Energy_in_subSaharan_Africa.pdf.
36 Zhang Yonghong, Liang Yijiang, Wang Tao, et al., "New Energy Cooperation Between China and Africa: Prospects, Challenges and Policies", *Journal of International Economic Cooperation*, No. 2, 2013.
37 Zong He, "Emerging Industries under Trade Protection", *China's Foreign Trade*, No. 9, 2013.
38 In 2010, three American solar companies claimed bankruptcy successively within a month. They were Evergreen Solar, Spectra Watt, and Solyndrat.
39 "Foreign Media: Li Keqiang Brings Sino-EU PV Negotiations to Success", August 5, 2013, http://poli-tics.people.com.cn/n/2013/0805/c1001-22450108.html.
40 Data from independent economic research institutes in Europe show that if EU imposes 20% punitive tariff on Chinese PV products, it will lose 175,500 jobs and EUR 18.4 billion value added in PV industry in the next three years; if the rate of punitive tariff reaches 60%, it will lose 242,000 jobs and EUR 27.2 billion value added in PV industry in the same period.
41 "European Commission Decides Not to Extend Anti-dumping and Countervailing Measures on Chinese Solar Panels", September 3, 2018, http://guangfu.bjx.com.cn/news/20180903/925126.shtml.
42 MOFCOM, "MOFCOM Makes Remarks on EU's Termination of Anti-dumping and Countervailing Measures on Chinese PV Products", September 3, 2018, http://guangfu.bjx.com.cn/news/20180903/925113.shtml.
43 Carbon tax is also called carbon border adjustment tax. It is a policy measure put forth by developed countries to avoid or mitigate the so-called carbon leakage that may arise from international trade and to keep their domestic products competitive.

4 Strategic positioning of clean energy diplomacy in major countries

An international comparison

Since the end of the 1990s, developing clean energy, represented by wind, solar, and biomass, and promoting international cooperation in this area has gained global recognition as a systematic plan for energy transition that will kill three birds with one stone – ensuring energy security, tackling climate change, and eradicating energy poverty. Especially in the 21st century, clean energy is regarded as a highly competitive option in many countries, enjoying rapid growth worldwide thanks to governments' supportive policy innovations, ever better financing channels, rising awareness of energy security and environmental protection, and more competitive green technologies. By analyzing the global development of clean energy diplomacy on the governance-driven dimension and competition-driven dimension, this book reviews and analyzes the stages of clean energy development and status of clean energy diplomacy in five typical or rising clean energy producers – Germany, America, Japan, India, and Brazil. It makes a historical analysis of each country and a lateral comparison of the five based on the different types of strategic position of clean energy diplomacy discussed in Chapter 2. It compares and summarizes the strategic positioning and features of their clean energy diplomacy to provide references for China in positioning its own and deciding how to carry it out. Facing mounting climate and energy challenges, many countries are stepping up innovation, promoting sustainable energy technologies, and strongly developing clean energy as an important national strategy. The measures they take are vital for accelerating the energy revolution and realizing a global energy transition.

An explanation must be given in the beginning why I chose the countries that are presented in this chapter. According to the data of 2015, there were 26 countries whose renewable capacity exceeded 10GW, 11 in Europe, 5 in Asia, 3 in North America and South America each, 2 in Eurasia, and 1 in Oceania and the Middle East respectively. The top three countries in Europe were Germany (105GW), Italy (54GW), and Spain (51GW), whose combined capacity accounted for 11% in the world. The top three countries in Asia were China (503GW), Japan (90GW), and India (82GW), with a combined capacity accounting for 34% in the world. The top three countries in North America were the US (215GW), Canada (94GW), and Mexico (18GW), collectively accounting for 17% in the world.[1] This chapter selects five typical countries from the global list and analyzes their clean energy policies and clean energy diplomacy status. Three of them are developed countries

DOI: 10.4324/9781003433903-6

Table 4.1 Installed capacity of renewable energy in major countries of different regions, 2015

Region	*Country*	*Installed capacity (MW)*	*Percentage in the region*
Asia	China	503796	90%
	Japan	90089	
	India	82117	
	Vietnam	16882	
	ROK	12708	
Europe	Germany	104986	65%
	Italy	54790	
	Spain	51316	
	France	43836	
	Norway	32235	
	Britain	32059	
North America	US	215117	100%
	Canada	94079	
	Mexico	17510	
South America	Brazil	116687	78%
	Venezuela	15190	
	Columbia	11757	
Eurasia	Russia	53047	94%
	Turkey	31704	
Oceania	Australia	18094	70%
Middle East	Iran	12024	78%
	Syria	1572	
Africa	South Africa	4877	30%
	Egypt	3506	
	Morocco	2609	

Source: IRENA2016.

leading in clean energy and low-carbon development, namely, Germany in Europe, the US in North America, and Japan in East Asia. The other two are major developing countries who have quickly caught up – India in South Asia and Brazil in Latin America. To analyze their clean energy development status and the features of their clean energy diplomacy in a more systematic way, this chapter studies each country in three areas: clean energy development and current status of energy transition, evolution of domestic policies on clean energy, and development and features of clean energy diplomacy. A comparative analysis of the five countries is conducted in the end in reference to the types of strategic positioning of clean energy diplomacy.

Section 1 Germany's clean energy diplomacy

Being the world's fifth-largest energy consumer and EU's largest economy, Germany is a "global paradigm" in the transition toward renewable energy particularly for the rapid development of its wind and PV power, drawing much attention for its performance and experience. In the past 20 years, the German federal government has adopted strong environmental, climatic, and energy policies to shift its industrial sector to the low-carbon end. A firm consensus across Germany is that to keep the country economically competitive in the long term, it is a must to adjust the economic structure toward higher efficiency in resource and energy use and greater climate friendliness.[2]

I. Germany's clean energy development and features of its energy transition

Being rich in coal but scant in petroleum and gas, Germany imported 95%–100% of petroleum and its natural gas import grew steadily from 75.6% in 1990 to 86.8% in 2013. To lead in climate governance and consolidate energy security, Germany began to shift to renewable energy as a key part of its energy strategy in the 1990s.[3] Since its first Erneuerbare-Energien-Gesetz (EEG, Renewable Energy Sources Act) in 2000, feed-in tariffs (FIT) for renewable electricity has been implemented in the country, around which other supportive policies have also given a strong push to the development of non-hydro renewable energy. Wind and PV are two pillars powering Germany's energy transition. The traditional power system must be remodeled from a large-scale architecture based on fossil fuels and centralized control to one with diverse fuels and distributed control, so as to accommodate the intermittence and fluctuation of wind and PV electricity.[4] Germany has developed relevant technologies and made innovative R&D throughout the whole power system to make it more flexible, with smart grid construction being a key step. In 2008, Germany launched the E-Energy program to build a self-regulated, intelligent "energy Internet" backed by information and communication technologies, aiming at smart energy production, transmission, consumption, and storage. Regarding power transmission, there was Europe's interconnected power grid, which was an indirect power storage system. When there was plenty of sunshine and wind, surplus electricity could be sold to neighboring countries; when wind and PV electricity was at an ebb during peak hours, electricity was bought from neighbors.[5]

In September 2010, Bundesministeriums für Wirtschaft und Energie (Federal Ministry of Economy and Energy) issued the Energy Concept for an Environmentally Sound, Reliable, and Affordable Energy Supply (ECG), an energy transition strategy aimed at a profound reform of energy supply. The strategy set the goals for renewables development, CO_2 emission reduction, and energy consumption reduction, and expounded on Germany's thought on medium- and long-term energy development, aiming at an environmentally sound, secure, and affordable energy supply system (Table 4.2). In 2011, Germany formally rolled out the "energy transition plan" to push the replacement of such fossil fuels as coal and natural gas by renewables such as solar and wind, intending to completely give up nuclear energy by 2022. The plan also vowed to have 80% electricity generated from renewables by 2050, with increased investment in the development of biomass, geothermal, and offshore wind energies.[6] In 2012, Germany issued the revised EEG-2012 and specified the medium- and long-term goals for renewable power through legislation. It set the goal that renewable energy would account for 35%, 50%, 65%, and

Table 4.2 Main goals in Germany's energy transition strategy

Category		*Goal*			
		2020	*2030*	*2040*	*2050*
GHG emission	GHG (compared with 1990)	– 40	– 55	– 70	– 80
Energy consumption	Primary energy consumption (compared with 2008)	– 20	–	–	– 50
	Power demand (compared with 2008)	– 10	–	–	– 25
	Residential heating	– 20	–	–	–
	Energy consumption in transport (compared with 2005)	– 10	–	–	– 40
Renewable energy development	Percentage in power consumption	35	50	65	80
	Percentage in end energy consumption	18	30	45	60

Source: Energy Transition in Germany, https://energytransition.org/.

80% of power supply by 2020, 2030, 2040, and 2050 respectively, and 60% of primary energy in 2050.[7]

Germany's energy transition is characterized by vigorous atmospheric and environmental protection. In June 2011, the German Parliament (Deutscher Bundestag) decided to guide the country's energy transition with three policy goals – environmentally compatible energy supply, affordable energy, and energy security, the first one receiving more attention. To meet all three criteria, Germany set about its energy transition with two main drivers: developing renewables and raising energy efficiency. After the EEG was issued in 2000, the percentage of renewables in the energy mix has kept rising – from 6.2% of electricity output in 2000 to 17% in 2010 to 27.8% in 2014 and 30% in 2015.[8] The environmental motive behind the energy transition is evident in Germany's narrow definition of clean energy and its decision to completely abandon nuclear energy by 2022. Though nuclear energy can help mitigate Germany's reliance on import, both the government and the public gave precedence to environmental issues related with the mitigation of risks of nuclear accidents and nuclear waste disposal over the security of energy supply. As a result, the percentage of nuclear energy fell quickly from 11.5% of primary energy consumption in 2000 to 7.1% in 2014.

Germany has not only given up nuclear power but also gradually scaled back on natural gas, a relatively clean fossil energy that the country refused to accept as clean energy, from 21.5% in 2000 to 20.5% in 2014. Despite the remarkable achievements with renewables, Germany's efforts to reduce the use of "unclean" energies such as coal and oil met resistance, which was a big challenge to its energy transition. The percentage of oil fell steadily from 38.9% in 2000 to 34.6% in 2007 but began to bounce back after that and hit 37% in 2009, while the percentage of coal dropped from 25.6% in 2000 to 23.3% in 2009 before starting to rebound and reaching 24.9% in 2014.[9]

In 2017, Angela Merkel was elected chancellor of Germany again in the coalition government comprising the Christlich Demokratische Union Deutschlands (CDU),

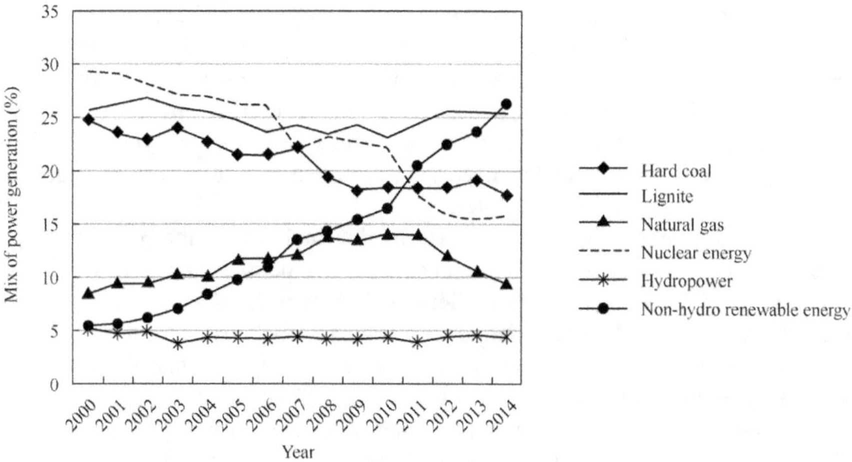

Figure 4.1 Germany's power generation mix 2000–2014

Source: AG Energieblanzen (AGEB).

Christian Social Union (CSU), and Sozialdemokratische Partei Deutschlands (SPD). With 38% of electricity generated from solar, wind, hydro, and biomass that year, the new government further raised the targets on renewables from 50% renewable electricity by 2030 – set by the previous administration – to 65%. Coal-fired power generation still accounted for 40% in Germany's power mix in 2018, higher than the average in EU. According to the agreement of the coalition government, it would decide on a timetable of phasing out coal in 2018, a task that had to be accomplished in 2025–2030 if Berlin was to meet the emission goal under the *Paris Agreement*. Germany was set to pass the climate protection law in 2019 to put in place a legal framework to guarantee the reduction in GHG emissions. It's worth noting that no strong emission-cutting measures were adopted in the industrial sector, whose emissions steadily made up 20% of the country's GHG emissions ever since 2010. The main reduction measure in the sector was EU's Emissions Trading System (EU ETS), but it hasn't fared well due to extremely low carbon price. Emission reduction and low-carbon development in the industrial sector will eventually decide whether Germany's energy transition will succeed.

II. Evolution of Germany's clean energy policies

The Chernobyl nuclear accident in 1986 prompted Germany to finally make up its mind to give up nuclear energy, which put nuclear supporters on the defensive. Led by the then chancellor Helmut Kohl and Minister for Environment Klaus Töpfer, the Committee on the Environment of the German Bundestag approved in 1987 the establishment of a committee of inquiry, which adopted measures for protecting the atmosphere. Soon after the reunification, the Kohl administration proposed to cut CO_2 emissions by 25%–30% in 2005 from the 1987 level. The policies underpinned by anti-nuclear movement and climate governance laid the groundwork for Germany's clean energy development. The *Electric Power Transmission Act* it promulgated in 1991 marked the legislative beginning of promoting the development of renewable energy. While ensuring grid synchronization for renewable electricity generators, the act, however, didn't offer enough incentives to enable a full-blown development of renewables.

Germany began to liberalize its power market in 1998, so the previous legal incentives had to be stepped up to introduce more competition to the market.[10] The EEG adopted in 2000, the center of Germany's federal legal system on renewables, stipulated detailed preferential policies that strongly boosted the development of clean energy. The law was revised five times since issued, and the revisions will be hereinafter referred to as EEG2004, EEG2009, EEG2012, EEG2014, and EEG2017. EEG2004 stipulated that renewable electricity should account for 12.5% in 2010 and 20% in 2020. EEG2009 came at a time when the development of renewable power generation exceeded expectations, so it further raised the target to having renewable electricity account for 30% of power consumption by 2020. It also rolled out a series of incentives, including priority and full purchase, classified and degressive power tariff, balanced apportionment of power tariff, information disclosure, and special reward for new technology.[11] The Fukushima nuclear leak in 2011 hastened Germany's steps to scale back on nuclear energy and gave another thrust to renewables. EEG2012 increased the 2020 target to 35% alongside longer-term goals – 50% by 2030, 65% by 2040, and 80% by 2050. In the meantime, given the reduced cost of renewable power generation and to lessen the burden of subsidies on the government, Germany continued to lower the feed-in tariff (FIT) of wind power and established a correlative mechanism between incremental PV capacity and power tariff adjustment. EEG2014, while strictly controlling the subsidy for renewable electricity, initiated a market-oriented and phased reform of PV power generation with clear priorities, on the basis of the bidding system for PV station construction. The revised edition was intended to lower the cost of renewable energy development and incentivize technological innovation. For example, the cap on annual increment in installed capacity expanded from PV to wind and biogas, FIT for renewables was decreased again, and subsidy was determined through a bidding process.

After the European Commission released the *2014 Guidelines on State Aid for Environmental Protection and Energy* in April 2014, Germany began to revise certain articles of EEG to comply with EU's institutional requirement, particularly to gradually cut the subsidies for renewable energy for greater competitiveness. Two supportive measures were taken for the policy reform. One was the introduction of the competitive bidding system for renewable power generation projects, and the other was the gradual replacement of fixed-amount subsidy with market premium. In this backdrop, the latest EEG2017 came into force on January 1, 2017, putting an end to the FIT policy that had been in force since 1990. The latest revision introduced a comprehensive bidding system for renewable power generation,[12] whereby the country could control the renewable capacity added every year to facilitate

Table 4.3 Main laws and regulations on renewable energy in Germany

Title of document		*Effective date or revision date*	*Main content*
General laws and regulations	Electricity Feed-in Act (Stromeinspeisungsgesetz – StrEG)	Effective date: January 1991	Introducing FIT to promote the synchronization of renewable electricity
	Renewable Energy Sources Act (Erneuerbare Energien Gesetz, EEG), six revisions	Effective: 2000 Revision: 2004, 2009, 2012, 2014, 2017, 2020	Promoting the development of renewable energy with clear goals. EEG2017 revised the FIT system, which eventually evolved into the FIP system (Feed-in Premium), and introduced the bidding system for renewable power generation.
General laws and regulations	Energy Industry Act (EnWG)	Issuance: July 2005 Revision: October 2008	Supplementary provisions to promote the grid synchronization of renewable electricity
	Renewable Energy Production Incentive Scheme (Stimuleringsregeling duurzame energieproductie, SDE)	Effective: April 2008 Revision: March 2009	Regulating the federal subsidy for renewable power generation
	Regulations on the Categorization of Sustainable Energy Generation (RAC 2009)	Effective: March 2009	Providing information on the classification of renewable energy products; standardizing the calculation of government subsidy
	General Conditions for the Allocation of Subsidies for Energy Use 2007	Effective: January 2008	Stipulating financial support for investment and research in renewables to promote tech improvement
Regulations on specific renewable energies	Ecological Tax Reform Act	Effective: 1999	Raising ecological tax on traditional fossil energy sources such as petroleum and natural gas, biofuel exempted
	Biomass Ordinance (BiomasseV)	Effective: June 2001 Revision: August 2005	Promoting biomass power generation
	German Biofuels Quota Law	Effective: January 2007	Developing tax-free policies for second-generation biofuel and pure biodiesel to increase bio-content in fuels
	Regulation on State Subsidies for Solar Cells 2009	Effective: July 2008	Stipulating government subsidy for investment in solar PV system

Source: Originally created by the author.

grid expansion. The marketization of renewable power generation in Germany proceeded in full swing.[13] Regarding regional development, the new revision not only enabled Germany to make safe, well-paced, and efficient plans for clean energy projects, but the unified standards also made it easier for surrounding countries to make better power generation plans as cross-border power transmission was commonplace across Europe. Compared with EEG2014, EEG2017 emphasized that the percentage of renewable electricity will reach 40%–45% by 2025, 55%–60% by 2035, and at least 80% by 2050. A bidding mechanism would be devised for each type of renewable power generation (e.g., solar, onshore wind power, offshore wind power, and biomass).

With EEG in the center, Germany also enacted specific laws concerning the development of different renewable energies, and all laws related to energy use included articles on preferential treatment and promoting the use of renewables. For example, the *Ecological Tax Reform Act* that took effect in 1999 and its revisions raised the ecological tax on traditional fossil energies such as oil and natural gas several times but exempted biofuel from this tax. The *EnEG* issued in 1976 and its revisions in 2005 and 2009 mandated the use of renewable energy (biomass, solar, and geothermal) in new buildings. Timely adjusting legal provisions according to actual situations and issuing targeted energy rules is an important piece of experience in Germany's energy transition. The *BiomasseV* that took effect in June 2001 and was revised in August 2005 was aimed at promoting power generation from biomass. The *Rules on Government Subsidy for Solar Cell 2009* coming into force in July 2008 built on the EEG to further stipulate that investment in solar PV system would be entitled to government subsidy.

III. Development of Germany's clean energy diplomacy and its strategic positioning

Germany's clean energy diplomacy is typically governance-driven. It establishes Germany's leadership in the new order of climate and energy governance by creating new institutions and systems in the international arena of clean energy.

First, Germany's governance-driven diplomacy is manifested in the establishment of IRENA.

As early as in the 1990s, German politician Hermann Scheer suggested creating an international organization on renewable energy to promote inter-state cooperation with Germany playing a leading part.[14] He was a key figure in the creation of International Renewable Energy Agency (IRENA). In addition to initiating the idea, he also introduced it into the joint agreement between the Greens and the Social Democratic Party (SPD) in the federal government after the 2002 election, proposing to create such an international agency.[15] The proposal was endorsed by other European countries, including Denmark and Spain, who, as pioneers in environmental protection, were dissatisfied that International Energy Agency (IEA), which stood for the interests of traditional fossil energy industries, played a leading part in global energy governance. Compared with restructuring the IEA, they would rather establish a new international agency dedicated to renewables in order to give clean energy sector a bigger say on the international stage. At the 2002 World Summit on Sustainable Development in Johannesburg, Germany proposed to set a goal of global clean energy development – a 10%–15% growth for renewable energy by 2010. After the proposal was vetoed by countries including the US, Germany pushed to form the Johannesburg Renewable Energy Coalition (JREC) as an alternative to continue to drive international action on clean energy development. The European Commission set up the JREC secretariat, and more than 80 countries joined the coalition.

Still at the 2002 Johannesburg Summit, the then German chancellor Gerhard Schröder extended a request to leaders of other countries to include the use of renewables in the formal agenda of a global conference for the first time. In June 2004, the first International Conference for Renewable Energies was held in Bonn, attended by representatives from 154 countries. The conference generated three political outcomes. For one, it passed a political statement deciding to enlarge the exploitation and utilization of renewables. For another, it adopted an international action plan to put the statement into practice, under which the governments of all countries might set goals and take actions on a voluntary basis. For a third, the participating countries shall create conditions for the development and utilization of renewables. However, the hollowness of these unsubstantial political outcomes disappointed many renewable energy supporters. Therefore, Germany decided to go another way. Instead of working on intergovernmental multilateral actions, it turned to form an "exclusive alliance of precursors" outside the framework of the United Nations.

At the Washington International Renewable Energy Conference in early 2008, the German government announced to kick off the negotiations on building the IRENA. The first preparatory meeting was held in Berlin in April 2008, at which 170 representatives from 60 countries expressed their unanimous support for the early establishment of the organization. The final preparatory meeting was held in Madrid in October 2008, at which the participating countries agreed on the draft *Statute of the International Renewable Energy Agency*. They also agreed on other important matters, such as the standards and procedures for the election of chief financial officer, acting director-general, and temporary headquarters. In January 2009, the inauguration conference of IRENA was held in Bonn, where representatives from 75 countries signed the IRENA Statute. Between 2009 and 2011, IRENA's preparatory committee held five meetings, and the second one in June 2009 designated Abu Dhabi as the host city of IRENA headquarters. An administrative committee was also formed at that meeting to ensure effective internal and external communication.

After the IRENA Statute came into force on July 8, 2010, IRENA held its first General Assembly in April 2011, which marked the official and full establishment of the organization after more than 20 years of planning, preparations, and hard negotiations.[16] Its establishment proved that institutional innovation through small-scale alliance of like-minded participants could be a good way to break the dilemma in collective action and that multilateral cooperation initiative could be postponed a little to facilitate the negotiations.[17] IRENA could become a pioneer in the global architecture of clean energy governance because it was appealing to both developed and developing countries. Industrialized countries in the West and emerging economies joined it because they were motivated to shape a global policy environment for renewables; developing and least developed countries joined it because they hoped to grow their green strengths by obtaining policy suggestions and related information concerning assessment on and capability building for clean energy resources. Basing the organization in Abu Dhabi, a city far away from the West, was good for securing global support.[18] Though established not for very long, IRENA had surprisingly had 158 member states and 24 applicants by August 2018.[19]

In addition to setting up basic units such as the General Assembly, the council, and the secretariat, Germany underscored IRENA's dedication to and authority in the research on renewable energies. The secretariat has three assistant organs. One is the Knowledge, Policy, and Finance Centre (KPFC). This is a global repository of renewable energy knowledge that provides a gateway for statistics on resource potential, investment cost along with research and information on policies, investment frameworks, and socioeconomic and environmental impact of renewable energy technologies. Another key project of the center is the Global Renewable Energy Atlas, the largest-ever initiative to assess renewable energy potential worldwide that provides important references concerning data, planning, policy development, and investment. Another assistant organ is the Country Support and Partnerships (CSP) division, which offers the Renewables Readiness Assessments (RRAs) to assess the policy measures adopted by different countries to boost renewable energy deployment and introduce and promote suitable incentive policies for certain countries.[20] It also has a Renewable Energy Policy Advice Network (REPAN), which assists IRENA in conducting renewables assessment, consulting on grid infrastructure, and other work, strengthening regional cooperation to increase the ratio of renewables in the energy mix. The third assistant organ is the Innovation and Technology Centre (IITC). Based in Bonn, Germany, the center provides cutting-edge information on renewable energy technologies and innovations and translates them into practical, policy-friendly tools for IRENA members.

Second, apart from establishing IRENA, Germany also hoped to advance governance innovations in different areas of clean energy development and promote its governance-driven concept in more international regimes. For instance, when the global financial crisis hit at the end of 2008, Germany, Norway, and European Commission jointly sponsored the Green Economy Initiative (GEI) with UN's support. The GEI was aimed at changing global economy through a green industrial revolution and boosting employment in the 21st century. Sectors that would benefit from the Green New Deal included clean energy and clean technology (including recycling technology), rural energy (including renewables and sustainable biomass), ecological infrastructure, and sustainable city (including planning, transport, and green buildings).[21] Germany proposed to set up an "international energy efficiency hub" at the 2016 G20 Summit in Hangzhou. During a bilateral meeting, the Chinese side said that energy efficiency cooperation within the G20 may not be able to proceed steadily and sustainedly as the annual rotating chair doesn't attach the same amount of attention to this work. In response, Germany asked if there was a possibility of creating a new mechanism like IRENA.

At the moment, the International Partnership for Energy Efficiency Cooperation (IPEEC) is already playing an important role in coordinating the implementation of the G20 Energy Efficiency Action Plan (EEAP). All G20 members are IPEEC members except Argentina, Saudi Arabia, and Indonesia, but the IPEEC Secretariat is understaffed and underfunded. Germany still proposed to set up an International Energy Efficiency Hub so all interested parties can equally participate in the decision-making process and benefit.[22] It hoped to reflect this initiative in the G20 Energy Ministerial Meeting Beijing Communique and the G20 Energy Efficiency Leading Programme:

> In order to strengthen the global voice for energy efficiency, G20 members support IPEEC working with the IEA and other international organizations, including IEF, OPEC, OECD, APEC, BRICS, SE4ALL and C2E2, and with stakeholders, and we will explore the feasibility of innovative collaborative arrangements for international cooperation on energy efficiency.

The initiative was endorsed by the EU, the US, Australia, Russia, ROK, and other countries and regions.

Third, although Germany adopted a typical governance-driven clean energy diplomacy, it attached great importance to technological competitiveness in clean energy and took that as the foundation for and starting point of its leading role in international clean energy governance. Environmental and energy technologies provide a way of creating new jobs, modernizing the economy, and taking us toward a better future. By establishing its leadership in technological innovation, a country is better positioned to develop the international standards for products. A study of German Environment Agency undertaken by the Lower Saxony Institute for Economic Research showed that in 2006, Germany's export of environmental technologies accounted for 16% of world total (EUR 56 billion) compared with America's 15% and Japan's 9%. German technologies were especially successful in the following areas: measurement, control, regulation, water supply and wastewater treatment, clean air, noise protection, and cyclic utilization. Former German Minister for Environment Sigmar Gabriel advocated a wise environmental policy driven by clean technology innovations. "The future market is green", and Germany has become the world's largest green technology exporter.[23] Many German corporations believed their future competitiveness will hinge on their ability to lead the world clean energy market. German Federal Ministry for the Environment made a plan in 2006 to help German companies enter the international market through its Export Initiative Recycling and Efficiency Technologies (EIRET).[24] The Federal Ministry for the Environment, Nature Conservation and Nuclear Safety (BMU), and Federal Ministry for Economic Affairs and Energy (BMWi) co-developed a "clean production" website to promote German environmental science and technologies to the global market. The Federal Ministry of Environment and Federal Ministry of Education and Research jointly rolled out a cabinet resolution titled "General

Plan for Environmental Technology" in November 2008, which underlined what policy makers should do to support German environmental protection industry in technology export. The central part of the plan consisted of research funds, intensified education and training, support for innovation by SMEs, transfer and spread of new technologies, and particularly international cooperation.[25]

In the meantime, EU's announcement in 2015 to start forming a European energy alliance provided an opportunity for Germany to further play its leading role in technological development and promote regional energy transition.[26] In February that year, the European Commission released the strategic program of the energy alliance, aiming to achieve the following purposes: establishing a fully integrated, competitive internal energy market; ensuring the security of energy supply; raising energy efficiency; lowering energy demand and strengthening the utilization of renewable resources; and stepping up research and innovation to develop green technologies. The EU is committed to building a clean, low-carbon, and environment-friendly economy. After the energy alliance was formed, renewables grew dramatically and were expected to account for 27% of EU's total energy consumption by 2030. Compared with the US and Japan, the EU has no advantage in clean, low-carbon technologies, which is all the more reason why Germany, a strong clean energy player, needs to step up and lead the union forward.

Section 2 America's clean energy diplomacy

The United States is the second-largest fossil energy consumer in the world after China. Since the oil crisis in the 1970s, all American administrations have adhered to the "energy independence" policy. When it comes to clean energy development, the country tops the world in clean energy technology, biomass, and geothermal energy, while also being one of the best in wind power and PV. Unlike Germany that gives priority to renewable energy, America's energy transition relies more on the development and utilization of such clean energies as natural gas, clean coal, and nuclear. Consistently striving for energy independence by actively promoting domestic energy supply to guarantee energy security is the primary motivation underpinning America's energy policy.

I. America's clean energy development and features of its energy transition

The US began producing renewable energy during the second oil crisis at the end of the 1970s. The oil price hike and its reliance on oil import prompted the US to finally make up its mind to develop renewables, optimize the energy mix, and guarantee national energy security. In the meantime, it released the *Clean Air Act* in 1970, its first milestone on promoting renewables, out of environmental considerations (in response to the "photochemical smog" event). From the late 1970s to the present day, America's energy transition towards energy independence has been driven in three ways. The first is encouraging the development of clean unconventional fossil energies, including nuclear, shale gas, coalbed methane (CBM), and clean utilization of coal. The second is strongly developing renewables, such as bioethanol and biodiesel, to make the transport sector less reliant on oil products, and boosting the development of wind and solar. The third is raising energy efficiency. Generally speaking, the US accelerated clean energy development after 2000 in the efforts of energy transition, with natural gas and nuclear as the transitional alternatives toward a renewable, sustainable energy system. Between 2000 and 2014, the percentage of natural gas rose from 26% to 30.2%, that of nuclear energy from 7.8% to 8.3%, and that of non-hydro renewables from 0.76% to 2.83%. In the same period, the percentage of oil and coal dropped steadily, the former from 38.2% to 36.4% and the latter from 24.6% to 19.7%. With only a mild increase in renewables, the US ensured a successful low-carbon transition thanks to the massive growth of natural gas and the steady increase of nuclear. In 2015, the percentage of clean energy as defined by the US in the broad sense reached 48% of total energy consumption, with 31% contributed by natural gas and 17% by nuclear.[27]

Of the series of measures adopted by the US to diversify domestic energy supply, the most significant was the shale gas revolution, a policy that lasted from the George W. Bush administration to the Obama administration to the Trump administration.[28] The US government began to support shale gas development during the first oil crisis. The government encouraged the prospecting and exploitation of shale gas and the research and development of relevant technologies, and medium- and small-sized oil companies took an active part. The appearance of horizontal drilling and hydro-fracture technologies after 2005 led to explosive increase in shale gas output, with an average annual growth rate of 30.9% in 2005–2014, generating half of the country's total natural gas output. The fast increase in tight oil output – with an average annual growth rate of 34.1% in 2008–2014 – led to the dramatic rebound of oil output after it bottomed out by quickly taking a share of 36%. The shale gas revolution largely reduced America's reliance on oil and gas import, which fell to 40% and 4.1% respectively in 2014, a drop of 44% and 72% from the peak. In 2016, the US could meet 87% of its energy demand. The Trump administration further enhanced the advantages of its shale gas industry by relaxing the regulation on natural gas projects and encouraging natural gas power generation and infrastructure construction. As a result, natural gas will remain the main clean energy source for quite some time to come.

The rapid development of renewable energy in the US should be credited to the Democratic Party. After winning the presidential election in 2008, Barack Obama went to great lengths to outline climate actions in quest for changes and innovations for a brighter, cleaner, more modern, and non-energy-dependent future. During his first week as president, Obama asked the Environmental Protection Agency (EPA) to review the Bush administration's decision to reject California's request to introduce the AB1493, which asked automakers to fulfill their obligation of minimizing CO_2 emissions. Wind energy and solar PV were renewables of great potential in the US. Since 2007, power generation from these two sources has registered the average annual growth rate of 27% and 69%, and their newly installed capacity accounted for 27% and 20% of the total increment of renewable capacity in 2014.

The US rolled out policies in transport, construction, and other sectors for raising energy efficiency. In transport, the *Energy Independence and Security Act* of

Table 4.4 Top five countries in cumulative installed capacity of and power output from different renewable energies

(By the end of 2016)

Ranking	*Renewable installed capacity (inc. hydropower)*	*Renewable installed capacity (exc. hydropower)*	*Wind installed capacity*	*Solar-thermal installed capacity (water heater)*	*PV installed capacity*	*Fuel ethanol output*	*Hydropower installed capacity*	*Renewable power and fuel investment (exc. hydropower stations larger than 50MW)*
1	China	China	China	China	China	US	China	China
2	US	US	US	Turkey	Japan	Brazil	Brazil	US
3	Brazil	Germany	Germany	Brazil	US	China	Turkey	Japan
4	Germany	Japan	Brazil	India	UK	Canada	India	UK
5	Canada	India	India	US	India	Thailand	Vietnam	India

Source: REN21, *Renewables 2017 Global Status Report*, pp. 16–18.

2007 stipulated that auto fuel consumption should be 40% lower than the current standards – down to 35 miles/gallon – in 2020. In May 2009, Obama announced the plan for developing new standards for fuel efficiency and set the federal standards for automobile GHG emission for the first time. The plan, with 2016 as the deadline, demanded that all automobiles produced after 2012 must meet the uniform fuel standard of 35.5 miles/gallon. The *Comprehensive Energy Strategy* of 2014 pledged to double the fuel efficiency of lightweight cars to 54.4 miles/gallon from 2010 to 2025 and raise the fuel efficiency of heavy-duty and midsize cars by 10%–20% by 2018. In construction, the *American Clean Energy and Security Act* of 2009 said energy efficiency standards would be raised by 50% for civil buildings built in 2014 and for commercial buildings built in 2015.[29] Thanks to the great efforts by the Obama administration, the number of clean energy patents granted by the United States Patent and Trademark Office (USPTO) saw exponential growth after 2009, much higher than in Japan, Germany, and ROK. In 2015, up to 3,613 clean energy technology patents were granted in the US.[30] In 2016, wind and solar power capacity accounted for about 62% of the newly installed capacity that year and was poised to maintain the high-speed growth for some time to come. According to a report from the US Department of Energy, the number of people working in the solar industry increased 24.5% in 2016 to approach 374,000, that in the wind energy industry increased 32% to approach 102,000, whereas only 187,000 people worked in the traditional fossil fuel industry.

By the end of 2016, the US ranked second in the world, after China, in terms of cumulative wind power capacity and renewable capacity (including hydropower), first in biomass (fuel ethanol and biodiesel) and geothermal energy. The main types of biofuels are fuel ethanol and biodiesel. Thanks to the strong policy support in various countries, biofuels reached a stable scale after a decade-long high-speed growth in the early 21st century, with its output growth starting to slow down in

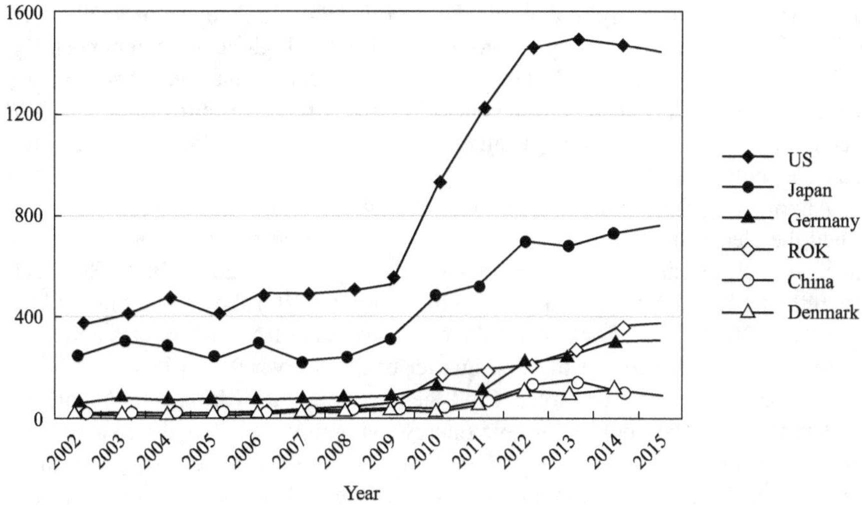

Figure 4.2 Top six countries in clean energy patent (2002–2015)
Source: The Clean Energy Patent Growth Index (CEPGI) 2015.

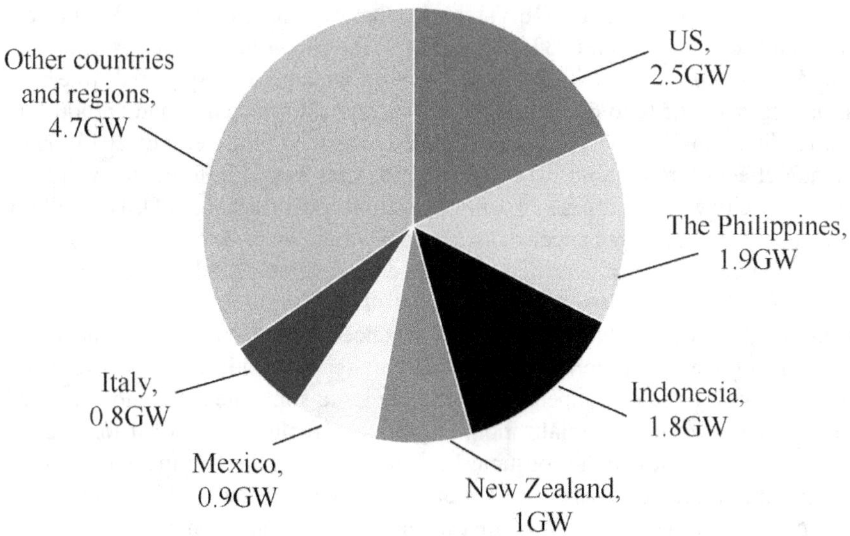

Figure 4.3 Top six countries in geothermal capacity, 2017
Source: REN21, Renewables Global Status Report 2018.

2014. In 2017, the world produced 1,060 × 10^8 liters of fuel ethanol, of which the US and Brazil were main producers and consumers; biodiesel production reached 310 × 10^8 liters, mostly from Europe, the US, and Brazil. Geothermal energy is very promising in the eyes of energy experts because of its huge global reserve and a usable size second only to that of solar energy. However, the use of geothermal energy has grown very slowly due to the consistently high development cost. By the end of 2017, altogether 1,700TWh geothermal energy had been used worldwide, a half-half between power generation and direct use; altogether 12.8GW geothermal capacity had been installed, to which the US, the Philippines, and Indonesia contributed the most.

Although the Trump administration withdrew from the *Paris Agreement*, abolished the clean power policy, and turned to boost the development of fossil fuels like coal, clean energy continued to see robust growth in 2017–2018. Statistics from the Federal Energy Regulatory Commission (FERC) showed that in the first quarter of 2017, 30% of newly installed capacity came from natural gas and 60% from renewable energy; in the first quarter of 2018, over 90% (95%) newly installed capacity came from solar, wind, geothermal, and hydropower. According to data from the National Renewable Energy Laboratory (NREL), the cost of solar power generation was down by 2/3 in 2010–2017, which gave a strong push to renewables. Lots of American power utilities chose to shut down coal power plants and turned to the cheaper and cleaner natural gas and renewables.

Trump's support for coal against the general clean trend proved futile, but his "de-climate" policies have undeniably caused some negative effects on the medium- and long-term development of clean energy. The *World Energy Outlook 2016* by International Energy Agency (IEA) reported that America's electricity output from wind and solar will reach 683TWh by 2030 if the *Clean Power Plan* is acted out, and 571TWh if the plan is abolished, with an average annual growth rate only shrinking from 7.5% to 6%. The federal "investment tax credit" and "production tax credit", which the US Congress decided to extend at the end of 2015, had a greater effect on renewables. If these two programs stayed in force, the wind and solar capacity would increase 56% in 2015–2020 and attract about USD 73 billion investment; if they were canceled, the capacity would increase only half as much.[31]

During Trump's term, America's clean energy development displayed three new trends. First, the new energy policy continued. The Trump administration remained committed to energy diversification and enhanced energy security and independence. The government continued to offer long-term subsidies for the use of renewable energy and developed tax credit policies to stimulate tech innovation and lower the cost of commercialization, to gradually replace traditional fossil energies with renewables on the consumer side. In particular, the Trump administration consistently increased the penetration of solar power for households, commercial, and public use. Second, the total investment in new energies, mainly clean energies, saw reduced growth, and new energy and low-carbon technologies became increasingly diversified. The international landscape of new energy investment, mainly clean energy, changed – with its slowdown in the US, China overtook it to become the world's largest new energy investor in 2017. Feeling uncertain about Trump's volatile new energy policy, the international financial market was on wait-and-watch and reduced R&D investment in the US. Third, new energy and low-carbon technologies progressed in multiple directions, with policy incentives being the key driving force. Applications for new energy patents were dominated by biomass, solar, and wind technologies, along with geothermal, nuclear, hydropower, and others. By 2017, biomass, solar and wind occupied the top three spots. In addition to breakthroughs in new energy patent technologies, low-carbon technologies aiming at higher energy efficiency also made remarkable progress, represented by low-energy lighting and fuel cell, the promotion of which would improve energy efficiency and lower carbon emission in construction and transport sectors.

II. Evolution of America's clean energy policies

The US released stimulus policies to boost the development of clean energy and renewable energy as early as the 1970s, mainly involving three categories – renewables, other clean energies, and smart grid and energy storage. Stimulus policies for renewables were most comprehensive, including such economic means as tax credit, fiscal subsidy, loan guarantee, accelerated depreciation, and fund grant, with tax credit being most frequently used. For example, investment in newly built, expanded, or renovated advanced energy production projects were entitled to a 30% tax credit. These projects basically covered all clean energy technology and equipment: storage, power transmission, fuel extraction, energy conservation, and carbon capture and sequestration. The production tax credit applied to various kinds of renewables, including biomass, wind, and PV, and the standard was USD 0.018/kWh. Consumption tax credit focused on biofuels. A consumption tax credit of USD 0.04/gallon of ethanol fuel was initiated in 1978, which was drastically increased in 2004 to USD 1/gallon for biodiesel made from oil-based plant and animal fats and USD 0.5/gallon for biodiesel made from recycled fats.

In the early 21st century, green energy got on a fast track powered by unprecedented economic incentives. The obligatory indicators and mandatory standards stipulated by relevant laws provided important policy guarantees for clean energy development. The *Energy Tax Incentives Act* of 2003 offered post-tax discounts for the purchase of new energy vehicles (NEVs). The *Energy Policy Act* of 2005, the most important energy act adopted in George W. Bush's term, was a milestone that, for the first time, systematically planned for green energy development. It comprehensively intensified the support for the research and development of clean energy technologies such as hydrogen energy, hybrid vehicle, and fuel cell, as well as for the production of such green energies as nuclear, solar, wind, and biomass power. It also encouraged the consumption of energy alternatives by demanding that the proportion of clean energy in power consumption shall be no less than 5% in 2010–2012 and no less than 7.5% after 2013. The *Advanced Energy Initiative* (AEI) of 2006 had two highlights. One was that it provided more financial support for the technological development and production of green energies and set the disruptive goal of changing the way how mankind used energy. The other was that it vowed to make ethanol fuel economically competitive and commercially viable. The "Twenty in Ten" initiative of 2007 set the long-term strategic goal of having clean energy account for 15% of total energy consumption by 2017, and the *Energy Independence and Security Act* (EISA) of the same year elevated bio-energy development to a strategic level never reached before.[32]

The US doesn't have renewable energy standards or energy conservation targets on the national level, and its efforts at climate change legislation have come to nothing. To date, the US federal government still hasn't formulated a law related to the quota of renewables. Instead, it is the states – nearly 30 of them – that have developed the Renewables Portfolio Standard (RPS), with California and Texas being the most successful cases. As an indispensable part of power reform, the RPS was first implemented in the 1990s. It set a general goal for the growth of renewables, broke it down among the electric power providers, and asked them to make sure a certain ratio of their electricity came from renewables. It is legally provided that grid operators must purchase a certain ratio of renewable electricity either through direct purchase or by buying quota from other entities that have bought more than required. More than 30 states have designed unique rules and elements for their RPS based on their own resource endowments and political and economic environment.[33] Many state governments have formed public funds to finance the research, development, and promotion of renewable energy and energy conservation technologies in the form of fixed subsidies, subsidized power tariffs, and low-interest loans, at a rate of 1%–3% of the retail power tariff. Regarding GHG emission reduction, there isn't a national cap or emission trading mechanism in the US, but a regional emission reduction market with states as main players has long existed. In 2005, America's first market-based mandatory regional emission reduction system – Regional Greenhouse Gas Initiative (RGGI) – came into being comprising ten states in the northeast and in the middle of the Atlantic coast. The trading entities were all the power generators in the region whose installed capacity exceeded 25MW, which were asked to reduce their emission by 10% in 2009–2018. In 2007, five Western states started the Western Climate Initiative, which, with 11 state members by 2009, aimed to cut regional GHG emissions by 15% from 2005 to 2020. This required concerted efforts across electricity generation, industry, business, transport, and domestic fuel use.[34]

To recover the American economy quickly from the 2015 financial crisis, the Obama administration picked clean energy as the green engine and a package solution to tackling the financial crisis, energy security, and climate change.

The *American Recovery and Reinvestment Act* issued in February 2009 initiated the idea of making massive investment in clean energy with investment tax credit. The act stressed providing direct fiscal subsidy for clean energy producers and consumers and proposed to allocate USD 3 billion to incentivize 5,000 biomass, solar, and wind power projects in the form of direct payment rather than tax credit. Regarding technological R&D, it planned to spend USD 23 billion supporting the R&D and promotion of clean energy technologies, in addition to doubling the federal research fund for developing clean coal technologies. Then the *American Clean Energy and Security Act* was enacted in June 2009, which was the first systematic plan targeting global warming. It laid down obligatory indicators in a larger scope, including power generation from renewables, energy efficiency, and GHG emission reduction. The act aimed to create jobs, facilitate economic recovery, and achieve energy independence by developing clean energy, striving to make the green industry a pillar industry in the future.

Table 4.5 RPS in American states

State	*Target (percentage in power sales)*	*Special requirement (percentage in power sales)*
Arizona	15% by 2025	4.5% distributed energy by 2012
California	33% by 2020	–
Colorado	Private power company: 20% by 2020 Power cooperative and public utility: 10% by 2020	Private power company: 0.4% solar power by 2010
Connecticut	23% by 2020	4% energy efficiency improvement and co-generation by 2010
District of Columbia	20% by 2020	0.4% solar power by 2022
Delaware	25% by 2025	2.005% solar power by 2019
Hawaii	40% by 2030	–
Iowa	105MW by 2025	–
Illinois	25% by 2025	18.75% wind power by 2013
Massachusetts	Type I: 4% by 2009 (annual increase of 1% afterwards) Type II: 3.6% of renewables and 3.5% of garbage power generation by 2009; 5% of alternatives by 2020 (annual increase of 0.25% afterwards)	Type II: 3.6% renewable and 3.5% garbage power generation by 2009
Maryland	20% by 2022	2% solar power by 2022
Maine	30% by 2000; additional increase of 10% by 2017	–
Michigan	10% by 2015	–
Minnesota	30% for Xcel by 2020; 25% for other power providers by 2025	25% wind power for Xcel
Missouri	15% by 2021	0.3% retail solar power by 2021
Montana	15% by 2015	–
North Dakota	10% by 2015	–
New Hampshire	23.8% by 2025; additional increase of 16.3%	0.3% solar power by 2025
New Jersey	22.5% by 2021	2.12% solar power by 2021
New Mexico	Private company: 20% by 2020 Rural power cooperative: 10% by 2020	4% wind, 4% solar, 2% biomass and geothermal, and 3% distributed new energy by 2020 (private company only)
Nevada	25% by 2025	1% solar power by 2015
New York	30% by 2015	0.154% by 2013
Ohio	25% new energy by 2025	1% solar power by 2025
Oregon	Large power company (with more than 3% of state's total power sales): 25% by 2025 Small power company: 5%–10% by 2025	Small power company: 5%–10% by 2025 (based on size)

(*Continued*)

Table 4.5 (Continued)

State	*Target (percentage in power sales)*	*Special requirement (percentage in power sales)*
Pennsylvania	18% new energy by May 31, 2021	0.5% solar power by 2025
Rhode Island	16% by 2020	–
South Dakota*	10% by 2015	–
Texas	10,000MW by 2025	At least 500MW renewable power other than wind power
Utah*	20% by 2025	–
Virginia*	12% of the 2007 sales volume by 2022	–
Vermont*	20% by 2017; annual increase of renewables in 2005–2012 up to standard (10% top)	–
State of Washington	15% by 2020	–
Wisconsin	10% by December 31, 2015	–

Note: * means the information is based on the latest DSIRE data.

Source: Xie Xuxuan, Wang Tian, Ren Dongming, "RPS in America: Latest Development and Lessons for China", *Energy of China*, No. 3, 2012.

It must be especially pointed out that the US also worked out a range of consumption plans, from buying clean electricity to using new energy in the transport sector to using solar energy in households, to ensure a successful transition toward green energy and economy. Although the US Congress didn't pass any national law on climate, it did form various public-private partnerships and research projects to support the development of clean energy and environmental technologies, with ever more federal R&D fund going that way. The White House was stepping up support for the industrial transformation toward a clean future too. In his State of the Union address in 2011, President Obama set the goal that 80% of power plants' output should be from clean energy (renewables, clean coal, and nuclear). In 2013, Obama, sidestepping the Congress, approved the *Climate Action Plan* through an executive order, which manifested his resolve to reestablish America's leadership in the governance of climate and clean energy. According to his ambitious "Clean Energy Plan" released in August 2015, American power plants needed to cut carbon emissions by 32% from 2005 to 2030, to push the energy transition strategy powered by clean energy development.

America's energy and climate policy took a U-turn after Trump came in office in January 2017 as the new president intended to clear out all political legacies left by Obama with respect to climate response and clean energy development. Trump took some actions regarding energy policy. He slashed the research funds for institutions related with energy and climate, he signed an Executive Order to restart the construction of Keystone XL oil pipeline, he allocated more capital to the nuclear industry, and he increased America's coal export.[35] On June 1, 2017, Trump announced that the US would withdraw from the *Paris Agreement*, citing its multiple negative effects on America's economy and employment. In October, he abolished Obama's "Clean Energy Plan" that was designed to cut GHG emissions by coal-fired power plants. In fact, Trump in March already ordered the Environmental Protection Agency (EPA) to review the plan and cancel it when necessary. The official abolishment meant that the US had completely given up the goal to reduce 32% GHG emissions by 2030 from the 2005 level, which took a serious toll on clean energy investment and development.[36] However, Trump shared the same view with Obama on "energy independence" and shale gas development, as was fully demonstrated in the "America First" Energy Plan rolled out by his administration in early 2017, which included three key points: accelerating the development of shale oil/gas at home, reviving the coal industry, and shedding the reliance on oil import. The US government also paid attention to environmental protection in the course of energy development and utilization. Although the "America First" Energy Plan negated Obama's *Climate Action Plan* and added uncertainty to global response to climate change, it proposed to develop clean coal technology and prioritize environmental protection in energy development. To further enlarge America's advantage in the shale gas industry, Trump administration also initiated the "public-private partnership" to finance the construction of natural gas infrastructure.

III. Development of America's clean energy diplomacy and its strategic positioning

Because of its two-party politics, the US, a major clean energy player, has seen periodic policy changes in its clean energy diplomacy but has maintained a degree of continuity notwithstanding. For instance, both Obama and Trump emphasized the competition-driven clean energy diplomacy, as reflected in their efforts to curb the development of clean energy in emerging countries by dint of anti-dumping and countervailing duty and trade friction. The US understands clean energy in the broad sense, placing emphasis not only on renewables, but also on nuclear energy, natural gas, and clean coal technology. All in all, America's primary motivation for advancing energy transition is to achieve energy security. As it doesn't pin all the hopes on renewables, natural gas, nuclear power, and clean coal utilization retain an important position in its transition strategy.

First, America's clean energy diplomacy displays periodic changes due to two-party politics. Clean energy diplomacy is so closely connected with climate change that America's clean energy diplomacy is largely affected by its two-party politics. Traditionally, the Democratic Party represented by Bill Clinton and Barack Obama has been very active about climate change, global environmental governance, and related topics. The Clinton administration played a vital role in the design and signing of the *Kyoto Protocol*, while the Obama administration, through close cooperation with China, was a key leader in pushing the signing and taking effect of the *Paris Agreement*. In particular, the clean energy cooperation between China and the US made significant breakthroughs. For instance, the China-U.S. Strategic and Economic Dialogue (S&ED) was jointly initiated by Chinese and American presidents in April 2009, which brought strategic and economic issues under an overall

Table 4.6 American policies for green energy development

Year	*Title*	*Key points*
2003	Energy Tax Incentives Act	Tax credit applies to the following: electricity production using required bioenergy equipment, livestock manure, geothermal energy, solar energy, local solid biomaterials, and recyclable sludge; small hydropower generator; and motor vehicles using alternative energy.
2005	Energy Policy Act	Developing non-conventional hydrocarbon energy; providing tax preferences for hybrid vehicles; funding accelerated R&D of hybrid power technologies; providing loan guarantee (up to 80% of total project cost) for projects applying innovative and advanced clean energy technologies; using 7.5 billion gallons of ethanol-based gasoline and biodiesel (about 3% of total gasoline consumption) annually by 2012; providing tax credit for household solar systems; developing projects under the "hydrogen energy initiative" with full-sum fund allocation to advance fuel cell technology and the production and storage of hydrogen energy.
2006	Advanced Energy Initiative	Increasing R&D fund for clean energy technology by 22%; supporting the R&D for new transport and new energy technologies; changing the way of energy use at American homes and offices by increasing the investment in coal-fired thermal power plants with zero emission, revolutionary solar and wind technologies, and clean and safe nuclear energy; developing hybrid cell and plug-in hybrid vehicles and accelerating the development of zero-emission and hydrogen-powered vehicles; making corn-based cellulosic ethanol fuel economically competitive by 2012.
2007	"Twenty in Ten" Initiative	Providing 35 billion gallons of renewable and alternative energies (15% of total energy consumption) by 2017; reducing America's oil consumption by 20% in the next decade; ensuring energy security with innovation and technology.
2007	Energy Independence and Security Act	First legislation to demand the development of biodiesel fuel, which shall not be commercialized unless its emissions are 50% lower than petroleum; increasing biofuel, as part of gasoline consumption, from 4.7 billion gallons in 2007 to 36 billion in 2022; subsidizing states with a small output of cellulosic biofuel in the research, development, and utilization of bioenergy technology.
2009	Recovery and Reinvestment Act	Investing USD 150 billion in renewable and alternative energies in the next decade; fostering advanced biofuel industry, hybrid vehicle and pure electric vehicle industry, high-efficiency storage cell, solar power, wind power, and other new energy sectors as new pillar industries for national economy.

(*Continued*)

Table 4.6 (Continued)

Year	*Title*	*Key points*
2009	Clean Energy and Security Act	Generating 15% (12% if an application is made and approved) of power supply from renewables in each state by 2020; formulating a national strategy on carbon capture and sequestration within a year, and clearing legal and regulatory obstacles in the commercialization of this technology; building infrastructure for plug-in vehicle on a large scale and asking every power company to make a plan supporting such vehicles; setting up a clean energy innovation center to guarantee America's leadership in energy technology; implementing the federal renewable power purchase plan, whereby government departments have the right to sign 30-year-long power purchase contract; transitioning toward clean energy and economy, creating more green jobs and helping workers shift to such jobs; setting up an "Energy Efficiency and Renewable Energy Worker Training Program".
2013	Climate Action Plan	Reaffirming America's commitment to cutting 17% GHG emissions by 2020 from the 2005 level; expounding the series of measures to be adopted by the federal government in three areas: reducing GHG emissions, coping with adverse effects of climate change, and leading international cooperation, which reflects America's determination to reshape its leadership in climate and clean energy governance.
2015	Clean Energy Plan	Reducing American power plants' carbon emissions by 32% in 2005–2030 to achieve the energy transition strategy based on clean energy development.

Source: Originally created by the author.

framework. The first session of S&ED made clean energy development a central topic, after which bilateral cooperation became increasingly institutionalized. The U.S.-China Clean Energy Research Center (CERC) was established to facilitate joint research in clean energy technology by Chinese and American scientists and engineers, in a bid to boost tech innovation, improve energy efficiency, and shift toward low-carbon economy at a faster pace.

In comparison, the Republican Party represented by Bush Junior and Trump has always been doubtful about climate change. Lacking interests in climate change and the global governance of clean energy, it is more focused on supporting traditional energies and keeping America's green hegemony through market competition. For instance, Bush Junior withdrew from the *Kyoto Protocol* as soon as he was sworn in, and Trump announced to exit the *Paris Agreement* soon after he became president, both casting a pall over the global climate governance and clean energy cooperation. The two parties taking turns in running the country has resulted in periodic changes in America's clean energy diplomacy.

The George W. Bush administration took *Kyoto Protocol* as a flawed system that would hurt both employment and the economy, but it made some efforts in developing clean technology for the purpose of energy independence and security. In 2002, the US Department of Energy launched a "climate change technology project" to develop low-emission or zero-emission technologies, reduce GHG emission from infrastructure, and strengthen the measurement and monitoring of GHG emission. The administration also initiated a regional cooperation mechanism titled Asia-Pacific Partnership on Clean Development and Climate (APPCDC) to promote research, development, and deployment of clean energy and environmental technologies based on public-private partnership, while strengthening the relations with Australia, Japan, Canada, India, and ROK.

Based on the *Clean Energy and Security Act* of 2009, President Obama put forth America's emission reduction plan at the 2009 Copenhagen Climate Change Conference. However, his Democratic Party lost the House majority after the midterm election in 2010 and continued to lose the Senate majority after the 2012 election.[37] Under such circumstance, Obama, to sidestep the Congress where he couldn't get a law passed, issued the *Climate Action Plan* by way of an Executive Order to reduce GHG emissions and promote clean energy. At this time, the US turned to focus on promoting a type of clean energy diplomacy centered on a hub-and-spoke system and the emission reduction by major countries. On the one hand, it called for creating a global emission market to exert its structural advantages in low-carbon economy and clean energy technology; on the other hand, it tried to form a model of "hub-and-spoke governance" based on the series of US-led climate and clean development partnerships in the Asia-Pacific region. It led the establishment of a slew of climate governance mechanisms outside the UNFCCC to challenge EU's leading role in this area. These mechanisms include the Asia-Pacific Partnership on Clean Development and Climate (APP, 2005), Major Economies Meeting on Energy Security and Climate Change (MEM, 2007), Major Economies Forum on Energy and Climate (MEF, 2009), and Climate and Clean Air Coalition (CCAC, 2012).

In August 2015, the Environmental Protection Agency (EPA), pushed by President Obama, released the *Clean Power Plan* to stimulate clean energy development.[38] On the international level, Obama strongly pushed the Clean Energy Ministerial (CEM) as a key part of his efforts to advance clean energy diplomacy. As early as in 2009, US Secretary of Energy Steve Chu advocated America's clean energy development plan at the Copenhagen Climate Change Conference, stressing the importance of helping southern countries develop sustainable energies and efficient energy technologies.[39] On July 20, 2010, the first CEM convened in Washington, and the 21 participating countries invited by the US government represented 80% of the world's clean energy market. Steve Chu, who chaired the meeting, called on all countries to work more closely together in clean energy technology to mitigate the environmental impacts of climate change. The creation and successful operation of the CEM, which currently covers the clean energy markets of 24 major countries and the EU, reflect the governance-driven side of clean energy diplomacy in President Obama's term. Even though Donald Trump pulled back from the *Paris Agreement* and abolished the *Clean Energy Plan*, the CEM, since its eighth session in Beijing, has been backed by the multilateral secretariat newly formed in the International Energy Agency (IEA) thanks to Obama. This means the CEM has come to a new stage of multilateral engagement, giving its members a greater sense of responsibility. Moreover, it was merged with the Mission Innovation (MI) co-founded by 20 major countries in December 2015 while the *Paris Agreement* was being concluded.[40] Such an integration made CEM much more institutionalized and internationally influential.

The Trump administration was consistently passive on clean energy diplomacy, especially international governance in clean energy. Domestically, President Trump changed the climate and energy policy chiefly by abolishing the *Clean Power Plan* through an executive order on energy independence. He also canceled the *Climate Action Plan* and the *Climate Action Plan: Strategy to Reduce Methane Emissions* issued by the Executive Office of President Obama, rescinded four of Obama's executive orders including the *Power Sector Carbon Pollution Standards* and *Climate Change and National Security*, and reviewed the carbon emission limits for newly built and renovated fossil fuel power plants. These regressive measures slashed America's emission reduction efforts for some time and led the country astray from the 2025 target in its intended nationally determined contributions. On the international level, Trump aggressively demonstrated America's resolution to counter globalization. He had no interests at all in global climate and clean energy governance, as proven by the announcement to withdraw from the *Paris Agreement* and giving up the leadership in CEM. He justified his action with the narrow-minded, utilitarian concept of "America first".[41] In particular, his refusal to fulfill the obligation of providing financial support for developing countries' climate actions and contributing capital to the Green Climate Fund may erode the global confidence in low-carbon investment. Since 2007, the surge of clean energy investment in the US has subsided because of Trump's passive actions and policies. It may also aggravate the negative effects of shale gas revolution as the growing output of fossil energies will very likely squeeze the space of renewable energy industry in the short term with an even lower price.

Second, America's clean energy diplomacy is highly competition-driven in all periods.

Obama and Trump treated clean energy in drastically different ways. The former advocated a clean energy diplomacy that was both high-governance-driven and high-competition-driven and oriented toward greater green strengths, while the latter adopted a clean energy diplomacy that was low-governance-driven and high-competition-driven. But despite the difference, high competition remained the persistent and dominant feature of the hegemon's clean energy diplomacy.

During Obama's term, the US was continuously enhancing its export capacity in the field of clean energy. For instance, Doris Matsui, a member of the US House representing California, proposed the "New Clean Energy Technology Manufacturing and Export Assistance Act" in January 2011. The Act called for setting up a special fund to ensure the development and implementation of a national strategy for clean energy technology export and assist American businesses in exporting their technologies. As China became a strong player in this field, the Obama administration, feeling concerned about the competition and strategically anxious, filed suits to the WTO against China for subsidizing its wind power manufacturers so as to keep its own edge in the field.[42] Speaking of competition, the US not only hurt China's export of PV and wind power products through anti-dumping and countervailing measures, but also began to vie for shares in the global clean energy market, especially Africa. Since 2012, clean energy has gradually become a key area witnessing economic and trade frictions between China and the US. Chinese wind power and PV industries have been subjected to America's anti-dumping sanction repeatedly. Regarding the competition for overseas market, the US tightened military control over Africa after 2012 and strengthened their new energy cooperation, in the attempt to launch an "enclosure movement" in the new energy sector. For instance, the US government provided USD 250 million to South Africa for developing solar energy, and America's Millennium Challenge Corporation provided new energy equipment for Tanzania.[43]

The competition became more conspicuous during Trump's term in the form of China-US trade frictions. On June 15, 2018, Trump slapped a 25% tariff on USD 50 billion worth of Chinese goods, including major industrial technologies. A statement issued by the US government declared that the tariff would come in two phases. The first phase of the 25% levy targeted 818 items worth USD 34 billion, including auto parts, information technology, aviation and aerospace, energy storage, medical apparatus, and other high-tech goods. The second phase would be imposed on 284 categories of Chinese goods worth about USD 16 billion, including semiconductors, swathes of electronic products, and chemical products. Energy-related products in the first batch of 818 items included nuclear reactors, steam boilers, electrical machinery, electric motors, power generator sets, and some cells. Much equipment could be categorized under the title of "energy and power", as defined in the broad sense, including wind turbines, and PV products were likely subject to a 55% superimposed tariff. BloombergNEF analyzed that a small number of Chinese manufacturers, such as Goldwind and China Shipbuilding Industry Group, might be affected. Import and installation of solar and wind equipment in the US would be more costly, and the tariff had a good chance of jeopardizing international trade system. As the sales of electric vehicles (EVs) grew, many of the fast-growing energy storage products (cells) were included in the first list. Certain EV models, especially BYD's electric bus, might be affected. On July 10, 2018, the US announced another 10% tariff on USD 200 billion worth of Chinese goods in retaliation to China's tariff hike on USD 50 billion worth of American exports. The new tariff items included photovoltaic inverters and AC components (solar panels with micro inverters), which made it much harder for Chinese PV industry to gain ground in more overseas markets.

Third, sub-national and non-state actors are gaining weight in America's clean energy diplomacy. Multilateral intergovernmental negotiations after the 2009 Copenhagen Climate Change Conference highlighted the dilemma of the *Kyoto Protocol*. Therefore, while America's climate policy was easily affected by the two-party politics, non-state actors in the country began to augment their influence by establishing partnership networks, as indicated by the formation of different coalitions of sub-national actors. There is the U.S. Climate Alliance comprising 14 states and Puerto Rico and the U.S. Climate Mayors covering 383 cities, each accounting for 36% and 23% of American population and 40% and 27% of its economy, respectively.[44] Just three days after Trump's announcement to exit the *Paris Agreement*, a one-of-a-kind coalition of non-state actors called We Are Still In was established on June 5, 2017. This more inclusive partnership gathered more than 1,200 participants from various states, cities, enterprises, civil groups, NGOs, universities, and research institutes. They signed the "We Are Still In" Declaration and hoped to draw more social and market forces through the network to support the realization of America's targets under the *Paris Agreement*. By October 2017, the network had quickly expanded to more than 2,300 members.[45] The undersigned actors, crossing the partisan boundary, stood for more than 130 million Americans (40% of population) across 50 states and USD 8.5 trillion worth of GDP (45% of national total).[46]

Leveraged on We Are Still In and joining hands with U.S. Climate Alliance and U.S. Climate Mayors, former New York City mayor Michael Bloomberg, who is also the UN special envoy on climate change, and governor of the State of California Jerry Brown jointly launched America's Pledge at the end of 2017. Being more broad-based than previous non-state coalitions, the new online initiative brought together 14 states, 252 cities and counties, 1,780 enterprises and investors, 339 colleges and universities, and nearly 300 social groups, who pledged to support the US in honoring its committed GHG emission targets in the *Paris Agreement* framework. Thanks to their social power and material power, non-state actors joining America's Pledge accounted for 49% of the American population (159 million people), 54% of GDP (USD 10.1 trillion), and 35% of CO_2 emissions (2.3 Gt equivalent). If we compare these states and cities supporting the *Paris Agreement*

Table 4.7 Networks of US non-state actors supporting *Paris Agreement*

Name of networks	*Type of entities*	*Number of entities*	*Population and percent of US total (2016)*		*GDP and percent of US total (2016)*		*Current GHG emissions and percent of US total (2016)*	
US Climate Alliance	States	14 states plus Puerto Rico	118 million	36%	$7.6 trillion	40%	1.5 Gt CO2e	23%
US Climate Mayors	Cities	383 cities	74 million	23%	$5.0 trillion	27%	1.0 Gt CO2e	15%
We Are Still In	All types	2,320 entities[47]	131 million	40%	$8.5 trillion	45%	1.8 Gt CO2e	27%
America's Pledge	All types	470 cities and states (including Puerto Rico)	159 million	49%	$10.1 trillion	54%	2.3 Gt CO2e	35%

Source: Bloomberg Philanthropies, *America's Pledge, Phase* 1 *Report States, Cities, and Businesses in the United States Are Stepping Up on Climate Action*, November 2017, p. 96.

to major countries on GDP, they as a group would rank third in the world after the US and China, with an economic aggregate twice as large as Japan's and nearly thrice Germany's. This speaks volumes for the rising structural power of non-state actors in global climate governance.

Given the general trend of low-carbon transition, whether a country can secure a vantage point in low-carbon technology and climate response will decide its future in the international landscape. Unlike before when climate governance was mainly negotiated, in the era post–*Paris Agreement*, local practices of climate governance and low-carbon standards will bear more heavily on climate negotiations.

The establishment of America's Pledge gave a fresh impetus to the networked governance mode involving multiple partners. The governance practices and the creation of standards by various non-state actors showcased America's commitment to endorsing the *Paris Agreement* and leading climate governance. With their respective strengths and specialties, the states, cities, universities, businesses, and other local actors across the US are taking it upon themselves to honor the commitment to climate response. For instance, American companies are transiting toward low-carbon economy, and almost half the corporations have at least one climate or clean energy objective or make emission reduction an integral part of their operation. American states are making more investment in green, sustainable infrastructure, proposing ambitious renewable energy targets, and pledging efforts to mitigate carbon pollution. Cities and counties are taking feasible measures to respond to climate change, ranging from using a larger proportion of renewables to setting active emission targets to investing in sustainable infrastructure. For example, in implementing the regulations, policies, and action plans in relation to climate change, the state government of California has adopted the work approach widely applied in international environmental organizations such as the International Council for Local Environmental Initiatives (ICLEI) and California Energy Alliance. This replicable, standard GHG control mechanism ensures the general synchrony of local governments in carrying out their climate plans.[48] American universities and colleges are developing clean energy technologies of the future, saying that institutions of higher education have the ability, potential, and necessity to shape a future where America is a climate leader. Social organizations tend to advocate new practices from a value-oriented perspective, such as facilitating negotiations on governance rules in the post–*Paris Agreement* age through constructive dialogues. In sum, these networks of local climate actions and the standards of climate governance they stand for will be more internationally influential as local forces acquire more leading power.

American non-state actors know how to spread their influence through global summits. California Governor Jerry Brown, in conjunction with the UNFCCC Secretariat, hosted the Global Climate Action Summit in San Francisco, California, in September 12–14, 2018. The summit gathered a broad range of participants including state leaders, local leaders, businesses, scientists, and nonprofit organizations to discuss how to respond to climate change together through enhanced decarbonization efforts worldwide.[49] Its invitations to the leaders and ministers of many countries were accepted. Attaching special importance to cooperating with

Table 4.8 Governance practices by non-state actors joining America's Pledge

Type of members	*Action tactics/ network*	*Governance practices and standards*
Businesses and investors	Science-based objectives	Businesses nationwide incorporate emission reduction in their development strategy to keep global temperature increase well below 2°C. Science-based objectives provide the basis for analysis and technical assistance to help businesses transit to the low-carbon mode.
	100% renewable energy target (e.g., RE100)	The more than 100 companies joining RE100 commit to using 100% renewable energy for faster energy transition.
	Higher energy productivity (e.g., EP100)	EP100 is a global initiative of businesses who want to reduce their carbon footprint and energy cost by doubling energy efficiency.
	Renewable Energy Buyers Alliance (RE-BA)	Businesses' energy demand is matched with the supply of renewables to accelerate the shift to clean, low-carbon energies.
	Investors: join the Portfolio Decarbonization Coalition (PDC)	PDC is a coalition that tries to reduce carbon emission by urging investors to phase down carbon in their portfolio.
	Signing Montreal Carbon Pledge	Investors pledge to measure and disclose the carbon footprint of their portfolio annually.
Cities and other sub-national actors	Global Covenant of Mayors for Climate and Energy (GCMCE)	This is the world's largest platform on which cities take climate actions together, including 175 American cities and more than 650 cities in the rest of the world. The cities pledge to reduce GHG emission and increase resilience/adaptation to climate change, trace their progress in an open and transparent manner, and promote learning of best practices with each other.
	Climate Mayors	This network comprises city mayors in the US who pledge to take actions in their communities and make joint efforts to support ambitious climate actions both on the federal and international level. More than 350 climate mayors signed a commitment to do their bit for implementing the *Paris Agreement*.
States	Under 2 Coalition	The undersigned states pledge to reduce 80%–95% of GHG emissions from the 1990 level, or limit the per capita CO_2 emission equivalent to 2 metric tons by 2050.
	US Climate Alliance	This is an alliance of states committed to achieving GHG emission targets consistent with those in the *Paris Agreement*.
	National Energy Efficiency Registry (NEER)	This is a state-level online platform. It helps the states achieve their energy and environmental targets, discloses the regulated organizations' performance, and encourages voluntary investment in energy efficiency and water/energy conservation initiatives.

(*Continued*)

Table 4.8 (Continued)

Type of members	*Action tactics/ network*	*Governance practices and standards*
Universities and colleges	Presidents' Climate Leadership Commitments (PCLC)	This is an online platform comprising colleges and universities committed to global climate issues and visible campus actions. The undersigned pledge to eliminate GHG emission on campus, improve their capability of climate adaptation and community building, and try to make research and education part of the efforts in response to climate change.
	Campus Cleantech Pilots	Universities and colleges can be platforms for testing new clean energy technologies, thus accelerating the transition toward a low-carbon economy. Not only will the world benefit from these innovations, but institutions of higher education can also acquire more opportunities of academic research and classroom study.
	Carbon Credit and Purchasing Program (C2P2)	This is an initiative supporting universities and colleges to develop and market carbon offset to speed up the process of campus carbon neutrality.
	Offset Network	This is a network of campus resources aimed at making carbon offset projects more innovative and adaptive to be suitable for large-scale application.
Social organizations	Coalition of Faith-based Organizations (213 faith-based organizations)	The Coalition of Faith-based Organizations believes it is a moral responsibility for humankind to change the way they live in order to balance the Earth's bearing capacity and protect the climate and environment.
	US Climate Action Network (US-CAN)	This is a network of 165 American NGOs active in the field of climate change. It is committed to enhancing local leadership and constructive dialogue in climate negotiations.

Source: Originally created by the author based on data in *America's Pledge* (2017), Bloomberg Philanthropies, *America's Pledge, Phase* 1 *Report States, Cities, and Businesses in the United States Are Stepping Up on Climate Action*, November 2017. www.bbhub.io/dotorg/sites/28/2017/11/AmericasPledgePhaseOneReportWeb.pdf.

international organizations such as the UN and with multinationals, the summit designed a co-chairing system involving several parties, including Governor Jerry Brown, UNFCCC Executive Secretary Patricia Espinosa, chairman of Indian auto giant Mahindra Group Anand Mahindra, and United Nations Special Envoy on Cities and Climate Change Bloomberg.[50] Though a local effort, the summit enhanced America's clout in climate change and clean energy governance internationally.

Section 3 Japan's clean energy diplomacy

Japan has been a global leader in energy efficiency and clean technology. Since the oil crisis in the 1970s, the resource-poor country has been seeking more energy independence. However, in the age of global environmental crisis, reflected by the rapid increase of energy demand and global warming, Japan's two major energy strategies – raising energy efficiency and developing nuclear power – have met greater challenges.[51] Therefore, ensuring stable and diversified energy supply is an important goal of Japan's energy strategy, diplomatic policies, and tech policies. Especially after the 2011 Fukushima nuclear accident, the country has seen a rising ratio of renewables in its energy mix, with the long-term strategy of fostering green energy into a pillar industry. It is also paying more attention to advancing a diversified clean energy diplomacy on the international level.

I. Japan's clean energy development and features of its energy transition

As a resource-poor country in serious lack of fossil energy reserve, Japan, with the fourth largest energy consumption in the world, is highly reliant on energy import. It is the third largest net importer of crude oil, second largest coal importer, and largest LNG importer. The uranium used by its nuclear power stations is 100% imported. With an energy self-sufficiency rate (other than nuclear power) as low as 4.3%, the lowest among developed countries, Japan has to meet its energy demand almost completely with import (99.7% oil import, 97.7% coal import, and 96.6% natural gas import).

Having experienced serious environmental pollution in the early stage of industrialization and two oil crises in the 1970s, Japan established a new energy strategy placing equal stress on energy security, environmental protection, and economic development. The Japanese government has been actively promoting an investment strategy and a medium- and long-term R&D system for clean technologies and energy efficiency. Between 1974 and 2009, the country spent USD 131.27 billion on R&D in the energy sector, second only to that of the US, and that gave Japan an all-round edge in the tech development, production, and consumption of green energy.

Japan initiated the Top Runner Program during the negotiations on *Kyoto Protocol* in the 1990s. The program set the highest energy-saving standards at the time for 11 products – namely, car, truck, air conditioner, fluorescent lamp, television receiver, copy machine, computer, HDD, VCR, fridge, and freezer.[52] As a result, many of Japan's high-efficiency and energy-saving products became technologically dominant. From 1988 to 2007, Japan had the world's largest number of patents in relation to clean energy and incubated a large group of industrial enterprises possessing key and core technologies. The "Cool Earth – Innovative Energy Technology Program" (CEIETP) it launched in 2008, which aimed at designing a road map of clean technology R&D for each sector,[53] involved 21 promising categories. They included innovative PV power, advanced nuclear power, high-efficiency natural gas power generation, high-efficiency coal-fired power generation, CO_2 capture and storage, hybrid car, innovative materials, high-efficiency superconducting power transmission, smart transport system, fuel cell vehicles, and high-efficiency buildings. Between 1990 and 2013, the energy consumption per unit GDP in Japan was consistently much lower than world average. In an international comparison, its primary energy consumption per unit GDP was only 1/1.9 that of the US, 1/1.7 of Europe, 1/7.2 of China, 1/16.3 of Russia, and 1/3.1 of world average.

Table 4.9 Distribution and licensing of clean energy technology patents worldwide – European Patent Office (EPO) (2009) Unit: Patent

Country/region	*Solar PV*	*Solar thermal*	*Wind energy*	*Geothermal*	*Hydro/ocean energy*	*Biofuel*	*Carbon capture*	*Carbon storage*	*IGCC*	*Selected clean energy sectors*	*Fossil fuel and nuclear energy*	*Total energy sectors*
Japan	3941	142	196	32	199	112	104	6	37	4672	5751	691751
US	1301	172	320	50	387	135	199	19	56	2508	5543	423187
Germany	931	450	649	44	259	133	79	4	27	2391	5840	334119
ROK	802	13	32	1	26	11	10	–	–	885	584	107001
France	242	88	84	10	104	45	60	9	4	607	2795	126924
UK	212	47	87	9	174	27	28	3	11	560	1039	84062
Italy	87	53	41	8	75	27	9	–	1	272	849	46492
The Netherlands	96	51	56	9	22	13	14	1	3	236	539	29009
Canada	51	39	49	11	59	22	17	3	2	233	549	35528
China Taiwan	160	11	9	2	14	4	–	–	–	195	122	20850
Switzerland	75	35	16	7	39	12	4	1	5	179	600	27081
Denmark	5	5	152	2	17	4	1	–	–	177	175	7929
Spain	29	42	90	1	25	6	2	1	–	174	176	10738
China	80	13	20	6	14	11	4	–	1	143	108	18892
Austria	39	35	20	11	37	11	1	–	2	137	416	19144
Sweden	23	18	34	7	35	6	1	–	7	122	719	27986
Norway	13	12	28	7	54	0.2	20	3	2	119	165	6362
Australia	41	43	11	1	22	7	3	–	3	112	132	10150
Finland	11	8	18	3	10	25	4	–	7	82	399	20178
Israel	19	38	9	14	16	3	2	–	3	82	59	11441
World total	8972	1639	2232	285	1902	731	616	54	190	15755	30235	2310472

Source: Ren Xiaoling, "Distribution and licensing of clean energy technology patents worldwide – EPO releases report on 'Patents and clean energy technologies'", *China Invention & Patent*, No. 1, 2011.

Leveraged on its advantages in clean energy technology, Japan has been in a leading position in areas related with renewables, such as solar cell and wind turbine manufacturing. The country began to support Japanese wind power equipment in 1997 and intensified the efforts in 2003 with the *Act on Special Measures Concerning New Energy Usage by Electric Utilities* (Act on Special Measures or RPS Act). Wind power has developed rather slowly in Japan due to the lack of flat terrain, complexity of landform, and insufficient power capacity.[54] Its newly installed wind power capacity in 2010 was only about 1/75 of China's. Even though the FIT system adopted in 2012 increased wind power capacity to some extent, the increase in wind power output was insignificant due to the long process of legal and environmental assessment, limited capacity of the grid system, and other factors. The Institute for Energy Economics and Financial Analysis (IEEFA) issued a report titled *Japan: Greater Energy Security Through Renewables* in 2017. The report pointed out that Japan, after the Fukushima accident, seemed inclined to replace nuclear power with fossil fuel, but that would cost it the opportunity of developing renewables – Japan has inestimable potential in renewable energy development, especially solar, wind, and geothermal energy. As of December 2013, its wind power capacity ranked eighteenth in the world, and its ratio in the 2030 power mix – the 30-year target released in July 2015 – was only 1.7%. While wind power developed faster than PV power in many other countries, onshore wind power in Japan has lagged behind limited by the land area. In 2016, solar power met 4.3% of Japan's electricity demand as opposed to 1.5% by wind power.[55] Large-scale solar power plants and wind farms require such a large land area that they are not suitable for Japan, a country of a small and narrow territory. Under such circumstances, stepping up the development of offshore wind power and solar power is an effective way of scaling up the use of renewables.[56]

Because the land suitable for wind power development is limited and it takes a long time to get an approval, onshore wind power has developed very slowly in Japan, but offshore wind power holds great potential with the fast-falling cost.[57] Japan has a potential offshore wind power capacity of 1,600GW, 378GW of which is technologically feasible, and 96GW is commercially and technologically feasible factoring in the grid demand and capacity, as well as other limitations. Japan has realized that to unleash the immense potential of offshore wind power, it must develop robust offshore wind turbines that can endure typhoon, and advanced technologies have guaranteed its leading position in renewable energy development. Meanwhile, its state-of-the-art manufacturing industry gives it a natural advantage in the production of wind turbine. For instance, Mitsubishi Heavy Industries (MHI) is developing offshore wind power technology and working with Vestas to provide offshore wind turbines. Offshore wind power doesn't need to worry about land limitation and has a utilization rate as high as 45%–50%. Now Japan's offshore wind power technology is already leading the world, and floating wind power is growing with an especially strong momentum. With financial support from the Ministry of the Environment and the Ministry of Economy, Trade, and Industry (METI), Japanese enterprises, universities, and research institutes have devoted huge amounts of research resources and, based on the many new concepts they put forth, have tested and synchronized several prototypes according to government-set targets. IEEFA estimated that Japan's offshore wind power capacity would reach 10GW by 2030 and 37GW by 2050, 19GW fixed and 18GW floating.

At the same time, Japan has made major breakthroughs in vertical axis wind turbine (VAWT) technology. The Magnus VAWT currently developed by Challenergy is able to generate electricity steadily in strong wind and turbulent flow. People have high hopes on this system, the first in the world adopting wind power technology suitable for remote islands and mountainous areas. Unlike traditional wind turbine, Magnus VAWT doesn't rely on the high-speed rotation of propellers, hence lowering the risk of accident and breakdown as well as the environmental impacts imposed by noises and bird collisions. In January 2018, Challenergy and SKY Perfect JSAT joined hands to provide services for countries and regions lacking in electricity and communications infrastructure by combining satellite communications services with wind power generation. Satellite communications services are suitable in remote islands and mountainous areas and for communications recovery after massive natural disasters, and ground communications equipment needs electric power. Magnus VAWT is able to provide steady power for the equipment in those hardly accessible regions and guarantee satellite communications services even after a disaster. The cooperation between Challenergy and SJC will augment satellite communications' advantage in providing connection services anytime, anywhere. SJC plans to reinforce its disaster-scenario communications solutions to meet the domestic demand in Japan. It also tries to provide communications services to areas around the world that suffer from the digital divide, such as Southeast Asia and Pacific Island states, where power and communications infrastructure is poor.

Regarding solar development, Japan began to promote solar energy as early as in the 1980s and propelled its growth with the FIT system. The production and

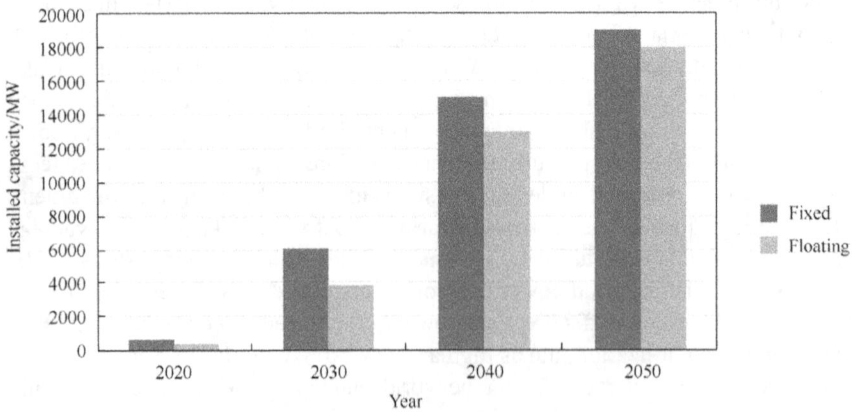

Figure 4.4 Japan's offshore wind power plan

Source: Wu Shaobo, Yin Haiqing, Zhang Kaihua, et al., "Floating Wind Power Technology in Japan: Current Status and Future Development", China Harbour Engineering, No. 6, 2017.

Figure 4.5 Japan's future offshore floating wind turbines

Source: SCIENCE & TECHNOLOGY: Energy, Innovation, Asia, https://ourworld.unu.edu/en/japans-next-generation-of-renewable-energy.

popularization of solar water heater reached a peak in the early 1980s, but the number of new installations decreased year by year after the 1990s because of low oil price and appreciated Japanese yen. Since then, especially with Japan's joining in the international climate negotiations, the country has attached more importance to solar development. The 2011 Fukushima nuclear accident stimulated Japan's investment in renewables to increase by 23% to reach USD 8.6 billion, over 90% of which was concentrated on solar power projects and other medium- and small-sized projects. In July 2012, Japan launched a clean energy stimulus program; in 2013, it was a top player in solar energy development; from 2013 to 2015, its PV installed capacity increased steadily from 7.1GW to 10.3GW to 12.3GW, the second largest in the world. In 2014, the Japanese government issued the *New Basic Energy Plan*, vowing to increase solar capacity to 53GW by 2030, which led to a peak PV installation of 14.3GW in 2016. Although wind power capacity hasn't taken off yet, PV capacity has been growing notably. While China remained the largest solar power generator, Japan was catching up quickly, with an all-year new capacity of 8,600MW and cumulative capacity of 42GW in 2016, beating Germany to rank second in the world. As Japan restructured its power industry, the percentage of solar PV in its power mix will rise from the current 4% to 12% in 2030. Thanks to the favorable policies for solar power and offshore wind power, the percentage of renewables in Japan's total power output is expected to double and reach 35% by 2030.[58]

In the meantime, Japan makes a point of developing renewable-based hydrogen technology. Hydrogen is drawing more attention as an important renewable energy, and hydrogen-based fuel cell realizes zero emission as it uses hydrogen and oxygen to produce electricity with water as the only byproduct. Statistics from Toshiba show that the global market of fuel cell power generation facilities fuel cell vehicles, and other hydrogen-related infrastructure will reach JPY 40 trillion in

2030 and JPY 160 trillion in 2050. Tempted by such an enormous market, Japanese government and enterprises began to pay close attention to the use of hydrogen energy and attempted to secure a vantage point in the international arena through renewable-based hydrogen production. In April 2015, Toshiba, a leading company in the field, held an unveiling ceremony of its "Hydrogen Research & Development Center" in Fuchu, Tokyo Prefecture. The center was tasked with producing hydrogen through renewable-based water electrolysis and using hydrogen byproduct from petrochemical and iron and steel industries to develop hydrogen-powered communities and raise Japan's energy self-sufficiency rate. It's worth noting that renewable-based hydrogen-producing technology has progressed by strides in Japan. Starting from 2013, the Japanese Ministry of the Environment has led the country's largest-ever experiment on offshore wind power generation off the coast of Kabashima, one of the Goto Islands in Nagasaki Prefecture. The surplus electricity was used to produce hydrogen that, stored in tanks in a liquid form, was used to fuel heating equipment in Fukue-shima, another of the Goto Islands. Solar power output is unstable, but if peak output is used to produce hydrogen, which is then stored and used to make fuel cell, the resulting electricity can meet demand for at least a week with a much lower cost. In June 2014, METI issued the *Strategic Roadmap for Hydrogen and Fuel Cells* with the aim of building an economy and society with hydrogen as the main energy source (the "Hydrogen Society"). The ministry then issued the *Basic Hydrogen Strategy* in December 2017, which further clarified the basic goals of building a hydrogen society by 2030 and the grand vision of realizing such a society in all respects by 2050.

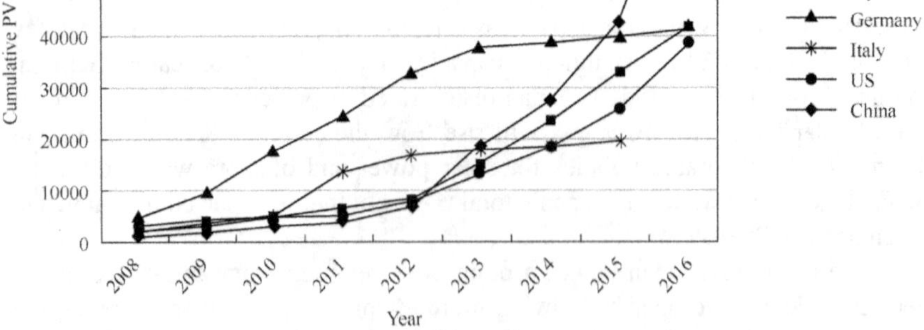

Figure 4.6 Cumulative PV capacity in different countries (2008–2016)

Source: JFS (Japan For Sustainability), "Current Status of Renewable Energy in Japan", JFS Newsletter No. 176, April 2017, https:///rww.japanfs.org/en/news/archives/news_id035824.html.

The *Blue Book of Japanese Economy: Annual Report on Japanese Economy and Sino-Japanese Economic & Trade Relations* released in 2015 pointed out that Japan is in the "midstream" of the global renewable sector. The country was more keenly conscious that in the context of the third technological revolution, new energy technology, primarily renewable energy technology, was increasingly blended with bio-technology, information technology, and new material technology in mutual promotion. Whoever controls clean energy technology would acquire a vantage point in the international system. As a resource-poor country, Japan had to pick up speed in the renewable sector in the next decade and more. The report titled *Japan: Greater Energy Security Through Renewables* issued by IEEFA in 2017 concluded that in the post-Fukushima era, Japan should not turn to fossil energy but should instead build a model of power transition based on renewables and accelerate the extensive application of clean energy technology. IEEFA also said with the shrinking power demand and growing renewable capacity, thermal power output in Japan will contract by 40% in 2030 compared with 2015, creating an important opportunity for the development of renewable energy.

II. Evolution of Japan's clean energy policies

The oil crisis in the 1970s spurred Japan to change its energy strategy more quickly and pay attention to green energy development. In 1974, the country kicked off the Sunshine Project and the Moonlight Project, the former focused on such renewables as solar and geothermal energy and the latter on the R&D of energy-saving technology. In 1980, Japan set up the New Energy and Industrial Technology Development Organization (NEDO) to promote more systematic development of green energy technologies. In 1994, it issued the New Energy Promotion Program to conduct education and publicity on green energy across the board. In 1997, the issuance of the New Energy Act marked the establishment of the basic guideline on new energy development, putting in place the policy guiding the development of relevant technologies and securing government fund.

In the 21st century, substantial progress was made in clean energy thanks to supportive government policy.[59] Japan made green energy a pillar industry and passed laws to mandate power generators to use renewables. Starting with technological R&D, its green energy development has expanded to the production and consumption of green energies backed by government support in funding, financing, and tax. In 2003, the Japanese government issued the Act on Special Measure, also known as the RPS Act, that required every power company to develop a certain amount of new energy for power generation. However, in general, the growth of renewables was undercut by Japan's emphasis on nuclear. In May 2006, the *New National Energy Strategy* drafted by METI pledged to increase the ratio of nuclear power to 30%–40% by 2030, cementing its crucial position in Japan's future energy market. In 2010, METI revised the *Strategic Energy Plan*, which specified the strategy of restructuring the power and energy sector to be focused on nuclear energy, with renewable and fossil energies as supplement.[60]

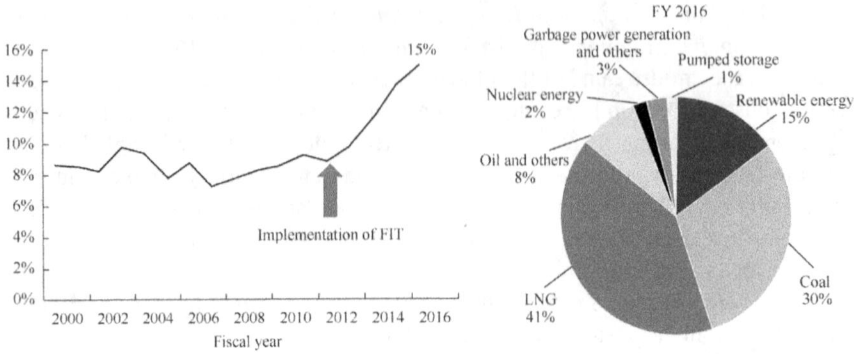

Figure 4.7 Percentage of renewable power before and after Japan implements FIT in 2012

Source: Keiji Kimura: Feed-in Tariffs in Japan: Five Years of Achievements and, Future Challen-ges, Renewable Energy Institute Report, September 2017.

The 2011 Fukushima nuclear accident prompted the Japanese government to announce the suspension of its nuclear development plan and to adjust its nuclear-centered energy strategy. As a result, a slew of research institutes and think tanks related to renewables were established, including the Renewable Energy Institute and Fukushima Renewable Energy Institute (FREA). In May 2011, SoftBank poured hundreds of millions of US dollars on the construction of large solar power plants, aiming to raise the percentage of renewable power to 30% by 2020. The Energy and Environment Council released the *Energy and Environment Innovation Strategy* in September 2012, making de-nuclearization the priority in Japan's post-Fukushima energy strategy.

To better implement this strategy, Japan made phased deployments for renewable development and energy conservation. First, it strove to increase the ratio of renewable power, the best alternative to nuclear power, from 10% in 2010 to 35% in 2035. To achieve that goal, Japan must speed up the development of renewable power and promote its massive use, especially by launching the FIT policy.[61] Its renewables, including wind and solar, indeed made remarkable progress after 2012, reaching 16% and 21% for all nonfossil energies in 2016. The shift of gravity from nuclear to renewable is a process full of challenges and opportunities for the Japanese government. The small size of territory makes it hard to build large solar plants and wind farms in Japan, so it must take advantage of its vast sea areas and strongly develop offshore wind and solar power to scale up the use of renewables.[62]

Japan formulated the *Long-term Energy Supply and Demand Outlook* in 2015 to simultaneously achieve energy security, stable supply, high efficiency, and environmental suitability. The energy supply and demand forecast for 2030 further specified that utmost efforts must be made to promote thorough energy conservation and use of renewables, so as to reduce the reliance on hydrocarbon energy and nuclear energy.[63] In 2016, the Japanese government drew up the *Fukushima Plan for a New Energy Society*, attempting to make Fukushima an advanced demonstration

Table 4.10 Japan's policies on clean energy development

Year	*Title*	*Content*
1974	Research and development project for new energy technology, or Sunshine Project	The government will invest JPY 1 trillion to develop and utilize solar, geothermal, synthetic natural gas, and hydrogen energy by 2000, focused on technologies for the exploitation, transmission, utilization, and storage of these green energies. Basic research on wind and ocean energy will be strengthened.
1978	R&D of energy saving technologies, or Moonlight Project	Developing high-efficiency energy use technology; promoting development of "large-scale energy-saving technology" such as fuel-cell-based power generation, heat pump, and superconducting power.
1980	Law Concerning the Promotion of Development and Introduction of Oil Alternative Energy	Setting up the New Energy and Industrial Technology Development Organisation (NEDO); strongly supporting the R&D, promotion, and use of practical new energy technologies.
1993	New Sunshine Project	Developing new technologies such as amorphous silicon solar cell and fuel cell through coordinated efforts of the government, enterprises, and universities; developing hydrogen usage, CO_2 fixation and storage, and other technologies.
1994	New Energy Promotion Program	Anyone engaged in the energy sector has the responsibility and obligation to fully promote renewables; new energy strategy must be communicated both on the national and regional level.
1997	Act on Special Measures for the Promotion of New Energy Usage	Strongly developing new and renewable energies such as wind, solar, and garbage power as well as fuel cell; determining the basic responsibilities of new energy suppliers, manufacturers, and users.
2002	Act on Special Measures concerning New Energy Usage by Electric Utilities	Electric utilities are obligated to use a certain amount of new energy. Every four years, the METI minister, in light of METI's policies, would formulate the new energy targets of electric utilities for the next eight years. Those who cannot meet the target must improve, and those who don't follow the improvement order will be fined JPY 1 million at most.
2004	Long-term Outlook for New Energy Industry	Efforts will be made to foster the new energy industry including solar and wind to be a pillar industry worth JPY 3 trillion in market value by 2030, with new energy accounting for 20% of total energy consumption. Green energy sector will provide jobs to about 310,000 people. Fuel cell industry will reach the market value of JPY 8 trillion by 2010.

(*Continued*)

Table 4.10 (Continued)

Year	*Title*	*Content*
2006	New National Energy Strategy	Supporting the independent development of new energy industry, energy technology development focused on new-generation accumulator, and creation of future energy (technology) parks; reducing the cost of solar power generation to be on a par with thermal power generation by 2030; promoting biomass power generation.
2010	Strategic Energy Plan	"Expanding the introduction of renewable energy" and "increasing nuclear power generation" as a way to achieve the national energy strategy.
2012	Energy and Environment Innovation Strategy	The post-Fukushima energy strategy focused on denuclearization. Japan made phased, detailed strategic deployments for renewable development and energy conservation, and adopted the FIT policy.
2014	Strategic Roadmap for Hydrogen and Fuel Cells	Setting the goal of building a "hydrogen society" with hydrogen as the main energy source.
2015	Long-term Energy Supply and Demand Outlook	Promoting energy conservation and use of renewable energy to the largest extent, reducing the reliance on hydrocarbon energy and nuclear energy, toward the goal of "stable supply, high efficiency and environmental suitability".
2016	Energy White Paper	An energy reform based on the *Paris Agreement*
2017	Basic Hydrogen Strategy	Proposing the basic road map for building a hydrogen society by 2030 and the grand vision of realizing such a society by 2050.
2018	Fifth Basic Energy Plan	Using renewable energy as a major economically independent and decarbonized power source toward 2050.

Source: Originally created by the author.

for renewables leveraged on the reconstruction and recovery efforts. The *Energy White Paper* also enacted in 2016 laid out three directions of energy strategy – ensuring future energy security in face of declining crude oil price, reforming nuclear policy in light of response to and reflection on the Fukushima accident, and reforming clean energy policy pursuant to the *Paris Agreement*. According to Japan's nationally determined contributions, it will cut GHG emissions by 26.0% from 2013 and meet the goal of 0.16kg CO_2 emission per unit GDP by 2030. The Japanese government put forth two pathways toward that goal. For one, it will set up a new power structure oriented toward slashing CO_2 emissions and assist in the establishment of institutions independently planned by the power sector (e.g., *Energy Conservation Act* and *Act on Sophisticated Methods of Energy Supply Structures*). For another, it will carry out an energy reform that balances environmental restriction with economic development, namely, thorough energy conservation, more renewables, more energy investment, and improved energy efficiency.[64] In 2018, Japan issued the *Fifth Basic Energy Plan*, which for the first time set out to use renewable energy as a major economically independent and decarbonized power source toward 2050. However, its 2030 target percentage of 22%–24% was widely criticized for being too low.

Besides, renewable energy is rather high-priced in Japan now. The actual cost of wind power averages JPY 13.9/kWh, 60% higher than the world average of JPY 8.8/kWh. Japan launched the FIT policy in 2017 and the Top Runner Program to help lower the cost, whereby the tariff of high-efficiency and low-cost Top Runner enterprises was taken as the benchmark to accelerate the reduction of renewable tariff and make it less subsidy-reliant. Japan drew on a series of practices adopted in Europe, from Sliding-Scale to Feed-in Premium (FIP) to direct trading of renewable electricity in the wholesale market. On that basis, it reformed the subsidizing scheme for renewable power, changed the FIT mode to FIP mode, and supplemented government support with market competition.[65]

III. Development of Japan's clean energy diplomacy and its strategic position

Although clean energy has developed rather slowly in Japan (especially wind power), the country has remained a world leader in terms of energy efficiency and green energy tech innovation. After the Fukushima nuclear accident, Japan has worked harder to promote clean energy and begun to emphasize its global leadership in clean energy technology, driving PV forward with extraordinary momentum and making constant innovations in offshore wind and PV technology. Japan's clean energy diplomacy is displaying a clear governance-driven tendency.

First, Japan is amplifying its influence in clean energy diplomacy by providing green economic aid.

Japan has made global environment a priority in its diplomatic agenda since the early 1990s. Globally, its official assistance mainly goes to environmental protection and green development. As one of the largest Official Development Assistance (ODA) providers in the world, Japan's foreign assistance is obviously tilted toward the environmental domain. The Official Development Assistance Charter enacted in 1992 had environmental protection as one of the four fundamental principles. In the meantime, Japan has played a key part in promoting the conclusion of major legally binding international agreements pertaining to environmental issues.[66] Former Japanese Prime Minister Junichiro Koizumi announced the Initiative for Development in East Asia (IDEA) at the World Summit on Sustainable Development in 2002. The Initiative underscored the importance of conducting environmental education, promoting the development of renewable energy, providing safe drinking water, and addressing global environmental issues, covering climate change, loss of biodiversity, and loss of forest. To strengthen the environmental capacity of developing countries in Asia and elsewhere, the Japanese government sponsored the establishment of environmental study, monitoring and training centers in China, Indonesia, Thailand, Chile, Mexico, and Egypt.[67] Through official economic assistance and outbound investment and trade in environment, Japan has been seeking helmsmanship in global environmental governance.

Promoting trade and investment and providing development assistance have been two decisive factors in Japan's economic diplomacy and clean energy diplomacy. The Ministry of Foreign Affairs' top responsibility is formulating the Official Development Assistance (ODA) policy, while the New Japan International Cooperation Agency (New JICA) is responsible for the three parts of bilateral assistance (tech cooperation, bilateral loan, and free aid). New JICA is an independent administrative agency formed in 2008 as a successor to JICA that was established in 2003 and responsible for tech cooperation.[68] New JICA has the following characteristics in carrying out foreign assistance. First, it applies the three approaches – tech cooperation, JPY loans, and free aid – in coordination to better promote cooperation. Second, it is the world's largest bilateral assistance organization with about 100 overseas offices in more than 150 countries and regions. Third, providing development assistance on behalf of the Japanese government, New JICA pools together private, local, academic, and civil societies at home and abroad to jointly advance the assistance initiatives.[69] Japan's trade and investment promotion policies are formulated by METI but are executed mainly by Japan External Trade Organization (JETRO), an entity established in 1958. The Japan Bank for International Cooperation (JBIC) drives the development of public-private partnership by providing financial plans for various ODA and commercial projects. Being at the core of what's called the "3JS" network, JICA, JETRO, and JBIC have all launched green initiatives in recent years.[70]

For example, JBIC launched the Leading Investment to Future Environment (LIFE) Initiative in 2009 to support environmental investment and meet the long-term goals for sustainable infrastructure in developing countries of Asia and other regions. The Japanese Ministry of the Environment is responsible for environmental cooperation initiatives but has limited influence because it's still too young, too small, and doesn't have executive bodies like JICA or JETRO. Other administrative organs engaged in Japan's green economic diplomacy include NEDO under METI and Nippon Export and Investment Insurance (NEXI). NEXI insures the losses resulting from political (strategic) and commercial risks, and NEDO as one of METI's largest administrative organs advocates environmental and energy technologies. The Innovation Network Corporation of Japan (INCJ) and Japan Climate Leaders' Partnership (JCLP) founded in 2009 further underline the government's efforts on international green cooperation and clean energy diplomacy. INCJ tries to stimulate low-carbon economy and green R&D by providing venture capital and industrial incentives, while JCLP aims to realize a sustainable, low-carbon society through commercialization. To drive growth with green innovation, Japan's R&D expenditure in 2007 accounted for 3.4% of GDP, the highest in G7 and most concentrated on the R&D of environment-related patents. Environmental technology is also a key element in Japan's foreign aid policy. Today, Japan is the top contributor to ODA in relation to climate change, providing over 1/3 of OECD's development and cooperation expenses in 2005–2007, cooperation in clean energy technology being an essential part.

Figure 4.8 The pyramid of Japan's economic and energy diplomacy

Source: Maaike Okano Heijmans, "Japan's 'Green' Economic Diplomacy: Environmental and Energy Technology and Foreign Relations", Pacific Review, 2012, Vol. 25, No. 3, p. 344.

METI's industrial policy is closely related to Japan's economic diplomacy and environmental diplomacy to form an all-round system of domestic, bilateral, and multilateral programs. Take the Cool Earth 50 initiative for example. It is a long-term strategy initiated by former Prime Minister Shinzo Abe in May 2007 to halve the global CO_2 emissions by 2050 and achieve the goals of *Kyoto Protocol*. Former Prime Minister Yasuo Fukuda announced the "Cool Earth Promotion Programme" in early 2008 to drive efforts toward those goals. Domestically, the "Cool Earth-Innovative Energy Technology Program" aimed to increase the use of clean energy to create a low-carbon economy, focused on 21 innovative energy industries. The technological progress resulting from this policy would be applied in Japan's clean energy diplomacy. Bilaterally, the Cool Earth Partnership provided developing countries with assistance in clean energy development, aiming at reducing GHG emissions and achieving economic growth in parallel. Multilaterally, climate change and man-nature coexistence were the focus of Japan's diplomatic efforts at the G8 Summit held in Hokkaido in July 2008. Moreover, when Japan was chairman of APEC in 2010, it put clean energy high on the agenda, advocated industrial strategy featuring public-private partnership, and promoted the application of Japan's advanced technologies in other countries. These policies were not temporary promises made by the Democratic Party or Liberal Democratic Party or any other party. They have been consistently carried out by all Japanese administrations because their importance is fully recognized in the political circle.

It's worth noting that other than economic assistance, New JICA also sets great store by "promoting mutual understanding". An important ODA executor, New JICA sent volunteers to assisted regions and supported local Japanese entities and NGOs in carrying out diverse friendly activities there. It also provided opportunities for people in the assisted countries to engage directly with Japanese people and learn Japanese culture. NGOs in Japan, leveraged on their technology and experience, would plan cooperative activities targeting developing countries, and New JICA would support these activities and join in the execution. Japan's implementation of ODA has given birth to many cross-national NGO networks dedicated to environmental protection, clean energy, and local governance and helped itself explore overseas markets for its clean energy technologies, make profits, and create investment opportunities for Japanese enterprises. On the other hand, sound economic development also increased the assisted countries' purchasing power, opening the door to huge overseas markets for Japan.[71]

Second, Japan is leveraging its influence in international organizations (e.g., IEA/IRENA) to improve its capability of clean energy diplomacy.

Given its sway in global energy governance and economic governance, Japan occupies an important position in many international organizations, such as International Energy Agency (IEA), Asian Development Bank (ADB), and International Renewable Energy Agency (IRENA). It also plays an active role in spurring these organizations to shift to the green and low-carbon track, intensify R&D in clean energy technology, and invest more in clean energy projects. Especially in IEA and ADB, not only is Japan a top capital contributor, but Japanese experts are also elected in leading positions, having a great say over their policies and decisions. Since IRENA was formed in 2009, IEA, facing the new competition, has increased input in clean energy research. In addition to releasing several annual reports – Renewables, Clean Energy Investment Trends, and Renewable Energy Market Update – it has intensified cooperation in renewable energy technology. Japan, with its capital and tech strengths, has played a leading role in IEA's clean energy technology cooperation and evaluation. For instance, it urged IEA to add the Tracking Clean Energy Progress service to provide comprehensive and rigorous evaluation on energy technologies and sectors critical for the world's clean energy development and low-carbon transition. According to IEA's sustainable development plan, the evaluation, which covers the latest tech information, aims to achieve the goal of the *Paris Agreement* to keep temperature rise within 2°C, provide universal energy access, and notably mitigate air pollution. As of 2017, some technologies had made remarkable progress, especially solar PV, LED, and electric vehicle (EV). But the improvement of energy efficiency has slowed down, and key technologies such as carbon capture and storage remain stagnant, calling for the united efforts of all countries.

Promoting clean energy is a primary goal of Asian Development Bank (ADB) and accounts for 1/4 of its loans. The Manila-based bank signed a geothermal power supply agreement with Advent Energy to make sure all its power comes from renewable energy. With that, 1,500MWh of its monthly power demand was met by the geothermal power plant in Tiwi of Albay Province, and the remaining 50MWh was from solar devices mounted on the bank's rooftop. ADB held the Asian Clean Energy Forum in 2017, the same year it announced a USD 200 million financial package to support renewable projects in the 11 smallest Pacific Island countries, namely, Cook Islands, Micronesia, Kiribati, Nauru, Palau, Marshall Islands, Samoa, Solomon Islands, Tonga, Tuvalu, and Vanuatu. It was the first such plan implemented by ADB in the Pacific region, with the objective of changing those countries' diesel-pivoted energy mix to be renewable-centered. Altogether 13 renewable energy projects will be carried out in nine of those countries over the next three years, with the first three – involving solar, wind, hydro, and grid renovation – to be deployed in Cook Islands, Tonga, and Vanuatu.

Nobuo Tanaka, Executive Director of IEA, said that considering the far-reaching effects caused by the current financial and economic crisis on energy security and climate change, and the significant dwindling in energy investment, it is necessary to take emergency measures worldwide to steer the global economy to a more sustainable path.

On January 14, 2018, Japanese Foreign Minister Taro Kono participated in the IRENA Assembly in Abu Dhabi, a first time for a Japanese foreign minister. When addressing the assembly, he stressed that Japan aimed to increase the percentage of renewable energy to 22%–24% of its energy mix by 2030, which, however, was lower than the current world average of 24%. He also said Japan should make great efforts to develop clean energy and set about renewable energy diplomacy in new ways.

In April 2018, Taro Kono invited Director-General of IRENA Adnan Z. Amin to Japan to discuss the era of renewable energy diplomacy and Japan's place within a global energy sector undergoing a rapid transformation. The invitation sent the important message that Japan believed establishing its global leadership in renewables could help expand the domestic low-carbon market. During his three-day stay, Adnan Z. Amin visited the Fukushima Renewable Energy Institute (FREA) and National Institute of Advanced Industrial Science and Technology (AIST) located in Koriyama. FREA specializes in the research and development of renewable energy and innovative technologies. Founded soon after the 2011 Fukushima nuclear accident, it symbolizes Japan's desire to develop a safe, pollution-free, and sustainable energy. Japan's international renewables leadership can help it scale-up domestic market, said the IRENA director-general.

As of the end of 2016, Japan had had more than 80,000 patents with respect to clean energy, accounting for more than 1/6 in the world and making Japan one of the three clean technology innovation centers. Later, Japan's Ministry of Foreign Affairs and Sasakawa Peace Foundation co-hosted an international seminar in the theme of "The Age of Renewable Energy Diplomacy and Japan's Course". As the price of solar PV, wind power, and accumulator products is taking a nosedive, renewable energy is quickly gaining ground across the globe. It and energy efficiency are considered two important contributors to the implementation of the *Paris Agreement*. In view of the robust momentum of renewable energy development, every country is making a careful strategic choice in this era of renewable diplomacy. At the seminar, IRENA director-general Adnan Z. Amin and Japanese government officials, experts, and businesspeople discussed the current momentum of global renewables development and how an active "renewable energy diplomacy" will affect the future energy landscape. They also exchanged views on what Japan should think and do about such a major subject, especially how to play a leading role in creating a future based on low-carbon renewables.

On July 3, 2017, the Japanese government and the African Development Bank (AfDB), on the sidelines of the African Union Summit held at the AU headquarters in Addis Ababa, signed a Letter of Intent to launch the Japan-Africa Energy

Initiative (JAEI) to provide significant support to the New Deal on Energy for Africa, which aims to achieve universal access to energy by 2025, using available energy sources and the most advanced technologies. Following discussions with African leaders during the Sixth Tokyo International Conference on African Development (TICAD-VI) held in Nairobi in 2016 and a follow-up visit of AfDB president Dr. Akinwumi Adesina to Japan, the government of Japan reaffirmed its commitment to supporting the development of Japan-Africa Energy Initiative. The Initiative would significantly contribute towards Africa's efforts to achieve universal access to energy and to transform its energy systems through a balanced and pragmatic least-cost energy mix that encompasses renewable and conventional energy. Under this Initiative, AfDB would take the lead in project development in close consultation with regional member countries. Japan would stand ready to provide up to USD 6 billion in both concessional and non-concessional finance for a variety of energy operations that would support the provision of electricity for homes, schools, hospitals, agriculture, industries, and clean cooking. The initiative would support the full range of activities associated with public and private sector energy projects – preparation, construction, and operations – through a mix of financing and technical assistance.[72]

Third, Japan strongly supports the establishment of official and nonofficial networks of clean energy diplomacy. As a country troubled by a dire scarcity of energy sources, Japan attaches great importance to securing steady energy supply by establishing global energy diplomacy networks. Facing both internal (rising fuel cost after the great east Japan earthquake) and external (fiercer competition for steady energy sources) challenges, METI appointed energy and mineral resource specialists at Japanese embassies and consulates in February 2013 and has assigned 56 officials to 50 countries so far. These specialists, making full use of the global diplomatic network, will promote Japan's energy diplomacy in countries around the world to help ensure stable and affordable supply of energy sources and mineral resources for their country, by collecting and analyzing relevant information and supporting private Japanese companies and organizations conducting businesses locally. To further push the effort, Prime Minister Shinzo Abe led the largest business delegation ever to visit major energy suppliers, including Russia, Saudi Arabia, UAE, and Turkey, in May 2013. They set out with three objectives in mind: Tightening the relation with these countries centered on oil trade and other energy topics, peddling nuclear technology in the post-Fukushima era regardless of strong opposition, and forging broader economic cooperation and political and cultural exchanges on multiple levels.

The first nuclear deal that Japan nailed after the Fukushima accident was the construction of Sinop nuclear power station in Turkey. Other than that, it is also pushing nuclear projects in Saudi Arabia, Vietnam, Finland, Jordan, and Lithuania.[73] At the "International Symposium: Energy Security and Investment in Asia" held in July 2017, the Japanese foreign minister gave a speech titled "Energy and Resource Diplomacy of Japan – Global Vision for a Shared Future". In the speech, he elaborated on the three primary pathways of Japan's energy and resource diplomacy amid the enormous changes in international energy sector. The first was intensifying the strategic pathway in which energy and resource subjects made an indispensable component of diplomacy, the second was meeting various demands through different approaches, and the third was solidifying Japan's "unique power" in the energy and resource field. The foreign minister emphasized that in implementing its energy and resource diplomacy, Japan's vision is to not only ensure the stable supply of energy resources but also contribute to responding to global energy challenges. To be specific, it will promote energy and free trade, establish intelligent market-adjusting mechanisms, and accelerate the process of ensuring energy availability in all regions around the world. It will also reduce environmental cost and raise energy efficiency, boost the development and deployment of new and renewable energies, and step up international emergency reserve of oil and gas as well as global energy governance. Evidently Japan is steering its energy diplomacy in the green direction and relying on the existing global network to promote clean energy diplomacy.

Japan's nonofficial network of clean energy diplomacy is also thriving. As early as in July 2009, Japan formed the Innovation Network Corporation (INC), a new public-private partnership company, to foster new-generation industrial innovations, including those pertaining to environment and energy, to reinforce Japan's long-term competitiveness in clean energy technology.[74] The Breakthrough Institute (BI) and the Information Technology and Innovation Foundation (ITIF) released the report "Rising Tigers, Sleeping Giant" in November 2009, which proclaimed that a race of clean technology was surging in Asia, in which China, Japan, and ROK were working hard to become global leaders. The three countries were almost on a par with the US in practically all clean energy technologies and were investing more in research and development at a faster pace.[75]

The Japan Council for Renewable Energy (JCRE) founded in 2007 has worked with National Institute of Advanced Industrial Science and Technology (AIST),

Table 4.11 Japan appoints "energy and mineral resource specialists" in its embassies and consulates worldwide

Region	Host country (where Japanese embassies and consulates are based)
Europe and Central Asia (6)	Azerbaijan, Uzbekistan, Kazakhstan, Kyrgyzstan, Turkmenistan, Russia
Middle East (6)	UAE, Iraq, Oman, Qatar, Kuwait, Saudi Arabia
Africa (17)	Algeria, Ghana, Guinea, Zambia, South Sudan, Burkina Faso, Madagascar, South Africa (Namibia), Rwanda, Angola, Gabon, Democratic Republic of Congo, Zimbabwe, Tanzania, Botswana, Malawi, Mozambique
Asia (8)	India, Indonesia, China, the Philippines, Vietnam, Myanmar, Mongolia, Laos
Oceania (6)	Australia, Sydney (consulate), Perth (consulate), Brisbane (consulate), Solomon, Papua New Guinea
North America (4)	The United States, Huston (consulate), Canada, Vancouver (consulate)
Latin America (7)	Argentina, Chile, Trinidad and Tobago, Brazil, Venezuela, Peru, Bolivia

Table 4.12 International clean energy conferences organized by JCRE

	2006	*2010*	*2014*	*2018*
Title	Renewable Energy 2006 International Conference	Renewable Energy 2010 International Conference	Renewable Energy 2014 International Conference	Renewable Energy 2018 International Conference
Time	Oct. 9–13	June 27–July 2	July 27–Aug. 1	June 17–22
Location	Makuhari Messe	Pacific Yokohama	Tokyo Big Sight	Pacific Yokohama
Participants	1,063 representatives from 55 countries	1,359 representatives from 66 countries	1,357 representatives from 48 countries	1,121 representatives from 47 countries
Papers submitted (exhibited)	663 (641)	986 (887)	974 (892)	713
Number of workshop participants	3,108	3,580	1,340	2,123
Outcomes	Report on discussions	Renewable Energy 2010 Digest Report RE2010 Communique	Grand Renewable Energy 2014 Digest Report GRE2014 Communique	GRE2018 Digest Report GRE2018 Communique

Source: www.renewableenergy.jp/council/english/activity.html#section3.

New Energy and Industrial Technology Development Organization (NEDO), and New Energy Foundation (NEF) to boost the R&D and deployment of renewable energy. After Japan hosted the first Renewable Energy 2006 International Conference and Exhibition, JCRE was founded in June 2007 with strong support from METI and was restructured into a nonprofit organization in January 2016. JCRE is engaged not only in specific technologies but also in renewables policies, new concepts, construction, hydrogen, energy network, among others, providing a panoramic view for integrating renewable energies. Since 2006, it has hosted four Renewable Energy International Conferences (once every four years, the latest one held in June 2018, Yokohama) and 13 International Renewable Energy Exhibitions and Forums (once every year), at which Japan showcased and shared its latest tech breakthroughs and the future trend of renewables.[76]

Section 4 India's clean energy diplomacy

India, the emerging developing country, is now the third largest oil consumer in Asia and likely to become the third largest energy consumer worldwide in 2030. It depends ever more heavily on energy sources overseas due to its fast increase of population and limited energy production at home. To ensure energy security and deal with environmental issues in the course of development, India is making great efforts to develop various clean energies represented by solar, wind, and ocean energy. It currently has a low availability of modern energy sources – 0.3 billion of its 1.3 billion people have no access to electricity, the largest number in the world. Soot from burning feces and timber and exhaust gas from kerosene stoves and coal-fired power stations result in 13 of the world's 20 most polluted cities. Providing the energy sources needed to sustain high-speed economic growth while achieving development and environmental targets is an immense challenge for the Indian government, prompting it to make clean energies such as solar and wind power the core solution. India has put forth an ambitious blueprint for clean energy development, aiming to have 175GW renewable capacity by 2022, thus laying the foundation to kick off its clean energy diplomacy as a major country.

I. India's clean energy development and features of its energy transition

India has experienced fast economic development in recent years, the fastest among the world's top 20 economies and faster than China, the regional power. With such a high growth rate, a huge population, and inadequate reserve of energy resources, India relies heavily on energy import, which accounts for up to 70% of its total energy consumption and is still rising. It is expected that India will become the fourth largest energy consumer in the world by 2025, following the US, China, and Japan. According to a forecast by its Planning Commission, the country's energy demand will triple, and its power demand will grow by five times by 2030 if the current high growth rate continues. At that time, energy shortage will curb national development, especially on power supply because India's fast-paced industrialization is posing an ever larger demand for electricity. Its average energy shortage rate is 10.3%, which increases to 15.4% at peak.[77] Because of mounting energy demand, clean energy is now regarded as an important strategic alternative with relevant technologies offering great potential, and Indian government is paying more attention to renewables.[78] But India is a latecomer in this field, and its renewable capacity accounts for only 16% of total installed capacity. At the moment, it is taking solar energy as an important breakthrough point, and it also has great potential in offshore wind power, tidal, and geothermal energy.[79]

India has the richest solar resources in the world with a first-ranking average insolation among the top 20 economies, and most areas across the country have 250–300 sunny days a year – an advantage that promises an inestimably large market if put to good use. India launched the National Solar Mission to strongly develop solar energy and expand the solar market and had installed 13GW solar capacity by 2008. Based on the favorable solar conditions, Indian Prime Minister Narendra Modi in 2017 put forth a more ambitious plan – to have 100GW solar capacity by 2022 and five times as much capacity as now by 2040. As of March 2017, India's solar capacity had increased by 81% to reach 12.3GW in the current fiscal year. Riding on the government's efforts to reach those goals, India's private sector quickly earned a good reputation in solar innovation as it was actively exploring a series of micro energy projects that could be promoted in other developing countries troubled by insufficient power supply. India's solar ambition has attracted overseas investors. For instance, the US company AES and Japan's Mitsubishi are building a 10MW solar energy storage base in Delhi for Tata Power.

The rich wind resources and their immense potential also make wind energy an appealing option. The most wind-rich regions are Karnataka, Gujarat, and Andhra Pradesh, which have 12,948MW, 11,364MW, and 10,015MW wind capacity respectively, and the country is likely to reach 100GW wind capacity with the use of larger turbines and intensified resource prospecting. In 2004, wind power only accounted for 3% of India's total installed capacity; in 2010, it exceeded 10GW, increasing by about 1% annually and 1.5% after 2010. At the end of 2012, wind capacity made up 11% in the power mix, four times more than its percentage in 2004. In 2016, Indian government pledged to meet 16% of the country's power demand with wind power by 2030.[80] Major wind turbine manufacturers, including VESTAS, GE, ENERCON, SIMENS, and GAMESA, have all built plants in India. The most well-known Indian wind turbine brand is Suzlan, which ranked 28th in the 2015 Top 500 list of new energy companies.[81]

A major agricultural country, India has 1/10 of the world's arable land and a forest coverage rate of 21.9%, with abundant biomass resources. But its bioenergy stays in the primitive stage – the most common biomasses are scrapped timber and agricultural wastes, and more than 800 million farmers use firewood and farm wastes for cooking and heating. A National Bioenergy Commission was formed to develop biomass energy technologies and formulate measures to incentivize biomass energy power generation. As a result, bio-power developed at a fast rate, reaching 1GW in 2010 and set to hit 10GW by 2020.[82]

Indian newspaper *The Pioneer* reported that New Delhi plans to have 175GW renewable capacity by 2022. As part of the efforts to implement its solar energy policy, India has handed out 280 million energy-saving lamps, which saved 4GWh electricity in the past three years, equivalent to saving USD 2 billion. As of the end of June 2017, India's power mix consisted of 220.58GW thermal power, 44.61GW hydropower, 58.30GW renewable power, and 6.78GW nuclear power. By the end of that year, the country had 330GW installed capacity in total, including 7,149MW solar capacity, a long way from reaching the 2022 renewable goal.[83] TERI (The Energy and Resources Institute) released a report titled "Transitions in the Indian Energy Sector – Macro Level Analysis of Demand and Supply Side Options". The report estimated that all new power capacity could be from renewable by 2023 provided they become cost-competitive compared with traditional energy sources and the grid is able to accommodate green electricity.[84]

II. Evolution of India's clean energy policies

In 1981, the Indian government set up a Commission for Additional Sources of Energy (CASE) under the Department of Science and Technology (DST) of the Ministry of Science and Technology. CASE was renamed the Department of Non-Conventional Energy Sources (DNES) in 1982 and further elevated to be the Ministry of Non-Conventional Energy Sources (MNES) in 1992, tasked with promoting commercialized or near-commercialized renewable energy technologies. In 1993,

MNES designed, developed, and implemented large-scale demonstration projects to promote renewable technologies and established many tech support centers to help manufacturers improve their technology.

Clean energy in India has developed at an accelerated rate in the 21st century. The issuance of the *Electricity Act* in 2003 paved the way for the establishment of Central Electricity Regulatory Commission (CERC) and stipulated renewables' role in the nation's power policy and independence system.[85] Aiming to create a favorable environment for the rapid development of the electric power industry, including new energy, the CERC requested electricity regulators to enforce the law on the synchronization of renewable power and made the FIT policy for renewable energies such as solar power.[86] The *National Electricity Policy* in 2005 required progressive development of power generation based on nontraditional energy sources. In 2006, the Ministry of Power underscored the necessity of setting renewable goals in the national tariff policy and applying preferential tariff to renewable power. The MNES was renamed Ministry of New and Renewable Energy (MNRE) also that year, which was responsible for all matters in relation to renewable energy, ranging from the formulation and execution of relevant policies to the organization and coordination of R&D projects to international exchange and cooperation. It is one of the few ministerial government bodies dedicated to the management of new and renewable energy. In August 2006, Indian Planning Commission enacted the *Integrated Energy Policy* that specified rules on subsidizing renewable energy and enforced grid connection of renewable power.

In 2008, Indian released its first National Action Plan on Climate Change (NAPCC), which focused on energy efficiency and renewables and underscored the research capability in response to climate change. In the same year, MNRE and Indian Renewable Energy Development Agency (IREDA) rolled out a series of plans to boost the development of wind power and PV power and ramped up national subsidy for the construction of renewable energy infrastructure. At the eleventh meeting for making the Five-Year Plan for new and renewable energies in 2008, India expressly vowed to have renewable power generation grow faster than conventional power generation (2008–2012). In 2009, CERC issued the *Renewable Energy Tariff Regulations* to explain how to calculate the tariff for renewable power projects, covering all renewable energy technologies. The tariff would be reviewed every three years and the baseline cost of PV and solar thermal projects reviewed every year.

As renewable energy made up a fast-rising proportion in energy mix, the Indian government introduced the Renewable Energy Certificates (RECs) system in 2011,[87] which was critical for the nation and public utilities groups to meet their voluntary goals for renewable portfolio. All Indian states were required to work out their own voluntary goals.[88] By March 2011, the National Load Dispatch Centre (NLDC) in charge of certifying renewable projects had issued 100 RECs to six projects.[89] Also that year, MNRE released the "Development of Solar Cities" program and the "National Solar Mission" successively. With "Development of Solar Cities", the first-phase target was building ten pilot solar cities, and the second-phase target was building solar cities in all states, with solar power technologies applied in small geographical entities such as campus and towns. "National Solar Mission" was a large-scale solar power plan that consists of three five-year periods, aimed at pushing large and small power plants to produce solar electricity to provide more accessible energy for the countryside. All parties should purchase solar electricity according to the RECs and fulfill their renewable obligation. The government also decided to lower the import tariff on the machinery, instruments, equipment, and apparatus used by PV and solar thermal plants down to 5%. "National Solar Mission" subsidized and rewarded young scientists for their innovations with a view to advancing the development and deployment of solar technologies as well as academic progress. At the fourth Clean Energy Ministerial (CEM) in 2013, former Indian Prime Minister Singh announced to give a further impetus to renewable energy with subsidy and incentives so as to double the capacity by 2017. He also encouraged enterprises to produce electricity from offshore wind farms and small hydropower stations.[90]

Table 4.13 Renewable energy policies in India

Time	*Title*	*Policy*
2003	Electricity Act	It specifies the role of renewable energy in national power policy and independence system to provide a favorable environment for the fast development of electric power industry, including new energy.
2005	National Electricity Policy	It stipulates the gradual development of nontraditional power.
2006	Integrated Energy Policy	This is a guidebook on energy policies that stipulates subsidy for renewables and enforced synchronization of renewable electricity.
2008	National Action Plan on Climate Change (NAPCC)	It pledges to develop clean energy to cope with climate change.
2009	Renewable Energy Tariff Regulations	It clarifies how to calculate the feed-in tariff of renewable power projects.
2011	Renewable Energy Certificates (RECs)	It is vital for the nation and public utilities groups to meet their voluntary goals for renewable portfolio.
2011	"Development of Solar Cities" program	First-phase goal: ten pilot solar cities; second-phase goal: solar cities in all states.
2011	National Solar Mission	It encourages large and small power plants to produce more solar electricity, vows to provide more accessible energy for the countryside, and supports tech innovation in solar power.
2015	Intended Nationally Determined Contribution (INDC)	It pledges to, with international support, increase the percentage of nonfossil power from the current 30% to 40% by 2030; install 175GW renewable capacity by 2022 and at least 200GW nonfossil capacity by 2030.
2016	International Solar Alliance (ISA)	It aims to create a common clean energy market based on shared values, experience, and resources.

Source: originally created by the author.

As the third largest emitter in the world that has difficulty in tackling climate change, India pronounced its new intended nationally determined contribution (INDC) in October 2015 prior to the Paris Climate Change Conference. According to the new INDC, it will increase the percentage of nonfossil power from the current 30% to 40% in 2030 with international support. This consists of two phased objectives – to install 175GW renewable capacity by 2022 and at least 200GW nonfossil capacity by 2030. Although coal and other fossil fuels will continue to be a key part of the energy mix in emerging countries represented by India for decades to come, the surge of clean energy is an irreversible trend.[91] However, the ambition to have 175GW renewable capacity by 2022 is facing no small challenges – India will have to surmount hurdles in capital, technology, policy, and many other aspects, especially international cooperation and support. Therefore, India formed the Prime Minister's Council on Climate Change, issued the National Action Plan on Climate Change (NAPCC), and put forth eight key programs covering solar power, energy efficiency, management, and use of water resources, sustainable living environment, afforestation, ecological environment on the Himalayas, sustainable agriculture, and climate change response. These provide strong policy guarantee for driving the energy transition in India.

III. Development of India's clean energy diplomacy and its strategic positioning

Well set to have the largest population in the world, India must meet the power demand of 1.45 billion people. While the US values clean energy's environmental benefits and highlight, along with Japan, its importance for energy independence and security, India emphasizes how clean energy can support energy availability in developing countries and help energy-poor population obtain modern electricity as soon as possible. It also begins to leverage its advantageous clean energies such as solar to underpin its dream to become a major country. India's clean energy diplomacy displays the following characteristics.

First, India takes advantage of international conferences and forms the International Solar Alliance (ISA) in the attempt to lead the clean energy sector.

When the Third India-Africa Forum Summit (IAFS), themed "Partners in Progress: Towards a Dynamic and Transformative Development Agenda", was held in New Delhi in October 2015, India as the host put clean energy, climate change, and technological development high on the agenda. At the summit, Indian Prime Minister Modi sent official invitations to about 110 countries to join the India-led ISA, saying that our goal was to make solar power an indispensable part of our lives and send it to villages and communities where grid connection was most difficult.[92] The full name of ISA is International Agency for Solar Policy and Application, and its members are fully or partly located between tropical zones and the Tropic of Capricorn. Some founding members were European countries (e.g., France), and the initiative was endorsed by countries like Australia, New Zealand, and Brazil. InSPA serves as a platform for countries to share technologies and best practices so they don't have to rely on the expensive transfer from the EU and the

US. It demonstrates India's wish to become a critical player in the global market and governance of solar energy.

On November 30, 2015, a day before the Paris Climate Change Conference, the India-led ISA comprising 121 member states (including all major countries from the tropics) was officially established under the witness of French president Hollande. The Alliance committed to providing USD 1 trillion to help achieve the emission targets for 2030. Arunabha Ghosh, chief executive officer of the Council on Energy, Environment, and Water (CEEW), said India was a natural leader of the alliance, and it aimed to install 175GW renewable capacity by 2022, including 100GW of solar. Hollande believed the establishment of ISA was a concrete step towards climate justice that could lever the public funds in developed countries and help universalize clean energy worldwide. In January 2016, India Prime Minister Modi and French President Hollande attended the groundbreaking ceremony of ISA (renamed from InSPA) in New Delhi, which indicated that the India-led Alliance would be formally established soon.

Founded on March 11, 2018, ISA is based at the National Institute of Solar Energy (NISE) in Gurgaon, a satellite city of India's capital, New Delhi, with the mission to create a common clean energy market based on shared values, experience, and resources. The heads of state and ministers of 43 countries, including French president Macron, who was visiting India at the time, attended ISA's inauguration ceremony and committed to providing the highest level of clean, affordable, and sustainable energy sources to respond to climate change. A total of 60 countries signed the ISA agreement at the meeting, and 32 of them ratified it. To show his commitment to the Alliance, Modi announced the plan to sponsor 27 solar projects in 15 countries, which amounted to USD 1.4 billion in worth, via the grant of credit. He also announced to set up a committee in charge of developing solar technologies and to build 500 training spots in the member states to lead R&D in solar energy. India's goal was to raise USD 1 trillion and install 1,000GW solar capacity by 2030. To achieve this goal, Modi rolled out a ten-point plan, including developing affordable solar technologies and creating common rules and standards to enable all countries to share solar energy. There are several corporate members, namely, Areva, ENEL, HSBC France, and India's Tata Steel. In particular, Yes Bank, a private Indian bank, agreed in 2018 to mobilize USD 5 billion by 2030 for solar projects nationwide. At the ISA meeting on the sidelines of the 2018 World Future Energy Summit in Abu Dhabi, Yes Bank announced that it would raise USD 1 billion by 2023 and USD 5 billion by 2030 to bankroll solar projects across India.[93] Before that, it had already signed a USD 400 million co-financing agreement with European Investment Bank (EIB) for the construction of new solar and wind power projects in India. It also drew up the road map toward realizing the vision of the Indian government at the 2018 Renewable Energy Investors Meet & Expo (Re-Invest 2018).

But the newly formed Alliance was facing challenges in multiple directions. For instance, Dubai in 2018 announced a solar program worth about USD 27 billion that aimed to put solar panels on top of all buildings, and that was just one of the many programs to make the city a global center of clean energy. Dubai's goal was to have clean energy account for 25% of its total electric output by 2030 and 75% by 2050, which was a signal that it will compete with India for international solar investment. In 2015, President of SoftBank Group Masayoshi Son expressed the intention to form a JV – SBGCleantech – with an Indian company and the Hon Hai Precision Industry Co., Ltd. based in China's Taiwan, and to invest USD 20 billion over the next decade to find a way to the Indian PV market. However, he later turned to sign an MOU with Crown Prince of Saudi Arabia Muhammad bin Salman in New York, whereby SoftBank would invest USD 25 billion in Saudi Arabia in the next three to four years with a plan to build a total of 200GW solar power stations through 2030. Such a massive investment would definitely affect SoftBank's previous plan for solar investment in India.[94]

Second, India attaches great importance to improving its ability of clean energy development and promoting industrial upgrade through bilateral and multilateral cooperation. A latecomer that has caught up quickly, India set great store by international exchanges and cooperation and tried to push renewable energy forward in higher intensity and speed through flexible international cooperation, bilateral or multilateral.

On the one hand, India seeks bilateral cooperation with Western countries strong in clean energy. In 2005, the US actively urged six Asian-Pacific countries, including India, to kick off the Asia-Pacific Partnership on Clean Development and Climate (APP) in Sydney, Australia.[95] India was active about this initiative because its main principles conformed with its own climate policies. In the same year, then Indian foreign minister Singh and then US secretary of state Condoleezza Rice met in New Delhi, where they stressed the possibility of jointly developing clean technologies to meet the mounting energy demand and adjust the energy mix. In 2009, the two countries signed an MOU to enhance cooperation on clean energy, energy efficiency, energy security, and climate change. As an institutional cooperation agreement between two countries, an MOU functions as a normative and binding document on their energy cooperation, playing an especially important role in the India-US cooperation on climate change and clean energy. When US President Barack Obama visited India in 2010, the two sides signed a joint statement on building a center of clean energy research and development in India with financial and technical support from the US. During their fourth round of strategic dialogue in 2013, the two countries reached a broad range of consensus, encompassing jointly tackling climate change, strongly promoting cooperation in clean energy, and working together on energy security. Efforts are already underway with regard to energy efficiency, development of renewables market, research on nuclear energy, and development of shale gas.

India and EU concluded the Joint Work Programme on Energy, Clean Development, and Climate Change in 2008, in a bid to strengthen pragmatic cooperation on climate and clean energy and carry out policy coordination and technology R&D cooperation through an institutional framework. In October 2017, they issued a leaders' joint statement regarding green energy and climate change for the better implementation of the *Paris Agreement*. Other than continued cooperation on clean energy, smart grid, energy efficiency, and offshore wind power, they would also work on solar power pump, energy storage, and biomass energy. India reached cooperation agreements with Britain and Norway on the development of ocean energy. In 2011, Atlantis Resources, a British company, and India's Gujarat State Electricity Corporation Limited (GSECL) signed an MOU to build a 50MW tidal power plant near the Gulf of Kachchh on the west coast of India, which would be the first commercial-scale tidal power plant in Asia. In 2012, Indian government and Norway's Ministry of Environment and International Development agreed to intensify the cooperation on offshore wind power development. India and Japan began to hold regular ministerial-level consultations on energy as early as in 2007, and their technological cooperation has driven India's tech transformation in relation to LED equipment, energy storage, and clean coal. At the 8th India-Japan Strategic Energy Dialogue in 2016, the two countries forged the "technology partnership" and issued a joint statement on cooperation regarding efficient and clean coal-based power generation, enhanced energy efficiency, and renewable energy technology.

On the other hand, the Indian government paid special attention to multilateral cooperation when promoting the establishment of ISA. India will inject a USD 30-million initial fund to ISA and build its headquarters in the country, with a view to raising USD 400 million from the member states and international organizations. When Modi and Hollande initiated to form the ISA on November 30, 2015, India set the ambitious goal of deploying 175GW renewable capacity by 2022, including 100GW solar. Thanks to the strong support from the Modi administration, the institutional organization of ISA was officially in place in March 2018, endorsed by French president Macron and leaders of many other countries and organizations.

At the inauguration ceremony of ISA in 2018, Mr. Adnan Z. Amin, Director-General of the International Renewable Energy Agency (IRENA), and ISA's acting Director-General Upendra Tripathy signed a joint statement vowing to deepen the two organizations' cooperation on solar energy. It was also agreed that IRENA would provide ISA with project facilitation tools and platforms, such as the Global Atlas for Renewable Energy, Project Navigator, and Sustainable Energy Marketplace, to support its operations in different countries. The long-term goal of ISA includes deploying more than 1,000GW solar capacity around the world and investing more than USD 1 trillion in solar by 2030. In March 2018, Asian Development Bank (ADB) and ISA signed a cooperation agreement on promoting solar energy deployment in the Asia-Pacific region, covering solar power generation, micro grid for solar power, and power transmission system that integrates solar power into the grid. The two sides would also join hands in promoting the sharing of knowledge in solar power and developing technology road maps.

In addition to solar and ocean energy, India also promotes international cooperation in nuclear energy. During Japanese prime minister Shinzo Abe's India visit in December 2015, the two sides signed an initial cooperation agreement for Japan to export nuclear technology to India to help it achieve its medium- and long-term nuclear development plan.[96] As a major nuclear power, France actively facilitated important nuclear cooperation agreement with India while promoting the cooperation with ISA. In March 2018, French and Indian electric power companies signed a letter of intent to the effect that France would provide six state-of-the-art civilian pressurized water reactors for the Jaitapur nuclear power station in Maharashtra State, India, and help the country increase its "nonfossil energy" to 40% of national energy output by 2030. On the one hand, developing nuclear power can help bring electricity to 1/4 of India's population; on the other hand, it may reshuffle the ranking list of clean energies in India's power mix. However, the security of nuclear technology is questioned by various social forces within the country.

Third, India keeps raising its position in South-South cooperation.

To begin with, India enhances its discourse power on green development as a major developing country through cooperation within the four-member BASIC and the five-member BRICS.

Since the UN climate change negotiations kicked off in 1992, India has paid close attention to cooperation with China and other major developing countries. The most prominent achievement was that China and India jointly established the principle of "common but differentiated responsibilities" and incorporated it in the normative system of global climate governance.[97] Shortly before the Copenhagen Climate Change Conference in 2009, representatives from Brazil, India, and South Africa gathered in Beijing, China, to discuss what basic stance the emerging developing countries should adopt collectively at the upcoming conference and agreed upon the BASIC Four cooperation mechanism. At the Copenhagen conference, the four countries declared their stance to the chairman, forced the "Denmark text" (referring to the draft Copenhagen Agreement) out of negotiations, and showed the developed world that developing countries were standing together to fight back. Since then, BASIC Four has become an important force representing developing countries in international climate negotiations. After China and the US announced their *Joint Statement on Climate Change* in 2014, India's passive attitude and conservative stance on climate change undermined the cooperation within BASIC Four. But Trump's retrogressive moves on climate change and clean energy after he was elected president in 2016 spurred the nations to come together again.

Although the China-India relation was shadowed after 2017, the BASIC Four – China, India, Brazil, and South Africa – was never more united than at the Bonn Climate Change Conference.[98] America's exit from the *Paris Agreement* tilted the BASIC Four toward India's stance (it was more inclined toward China before), which further intensified India's willingness to lead the climate movement. During the conference in Bonn, BASIC Four released a joint statement one day before the High-Level Ministerial Meeting. The 22-page, 3,500-word statement demanded tracking and auditing the climate funds provided by developed countries, and that climate negotiations should continue to respect the principles of "common but differentiated responsibilities" and respective capacities. At the 27th BASIC Ministerial Meeting on Climate Change held in New Delhi, India, in 2018, the four countries consulted on such topics as equity, transparency, actions and commitments, and high-level dialogue on climate funds. This gave an impetus to negotiating the implementation rules for the *Paris Agreement* at the United Nations Climate Change Conference in Katowice at the end of that year.[99]

At the same time, India attaches great importance to its green leadership among BRICS countries. It ranks third in BRICS in terms of clean energy development, equivalent to the second-ranking Brazil in aggregate, with an ambitious plan for solar. When addressing the BRICS Summit held in Fortaleza, Brazil, in 2014, Indian prime minister Modi proposed to create more diverse, multilayered dialogue and exchange mechanisms in addition to the summit, such as cultural, social, and youth exchanges among BRICS countries and multilateral cooperation in such areas as clean energy, disaster relief, and tourism involving multiple stakeholders. India also took an active part in preparing for the New Development Bank (NDB) and appointed Kamath, chairman of ICICI bank, the largest private bank in India, to be the first president of NDB when it was inaugurated in 2015. Taking clean energy as a key area of development, NDB allocated its first batch of loans to energy enterprises engaged in energy conservation and environmental protection. About 60% of the special loans went to clean energy, with USD 811 million granted for four projects in Brazil, China, North Africa, and India respectively. The 9th BRICS Summit convened in Xiamen, China, in September 2017 announced a master strategy for the next five years, according to which the NDB would focus on sustainable development, with more than 60% of its loans expected to go to infrastructure construction for that purpose.[100] In July 2018, the 10th BRICS Summit took place in Johannesburg, South Africa. At this summit, the Indian government gave approval for its Exim Bank to sign an agreement on collaborative research on Distributed Ledger/Blockchain Technology with Brazilian Development Bank, China Development Bank, Russian National Development Bank, and Development Bank of Southern Africa. Still focused on economic cooperation and development, BRICS planned to refine management and promote sustainable development through technological innovation in the face of the fourth Industrial Revolution.

Apart from working with major developing countries under the South-South cooperation framework, India also communicates with other developing countries for clean energy innovation. For instance, sponsored by the Ministry of New and Renewable Energy (MNRE), it hosted the Renewable Energy India Expo 2017, which provided an opportunity for energy industry stakeholders from India and the rest of the world, from industry entities and government officials to power station operators and private business managers, to have in-depth exchanges and share their experience. The expo not only helped India promote its achievements and experience in clean energy development but also augmented its international influence in this field. While cooperating with other developing countries, India made a point of adding clean energy topics into traditional energy cooperation. At the second India-Brazil-South Africa (IBSA) Summit in 2007, the three countries agreed to jointly promote nuclear energy, clean energy technologies, and other renewables and mitigate climate change. The *India-Brazil-South Africa Declaration on Clean Energy* listed some key areas of cooperation: clean coal technology and renewable energies such as biomass and innovative ways to transfer, develop, and commercialize clean energy.[101] When the vice president of India Mohammad Hamid Ansari visited Indonesia in November 2015, the two sides signed a spate of MOUs on cooperation in economy and trade, energy, climate change, and other areas. India has always viewed Indonesia as a strategic partner, and the two countries also inked an MOU on new and renewable energies this time to share their concepts and best practices in developing environment-friendly energies and establish a framework for tech cooperation.[102] While preparing for the ISA, India kept emphasizing that ISA members were developing countries fully or partly located between the tropical zone and the Tropic of Capricorn, in a bid to share experience with other developing countries and least developed countries in the tropical zone while developing its own solar energy.

Section 5 Brazil's clean energy diplomacy

Blessed with bountiful resources, Brazil has been actively developing and utilizing clean energies such as biofuel and wind energy since the 1970s to make up for the shortage of traditional energy sources. Today, being the world's second-largest producer and biggest exporter of ethanol fuel, Brazil has become a global leader in the utilization of clean energy. As far as electric power mix is concerned, renewable energy accounts for 3/4, among the highest percentage in all major economies. By adopting effective policies, the country has blazed a green, sustainable path of clean energy development and laid a solid foundation for implementing its ambitious clean energy diplomacy.

I. Brazil's clean energy development and features of its energy transition

Biomass energy and hydro energy take the largest proportion in Brazil's clean energy portfolio, while wind and PV also develop at a fast pace. Boasting rich experience in the field of renewables, Brazil is the second-largest bioenergy producer after the US and is superior to it and Europe in the production cost, selling price, and production technology of bioethanol and biodiesel.[103] From 1968 to 1975, Brazil created a miracle by maintaining an average annual economic growth rate as high as 11%, but the outbreak of the first oil crisis in 1973 lent a heavy blow to its economy, and inadequate oil supply in the international market quickly widened the demand-supply gap in the country. This spurred Brazil to strongly boost the development of biofuel based on its resources.

Located in the tropical and sub-tropical zones, most of the country features warm and rainy weather as well as fertile soil, creating favorable natural conditions for the growth of soybeans, sugarcane, corn, and other crops. The abundant output of raw materials provides the perfect conditions for extracting bioethanol (whose main raw material is sugarcane) and biodiesel (whose main raw material is soybean).[104] The National Ethanol Program launched in 1975 and the Biodiesel Program in the 1980s made Brazil a major producer of biomass energy and the first one that realized sustainable use of biofuel. In 2010, its bioenergy output accounted for 1/3 of the world total. Bioethanol, biodiesel, and other alternative energies made up almost half (45.3%) of its total energy consumption, a ratio much higher than in developed countries such as the US, Japan, and Germany. Its utilization rate of clean energy also topped the world. Through 30 years of unremitting efforts in terms of policy guarantee, industry chain, and financial support, Brazil has established a full industry chain, from planting sugarcane to producing ethanol fuel, from manufacturing ethanol-fuel-powered cars to building fuel supply stations. A national production and sales network is well in place.[105]

Hydropower is a vital renewable energy in Brazil. Thanks to a hydro-dominated and high-efficiency energy mix (over 90% of electricity is generated from hydropower), the modern economic sectors, such as industry, energy, transport, housing, and large-scale agricultural operation, generate only a small proportion of GHG emissions. The Itaipu hydropower station that started producing electricity in 1984 was at the time the second largest in the world following China's Gezhouba station, with an output enough to power the whole world for about 40 days. In 2014, Brazil produced 373TWh electricity from hydropower, 3/4 of its total output. However, hydropower is often affected by the dry season and climate change. Dwindling precipitation has slashed the amount of electricity generated, and a growing number of people, worried about the destruction of rainforest ecology, begin to resist hydropower and turn to the cleaner wind energy. With a 7,400 km long coastline, Brazil's wind resources are concentrated in the northeast inshore areas, with an average speed of up to 8 m/s in stable direction. According to the latest forecast by German Wind Energy Institute (DEWI), Brazil has a potential wind energy of 5×10^8kW, offshore resources excluded. Its wind power has grown since 2011 at a much higher rate than other energy sources. Especially, wind power accounted for 4/5 of the power supply contracts in 2016. The increment of wind power capacity in Brazil is likely to exceed the combined increment in other Latin American countries in the next few years.

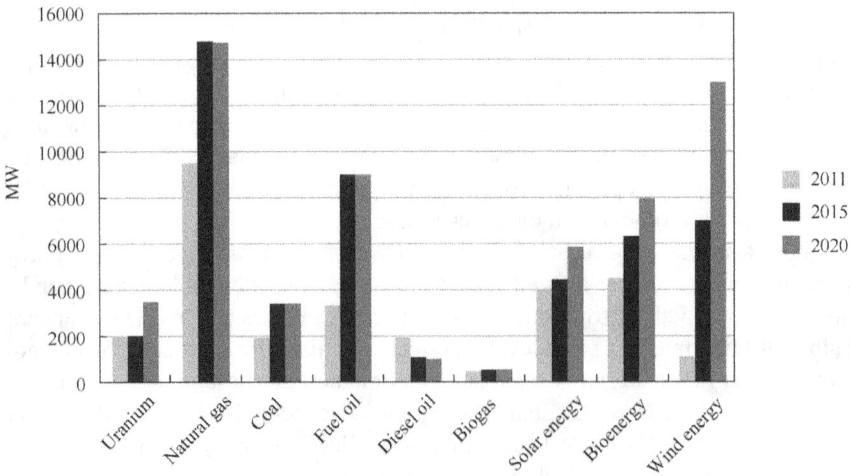

Figure 4.9 Planned installed capacity from different energy sources in Brazil (2011, 2015, 2020)

Source: Jiang He, "Brazil's Development and Utilization of Renewable Energy: Achievements and Lessons", Journal of Jiangsu Normal University (Philosophy and Social Sciences Edition), No. 2, 2017.

Brazil boasts the best solar radiation in the world, especially its northeast region that has an average daily radiation of about 5.9 kWh/m^2 and an average annual sun exposure of 2,500–2,900 hours. However, solar energy started quite late in Brazil, and its solar capacity was less than 35MW in 2014. Later as solar technology progressed and the cost of solar power generation kept falling, the Brazilian government began to pay attention to PV projects. In 2015, Brazil suffered the most serious drought in 80 years because of climate change, which exposed the heavily hydropower-dependent country to a dire shortage of power supply. This prompted the government to expedite the adjustment of its power mix, not only strongly developing wind power, but also stepping up the support for PV. For instance, the government adopted a solar power auction system that not only lured enterprises to participate but also stimulated them to make investment attempted by ensured yields. In April 2015, Brazil announced to build a 350MW floating solar power station at the Balbina reservoir on the Amazon, which would be the largest of its kind worldwide. To support a green and sustainable Olympic Games in 2016, the State of Piauí in northeast Brazil built a 292MW PV station, the largest in Latin America, that could power 300,000 households simultaneously. The Brazilian government also propelled the construction of several off-grid solar projects smaller than 1MW to increase the availability of modern energy in remote areas.

Overall, clean energy is growing apace in Brazil. According to an annual report on national energy balance in 2016 released by a Brazilian energy research institute, from 2015 to 2016, hydropower supply decreased by 3.2%, but the percentage of renewable power rose from 74.6% to 75.5% thanks to the increase of biomass power and wind power, the latter growing even faster (77.1%) than nuclear power, while the use of bioenergy grew from 18% in 2014 to 21% in 2016. A 2017 report released by Brazilian Ministry of Mines and Energy (MME) showed that renewable energy contributed to 43.5% of the country's energy supply in 2016, up 2.2% from 2015. Of the supply of renewable energy in 2016, bioethanol ranked first (40.1%), followed by hydropower (28.9%) and other energy sources (29%). The percentage of renewables was more than four times the average level of members of the Organization for Economic Co-operation and Development (OECD) and more than three times the world average.[106]

II. Evolution of Brazil's clean energy policies

Brazil is one of the first countries to implement clean energy policies. After the oil crisis in the 1970s, Brazil, in consideration for its energy security and economic development, began to strongly promote the development of biomass energy/biofuel leveraged on its advantages in agricultural production.

The first oil crisis in 1973 lent a heavy blow to Brazil that was in the middle of its "economic miracle". The country officially announced its National Ethanol Program (PROALCOOL) in 1975, under which sugarcane was used to produce ethanol as an alternative to fossil fuel and steps were quickened to develop ethanol-fueled vehicles. Under the program, a mix of measures were taken to create conditions for the promotion of biofuels, including provision of direct subsidy, allocation of quota, collective purchase of biofuel by governments and enterprises, price regulation, and legislative and administrative intervention. Brazilian law stipulated that gas-fueled vehicles must use gas containing 20%–25% ethanol fuel. After the second oil crisis broke out in 1979, the Brazilian government implemented PROALCOOL at a faster pace. It transferred state-funded technologies to automakers for free and applied special policies and financial support, such as subsidy, quota, and collective purpose, to encourage the use of ethanol fuel. The Department of Environment formed in 1990 and elevated to be the Ministry of Environment two years later was responsible for formulating guidelines and policies on environmental issues and the utilization of natural resources and coordinating the actions of relevant sectors. The Brazilian Institute of Environment and Renewable Natural Resources (IBAMA), an executive arm under the Ministry of Environment, was tasked with developing clean energy. After President Luiz Inácio Lula da Silva came into power in 2003, Brazil took a positive turn in its stance and policies in relation to climate change and gave a further push to the development of clean energy. That same year, it developed the first "flex-fuel" vehicle that could use a mixed fuel of any gas-ethanol ratio. In the meantime, the government demanded the gradual increase of ethanol in gas products in the market, and the percentage hit 27% in 2015.[107] In the past few years, the Brazilian government has actively supported the development of second-generation ethanol fuel technology – the technology that extracts ethanol from agricultural and forestry wastes such as straw stalk, bagasse, and rice husk. It has also made breakthroughs in producing bioethanol using enzyme and extracting ethanol from plant fiber.

Regarding biofuel, thanks to the success of PROALCOOL, Brazil launched the National Biodiesel Program (PNPB) and carried out small-scale experimental production in the 1980s, along with guarantee and tax break to boost the biodiesel industry. However, excessive cost prevented it from scaling up the program.[108] The Ministry of Science and Technology 2002 put the biodiesel technology project on the agenda again, fostered the biofuel market, and built the network of application. Advocated by Professor Miguel Joaquim Dabdoub and his clean technology laboratory at the University of São Paulo, the Brazilian president issued a decree in 2003 to form an inter-ministerial work group to restart the PNPB program, providing guarantee and tax break for biodiesel development. It's safe to say that Brazil has state-of-the-art biodiesel technology and has gathered rich experience in promoting its application. In 2005, the country launched the National Biodiesel Production and Use Program. According to the program, it would start using B2 diesel (2% biodiesel + 98% petroleum diesel) nationwide from January 2008 and gradually increase the ratio of biodiesel to 5% by 2013. In March 2017, Brazil enforced the use of B6 diesel and expected to start using B9 in March 2018 and B10 one year later, meaning 10% of biodiesel would be added.[109] Supported by PNPB, Brazil has built a network of biodiesel technology development and a system of biodiesel stations in more than 20 states across the country. At present, Petrobras alone has nearly 4,000 gas stations selling mixed biodiesel oil.

Having made breakthroughs in bioenergy, the Brazilian government put forth the Alternative Energy Sources Incentive Program (PROINFA) in 2002, aimed to diversify the power mix by increasing the use of wind energy and establish an integrated power system of both renewable and traditional energy sources.[110] Under PROINFA, wind power policies were developed through legislation, allowing renewable energy projects to use preferential loans. It was also proposed that Eleterobrás signed, through bidding and at a highly competitive price, 20-year-long purchase agreements with the wind farms in order to promote the use of wind power with FIT. An executive committee comprising officials from government departments, including the Ministry of Science and Technology, Ministry of Mines and Energy, and National Electric Power Agency (ANEEL), was also created under PROINFA to supervise work on renewable energy and energy efficiency, in hopes of making the electric sector more competitive. Wind power in Brazil increased at a high speed after 2011. While the total power capacity amounted to 140GW in 2015, wind capacity is expected to reach 13GW in 2020, 7.6% of the total.[111]

Of all the three programs – PROALCOOL, PNPB, and PROINFA – the government has played an important part from the beginning to the end. For one thing, the government preluded the implementation of the programs with specific laws and escorted it with standard management. It revised relevant laws, issued corresponding policy measures, and provided tax adjustments and preferences to clear the way for implementation, and the institutional adjustment was fixated in a legal form. For another, to advance the three programs, the government, by dint of presidential decree, set up a cross-sectoral committee as a powerful organizational guarantee for implementing the supportive policies. Moreover, the government consistently carried out differentiated tax rate. It provided continuous tax preferences for enterprises, agricultural cooperatives, and other economic entities that joined the programs, stimulating them with economic benefits.[112] Partly thanks to its clean energy endowments, Brazil is the first major developing country that committed to absolute emission reduction targets – rather than reducing planned emissions or emission intensity – starting from the base year. According to the Intended Nationally Determined Contributions (INDC) it submitted in 2015, Brazil would reduce 37% of GHG emissions by 2025 compared with 2005 and 43% by 2030, when renewable power other than hydropower will add up to 23%. At present, hydropower accounts for 66% of Brazil's power output while other forms of renewables less than 10%, which means solar, wind, and biomass energies will play an important part in the power mix.

III. Development of Brazil's clean energy diplomacy and its strategic positioning

The quick rise of Brazil's clean energy diplomacy is ascribed to its unique advantages in clean energy. Thanks to the rapid development of biofuel, hydropower, wind power, and other clean energy sources, Brazil has become a developing country with one of the highest clean energy percentages. In this process, the restructuring of international interest structure is inevitable with the collective emergence of new forces. Following this trend, Brazil has actively engaged in global affairs to seek a prominent position as a major country. This is conducive to balancing the global power structure, establishing the new international political and economic order, and pushing developing countries from the margin to the center of the international arena. Brazil's clean energy diplomacy displays the following characteristics.

First, its clean energy diplomacy and climate diplomacy are closely linked and promote each other through two-way alliance. The high percentage of clean energy sources lays the foundation for Brazil's positive attitude during climate negotiations, and the increasingly aggressive negotiations are good for establishing Brazil's position as a major country of bioenergy.

Celso Amorim, a senior Brazilian diplomat, said many times that Brazil is an important player on the international stage with diverse advantages in territory, political democracy, economic strengths, and other respects. But it is also a developing country facing serious economic and social fragility.[113] Brazil sees itself as a "developing country that can play an important role", by which it means it should engage in the international decision-making mechanism as much as possible, seek diverse, effective paths to participate in global governance, and manifest and enhance its voice and influence in international affairs. Brazil's efforts in this respect are first and foremost reflected in global climate governance.

As renewable energy makes up 38% in Brazil's energy mix, the main source of its GHG emissions isn't the use of fossil fuel but the deforestation resulting from enlarging farmland and urban construction. Besides, the Brazilian society pays close attention to protecting the environment and coping with climate change – a high level of attention not often seen in the world. The private sector, NGOs, and other social groups have all played an important part in the process of tackling climate change. Therefore, Brazil is very ambitious in this field and has adopted the approach of two-way alliance in international climate negotiations.

On the one hand, Brazil positions itself as an "emerging developing country" on the diplomatic front. Believing that it shoulders fewer historical responsibilities for climate change than developed countries, it upholds the principle of "common but differentiated responsibilities", based on which it asks developed countries to provide financial and technological assistance for developing ones. As a developing country, it also coordinates with other major developing countries in actions. In June 1997, Brazil proposed to set up the Clean Development Fund (CDF), which required developed countries failing to meet their emission goals to pay fines to support the emission reduction projects in developing countries, but this proposal was unanimously rejected by the developed world. However, the US and Brazil jointly proposed the Clean Development Mechanism (CDM) in October 1997 based on that proposal. The new mechanism, a revised edition of Brazil's original proposal, got rid of the punitive terms and respected the free will of countries. It was a flexible mechanism for cooperation in emission reduction between developed and developing countries, deemed as a major innovation in the *Kyoto Protocol*. Brazil insisted that developed countries should provide necessary financial assistance to help developing ones achieve clean development.[114] At the 2009 Copenhagen Climate Change Conference, Brazil coordinated with South Africa, India, and China for strengthened solidarity and cooperation within the BRICS.

Meanwhile, the Bolivarian Alliance for the Peoples of Our America (ALBA), of which Brazil is also a member, insisted on developing countries making emission reduction commitments and providing international aid, emphasizing social justice while responding to climate change.

On the other hand, Brazil wishes to play a special leading part in climate diplomacy by setting ambitious targets for clean energy development. During climate negotiations, it, leveraged on its favorable energy mix, set higher-than-average emission targets and adopted a similar stance to that of developed countries. Brazil stands between developed and developing countries on climate change – a dual stance intended to maximize its interests and enhance its discourse power regarding environmental issues. By actively coordinating between the two sides, Brazil expects to gain their recognition of its "leading" part in the negotiations.[115] The 2009 Conference of the Parties to the UNFCCC set the stage for Brazil to make a difference. Before the Copenhagen conference convened, Brazil was the first developing country to put the emission reduction initiative on the negotiating table, a move that put other developing countries such as China and India in a passive situation. In December 2009, Brazil took the lead in adopting the *National Plan for Adaptation to Climate Change (PNA)*, which specified the targets, principles, and tools of the national climate change policy and incorporated the voluntary emission targets it previously committed to at the climate change conference.[116] The then Brazilian president Dilma Rousseff announced the report on intended nationally determined contributions at the United Nations Sustainable Development Summit 2015. The report listed the following targets and indicators of emission reduction for the next stage: GHG emission will be reduced by 37% from 2005 to 2025 and by 43% to 2030, the percentage of sustainable bioenergy in the energy mix will rise up to 18%, power output from other renewables than hydropower will increase to 23%, and renewable energy will account for 45% of energy mix. For the first time, Brazil pledged to reduce the absolute amount of emissions starting from the base year, which signified a shift in its attitude on the negotiations – from "developing countries have the right to pollute" to "developing countries also share the responsibility for emission reduction". It's clear that Brazil intended to have more say on the negotiations by putting forward ambitious targets for emission reduction and clean energy development,[117] and it would impose more pressure on other major emitters. From a national interests point of view, Brazil was working to create a global bioenergy market by advancing the climate change negotiations so it could enlarge the export of its highly competitive bioenergy and consequently secure a leading position for itself in bioenergy development.[118]

Second, Brazil reinforces its leading role in South-South cooperation, especially in BRICS, through clean energy development.

The Brazil-initiated South-South cooperation on climate change has two characteristics. To begin with, it has clear-cut focuses. Revolving around two dominant themes – developing clean energy and protecting the Amazon Rainforest, Brazil concentrated efforts on creating distinctive cooperation brands, thus laying a solid foundation for promoting and deepening relevant cooperation and attracting more financial and technological resources. Regarding the development of renewable energy, Brazil, leveraged on its advantageous resources, has gathered rich experience and grasped advanced technologies. It actively cooperated with major developing countries in this area to seek complementarity and boost relevant industries. In 2004, it signed a Memorandum on the Cooperation in New and Clean Energies with China; in 2009, the Brazil-China Center for Climate Change and Energy Technology Innovation was established. In the meantime, Brazil provided a great deal of substantive assistance to underdeveloped countries. In 2007, it provided Nigeria with the first batch of up to USD 100 million investment loans for the construction of its "Biofuels City"; in 2009, it signed a USD 6 billion agreement with Mozambique to assist in its bioenergy development. Playing an irreplaceable role in regulating climate and fixating carbon dioxide, the Amazon Rainforest is essential for regional ecology and environment and the livelihood of local residents. As a regional power and an emerging developing country, Brazil is obligated to protect the Amazon and cope with local crisis and global climate change.[119] At the same time, it encourages the private sector and NGOs to take part to bring into full play the strengths of different stakeholders and make cooperation more fruitful. Therefore, when the government is taking actions, the private sector and NGOs also play an important role in promoting South-South cooperation on climate change. Their participation has helped translate many potential cooperation opportunities into pragmatic projects, and promoted, in flexible ways, Brazil's communication with its partners. The resulting multilayered cooperation system enables Brazil to double the outcomes of the cooperation with half the efforts.

Brazil's diplomatic considerations for BRICS cooperation epitomize its diplomatic strategy that gives precedence to South-South cooperation. The strategic motive behind its active participation in BRICS cooperation is that the mechanism provides a major external pathway to national development and a great platform for it to participate in multilateral cooperation. Judging from the results, Brazil has achieved its objectives through BRICS cooperation – strengthening the economic and trade bonds with several important emerging countries, and enhancing its international clout in climate and clean energy. In this process, Brazil was especially supportive of establishing the New Development Bank (NDB) and contributed USD 28 billion to the bank and the BRICS Contingent Reserve Arrangement.[120] Since inaugurated on July 16, 2014, with an initial capital of USD 50 billion, NDB has paid special attention to clean energy, and the first batch of projects it rolled out in April 2016 was focused on energy, particularly clean energy and renewable energy. The Brazilian National Bank for Economic and Social Development (BNDES) was granted one of NDB's first loans to support the development of 600MW renewable capacity in Brazil.

Third, Brazil's clean energy diplomacy is development-oriented. Through international platforms, it strives to become more competitive in the bioenergy market and lead the formulation of industrial standards.

Brazil emphasizes enhancing its structural influence by taking an active part in various multilateral mechanisms, such as the Clean Development Mechanism (CDM) and Clean Energy Ministerial (CEM). By the end of March 2017, it had the third largest number of ongoing CDM projects in the world. It also actively participated in the initiatives proposed by CEM, including the bioenergy work group, 21st Century Power Partnership, Multilateral Solar and Wind Working Group, Super-Efficient Equipment and Appliance Deployment Initiative, and the challenge to flexible supply of advanced energy sources. In November 2008, Brazil convened an International Conference on Biofuels in Sao Paulo at the suggestion of then President Lula. The conference, themed "Biofuels as a Driving Force of Sustainable Development", gathered representatives from 90 countries and 24 international organizations. In response to the international community's doubts that bioenergy production might affect food security, then Minister of Civil Affairs Dilma Rousseff pointed out that biofuels in Brazil stemmed from sugarcane, whose planting area accounted for only 0.5% of the national land area. She encouraged poor countries and regions suitable for sugarcane planting to scale up the production of alcohol using sugarcane as raw materials and announced that Brazil would launch an agricultural program to make sure crops grown in Latin America could guarantee both energy and grain supply simultaneously.

Meanwhile, leveraged on its superior bioenergy technologies, Brazil strongly promoted second-generation biofuels represented by cellulosic ethanol. With second-generation biofuels, food crops were no longer used as raw materials, so biofuels didn't have to "vie for crops" anymore. Instead, agricultural and forestry wastes such as bagasse, straw stalks, grass, and scrapped timber were used to produce biofuel – cellulosic ethanol to be specific using bio-cellulose. Brazilian government vowed to give a strong push to the production of second-generation biofuels with cellulose and bagasse, especially to provide policy and financial support for technological advancement, commercialization, and application of second-generation bioethanol. GranBio and Raízen, two Brazilian companies, announced in 2014 their success in using bagasse cellulose to mass-produce second-generation ethanol fuels.[121] After the *Paris Agreement* was signed, to use bioethanol as an alternative energy source in the global transport sector, Brazil took the lead in 2016 to establish the "Biofuture Platform" in conjunction with 20 countries. Stressing the important role of bioenergy in meeting the targets set in the *Paris Agreement*, Brazil, with its technological superiority and advanced emission goals, endeavored to create a new international image for itself with enhanced international influence. It's evident that Brazil took bioenergy as a key toehold of its diplomatic efforts. Domestically, it actively utilized foreign capital to expedite technological innovation for clean energy development. Internationally, it tried to highlight its role on global climate issues to drive forward its "major country strategy". Brazil not only forced developed countries to lower the import tariff for bioenergy but also promoted relevant technologies to developing countries in Asia, Africa, and Latin America and fostered new bioenergy markets there.

Section 6 Comparison of the five countries' clean energy development and diplomatic strategy

This chapter analyzes how the five major countries of clean energy development have proceeded with their energy transition, how their clean energy policies have evolved, and the characteristics of their clean energy diplomacy amid the changing global strategic landscape of climate and energy. The five countries are Germany, a traditional pioneer in clean energy; the US and Japan, strong players in clean energy innovation; and India and Brazil, emerging developing countries that have performed superbly in clean energy.

I. Five-country comparison: characteristics of energy transition and clean energy policies

First, let's look at the tendency of the five countries' energy transition and their targets of clean energy development. Aimed at climate friendliness and environmental protection, the German government made it clear that its energy transition would be pivoted on the "strong development of renewable energy". Germany officially put forth the "Energy Transition Plan" in 2011, aiming to, in addition to completely giving up nuclear energy in 2022, have renewable energy account for 60% of end energy consumption and 80% of total power output by 2050. The government also developed laws and standards in relation to clean energy and supported the shift toward a low-carbon economy with preferential policies centered on "feed-in premiums (FIP)".[122] In 2017, Germany's CDU/CSU (Christlich Demokratische Union/Christian Social Union) and SPD (Sozialdemokratische Partei Deutschlands) reached a new coalition agreement that raised the target for 2030 to 65%, and Merkel was elected German chancellor again.

America's energy transition is driven by the desire for energy independence. It launched a shale gas revolution to advance the energy transformation with natural gas and nuclear energy as transitional options. Even today, the US government still hasn't put forth a strategy with renewable energy as the only or primary direction. The "boldest" target it has set so far was brought up by Barack Obama in his 2011 State of the Union Address – 80% of electricity in the US would come from clean energy comprising renewables, natural gas, and nuclear energy by 2035. However, the *Clean Energy Plan* was abolished during Trump's term, although efforts by sub-national entities, especially the targets by states and cities, have ensured America's leadership in the innovation in and production of clean energy. Unlike Germany that energetically developed renewable energy, the US placed more emphasis on the development and use of natural gas, clean coal, nuclear power, and other clean energies in pushing the energy shift. With the long-term goal of energy independence, actively promoting domestic energy supply to guarantee energy security remains the primary and central goal of America's energy policy.

As an island country, Japan is destitute of resources and has a high reliance on energy import, but its energy efficiency is among the best in the world. Japan adopted an energy transition strategy that emphasized energy supply and safe use. Nuclear energy was dominant in its clean energy portfolio, while wind and PV could hardly develop on a large scale or at a high speed because of the narrow and small territory, but significant technological progress has been made in offshore wind and PV. After the Fukushima nuclear crisis in 2011, Japan issued the *Energy and Environment Innovation Strategy* on September 14, 2012, pledging to increase

Table 4.14 Tendency of energy transition and clean energy targets of the five countries

Country	*Type of transition*	*Clean energy target*
Germany	Oriented toward climate friendliness and environmental governance	In 2012, Germany revised the Erneuerbare-Energien-Gesetz (EEG-2012, meaning Renewable Energy Law) to lay down the medium- and long-term goals for renewable energy development in a legal form. The new EEG vowed to have renewable energy account for 35%, 50%, 65%, and 80% of Germany's power supply in 2020, 2030, 2040, and 2050. In 2017, Germany's CDU/CSU and SPD reached a new coalition agreement that raised the 2030 target to 65%, and Merkel was elected German chancellor again.
US	Oriented toward energy independence	Barack Obama proclaimed his ambitious *Clean Energy Plan* in August 2015, according to which American power plants must cut their carbon emissions by 32% in 2030 from the 2005 levels as part of the efforts to drive an energy transition strategy powered by renewable energy, natural gas, and nuclear energy. Although Trump abolished the plan during his term, the states had set their own targets for clean development. Besides, Trump, like Obama, also emphasized achieving energy independence through the shale gas revolution.
Japan	Oriented toward energy supply and safety of use	Japan released the *Energy and Environment Innovation Strategy* on September 14, 2012, planning to increase the percentage of renewables, the best alternative to nuclear energy, to 35% of power mix by 2030 from 10% in 2010. In 2018, it issued the Fifth Basic Energy Plan and, for the first time, decided to use renewable energy as a major economically independent and decarbonized power source toward 2050. However, the plan lowered the 2030 renewable target to 22%–24%.
India	Oriented toward availability of modern energy	According to its intended nationally determined contributions submitted in 2015, India, with international support, would increase the percentage of nonfossil energy in its power mix from the current 30% to 40% in 2030. It planned to have 175GW renewable capacity by 2022 and at least 200GW nonfossil capacity by 2030.
Brazil	Oriented toward climate friendliness and clean development	Brazil vowed to reduce 43% of GHG emissions, have renewable energy account for 45% of energy mix, and increase renewable power other than hydropower to 23% by 2030. At present, hydropower accounts for 66% of Brazil's power output while other forms of renewables less than 10%, which indicates that solar, wind, and biomass energies will play an important part in its future power mix.

Source: Originally created by the author.

the percentage of renewable energy, the best alternative to nuclear energy, from 10% of the power mix in 2010 to 35% in 2030. In 2018, Japan issued the Fifth Basic Energy Plan and, for the first time, decided to use renewable energy as a major economically independent and decarbonized power source toward 2050. However, the plan drew severe criticism because it lowered the 2030 renewable target to 22%–24%.

India's energy transition strategy aims to ensure the availability of modern energy. A report by World Bank showed that economic losses caused by electricity scarcity to India amounted to around 7% of its GDP. A quarter of all the population without access to electricity yet live in India, the largest percentage of all countries. As of the second half of last year, about 304 million Indians – 23% of the national population – lived without electricity. Therefore, India takes clean energy development as an important way to increase energy availability, ensure energy security, and realize sustainable development. At the Paris Climate Change Conference in 2015, India submitted an ambitious Intended Nationally Determined Contributions, pledging to increase the percentage of renewable energy in its power mix to 40% and to have at least 200GW nonfossil capacity by 2030. India's goal was to become a major clean energy country – indeed a leader and core player in the global solar industry.

Brazil is a developing country whose percentage of clean energy leaves other countries far behind. Making full use of its advantages in climate negotiations, it adopted an energy transition strategy oriented toward climate friendliness and clean development. The Brazilian government proposed in 2015 to reduce 43% of its GHG emissions and have renewable energy account for 45% in its energy mix by 2030. Considering that the percentage of renewables was already close to that goal in 2016, it was not a very ambitious plan for Brazil. What was significant was that Brazil decided to increase the percentage of other renewable power than hydropower from less than 10% to 23%, meaning solar and wind energies will play an ever-bigger role in the future energy mix.

The five countries vary greatly in clean energy policies and in their clean energy development. Germany is a traditional power of clean energy and a pioneer in relevant technologies and policies. It first put forth the energy transition strategy in 2010 and set the agenda to abandon nuclear power in 2022, thus further boosting the momentum of wind and PV. Germany enacted the first EEG in 2000, with which the FIT policy for renewable power was promoted in the country and emulated by many countries around the world. The EEG was revised six times from its enactment in 2000 to 2017, indicating that people's understanding of renewable energy was progressive, and that called for special attention to the stability and adjustment of relevant laws and policies. To make sure the legal adjustment was valid and effective, Germany timely modified the legislative provisions to guarantee the sound development of renewables.[123]

Though two-party politics have hurt America's clean energy policies, the country remains a major innovator of clean energy technology. It ranks first in terms of the use of biofuels and geothermal energy, and its wind and PV development is also leading the world. Setting great store by energy security, the US has coupled its shale gas revolution with the utilization of renewable energy. Nowadays, more than 30 states across the country are enforcing the renewables portfolio standard (RPS), and five of them have set renewable targets. Even if the country hasn't passed the RPS on the federal level yet, a host of federal bills are related with compulsory RPS, which is a means of market transaction under administrative regulation. Efforts on the state level have never stopped even after Trump came in office. In contrast to the federal government, many state governments are enthusiastic about developing renewable energy and have put in place a string of effective incentives. Since RPS features efficient, market-based allocation of resources, more and more countries have begun to design their own clean energy development plan in reference to it.

Japan boasts the highest energy efficiency and the largest number of clean energy innovations and IPs in the world. In particular, it leaves other countries far behind in offshore wind power and PV as well as solar-based production of hydrogen. In 2003, the Japanese government issued the *Act on Special Measures Concerning New Energy Usage by Electric Utilities* (Act on Special Measures or RPS Act) to impel the rational development and utilization of new energy. The act required every electric power company to develop a certain amount of new energy sources for power generation. Although the FIT system for renewables starting in

Table 4.15 Comparison of the five countries' renewable energy policies and features of their clean energy development

Country	*Clean energy policy*	*Features of clean energy development*
Germany	FIT-FIP	Germany is a traditional clean energy power and a pioneer in relevant technologies and policies. It put forth the energy transition strategy and set the agenda to abandon nuclear power in 2022, thus further boosting the momentum of wind and PV.
US	RPS, more upbeat policies on the state level	The US is a major innovator of clean energy technology. It ranks first in terms of the use of biofuel and geothermal energy, and its wind and PV development is leading the world. Setting great store by energy security, the US has coupled its shale gas revolution with the utilization of renewable energy.
Japan	FIT	Japan boasts the highest energy efficiency and the largest number of clean energy innovations and IPs in the world. In particular, it leaves other countries far behind in offshore wind power and PV as well as solar-based production of hydrogen.
India	RECs	India has an ambitious solar plan and its wind power tops all developing countries.
Brazil	Systematic national support	Brazil has the world's highest percentage of clean energy in energy mix (biomass and hydro). It is a major biofuel developer with fast-developing wind and PV as well.

Source: Originally created by the author.

2012 increased wind power equipment in Japan, the capacity only ranked eighteenth worldwide as of December 2013 because of the narrow and small territory. In the 2030 power mix released by the government in July 2015, wind power only accounted for 1.7%. Unlike many other countries where wind power developed faster than PV, Japan's PV developed much faster, and the country took offshore wind and PV as the future area for technological breakthroughs.

India started late in the development of clean energy but has shown robust growth momentum in recent years. It has put forth an ambitious solar plan and formed the International Solar Alliance (ISA), and its wind power develops fastest in developing countries. As the percentage of renewable energy expanded quickly after 2011, the Indian government adopted the Renewable Energy Certificates (RECs), a system that was critical for the nation and public utilities to meet their voluntary goals for renewable energy portfolio. All Indian states were required to work out their own voluntary goals. The INDC submitted by India in 2015 included targets for clean energy, whereby the country planned to build 175GW renewable capacity by 2022 with international support, thus establishing its international position as a major clean energy power.

Brazil has the world's highest percentage of clean energy, with biofuels and hydropower leading the world and wind and PV growing at a fast rate. It didn't adopt the FIT system in Germany and Japan or the RPS system in the US, which were systematic policies on clean energy development. Instead, the rapid development of its clean energy is mainly attributed to three programs – PROALCOOL, PNPB, and PROINFA (also called Alternative Energy Sources Incentive Program). To lead by example, the federal government of Brazil has earnestly implemented the three programs in government procurement. It purchased new energy vehicles and other related products as much as possible and encouraged state governments to join the programs. We can say that the government's all-out support for new energy strategies and plans and earnest implementation of every specific policy is the key reason why Brazil has been so successful in developing new energy sources.

II. Five-country comparison: strategic positioning of clean energy diplomacy

We have so far compared the energy transition strategies of the five countries, their renewable energy policies, and features of their energy development. It's evident that they all draw up their clean energy diplomacy strategies based on their specific conditions and endowments, and these strategies basically conform with the four types discussed in Chapter 2 – theoretical analysis. Germany's clean energy diplomacy is typically driven by governance. Clean energy diplomacy of the Obama administration is typically driven by green hegemony, while that of the Trump administration is typically competition-driven – both are high on the competition dimension despite wildly different policies. Japan adopts a competition-driven clean energy diplomacy that places more stress on energy security, while that of India and Brazil is driven by green development, with slight difference on governance and competition dimensions. A comparison of the five countries' clean energy diplomacy strategies is made in Table 4.17.

Table 4.16 Comparison of the five countries' renewable energy policies

Five major countries of clean energy development		*National goal of clean energy development*	*Clean energy targets in INDC*	*Regulatory policies*							*Fiscal incentives & public financing policies*			
				FIT	*RPS*	*Net metering/ net billing*	*Green transport regulations*	*Green heating regulations*	*Tradable REC*	*Bidding of clean energy projects*	*Subsidy, loan, rebate*	*Investment/ production tax credit*	*Tax credit for sales/VAT on energy consumption*	*Public investment, preferential loan or special fund*
Developed countries	Germany	0		R			0	0	0	H	0	0		R
	US	R*		·	R*	R*	R	·	·		R	0		R
	Japan	0	0	R					0	H		0		0
Developing countries	India		0	0	R				0	R	0	0		0
	Brazil	0	0			R	0	·		R	0	0		0

Note:
0 means current national policies (including on sub-national level)
• means current sub-national policies (excluding on national level)
R means refined national policies (one or several policies of the same type)
R* means refined sub-national policies (one or several policies of the same type)
H means bidding projects on national level

Source: Originally created by the author based on *Global Report* 2017 released by REN21.

Table 4.17 Main drivers and characteristics of the five countries' clean energy diplomacy

Country	*Driver of clean energy diplomacy*	*Characteristics of clean energy diplomacy*
Germany	Governance regime	Germany tries to enhance its leadership in the new order of climate and energy governance by establishing new international mechanisms and systems in the field of clean energy. This diplomatic strategy – pursuing leadership in governance – is first reflected in the establishment of IRENA. In addition to that, Germany also hopes to advance governance innovation in different areas of clean energy, so as to promote its governance-driven concepts on more international platforms.
US	A mixture of green hegemony and market competition	American's clean energy diplomacy displays periodic changes because of its two-party politics but maintains a certain level of continuity anyway. For example, both President Obama and President Trump emphasize the competition-driven clean energy diplomacy. Sub-national and non-national actors are gaining weight in America's clean energy diplomacy. Local practices of climate governance and the low-carbon standards they implement will largely advance and affect climate negotiations.
Japan	Market competition with special emphasis on energy security	Attaching great importance to world leadership in clean energy technology, Japan tries to enhance its influence in clean energy diplomacy by assisting other countries in green economic development. It is good at improving its abilities of clean energy diplomacy leveraging its influence in international organizations such as IEA/IRENA. It also supports the establishment of both formal and informal networks of clean energy diplomacy.
India	Green economic development with a governance-driven tendency	India seeks leadership in clean energy by creating the ISA and takes advantage of international conferences to enhance its international influence. It also tries to improve its ability of clean energy development and promote industrial upgrade through bilateral and multilateral cooperation. While making continuous efforts to elevate its position in South-South cooperation, India actively works with other developing countries in clean energy exchanges and innovations.
Brazil	Green economic development coupled with climate diplomacy	For Brazil, its clean energy diplomacy and climate diplomacy are closely linked in mutual promotion. Brazil reinforces its leading role in South-South cooperation, especially in BRICS regime, through clean energy development. Its clean energy diplomacy is more development-oriented as it tries to be more competitive in the bioenergy market and lead the formulation of industrial standards through international platforms.

Source: Originally created by the author.

In light of the characteristics of the five countries' clean energy diplomacy, a graph depicting the types of their diplomacy strategy is developed in this chapter. Figure 4.10 displays two dimensions – the governance-driven dimension on the vertical axis and the competition-driven dimension on the lateral axis. The clean energy diplomacy of the US is divided into the Obama period and the Trump period considering its discontinuity caused by two-party politics.

To begin with, on the governance-driven dimension, Germany adopted a clean energy diplomacy that's typically governance-oriented. The country attempted to lead the new order of clean energy governance by establishing the IRENA. In the US, clean energy diplomacy during Obama's term was oriented toward green hegemony, standing at a high level both on the governance-driven and competition-driven dimensions. In that period, the US sought leadership and rules-making power in the global clean energy domain through the creation of Clean Energy Ministerial (CEM). At the same time, it stressed competition in the international clean energy market and ensured its interests by making relevant rules, carrying out the IP "enclosure movement" and implementing protective trade policies. On the competition-driven dimension, the clean energy diplomacy during Trump's term was obviously oriented toward market competition. During that period, the US

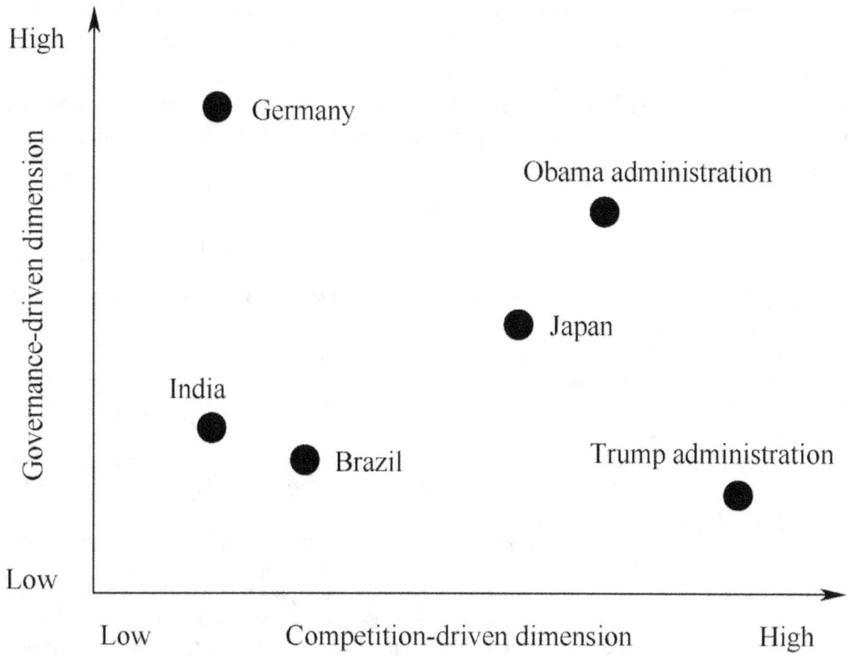

Figure 4.10 Types of the five countries' clean energy diplomacy strategies

Source: Originally created by the author.

government, interested solely in protecting and occupying the clean energy market, resorted to some extreme means to ensure its own interests, including restricting the free flow of technological personnel, restricting the export of high technologies, and stirring up the trade war with China.

Japan comes next after the Obama administration on the competition-driven dimension. It sought global leadership in clean energy technology and market by providing economic assistance worldwide and forging networks of traditional energy diplomacy. It also supported the establishment of formal and informal clean energy partnerships, especially strengthening the interaction with IRENA and IEA, so as to gain more say and rules-making power in global clean energy governance. India and Brazil, developing countries strong in clean energy, have adopted a clean energy diplomacy oriented toward green economy, meaning their capability of green development is enhanced through clean energy diplomacy. India pays special attention to obtaining more financial and technological support through bilateral and multilateral cooperation, but there have been signs of it turning to the governance-driven dimension. For example, it actively promoted the establishment of ISA with the purpose of augmenting its international influence in clean energy development and making better use of international resources to increase energy availability at home. In comparison, Brazil is endowed with better and more clean energy resources. Boasting the highest percentage of renewables, Brazil's clean energy diplomacy and climate diplomacy are closely linked, and it makes full use of its advantages in bioenergy technology to explore the international market. Therefore, its clean energy diplomacy is more competition-driven than India's. Besides, India and Brazil set greater store than developed countries by clean energy cooperation within the BRICS framework and the South-South cooperation framework.

Notes

1 Wang Bo, Li Chaoqian, "Global Status and Trend of Renewable Energy Development", *China Prices*, No. 5, 2018.

2 Martin Seiwert, Matthias Hohensee, Matthias Kamp, "Hot Technology to Protect the Earth", *German News*, No. 1/27, 2007, p. 19.

3 Zhu Tong, Wang Lei, *National Energy Transition*, Hangzhou: Zhejiang University Press, 2015.

4 Wen Jing, "Renewable Energy Development in Germany: Policy Environment, Main Achievements, and Lessons", *Agriculture Engineering Technology: New Energy Industry*, No. 11, 2011.

5 Guo Jiwei, Wang Xiaolu, "Energy Transition in Germany: Experience, Challenges, and Lessons", *Global Science, Technology and Economy Outlook*, No. 1, 2014.

6 The ECG postponed the time of shutting down nuclear power plants (NPPs) from 2022 to the end of their service life, but after Japan's Fukushima nuclear accident in 2011, the German government decided to give up nuclear power altogether and to shut down all 17 NPPs within its borders by 2022.

7 Liu Mingde, Yang Yuhua, "Reference Value of Key Projects in Germany's Energy Transition for China's Energy Policy", *Journal of North China Electric Power University* (Social Sciences), No. 6, 2015.

8 Miranda Schreurs, Li Qing, "On Germany's Energy Transition and Demand for New Governance Modes", *Journal of Nanjing Tech University* (Social Science Edition), No. 2, 2015.
9 Zhu Tong, "Comparative Analysis of Energy Transition in Germany and the US", *International Petroleum Economics*, No. 5, 2016.
10 Zhang Lifeng, Feng Hongxia, "Evolution of Germany's EEG and Lessons for China", *Hebei Law Science*, No. 10, 2017.
11 Du Qun, Liao Jiankai, "Comparative Study of New Energy Law in Germany and Britain and Lessons for China", *Law Review*, No. 6, 2011.
12 Wang Zhongying, Ren Dongming, Qin Haiyan, et al., eds. and trans., *The World Renewable Energy Policies and Regulations Compilation*, Beijing: China Economic Publishing House, 2013.
13 Xu Yao, "Age 3.0 for Renewable Energy – Germany Revises EEG", *China Electric Power News*, June 25, 2016.
14 Sebastian Oberthür, Stephanie Pfahl, Dennis Tänzler, "Renewable Energy Needs International Cooperation", *World Economics and Politics*, No. 4, 2005.
15 G. Wright, "The International Renewable Energy Agency: A Global Voice for the Renewable Energy Era?", *Renewable Energy Law & Poly Review*, November 4, 2012, pp. 251–268.
16 Wang Qingsong, "Study of the Legal System of IRENA", *Social Sciences in Xinjiang*, No. 3, 2015.
17 The establishment of IRENA was prompted by an important window of opportunity in international politics. The oil price in the international market quadrupled in 2004–2008 to hit a new high of almost USD 150 per barrel. One year later, IRENA was established.
18 Johannes Urpelainen, Thijs Van de Graaf, Lin Xuefei, "The International Renewable Energy Agency: A Successful Institutional Innovation?", *Foreign Theoretical Trends*, No. 2, 2017.
19 IRENA, www.irena.org/irenamembership.
20 G. Wright, "The International Renewable Energy Agency: A Global Voice for the Renewable Energy Era?", *Renewable Energy Law & Poly Review*, November 4, 2012, pp. 251–268.
21 United Nations Environment Programme, "'Global Green New Deal': Environmentally-Focused Investment Historic Opportunity for 21st Century Prosperity and Job Creation", *Press Release*, October 22, 2008.
22 Zhang Jianguo, Bai Quan, "G20 Energy Ministers' Meeting: Countries' Priorities for Improved Energy Efficiency", *Energy of China*, No. 11, 2016.
23 Euractiv, "German Minister Urges 'New Deal' on Economy, Environment, Jobs", www.euractiv.com/en/innovation/german-minister-urges-new-deal-economy-environment-jobs/article-159321.
24 Federal Ministry for the Environment, "Recycling and Efficiency Technologies: Made in Germany", March 2008.
25 Federal Ministry of Education and Research, "Federal Government to Open Lead Markets for the Environment", November 12, 2008.
26 In February 2015, the EU announced to build a unified energy market, improve energy efficiency, and guarantee energy security. The Ukraine crisis exposed EU's serious reliance on energy export from Russia, prompting the union to form an energy alliance.
27 Lin Lyu, Wu Yanan, Dong Zhanfeng, et al., "Policy Innovation in Germany and America's Energy Transition and Lessons for China", *Environmental Protection*, No. 19, 2017.
28 Daniel Yergin, "America's New Energy Security: Thanks to New Technology, the U. S. has Become Less Dependent on Petroleum Imports from Unstable Countries", *The Wall Street Journal*, December 12, 2011.

29 White House Press Office, "Press Background Briefing on White House Announcement on Auto Emission and Efficiency Standards", May 18, 2009, www.whitehouse.gov/the_press_office/Background-Briefing-on-Auto-Emissions-and-Efficiency-Standards.
30 The Cleantech Group-Heslin Rothenberg Farley & Mesiti P. C., *Clean Energy Patent Growth Index (CEPGI)*, 2015, www.cleantechintellectualproperty.com; www.cepgi.com.
31 Wang Ruibin, "Shift in America's Climate and Energy Policy and Its Effects", *International Petroleum Economics*, No. 4, 2017.
32 Zheng Yanting, Xu Ligang, "How Developed Countries Promote Green Energy: Experiences and Lessons", *Resources Science*, No. 10, 2012.
33 Xie Xuxuan, Wang Tian, Ren Dongming, "RPS in America: Latest Development and Lessons for China", *Energy of China*, No. 3, 2012.
34 Lin Lyu, Wu Yanan, Dong Zhanfeng, et al., "Policy Innovation in Germany and America's Energy Transition and Lessons for China", *Environmental Protection*, No. 19, 2017.
35 David K. Gattie, "Incorporating Stability and Resilience in Energy Policy for the U. S. Power Sector: Recommendations for the Trump Administration", *The Electricity Journal*, No. 30, 2017, pp. 47–54.
36 It must be noted that the production tax credit (PTC) and investment tax credit (ITC), two federal tax preferences that gave a strong impetus to the development of wind power and solar energy, are still at play and will continue to be till the end of Trump's term because he cannot get enough votes at the Congress to abolish in advance these two Democrat-backed policies.
37 Jeff Goodell, "Obama's Climate Challenge", *Rolling Stone*, Vol. 1175, January 31, 2013, pp. 41–45.
38 Zhou Qi, Fu Suixin, "America's Clean Power Plan and Its Effects on American Energy Industry", *International Petroleum Economics*, No. 10, 2015.
39 Steve Chu announced at the conference that Washington will host the first CEM in 2010, and energy officials from relevant countries will gather and discuss future energy development and climate measures. To make the meeting more influential, representatives of multiple stakeholders – governments, enterprises, and NGOs – were invited, and Steve Chu's speech was broadcast at parallel sessions in Berlin, Beijing, and London.
40 The Mission Innovation Ministerial is a standing high-level international forum/cooperation mechanism tasked with carrying out the Joint Launch Statement released by the heads of state and representatives of members during the UN Climate Change Conference Paris 2015. The meeting aimed to increase the global investment in R&D and innovation of clean energy technology, double government-made or government-guided investment in clean energy R&D in the next five years, and encourage private investment in the shift to clean energy.
41 Trump thought *Paris Agreement* is a punishment on the US because if the US is to meet the carbon cut commitment in it, it will lose about USD 3 trillion in GDP and 6.5 million jobs.
42 China's special fund for the wind power manufacturing sector demands the beneficiaries must use China-made parts and components, which the US deems as breaking WTO rules. This reflects the rising tension between the two countries in clean energy trade. Sewell Chan, "U. S. Says, Chinese Fund Breaks Rules", *New York Times*, December 22, 2010.
43 Zhang Yonghong, Liang Yijian, Wang Tao, et al., "New Energy Cooperation Between China and Africa: Prospects, Challenges and Policies", *Journal of International Economic Cooperation*, No. 2, 2013.
44 Bloomberg Philanthropies, *America's Pledge, Phase 1 Report States, Cities, and Businesses in the United States Are Stepping Up on Climate Action*, November 2017, p. 96, www.bbhub.io/dotorg/sites/28/2017/11/AmericasPledgePhaseOneReportWeb.pdf.

45 Reflecting the concept of multi-party governance involving multiple stakeholders, this partnership network brings together public sector, private sector, and social groups. It organizes and coordinates actions through American Sustainable Business Council (ASBC), Bloomberg Philanthropies, Center for American Progress (CAP), C40 Cities Climate Leadership Group (C40), Environmental Entrepreneurs, International Council for Local Environmental Initiatives (ICLEI), Rocky Mountain Institute, and World Wildlife Fund (WWF).

46 Bloomberg Philanthropies, *America's Pledge, Phase 1 Report States, Cities, and Businesses in the United States Are Stepping Up on Climate Action*, November 2017, pp. 13–14, www.bbhub.io/dotorg/sites/28/2017/11/AmericasPledgePhaseOneReport-Web.pdf.

47 There are 9 states, 239 cities and counties, 1,747 enterprises, and 325 universities.

48 The paradigmatic GHG control mechanism includes developing baseline GHG list, setting emission-cutting goals, making plans, implementing measures, monitoring the progress, and evaluating the results. Lin Xuanchen, Li Yan, Li Changsheng, "California's Experience and Reference in Responding to Climate Change", *Macroeconomic Management*, No. 4, 2017.

49 The website of Global Climate Action Summit, https://globalclimateactionsummit.org/events/2018/9/12/global-climate-action-summit.

50 The advisory committees also involve multiple stakeholders: C40's executive director Mark Watts, executive director of Climate Action Network International Wael Hmaidan, BSR President Aron Cramer, The Climate Group CEO Helen Clarkson, WWF's Global Leader of Climate & Energy Manuel Pulgar-Vidal, and President Mindy Lubber of Ceres, an alliance of American investors and environmental leaders committed to improving corporate environment, society, and governance practices.

51 Feng Zhaokui, "International Energy Landscape in Early 21st Century and Its Medium- and Long-term Changes – Japan's Dilemma in Energy Security and Its Way Out", *Journal of International Security Studies*, No. 6, 2013.

52 Jun Aruma, "Top Runner Program: Japan", *Paper Presented at Workshop on Best Practices in Policies and Measures*, Copenhagen, April 11–13, 2000.

53 Ministry of Economy, Trade and Industry, "Cool Earth-Innovative Energy Technology Program", March 2008, www.iae.or.jp/wp/wp-content/uploads/2014/09/Cool_Earth08_e/CoolEarth_RM.pdf.

54 Li Jun, Wang Xuchun, Li Xiaozhao, "Energy Situation and Use of Renewable Energy in Japan", *Solar Energy*, No. 12, 2017.

55 The life cycle of a nuclear power station is usually 40 years. The nuclear power stations in Japan are mostly built in the 1980s, which means there will be a peak of decommissioning in the 2020s and 2030s. Therefore, power generators need to determine alternative energy sources as soon as possible to make up for the nearly 30% power shortfall stemming from the decommissioning, but that will be difficult given that renewable energy only accounts for 9% of Japan's power mix now.

56 Fan Liuyan, Qu Delin, Wang Haibo, et al., "Japan's New Energy Situation in the Post-Fukushima Era: Changes and Lessons", *Renewable Energy Resources*, No. 5, 2011.

57 There were three reasons why Japan reduced the subsidy for solar power. First, the relaunch of nuclear power made it less motivated to promote renewables. PV accounts for 7% of the latest 2030 energy mix as opposed to nuclear power's 20%–30%. Second, solar power has too high a percentage (higher than 90%) in renewables, and Japan needs to mitigate the fast PV growth to balance different kinds of renewable energies. Third, renewable electricity is too expensive. It is purchased by power companies, but the cost is eventually borne by consumers.

58 Zhang Qian, "Japan Strongly Develops Renewable Energy; Solar Power and Offshore Wind Power Have Obvious Advantages", *China Environment News*, May 1, 2017.

59 Hideo Matsuoka, "Global Environmental Issues and Space Solar Power Generation: Promoting the SPS 2000 Project in Japan", *Technology in Society*, No. 21, 1999, pp. 1–17.

60 Fan Liuyan, Qu Delin, Wang Haibo, et al., "Japan's New Energy Situation in the Post-Fukushima Era: Changes and Lessons", *Sino-Global Energy*, No. 8, 2011.
61 Li Meiyan, Feng Lianyong, "Impacts on and Lessons for Japan's Energy Strategy from Fukushima Nuclear Crisis", *Sino-Global Energy*, No. 3, 2013.
62 Fan Liuyan, Qu Delin, Wang Haibo, et al., "Japan's New Energy Situation in the Post-Fukushima Era: Changes and Lessons", *Sino-Global Energy*, No. 8, 2011.
63 Wang Zhongying, Ren Dongming, Qin Haiyan, et al., ed. and trans., *The World Renewable Energy Policies and Regulations Compilation*, Beijing: China Economic Publishing House, 2013.
64 Li Jun, Wang Xuchun, Li Xiaozhao, "Energy Situation and Use of Renewable Energy in Japan", *Solar Energy*, No. 12, 2017.
65 Zhou Jie, "How Japan Breaks Bottleneck on Development of Renewable Energy", August 13, 2018, http://news.bjx.com.cn/html/20180813/920419-2.shtml.
66 M. H. Moni, "Why Japan's Development Aid Matters Most for Dealing with Global Environmental Problems", *Asia-Pacific Review*, Vol. 16, No. 1, 2009, pp. 8–36.
67 M. A. Schreurs, "Assessing Japan's Role as a Global Environmental Leader", *Policy & Society*, Vol. 23, No. 1, 2004, pp. 88–110.
68 The Japan International Cooperation Agency (JICA) was established in 2003 as the successor to a namesake group founded in 1974. A government agency directly affiliated to the Ministry of Foreign Affairs, JICA carries out international cooperation with the aim of fostering talent, providing gratuitous assistance to developing countries for economic development, and improving social well-being. In the 21st century, the Japanese government has repositioned government development assistance and formed the integrated New JICA to be responsible for that.
69 Gong Na, "NEW JICA and Japan's Soft Power", *Japan Studies*, No. 4, 2012.
70 Maaike Okano Heijmans, "Japan's 'Green' Economic Diplomacy: Environmental and Energy Technology and Foreign Relations", *Pacific Review*, Vol. 25, No. 3, 2012, pp. 339–364.
71 Japanese loans usually come with strings attached. For instance, successful bidders must be Japanese enterprises, and construction materials or machinery and equipment must be purchased from Japan. See Gong Na, "NEW JICA and Japan's Soft Power", *Japan Studies*, No. 4, 2012.
72 "AfDB and Government of Japan Launch Japan-Africa Energy Initiative", July 31, 2017, www.in-en.com/article/html/energy-2262472.shtml.
73 According to the forecast by International Atomic Energy Agency (IAEA), a total of 90 to 370 nuclear reactors will be built on top of the current fleet by 2030. Huang Lijun, "Abe Promotes Energy Diplomacy by Haggling and Peddling", *China Business News*, May 6, 2013.
74 "Innovation Network Corporation Japan: A New Initiative to Drive Next-generation Businesses", *INCJ New Release*, September 27, 2007.
75 Rob Atkinson et al., *Rising Tiger, Sleeping Giant: Asian Nation Set to Dominate the Clean Energy Race by Out-Investing the United States*, Breakthrough Institute and The Information Technology and Innovation Foundation, November 2009.
76 Japan Council for Renewable Energy, www.renewableenergy.jp/council/english/about_jcre.html#section1.
77 Kumar, A. A., and K. Karthick. "Clean Energy Resources Available in India", *International Journal of Environmental Science & Development*, 2011, pp. 1–7.
78 Fu Xueqian, Deng Guangchang, "Renewable Energy in India", *Power Demand Side Management*, No. 1, 2013.
79 Cecilia Tortajada, Udisha Saklani, "Hydropower-based Collaboration in South Asia: The Case of India and Bhutan", *Energy Policy*, No. 43, Vol. 117, 2018, pp. 316–325.
80 He Tingting, "India to Have 16% of Electric Power from Wind Energy in 2030", *Wind Energy*, No. 11, 2017.

81 China National Renewable Energy Center (CNREC), Center for Renewable Energy Development, Energy Research Institute of NDRC, eds., *International Renewable Energy Development Report (2017)*, Beijing: China Environmental Science Press, 2017, p. 143.
82 Fu Xueqian, Deng Guangchang, "Renewable Energy in India", *Power Demand Side Management*, No. 1, 2013.
83 "International Solar Alliance Established in India", March 14, 2018, www.in-en.com/article/html/energy-2266363.shtml.
84 Kumar, A. A., and K. Karthick. "Clean Energy Resources Available in India", *International Journal of Environmental Science & Development*, 2011, pp. 1–7.
85 Wang Zhongying, Ren Dongming, Qin Haiyan et al., *The World Renewable Energy Policies and Regulations Compilation*, Beijing: China Economic Publishing House, 2013, pp. 876–879.
86 China National Renewable Energy Center (CNREC), Center for Renewable Energy Development, Energy Research Institute of NDRC, eds., *International Renewable Energy Development Report (2017)*, Beijing: China Environmental Science Press, 2017, p. 139.
87 Kumar, A. A., and K. Karthick. "Clean Energy Resources Available in India", *International Journal of Environmental Science & Development*, 2011, pp. 1–7.
88 In 2010, some states in India, such as Karnataka and Tamil Nadu, more than accomplished their renewable targets, while other states such as Punjab and Haryana had difficulty meeting their targets, who then could buy Renewable Energy Certificates (RECs) from the state to make up for the gap.
89 Wang Zhongying, Ren Dongming, Qin Haiyan, et al., *The World Renewable Energy Policies and Regulations Compilation*, Beijing: China Economic Publishing House, 2013, pp. 872–876.
90 Wang Zhongying, Ren Dongming, Qin Haiyan, et al., *The World Renewable Energy Policies and Regulations Compilation*, Beijing: China Economic Publishing House, 2013, pp. 863–869.
91 Kari-Anne Isaksen, Kristian Stokke, "Changing Climate Discourse and Politics in India. Climate Change as Challenge and Opportunity for Diplomacy and Development", *Geoforum*, No. 57, 2014, pp. 110–119.
92 International Solar Alliance website, www.isolaralliance.org/.
93 To meet this goal, the bank signed five letters of intent (LOI) on co-financing for solar energy respectively with Hero Future Energy (1.5GW), Greenko Group (10GW), Amplus Solar (1GW), Jakson Group (1GW), and Tata Power Delhi Distribution Ltd. (10MW). These projects will be completed by 2023. The announcement was part of Yes Bank's efforts to support ISA's vision of creating a global solar ecosystem and to help the Indian government achieve the goal of 100GW solar capacity by 2022.
94 "Masayoshi Son Invests USD 200 Billion in Saudi Arabia, India's Solar Energy Plan Meets Setback", March 30, 2018, http://mini.eastday.com/a/180330003858719.html.
95 The six members of Asia-Pacific Partnership on Clean Development and Climate (APP) account for about half of the world's GHG emissions, energy consumption, economic aggregate, and population.
96 According to India's nuclear development plan, it will have 14.6GW nuclear capacity by 2024 and 63GW by 2032. The percentage of nuclear power in its power mix will increase from the current 5.3% to 25% in 2050.
97 Kari-Anne Isaksen, Kristian Stokke, "Changing Climate Discourse and Politics in India. Climate Change as Challenge and Opportunity for Diplomacy and Development", *Geoforum*, No. 57, 2014, pp. 110–119.
98 A series of events in 2017 cast a shadow over China-India relations. First, disgruntled by the "China-Pakistan Economic Corridor", India refused to participate in the first Belt and Road Forum for International Cooperation held in Beijing in May. Then the

Chinese and Indian troops had an intense standoff in Donglang (Doklam) in June–July. But Indian prime minister Modi finally attended the BRICS Summit in Xiamen, China, in September.

99 At the BASIC Ministerial Meeting on Climate Change, the member states emphasized that equity was a basic element that must be considered when reviewing the overall progress and efforts on mitigation, adaptation, and support. The transparency principle must allow flexibility for developing countries in light of their national circumstances and capacities, which should be a guiding principle for the modalities, procedures, and guidelines (MPGs) of the enhanced transparency framework.

100 The Chinese Ministry of Finance signed an agreement with NDB to provide sovereign loans to Fujian, Hunan, and Jiangxi provinces. The RMB 2 billion loan for Fujian Province will all be spent on the Pinghaiwan offshore wind power project in Putian, a clean energy project under Fujian Investment Group, to assist the province in green development.

101 Wang Zhongying, Ren Dongming, Qin Haiyan, et al., *The World Renewable Energy Policies and Regulations Compilation*, Beijing: China Economic Publishing House, 2013, p. 648.

102 In September 2015, Indonesia announced a plan to cut 29% of its GHG emissions by 2030. In October, the Indian government announced its goal to reduce GHG emissions by 33%–35% in 2015–2030 in addition to setting up a fund for coping with climate change at home. The signing of the MOU on new and renewable energies marked an important step toward meeting their emission goals.

103 Brazil has a forest coverage of 57% and timber reserve of 658×10^8 m^3. It produces more than $5{,}500 \times 10^4$ tons of biomass residues from the forestry industry every year.

104 Data released by Brazilian Institute of Geography and Statistics in 2017 showed that Brazil harvested a record-breaking 242 million tons of grains, beans, and oil crops, up 30.3% year-on-year. The output of sugarcane and rice also increased.

105 Li Renfang, Shan Dan, "New Energy Policies in Brazil and Their Effects", *Journal of Southwest University of Science and Technology* (Philosophy and Social Science Edition), No. 5, 2013.

106 Wang Lei, "Clean Energy Development in Brazil: Policies and Practices", *Global Science, Technology and Economy Outlook*, No. 10, 2017.

107 According to the latest OECD-FAO Agricultural Outlook, the output of sugarcane-based ethanol in Brazil is expected to increase to 50 billion liters in 2023 with 11 billion liters exported.

108 The main raw materials used by Brazil to produce biodiesel include soybeans (80%), cotton seeds, castor-oil plants, palm, sunflower, and corn.

109 Wang Lei, "Clean Energy Development in Brazil: Policies and Practices", *Global Science, Technology and Economy Outlook*, No. 10, 2017.

110 Wang Zhongying, Ren Dongming, Qin Haiyan, et al., *The World Renewable Energy Policies and Regulations Compilation*, Beijing: China Economic Publishing House, 2013.

111 Jiang He, "Brazil's Development and Utilization of Renewable Energy: Achievements and Lessons", *Journal of Jiangsu Normal University* (Philosophy and Social Sciences Edition), No. 2, 2017.

112 Li Renfang, Shan Dan, "New Energy Policies in Brazil and Their Effects", *Journal of Southwest University of Science and Technology* (Philosophy and Social Science Edition), No. 5, 2013.

113 Zhou Zhiwei, "Brazil's Participation in BRICS Cooperation: Strategic Considerations and Effects", *Journal of Latin American Studies*, No. 4, 2017.

114 Sybille Roehrkasten, *Global Governance on Renewable Energy: Contrasting the Ideas of the German and the Brazilian Governments*, Wiesbaden: Springer VS, 2015, pp. 171–192.

115 Lars Friberg, "Varieties of Carbon Governance: The Clean Development Mechanism in Brazil – A Success Story Challenged", *The Journal* of *Environment & Development*, Vol. 18, No. 4, 2009, pp. 398–399.
116 Brazil will reduce its GHG emissions by 36.1%–38.9% in 2020 from the current level and promote the development of its renewable energy industry that's highly competitive in the international market.
117 World Resources Institute, *A Closer Look at Brazil's New Climate Plan* (INDC), March 18, 2016, www.wri.org.cn/en/node/41350.
118 Sybille Roehrkasten, *Global Governance on Renewable Energy: Contrasting the Ideas of the German and the Brazilian Governments*, Wiesbaden: Springer VS, 2015, pp. 171–192.
119 Qi Yue, Fan Yichun, "BASIC Four's South-South Cooperation on Climate Change: Policies, Actions and Lessons", *World Environment*, No. 1, 2017.
120 The New Development Bank (NDB) has a capital base of USD 50 billion, equally contributed by each member, and an additional USD 8 billion as contingency fund. The BRICS Contingent Reserve Arrangement has USD 100 billion, with Brazil, India, and Russia each contributing USD 18 billion, China USD 41 billion, and South Africa USD 5 billion.
121 This makes Brazil the third country to commercialize second-generation bioethanol after the US and Italy.
122 Miranda Schreurs, Wang Congcong, "Competition for Leadership in Clean Energy and Environmental Technologies", *Green Leaf*, No. 3, 2012.
123 Zhang Lifeng, Feng Hongxia, "Evolution of Germany's EEG and Lessons for China", *Hebei Law Science*, No. 10, 2017, pp. 119–127.

Part II

China's practices and policies

5 Clean energy diplomacy of China

Path of development and mode of operation

Energy supply is considered the essential "vitamin" for national development. To realize sustainable energy development, it is necessary to strongly develop clean energy sources represented by wind, solar, hydro, biomass, and nuclear, and blaze a sustainable path of energy development that is clean, safe, and efficient. The clean energy industry will be an important pivot to steer international energy cooperation to a new, green, and low-carbon course, and provide inexhaustible momentum for the establishment of a new order of global energy governance.[1] In this chapter, we will analyze China's switch to energy security and its clean energy development against the background of the changing international strategic landscape of energy and climate. On that basis, we will systematically comb through, track, and study the developing trajectory of China's clean energy diplomacy since the 1990s, make a "vertical" comparison of different development stages, and generalize the characteristics in each stage. In the end, we, in reference to the main forms of China's clean energy diplomacy, will analyze the unique path it has taken and the special driving mechanism behind it.

Section 1 China's low-carbon transition and clean development amid the changing international strategic landscape of energy and climate

As the global strategic landscape of energy and climate is changing, the climate and energy policies of different countries are affected to varying degrees. China's energy security outlook has also undergone an important green transition as the country engages in global climate and energy governance. A latecomer in clean energy development, China has continuously advanced the low-carbon switch in energy governance through the adjustment and innovation of domestic clean energy policies.[2] Since 2009, its installed capacity and investment in wind, solar, PV, hydro and new energy vehicles (NEV) have both been leading the world. This has stimulated the rapid development of related green industries in the upstream and downstream of the industry chain. Such effects of driving regional low-carbon development have enabled and empowered China to carry out clean energy diplomacy.

DOI: 10.4324/9781003433903-8

I Evolution of China's stance and perception on global climate governance

How a country responds to climate change and what energy policies it develops is not just a domestic political issue but will bear heavily on other countries. Academics in China and abroad are paying growing attention to China's stance on the climate change regime and what its interests are. The center of the discussions is whether China has kept its climate policies unchanged or not. Some Western scholars used to stress that economic development remained the mainstream narrative of the Chinese leadership and the highest item on its political agenda. Although climate change has drawn more attention, it has not replaced economic development to become the country's most important strategic consideration. Given the vital importance of economic growth for the political regime and social stability, China's stance on climate change has a consistent side.[3] However, more scholars have begun to emphasize the gradual change in China's stance on climate change negotiations – it remains cautious about the reduction of the absolute amount of emissions, but that doesn't mean it still sticks to the original stance. At the very beginning, China was highly defensive regarding the topic of global warming and its mitigation, but now climate change subjects have been included in the strategic goal of green transition set in the 12th and 13th Five-Year Plans. Ever since the early 1990s, its stance on climate change has been evolving while maintaining general consistency.[4] A marked trend is that as China is more deeply engaged in climate change mechanisms, its attitude has gone from conservative and doubtful to more proactive, flexible, and open.

Table 5.1 shows China's changing attitude on climate change – from doubtful and ambivalent to proactive and confident, which reflects the country's change of preferences. When the *Montreal Protocol on Substances that Deplete the Ozone Layer* (The *Montreal Protocol*) was signed, China was just an observer; later it became a signatory of the *United Nations Framework Convention on Climate Change* (UNFCCC); then it was an active leader of G77 when *Kyoto Protocol* was concluded. After that, it was a key member at the Bali Conference and a significant participant in the Copenhagen Climate Change Conference; finally, it was the leader at the Paris Conference. As climate change gained more importance on the political agenda, environmental issues at home, such as environmental pollution and water administration, have received more attention. In particular, the frequent occurrence of extreme environmental events in recent years, such as the massive PM2.5 pollution in northern China, has further prompted the blending of domestic environmental issues with international climate governance. The Chinese government has realized that including climate change in the national master plan for social and economic development is conducive to realizing the low-carbon shift of economic structure and building an environment-friendly society.

To be specific, the negotiations on *Montreal Protocol* in 1987, which revolved around ozone-depleting substances, indicated that the international community began to pay attention to atmospheric and environmental issues. Although China participated in the negotiations, it was just an observer and played no part in concluding the protocol.[7] The Chinese government didn't attach enough importance to

Table 5.1 China's stance on climate negotiations – consistency and change

Topic	1991	1997	2001	2005	2007	2009	2011	2012	2013	2014	2015	2016
Does it require developed countries to provide financial and technological assistance?	Yes	Yes	Yes	Yes	Yes	Yes	Yes	Yes	Yes	Yes	Yes	Yes
Does it mention promoting the development of renewable energy?	No	Unclear information	Yes	Yes	Yes	Yes	Yes	Yes	Yes	Yes	Yes	Yes
Does it support CDM?	No	Hesitant	Yes	Yes[5]	Yes	Yes	Yes	Yes	Yes	Yes	Yes	Yes
Does it make a (voluntary) commitment to reducing GHG emissions?	No	No	No	No	Yes[6]	Yes	Yes	Yes	Yes	Yes	Yes	Yes
Does it have a national climate change plan?	No	No	No	Under planning	Yes	Yes	Yes	Yes	Yes	Yes	Yes	Yes
Does it have a quantitative target of carbon intensity reduction?	No	No	No	No	No	No	Yes	Yes	Yes	Yes	Yes	Yes
Does it have a national-level legal framework on climate change?	No	No	No	No	No	Under planning	Under preparation	Draft	Soliciting opinions	Soliciting opinions	Soliciting opinions	Soliciting opinions

(*Continued*)

Table 5.1 (Continued)

Topic	*1991*	*1997*	*2001*	*2005*	*2007*	*2009*	*2011*	*2012*	*2013*	*2014*	*2015*	*2016*
Is it ready to accept legally binding commitments?	No	No	No	No	No	No	Under planning	Yes	Yes	Yes	Yes	Yes
Does it concede to the shift from dual-track to single-track negotiations?	No	No	No	No	Unclear information	Yes	Yes	Yes	Yes	Yes	Yes	Yes
Does it agree with the system of carbon tax or carbon trade?	No	No	No	No	No	To be discussed	Under designing	Yes	Yes	Yes	Yes	Yes
Does it express the wish to play a leading role in climate governance?	No	No	No	No	No	No	No	No	No	Initial intention	Yes	Yes
Does it formally set the time for carbon peaking (2030 or earlier)?	No	No	No	No	No	No	No	Unclear information	Unclear attitude	Yes	Yes	Yes

Source: Data of 2007–2016 are collected by the author; data of 1991–2005 are from Zhang Haibin (2006).

the atmospheric issue at the time either, which was the reason for insufficient input in scientific research, inadequate tech support, and insufficient supply of monitoring data. China joined the climate change mechanism in the early 1990s for diplomatic purposes – to break the diplomatic isolation of the West and deal with international issues in cooperation with other developing countries. At the early stage of participating in the climate change mechanism, it didn't understand what climate change really meant for its energy regulation and economic development. At the third session of the Conference of the Parties (COP 3) in 1997, the *Tokyo Protocol*, the first international treaty that imposed legally binding obligations of GHG emission reduction on developed countries, was concluded, which was signed by China in May 1998. Compared with when it participated in the UNFCCC negotiations and approved it, China was more conservative and prudent now because its leaders began to realize how climate change might affect the country's structure of energy consumption and economic development.

In this process, China increasingly realized the importance of actively participating in international climate cooperation and making good use of financial and technological assistance both inside and outside the UN framework. International investments and best managerial practices could also help with its transition toward a low-carbon economy. Because of the energy-intensive development model and lagging innovation in clean energy technology, China's high-speed economic development in the past 30 years has caused serious environmental pollution in the country.[8] By taking part in bilateral and multilateral climate projects, it could learn best practices and experience in the world and obtain more financial and technological support for its sustainable development, which was good for changing its economic development model. Participating in international cooperation on climate change could also establish China's image as an environmentally responsible country and push for the achievement of its diplomatic targets. For instance, the development of large-scale clean energy projects in China in the early stage was largely driven by the Clean Development Mechanism (CDM) in the UN framework of climate negotiations.

At first, China had doubts and reservations about the three flexible mechanisms under *Kyoto Protocol* for fear that developed countries would shirk their historical responsibilities and induce developing countries to join the emission reduction.[9] However, after the Bonn Climate Change Conference in 1999 further explained the flexible mechanisms, China began to change its attitude in 2001, realizing that CDM could provide investment and technology for emission-cutting projects in developing countries, thus creating opportunities for the development of clean energy.[10] It ratified *Kyoto Protocol* and launched the first CDM project in 2002, which has since been fast-tracked, propelling China to beat India and Brazil in 2006 as the country hosting the largest number of CDM projects, mostly in renewables. By June 2014, China topped the world by housing more than 60% of CDM projects. In the meantime, the CDM capacity building programs in China sponsored by United Nations Development Programme (UNDP) and United Nations Fund (UNF) have made the projects more standardized through policy research, capacity training, and project demonstration. Moreover, the China Renewable Energy Development

Project (REDP) and China-Renewable Energy Scale-up Program (CRESP) – external incentive mechanisms within the UN framework – also stimulated the scale-up of clean energy development in China in the early stage and improved its governance capability in the field.

Ever since joining the international climate change regime in the early 1990s, China has faced immense challenges and opportunities. Especially after it became the largest GHG emitter in 2007, the country has been considered a key participant in global climate dialogue[11] and is facing mounting pressure from the international community demanding it make legally binding commitments to reducing GHG emissions. As the subject of climate change finds its way to international systems and bilateral/multilateral cooperation, the climate change regime is putting more limitations on national behaviors. Unprecedented pressure concerning the country's reputation forces Chinese leaders to take more seriously their voluntary emission reduction commitments. The Bali Conference held in December 2007 marked the beginning of the international community's efforts to officially work out a post-Kyoto framework, and the formulation of the Bali Roadmap paved the way for the negotiations toward that goal. The Bali Conference was such a significant watershed in climate negotiations because, for the first time, developing countries sat at the negotiating table and expressed willingness to discuss their emission reductions (voluntary commitments).

Changing its tough stance since 1997, China acted in a more proactive and flexible way during the Bali climate negotiations. It was the first time that China and other developing countries agreed to "discuss voluntary mitigation actions suitable for each country in the context of sustainable development, supported and enabled by technology, financing, and capacity-building, in a measurable, reportable and verifiable manner". For instance, although China still insisted on the principle of "common but differentiated responsibilities" and objected taking any legal accountability for quantifiable emission reductions, Chinese leaders considered using voluntary targets (instead of absolute obligations) to demonstrate its compliance, at least to some extent, to the climate change regime. That also in a way eased the pressure from the international community. What's worth special attention is that China's National Development and Reform Commission (NDRC), the leading government department participating in climate change negotiations, released the *National Plan on Climate Change* in June 2007. As the first policy initiative on global warming released by China, the plan expounded on its stance on international climate cooperation, including the guidelines, principles, and targets of climate response.

Compared with previous climate negotiations, the biggest change at the 2009 Copenhagen Conference was that it questioned the dual-track approach to negotiation and exerted more pressure on emerging developing countries. China's engagement in the conference drew special attention. As Hodgson said, if China was an observer to the *Montreal Protocol* negotiations and a participant in the *Kyoto Protocol* negotiations, it had become a main actor in the *Copenhagen Accord*.[12] In Copenhagen, China announced its voluntary, quantified climate action targets for the first time – to reduce its CO_2 emission per unit GDP (carbon intensity) by 40%–45% in 2020 from the 2005 level and increase the percentage of nonfossil fuels in the energy mix to 15% by then. Yet this voluntary target was still considered to fall short of the expectations of the Copenhagen Conference. British Secretary of State for Energy and Climate Change Ed Miliband published an article in *The Guardian*, dated December 20, 2009, accusing China of hijacking the negotiations at Copenhagen, which exposed China to a crisis.[13]

Learning a lesson from the setback at Copenhagen in 2009, the Cancun Conference in 2010 worked hard to save the multilateral climate negotiation, and the Durban Conference in 2011 was an important turning point as the establishment of the Durban Platform for Enhanced Action (ADP) cleared the way for planning for the post-Kyoto era. At the Durban Conference, Xie Zhenhua, then deputy director of NDRC and head of the Chinese delegation, announced China's decision to accept, conditionally, legally binding emission reduction arrangements. It was the first time that China was willing to bear legally binding responsibilities that were commensurate with its economic development level and capacity. The announcement by Xie was considered a sign of China's positive attitude toward participating in global negotiations and making legally binding emission reduction plans.

After the 2009 Copenhagen Conference, China changed its conservative attitude toward carbon tax, carbon budget, and carbon trade.[14] Given the global trend of developing carbon markets, especially inspired by the EU Emissions Trading System (EU ETS) and the CDM projects, NDRC released the *Notice of Piloting Carbon Trade* in October 2011 and kicked off a batch of municipal and provincial-level pilot projects. According to the plan, during the 12th Five-Year Plan Period, or by 2015, the "emission restriction, trading and licensing" mechanism would be introduced nationwide. Energy-related emission in China mostly comes from coal (over 80%). A total of 77GW thermal power was shut down during the 11th Five-Year Plan period (2005–2010), to be followed by another 20GW in the 12th Five-Year Plan period (2010–2015). In 2014, coal consumption shrank for the first time in decades, and so did CO_2 emission, also for the first time since 1999. According to studies by IEA, energy-related carbon emissions in China reached 8.6 billion tons in 2014, the largest amount in the world, but that was less than in previous years, indicating a delinking trend between economic growth and emission increase – although they were not completely delinked yet. China tended to rely on market-oriented measures to combine green growth with climate mitigation and take climate change as an opportunity to promote economic restructuring. The global competition in low-carbon technology is another factor pushing climate change negotiations. Boyd said, "The idea of low-carbon leadership has reframed China's global role and supported China's emergence at the forefront of low-carbon markets."[15] The Chinese government is glad to see China with outstanding competitiveness and leadership in the global market of low-carbon energy.[16] Green development was made one of the main strategies in the next five-year plan at the fifth plenary session of the 18th CPC Central Committee in 2015. The *Suggestions of the CPC Central Committee on Formulating the 13th Five-Year Plan for National Economic and Social Development* released in November that year pledged that China will actively participate in global climate change negotiations and deliver its emission commitments on the principle of fairness and respective capabilities.

With its growing green strengths, China stepped up efforts on climate diplomacy. It not only repeatedly declared its positive attitude toward global climate actions on international occasions but also demonstrated its resolve to take a path of green, low-carbon, and circular development characterized by the transition in growth model, energy mix, and consumption model. When Premier Li Keqiang met with the French president in Paris in 2015, he said the world's largest GHG emitter would strive to peak its CO_2 emissions by 2030. In June that year, the Chinese government submitted its intended nationally determined contributions (INDC) to the UNFCCC secretariat, pledging to lower CO_2 emissions per unit of GDP by 60–65% from 2005 levels by 2030. The INDC also reaffirmed the previous goal of increasing the share of renewable energy in the primary energy supply to around 20% by 2030. During President Xi Jinping's state visit to the US in September 2015, leaders of the two countries proposed a joint vision on the outcomes of the upcoming Paris Conference and announced their domestic policy measures and cooperation initiatives in response to climate change as well as important progress on funding. This set the stage for a successful Paris Conference that year. The signing of the *Paris Agreement* at the end of 2015 marked the inking of a global commitment to responding to climate change and sent a strong signal that the world needed to quickly switch to a low-carbon and climate-adaptive economy.[17]

In March 2016, the *U.S.-China Joint Presidential Statement on Climate Change* was signed, with which the two countries pledged to promote the *Kigali Amendment to the Montreal Protocol on Substances that Deplete the Ozone Layer* that complied with the "Dubai route" and the global market measures adopted by the Congress of the International Civil Aviation Organization (ICAO) in response to GHG emission from international aviation. To expedite innovation and application of clean energy, the two sides would make joint efforts to deliver the objectives of the Mission Innovation initiative announced at the Paris Conference. When the G20 Summit kicked off in Hangzhou in September 2016, China, the rotating chair hosting the summit for the first time, released a host of positive signals to promote sustainable global development, such as climate response and the development of green finance and clean energy. During the summit, China and the US jointly announced the completion of their domestic procedures for ratifying the *Paris Agreement*, which officially took effect on November 4, demonstrating strong leadership in pushing the global climate response. At the Marrakech Conference in December, Special Envoy of China Xie Zhenhua stressed that the global trend of green development and low-carbon transformation wouldn't change despite recent uncertainties to multilateral climate actions caused by new changes in the international situation (e.g., the election of US President Trump). He added that China, leveraging on its influence, would continue to play a positive and constructive role when participating in and leading the climate negotiations.

Global climate governance has come to a new stage of "dual transition" – the transition of cooperation landscape and emission reduction model. This presents new opportunities and challenges to China. Regarding the transition of the emission reduction model, on the one hand, China has done a good job delivering its INDC with improved methodology and transparency. On the other hand, while meeting its own targets, China should also help other countries meet theirs, which requires refining the emission reduction model, and implementing evaluation, supervision, and other institutional arrangements through example.[18] Regarding the transition of the cooperation landscape, for one thing, the international community has expectations for China, and the achievements of global climate governance have in a way contributed to the Belt and Road Initiative. For another, China needs to take international expectations with a sober mind and blaze out a path with Chinese characteristics amid the complex international environment, to avoid straining itself and undermining its efforts to restructure the domestic economy and deeply engage in global governance. At the Bonn Conference in 2017, China put forth a plan to bridge divergences among the parties and pushed the early conclusion of implementation rules of the *Paris Agreement*. It also released the *China Renewable Energy Outlook* at the conference, in which it analyzed the development status and future plan for renewable energy, and showcased its confidence to shift to green, low-carbon development at home and resolve to lead clean development internationally. China is playing out its unique helmsmanship in international climate governance.

In promoting multilateral cooperation, China convened the 25th BASIC Ministerial Meeting on Climate Change during the Bonn Conference, and the participating countries issued a joint statement. The ministers underlined BASIC's highest political commitment to the full, effective, and sustained implementation of the Convention, its *Kyoto Protocol*, and the *Paris Agreement* in all their aspects. They also highlighted BASIC's willingness to work together with all parties and stakeholders to promote global low greenhouse gas emissions and climate-resilient and sustainable development. The unprecedented unity within BASIC was a strong driving force of international climate negotiations.[19] While the US became more passive about climate action, China, in addition to uniting with BASIC countries, also paid close attention to cooperation with the EU and made major headway there. In light of new developments in international climate governance and changes within the EU, China should strengthen dialogue with it in a bid to maintain and uplift their cooperation. The *EU-China Joint Statement on Climate Change* was released in 2015, followed by *EU-China Roadmap on Energy Cooperation* in 2016 and the *Leaders' Statement on Climate Change and Clean Energy* in 2018. These three documents showed that the two sides shared important, strategic interests in climate change and clean energy, and that only intensified that political, technological, economic, and scientific cooperation could carry forward the global transformation toward a resource-intensive and climate-resilient economy and society. Regarding the development of clean energy, in particular, China and the EU can carry out pragmatic cooperation in a range of areas, including power generation, high-efficiency and large-scale co-generation plants, energy regulations, and market design. They have already reached a consensus on enhancing the interconnectivity of energy infrastructure and boosting the multilateral energy cooperation mechanisms represented by the G20 and CEM.[20] They have also jointly witnessed the signing of six cooperation documents, including the *Memorandum of Understanding on Circular Economy Cooperation* and the *MOU to Enhance Cooperation on Emission Trading*.

II Fast rise of clean energy in China

With a vast territory, China abounds in clean energy resources, with an enormous reserve of hydro, wind (onshore and offshore), solar (solar-thermal and PV), biomass, geothermal, and marine energy (tidal energy) (Table 5.2), but its mass development of clean energy started quite late. Compared with Western pioneers, China is a latecomer that, however, has overtaken those "early birds" in ten years by studying and innovating renewable policies.

Now it is a global leader in this field, ranking first in terms of cumulative installed capacity, equipment manufacturing, green investment, and market size.

China has a typical coal-dominated energy supply structure, with coal accounting for a steady 70% of total energy consumption. In the 1990s, only traditional hydropower contributed to the power supply, whereas wind, solar, and nuclear were basically a blank. From a historical point of view, the nearly 30 years from 1990 have witnessed China's clean energy growing from scratch at an ever higher rate (Table 5.3). Regarding installed capacity, the amount of clean energy at the end of 2016 stood at 591.87GW, 16 times the amount at the end of 1990 (36.05GW, mainly hydropower); regarding annual electricity output, 1,705.42TWh electricity was generated from clean energy in 2016, 13 times the output in 1990 (126.35TWh).[21] In the 21st century, clean energy in China has increased year by year, driven by the launch of large-scale wind and solar projects, and it got on the fast track, especially after the *Renewable Energy Law* was enacted in 2005. Following the enactment of the *Amendment to the Renewable Energy Law* in 2009, the State Council released the *Decisions on Accelerating the Cultivation and Development of Strategic Emerging Industries* in 2010, which affirmed renewable energy as an important strategic industry, and emphasized promoting its grid access and transmission through the quota system. As the Chinese economy enters the new normal, China has been taking faster steps to adjust its energy mix, and has come to a new stage when quantitative expansion takes the back seat after enhanced quality and efficiency. A pressing task facing the country is earnestly implementing a revolution of energy production and consumption, quickening the adjustment of the fossil-dominant energy mix, and further scaling up the development and use of clean energy.

In 2016, NDRC and National Energy Administration (NEA) issued the *13th Five-Year Plan for Energy Development*, *Energy Production and Consumption Revolution Strategy (2016–2030)*, and the *13th Five-Year Plan for Renewable Energy Development*. The documents reaffirmed the green and low-carbon direction, set phased targets for nonfossil energy development, and pledged to meet half the energy demand with nonfossil energy, including renewables, by the mid-21st century.

According to data in *China Renewable Energy Outlook 2017*, China used 4.36 billion tons of standard coal in 2016, 65% of which was coal, 21% petroleum, 6% natural gas, 13% nonfossil energy, and 11% renewables. In the electric power sector, renewables contributed 26% of the total electricity output in 2016 and nonfossil energy 29.6%, while 67% was from coal and 3% from natural gas. On the whole, coal remains the backbone of China's energy consumption, while renewables only

Table 5.2 Renewable energy reserve in China

		Installed capacity (GW)	Annual output (TWh)	
Hydro	Theoretical reserve	694.40	6082.9	
	Technically exploitable	541.64	2474.0	
	Economically exploitable	401.80	1753.4	
	Exploitable small hydropower (<50MW)	128.03	535.0	
		Available	Usable	
Biomass	Crop straw	546 Mt	138 Mt	69 Mtce
	Timber residue	125 Mt	125 Mt	63 Mtce
	Animal dung	239 Mt	239 Mt	107 Mtce
	Industrial organic waste	50 billion m^3 biogas	50 billion m^3 biogas	39 Mtce
	Urban organic waste	150 Mt	150 Mt	2 Mtce
Solar	Resources	Usable capacity		
	1,700 billion TCE	2,200GW/a		
Wind		Potential capacity (GW)	Technically exploitable (GW)	
	Onshore Height from ground/m			
	50	2,560	2,050	
	70	3,050	2,570	
	100	3,920	3,370	
	Offshore	Wind power density > $400W/m^2$	> $300W/m^2$	
	< 50km from the coast	230	380	
	< 20km	70	140	
	5–25m underwater	90	190	
Geothermal	Medium/low-temperature		2,210 Mtce	
	Exploitable		282 Mtce	
	Exploitable geothermal fluid		$372m^3/a$	
	Usable shallow geothermal energy in 31 provincial capitals nationwide		467 Mtce	
Marine energy	Offshore reserve (GW)		1,495	
	Including			
	Tidal energy		22	
	Wave energy		13	
	Tidal current energy		14	
	Salinity gradient energy		125	
	Temperature-difference energy		1,321	

Sources: China Renewable Energy Industry Development Report, compiled by China National Renewable Energy Center and Center for Renewable Energy Development of NDRC Energy Research Institute, China Economic Publishing House, 2017.

Table 5.3 Installed capacity and electricity output of different types of clean energy in China (1990–2016)

	1990	*2000*	*2010*	*2012*	*2013*	*2014*	*2015*	*2016*
Year-end capacity/GW	137.89	319.32	966.41	1146.76	1257.68	1370.18	1508.28	1645.75
Inc. Hydro	36.05	79.35	216.06	249.47	280.44	304.86	319.37	332.11
Thermal	101.84	237.54	709.67	819.68	870.09	923.63	990.21	1053.88
Nuclear	–	2.10	10.82	12.57	14.66	20.08	26.08	33.64
Wind		0.35	44.7	75.3	91.4	114.8	145.4	168.7
Electricity output/TWh	621.32	1386.5	4207.2	4937.8	5397.59	5649.58	5810.58	6142.49
Inc. Hydro	126.35	243.1	722.2	860.9	911.64	1064.34	1126.42	1193.07
Thermal	494.97	1107.9	3331.9	3910.8	4235.87	4233.73	4242.04	4437.07
Nuclear	–	16.7	73.9	98.3	111.5	132.54	170.79	213.29
Wind			72.2	124.3	159.8	200.3	251.2	294.4

Sources: National Bureau of Statistics, China Electricity Council.

make up a small part.[22] Although clean energy has grown at a high speed in the past decade, China's energy mix is still carbon-dominated, a long way from its goal of sustainable and green energy development that is clean, efficient, and safe. According to the *13th Five-Year Plan for Renewable Energy Development*, the amount of newly installed clean energy capacity will reach 210GW in 2016–2020, including 60GW hydro, 80GW wind, and 70GW solar, with an estimated investment of RMB 2.5 trillion in renewables.

On the global level, China overtook Germany and the US to be the country with the largest amount of clean energy capacity in 2010, with a world-leading growth rate in wind and PV in particular. At the end of 2014, it had 476.6GW clean energy capacity, accounting for 37% worldwide from 28% in 2008. In comparison, the percentage of the US contracted from 14% to 11% in the same period, with only 1/4 of China's annual production capacity. China's current investment in the clean energy industry is more than that of the US and Europe combined.[23] All these have laid a solid foundation for its clean energy diplomacy.

IEA's *Renewables 2017* showed that in 2016, nearly 165GW renewable capacity was installed across the world, accounting for about 2/3 of the world's new capacity thanks to the fast-rising PV market as global PV capacity increased by 50%, over half contributed by China. IEA explained that China's contribution to over 2/5 of global renewable additions was largely credited to its resolve to address air pollution and its efforts to achieve the clean energy targets set in the 13th Five-Year Plan. In terms of PV, China develops much faster than the world average and has achieved its 2020 goals three years ahead of schedule. It has also grown into a global leader in biomass-based power generation and heating as well as electric vehicles (EV). BP's *Statistical Review of World Energy 2018* showed that China spearheaded the global consumption of renewable energy in

Table 5.4 Renewable energy development in China (2000–2016)

Unit	*2000*	*2005*	*2010*	*2013*	*2014*	*2015*	*2016*
Hydro/GW	79.4	117.4	213.4	280.0	301.8	319.4	332.1
TWh	243.1	397.0	722.2	911.6	1064.3	1126.4	1193.4
Mtce	88.2	136.2	225.3	276.2	319.3	335.6	352.1
Inc. Small hydro/GW	24.8	38.5	59.0	68.0	70.0	75.0	77.9
TWh	80.0	120.9	202.3	227.3	233.7	240.0	268.2
Mtce	29.0	41.5	63.1	68.9	70.1	71.5	79.1
Solar/TCE	3.1	9.6	22.6	44.5	55.6	64.6	75.1
PV/10MW	1.8	7.0	122.0	1745.0	2805.0	4318.0	7742.0
100GWh	0.19	0.74	12.9	238.8	250.0	392.0	662.0
Mtce	0.01	0.03	0.40	7.24	7.50	11.64	19.53
Water heater/10,000m^2	2600	8000	18500	31000	41400	44200	46400
Mtce	3.1	9.6	22.2	37.2	48.1	53.0	55.6
Wind/GW	0.34	1.22	44.78	91.41	114.61	145.4	168.7
TWh	0.5	2.0	72.2	159.8	200.3	251.2	294.4
Mtce	0.2	0.7	22.5	48.4	60.1	74.6	86.8
Rural biogas/100 million m^3	23	86	145	158	160	168	174
Mtce	1.6	6.1	10.4	11.3	11.4	12.0	12.4
Biomass and garbage-to-power/GW	0.8	2.0	6.7	9.0	9.8	16.0	17.7
TWh	3.5	8.7	29.0	38.3	41.9	68.9	92.7
Mtce	1.3	3.0	9.0	11.6	12.6	20.4	27.3
Geothermal/Mtce	0.7	1.2	6.7	14.4	17.6	24.1	31.3
Total	86.3	197.8	284.3	409.1	476.6	491.1	580.5

Source: National Bureau of Statistics; *China Energy Statistical Yearbook 2016*; NDRC; NEA; Ministry of Water Resources; Ministry of Agriculture; Ministry of Housing and Urban-Rural Development; Ministry of Land and Resources; China Electricity Council; China Renewable Energy Society; China Association of Rural Energy Industry; China Energy Saving Association; China Wind Energy Association; National Geothermal Energy Center.

2017 by contributing 36% of the growth. It is playing a vital role in the low-carbon transition of the world and will remain an indisputable leader in renewables growth for the next five years. BP's report also forecast China to account for roughly 36% of global hydropower, 40% of wind power, and 36% of solar power in 2015–2021.

In addition to topping the world in renewable capacity and green energy investment, China also boasts at least five world-leading technologies, namely, ultra-high-voltage (UHV) power transmission, NEV, ultra-supercritical (USC) thermal power generation, nuclear power, and supercomputer. In 2017, it built 15 UHV power transmission lines, setting the stage for energy networking and the transmission of clean power over a long distance. In 2016, China sold 409,000 pure EVs with a car parc of 740,000, and sold 98,000 hybrid cars with a car parc of 350,000. The total sales volume of 507,000 NEVs, more than America's 446,000, made China the largest NEV market. USC thermal power generation technology

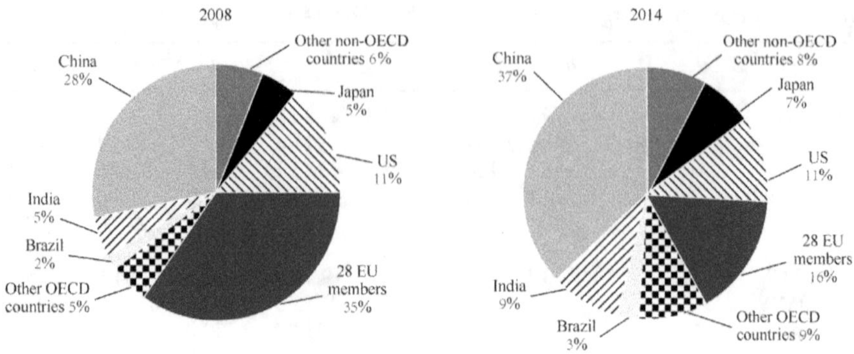

Figure 5.1 Percentage of annual non-hydro renewable capacity worldwide (2008/2014)

Sources: IEA, Medium-Term Renewable Energy Market Report, 2016.

is crucial for the clean utilization of coal. In 2016, China had 100 USC units larger than 1GW in operation, more than the combined capacity of the rest of the world. It also made major headway in coal-water-mixture (CWM), circulating fluidized bed boiler (CFB), and Integrated Gasification Combined Cycle (IGCC) technologies.

In terms of nuclear power, in 2016, China had 36 nuclear units in operation with a total capacity of 33.5GW; it also had 20 units under construction with a total capacity of 23.1GW, more than America's five totaling 6.2GW. As to supercomputers, the China-developed "Sunway Taihu Light" supercomputer is capable of 93 petaflops, or quadrillion calculations per second. It topped the TOP 500 list of supercomputers released on September 14, 2017, repeating the feat for the fourth consecutive year, followed by China's Tianhe-2 in the second position and supercomputers from Switzerland, Japan, and the US in the following three spots. Being able to simulate highly complicated systems and processes by running meticulous models, supercomputers can facilitate breakthroughs in a series of domains, from energy efficiency to wind and PV to auto technology.[24]

As shown in Table 5.5, by the end of 2017, China topped the world in terms of investment in hydropower, PV, solar-thermal, and renewables, with a critical structural influence on the whole clean energy development system. The rapid development of clean energy laid a solid foundation for China's clean energy diplomacy. Especially after 2013, clean energy diplomacy has been increasingly integrated with China's traditional energy diplomacy, neighborhood diplomacy, and the forging of a new-model major-country relationship. It is also merged into various multilateral cooperation platforms, serving as an important instrument with which China actively participates in global governance on multiple dimensions and advances the BRI on all fronts.

Section 2 Evolution of China's clean energy diplomacy

Major structural changes in the international system are usually caused by changes in the global energy and power structure. Renewable energy, dominant in the

Table 5.5 Top five countries in renewable investment/net capacity/output, 2017

Ranking	*1*	*2*	*3*	*4*	*5*
Investment in renewables and fuels (exc. hydropower larger than 50MW)	China	US	Japan	India	Germany
Percentage of renewables and fuels investment in unit GDP	Marshall Islands	Rwanda	Solomon Islands	Guinea-Bissau	Serbia
Geothermal capacity	Indonesia	Turkey	Chile	Iceland	Honduras
Hydropower capacity	China	Brazil	India	Angola	Turkey
PV capacity	China	US	India	Japan	Turkey
Concentrated solar power (CSP) capacity	South Africa	–	–	–	–
Wind power capacity	China	US	Germany	UK	India
Solar-thermal capacity	China	Turkey	India	Brazil	US
Biodiesel products	US	Brazil	Germany	Argentina	Indonesia
Ethanol products	US	Brazil	China	Canada	Thailand

Sources: REN21 Global Report 2018.

next-generation energy system, is getting increasingly important in the struggle for dominance in the future strategic energy and climate landscape.[25] The evolving landscape has already pushed the development of a low-carbon economy amidst the international transition and put more low-carbon restrictions on national development. In this process, countries that seize the low-carbon initiative are sure to be better positioned. Generally speaking, the low-carbon transition of international order should be based on a green energy mix, especially the development of clean energy. China started quite late in this field, almost ten years later than the Western pioneers. However, it has established systematic renewable energy policies almost from scratch, providing a fundamental guarantee for the high-speed development of green industries. In the 21st century, its massive clean energy development has also registered remarkable progress, during which its clean energy diplomacy has evolved through five stages.

I. Stage of gestation (1978–1990)

In the first stage of gestation, there was basically no domestic policy on renewables, and the renewable projects aimed to provide energy for the countryside were too scattered and of a small scale. Internationally, China began to participate in the global governance on climate change and sustainable development to further merge into the international community.

(I) Domestically: a blank of renewable energy policy

After reform and opening up was launched in 1978, renewable energy (especially small-scale biogas, solar cooker, and solar water heater) was mainly considered a supplement to energy supply in rural areas. The Ministry of Agriculture played a vital part in advancing the demonstration and use of renewables in the countryside. For instance, in 1979, the fourth plenary session of the 11th CPC Central Committee released the decision on accelerating agricultural development, which underlined the importance of promoting biogas to meet rural energy demand. In 1986, the former National Economic Committee issued the *Opinions on Strengthening Energy Development in Rural Areas*, which asked all provinces and autonomous regions to work out their own long-term plan to achieve that goal. The measures included "promoting the use of new-type energy-saving cookers, biogas, forestry resources, small-scale hydropower and thermal power, straw, solar cooker, wind power, and geothermal energy".[26] In this stage, fiscal input in the field mainly went to promoting traditional, small-scale renewable projects. During the 7th Five-Year Plan, for example, the Ministry of Finance allocated RMB 3 million loans to support rural energy development, focused on popularizing small-scale biogas and solar cookers. However, there was basically no policy or regulation on renewable energy development at this stage, and the energy itself was regarded more as a supplement to rural energy supply than as an important alternative to traditional energy sources.

Nevertheless, nongovernment actors such as renewable energy societies and communities emerged in this stage. In October 1980, the China Biogas Society was founded and held the first National Rural Energy Seminar in Beijing. In 1983, the society issued the national standards on domestic biogas cookers. In June 1992, the China Association of Rural Energy Industry was formed, and it gave a strong impetus to the wider use of biogas in rural areas. In the 1980s, China launched a large number of small wind power projects (mostly off-grid) to ensure the supply of energy and electricity in remote areas. In 1984, the Chinese Society for Electrical Engineering formed a Wind Energy Committee, which issued the national standards for small wind turbine generator sets in 1989.

From 1978 to 1992, the solar water heater industry developed quickly. After the Chinese Solar Energy Society was formed in 1979, more attention was paid to the R&D of solar water heaters. During the 6th Five-Year Plan period (1981–1985), renewable technology was included in the national R&D plan for the first time, though the plan was only granted RMB 3 million. During the 7th Five-Year Plan period, the State Scientific and Technological Commission and the Ministry of Agriculture jointly advanced the commercialization and application of solar power in rural areas. In 1987, the Beijing Solar Energy Research Institute introduced from Canada a production line of copper-aluminum composite panels and successfully developed multifunction energy-saving solar panels, injecting a strong impetus into the promotion of solar water heaters.[27]

In sum, renewable energy development in this stage was rather dispersive and of a small scale, with the main purpose of promoting rural energy access under the lead of the Ministry of Agriculture. Therefore, there was no special policy or regulation on the subject then, let alone promoting large-scale renewable projects. The highlight of this stage was the rapid development and spread of solar water heaters driven by private entities, such as renewable energy associations, research institutes, and universities, who played a positive role in the commercialization of solar water heaters (even without national grant or loan). Due to the lack of favorable policies and government support, there were no large-scale renewable projects at this stage.

(II) Internationally: participation in global governance on climate change and sustainable development

In March 1980, at the initiation of the United Nations Environment Programme (UNEP), the International Union for Conservation of Nature and Natural Resources (IUCN), and World Wildlife Fund (WWF), officials and scientists from multiple countries jointly formulated the *World Conservation Strategy: Living Resources Conservation for Sustainable Development*. The document officially used the term "sustainable development" as representing the "light green" ecological thought. It was defined as follows: "The management of human use of the biosphere so that it may yield the greatest sustainable benefit to present generations while maintaining its potential to meet the needs and aspirations of future generations".[28] Thanks to the efforts of IUCN and other international organizations, the 38th UN General Assembly (UNGA) in November 1983 adopted the Resolution 38/161, whereby the World Commission on Environment and Development (WCED) was founded under the lead of Norway's first female prime minister, Gro Harlem Brundtland, and a Global Agenda for Change was developed under the framework of "Sustainable Development". The formation of WCED provided an institutional platform to make sustainable development theories more systematic and comprehensive. After four years of efforts, the commission submitted the famous Brundtland Report – *Our Common Future* – to the 42nd UNGA in 1987, and released the *Tokyo Declaration* simultaneously calling on all countries to incorporate the concept and model of sustainable development into their development objectives. The Brundtland Report refined the sustainable development concept as follows: "It meets the needs of the present without compromising the ability of future generations to meet their own needs".[29] This is so far the most influential and widespread definition of the concept. It means the narrative of sustainable development has been widely accepted as an important consensus around the world – we must work to achieve economic goals while ensuring harmony with nature and the environment that human beings depend on for survival so that our offspring can last and sustain. This idea was reiterated in the *Declaration on Sustainable Development* issued by the fifteenth session of the Governing Council of UNEP in 1989.[30] All of these paved the way for the Earth Summit to be held in Rio de Janeiro, Brazil, in June 1992.

At the same time, sustainable development movements surged across the globe, especially in Europe, the US, and other developed countries such as Germany, the Netherlands, Denmark, and Britain. Leveraged on their advanced technologies and bountiful capital, these countries, by developing green technology and green market, continuously promoted theories and practices of ecological modernization that accommodated economic growth and environmental protection. The abstract theories were therefore filled with more concrete connotations. Developing countries might understand the theory of sustainable development differently from developed countries – they placed more emphasis on the right to development and demanded developed countries make due "ecological compensation". However, the global diffusion of innovative green policy tools, including the FIT and Quota System designed to boost renewables and the environmental information disclosure system, demonstrated developing countries' active response to and implementation of the sustainable strategy. In this stage, China gradually accepted the idea of sustainable development. It began to pay attention to subjects of international cooperation such as climate change and clean energy and took actions to join the global environmental governance.

China's cooperation with Europe and the US can date back to the early 1980s. For example, the biogas project and small solar demonstration project between China and Germany back then were intended to equip remote rural areas in China with small and practical biomass, solar, and wind facilities and devices. At the end of the 1980s, the two countries set down specific provisions on the principles, content, and forms of their renewable cooperation in the framework of scientific and technological cooperation. In the 1990s, they not only renewed the renewable energy cooperation agreement but also included its clauses in their agenda of climate cooperation and other environmental cooperation.[31] In October 1978, US Secretary of Energy James Schlesinger visited China and discussed the possibility of working together on hydropower, renewables, and nuclear energy after a formal diplomatic relation was established. Soon after the diplomatic ties were forged, Deng Xiaoping, then vice premier of the State Council, led the first delegation of the PRC to visit the US, where he signed the *Agreement Between the Government of the United States of America and the Government of the People's Republic of China on Cooperation in Science and Technology* with then US president Jimmy Carter. The agreement set up the stage for the two countries to carry out joint sci-tech R&D and cooperation in clean energy.[32] However, bilateral clean energy cooperation at that time was tentative and sporadic without an institutional and interactive platform.

II. Stage of germination (1990–1997)

The second stage was one of germination. Domestically, renewable energy policies began to be formulated, and scattered, small-scale use of renewables as a supplement to rural energy supply evolved into medium- and large-scale modern renewable projects. Internationally, although China joined the United Nations Framework

Convention on Climate Change (UNFCCC), it didn't fully understand the scientific principles and significance of climate response and therefore didn't pay enough attention to the development of clean energy. At that time, it began to carry out bilateral or multilateral renewable cooperation (e.g., experiments on large-scale wind power projects) making full use of international resources and sold its solar water heaters and other products in the international market, but international cooperation remained sporadic and unsystematic.

(I) Domestically: formulation of renewable energy policies

In this stage, support for renewable energy gradually became a consensus domestically and internationally. China evolved from a net oil exporter in 1993 to a net importer, marking the end of its energy self-sufficiency, and its import shot up dramatically since then. Massive renewable development began to draw more attention, although the voice that emphasized the "secure supply" of traditional fossil energy remained prevalent. In 1993, China enacted the *Scientific and Technological Progress Law*, which gave more support to the R&D of renewable energy technology.

In January 1995, the former National Planning Committee, National Scientific Committee, and National Economic and Trade Committee proposed the *Guideline of China on the Development of New Energy and Renewable Energy* (1960–2010) as an important document guiding the development of renewables. The *Electric Power Law* enacted in 1995 was the first law discussing energy policies in China, which stated that "the Chinese government encourages the development and use of new and renewable energy resources", a principle that was reaffirmed in the *Energy Conservation Law* in 1998. As a result, starting from the early 1990s, the development of renewable energy evolved from scattered and small-scale use as a supplement to rural energy supply to medium- and large-scale modern projects. By then, China had begun to conduct bilateral or multilateral cooperation (e.g., experiment on large-scale wind power projects) using international resources, and sold its solar water heaters and other products on the international market. In this stage, medium- and large-scale wind and solar projects gained ground, and international renewable cooperation projects kicked off. For example, in December 1993, China and Germany signed an agreement to jointly produce the 250kW on-grid wind turbine; also that year, the Xinjiang Electric Power Bureau installed 4 × 450kW wind turbines at Chaigoubao wind farm using loans from Denmark and investment at home. From 1990 to 1998, wind capacity reached 224MW at an average annual growth rate of more than 60%. With regard to solar power, a 10kW PV station was installed in Geji, Tibet, in October 1993, the first large PV power station in the autonomous region. Besides, the solar-thermal industry saw remarkable advancement and started large-scale industrialization. In 1998, there were more than 2,000 solar water heater producers in China, and the total installed capacity of the product amounted to 15 million cubic meters, the largest volume in the world.[33]

However, compared with developed Western countries, the renewable energy industry in China didn't get sufficient political attention or policy support in the 1990s. There were no systematic policies (specific policy tools or related administrative regulations) to promote large-scale projects. For example, large-scale wind power projects were sporadic, and the solar industry was focused on low-tech solar water heater with little heed to the research and development of PV power technology. Moreover, the emphasis on traditional energy security, focused on the supply side, remained dominant. China took long-term oil imports at a reasonable price as the key to ensuring energy security. During the 9th (1995–2000) and 10th Five-Year Plan (2001–2005), priority was given to "strengthening maritime prospecting, tapping energy sources overseas, building overseas oil and natural gas bases, and diversifying the channels of oil supply".

(II) Internationally: China's passive clean energy diplomacy with Europe and the US centered on energy technology cooperation

On the international level, China interacted more frequently with the international community on environmental issues in the early 1990s and joined the *Montreal Protocol* and the UNFCCC. Against this background, people were paying more attention to sustainable development and energy conservation, which created a favorable international environment for the development of renewables. After the United Nations Conference on Environment and Development (UNCED) in 1992, China released its *21st Century Agenda* in 1994 to impel sustainable development and rational use of resources. Also in 1994, the State Council adopted the *White Paper on China's Population, Environment and Development of 21st Century*, vowing that "China should develop new and renewable energy sources based on local conditions".

At this stage, China didn't fully realize yet how climate negotiations would affect its energy mix and consumption model. Therefore, its clean energy diplomacy was still focused on international cooperation on energy technology, and China, due to backward technology and insufficient capital, was the receiving end in such cooperation.

In their cooperation in the early period, China was the recipient of European and American energy technologies (technology transfer). On the one hand, it imported clean energy technologies and products from the EU or the US to enhance its own technological strength; on the other hand, European and American energy companies sometimes would transfer clean energy technology to their Chinese counterparts in exchange for the Chinese market. Besides, the EU began to turn its eyes to environmental and energy cooperation while providing government aid to China, so China could obtain some non-core clean energy technologies gratuitously through EU-aided demonstration projects. In 1994, the European Commission and the Chinese Ministry of Science and Technology hosted the China-EU Energy Cooperation Conference. This conference, of the largest scale and the highest level in bilateral energy cooperation, provided an official channel for the two sides to communicate energy-related issues as well as a platform for their energy companies to exchange views regularly.[34] In 1997, the EU-China High Level Energy Working Group was formed and had its first meeting. An important platform tasked to guide, coordinate, and supervise energy cooperation between China and the EU, the working group held a meeting every two to three years. In the meantime, the EU uplifted its aid to China by shifting the focus from poverty alleviation to providing technological assistance and intelligent support.

China and the US signed the *Cooperation Agreement on Renewable Energy* in February 1995, and then the *China-US Energy Efficiency and Renewable Energy Protocol* (first signed in 1995, renewed in 2000; revised in 2005 and renewed in 2006). Then the *China-US Energy and Environment Cooperation Initiative* was concluded in October 1997, which highlighted cooperation in energy conservation, environmental protection, and renewable energy technology. The two countries continued to sign the *China-US Agreement on the Peaceful Uses of Nuclear Energy* in January and the *Peaceful Uses of Nuclear Technology Agreement* in June 1998. At the China-US Forum on Environment and Development later, the two sides determined three priority areas of cooperation – access to electricity in rural areas, clean energy and energy efficiency, and air quality in cities.

III. Stage of initial exploration (1998–2004)

The third stage was one of initial exploration. The signing of the *Kyoto Protocol* in 1997 made China realize that climate had a great bearing on a country's economic development and energy consumption structure. Therefore, the National Development and Planning Commission formed a National Coordinating Group on Climate Policies in 1998 to be in charge of climate negotiations, and the country signed *Kyoto Protocol* the same year, moving up climate and clean energy subjects on the domestic political agenda.[35] Thanks to Clean Development Mechanism (CDM), China had gained more experience in the development and foreign interactions on clean energy.

(I) Domestically: a franchised tendering system for renewables

The year 1998 was essential for advancing the development of renewable energy because in that year, the National Development and Planning Commission (predecessor of the National Development and Reform Commission, or NDRC), the regulator responsible for planning the macro-economy and regulating the energy sector, was officially tasked with conducting climate negotiations and signed *Kyoto Protocol* on behalf of China. This institutional change reflected China's growing awareness of climate change's significant influences on domestic economic development and energy use structure. Moreover, to support climate negotiations and further deliberate the flexible mechanisms under *Kyoto Protocol*, the National Development and Planning Commission set up a Climate Change Center and Renewable Energy Research Center under its Energy Research Institute. China's ratification of the *Kyoto Protocol* in 2002 signaled its readiness to engage more deeply in the international regime in response to climate change. What was most noteworthy in this stage was that China no longer doubted the "flexible mechanisms" under the protocol and began to show interest in CDM around 2002, a mechanism that played a significant role in scaling up renewable energy development (especially large wind power projects) and accelerating the modernization of this industry. On the domestic level, former president Hu Jintao made the political commitment to optimizing the country's development path by advancing the low-carbon transformation. He also put forth the "Scientific Outlook on Development", which laid special stress on balanced and sustainable social development and conservation of energy sources and resources.

Against such a background, China rolled out more laws and policies concerning the environment and clean energy, including the *Law on Environmental Impact Assessment* in 2002 and the *Law on Promoting Clean Production* in 2003. It also began to formulate national renewables policies and attached greater importance to the modernization of this sector on a large scale. Such a shift in attitude was primarily manifested in the reduction of VAT for wind farms from 17% to less than 8% in 2002[36] to encourage developers to engage in wind power generation. The NDRC knew that short-term VAT reduction was not as effective as creating a renewable energy market through relevant policies. Therefore, drawing on the British experience, it adopted the franchised tendering policy in 2002 and put it into action in 2003. With this policy, "the most cost-effective project is selected through competitive bidding". To be more specific, "different renewable energy developers submit their bidding documents about the facilities they will build along with the acceptable construction cost, and the lowest bidder would be selected". The main purpose of this policy was to drive the scale-up of renewable projects and have a better idea of the low-end cost of production.

In 2003, NDRC released the *Plan for Franchised Wind Power Operation* to further stimulate international and domestic investors to step up the construction of large wind farms through franchised tendering. It also encouraged investors, under the government's supervision, to lower the cost of wind power generation through technological improvement, so it could better control the production cost. All eligible companies, Chinese and foreign, were invited to bid for the franchised, large-scale wind power projects (100–200MW), and the bid would be granted based on the cost per kWh electricity and the ratio of China-made components used at the wind farm.[37] Between 2003 and 2008, NDRC organized five rounds of franchised bidding, giving more weight to the ratio of localization of wind turbine generator set when screening the bidders.

Although the franchising policy was intended to find a reasonable base price for the future FIT policy, it aggravated a price war, as evidenced by the fact that the price quoted by some bidders was far lower than the reasonable price range (even as low as the price for coal-fired power generation – RMB 0.382/kWh). Besides, deep-pocketed state-owned energy enterprises could win the bid at a very low price regardless of limited profits, while medium and small-sized private companies were marginalized in this green market. As the franchising policy couldn't guarantee a reasonable price for renewable energy development, it was gradually replaced by FIT after the *Renewable Energy Law* was enacted in 2005. Starting from 2009, franchised tendering only applied to offshore wind farm projects and large-scale PV projects, whose power generation cost was relatively high. For instance, in March 2009, the National Energy Administration (NEA) organized bidding for large franchised PV projects in Dunhuang, Gansu Province, and the price was set at RMB 1.09/kWh. The accumulation of basic data regarding PV power generation provided scientific references for designing the on-grid tariff for PV power.

The policy of franchised tendering laid the foundation for introducing specific renewable energy policies. Kicking off CDM and implementing franchised projects gave a strong impetus to massive renewables development, particularly large-scale wind power projects. Franchised tendering also gave the government a chance to learn about the reasonable price of renewable power generation and consequently helped it design the future FIT policy. In sum, the successful experience with franchised tendering paved the way for the inclusion of FIT in the *Renewable Energy Law*.

(II) Internationally: clean energy diplomacy driven by external aid and integrating energy and environment

Generally speaking, China's clean energy diplomacy in the early stage was quite passive. The co-development of large-scale clean energy projects was to a large extent motivated by CDM under the UN framework, and diplomatic efforts were focused on mobilizing international resources to enhance its own capability of clean energy development. At first, China had doubts and reservations about the three flexible mechanisms of the *Kyoto Protocol* lest developed countries would shirk their historical responsibilities and induce developing countries to join the emission reduction. After the flexible mechanisms were further clarified at the Bonn Conference in 1999, China began to change its attitude in 2001 as it recognized that CDM offered it the opportunity to develop clean energy sources by cooperating with developed countries, in investment or technology, on emission reduction.[38] After it ratified *Kyoto Protocol* and carried out the first CDM project in 2002, more CDM projects were launched at a high speed, and China overtook India and Brazil in 2006 to host the most CDM projects, mostly renewables. As of June 2014, the cumulative Certified Emission Reduction (CER) from China-based CDM projects amounted to 880 million tons, the most in the world making up 60% of the total. In the meantime, the United Nations Development Programme (UNDP) and United Nations Foundation (UNF) sponsored a program to enhance China's capacity for developing and managing CDM projects, in the attempt to standardize the projects by way of policy study, capacity training, and demonstration. In addition to CDM, the China-Renewable Energy Scale-Up Program (CRESP) and Renewable Energy Development Programme (REDP) in the UN climate and environmental governance framework were also external incentives to scale up clean energy development in China. The CRESP (2006–2018) was a project jointly undertaken by NDRC's Center for Renewable Energy Development, World Bank, and Global Environment Fund (GEF). It was unique in that it shifted the focus from helping build projects to refining the policy system – it helped the Chinese government establish and improve auxiliary regulations and policies in support of the *Renewable Energy Law* by drawing on developed countries' experience. The REDP (2001–2008) aimed to support China in building on-grid, large-scale wind farms with commercial prospects and promote the PV market and industrialization using GEF grants and World Bank loans.

In sum, the external incentives provided by various UN projects strongly impelled China's clean energy scale-up and enhanced its capability of clean energy governance in the early stage. However, this model was unstable and inconsistent. For example, as emerging countries grew and the EU carbon market withered, the number of CDM projects in China plummeted after 2013, and the external incentives weakened.[39] However, as China became more capable of clean energy development in its own right, its clean energy diplomacy began to rely less on external drives than on internal motivation.

In the 21st century, China has put energy and environmental protection on the same track when cooperating with Europe and the US. Boosting environmental protection and sustainable development is one of the three priority areas in China-EU cooperation, and the EU aids China in this field in two ways. One is sponsoring clean energy projects; the other is training Chinese energy personnel – with financial or technical support. Moreover, the China-EU Energy Cooperation Conference kicked off the EU-China Energy and Environment Program (EEP) (November 2004–end of 2009) to reinforce the security of energy supply and the capacity for environmentally sustainable development. An important program launched by the Chinese government and European Commission pursuant to the previously signed agreement, the EEP highlighted energy and environmental cooperation in three areas – policy formulation, capacity building, and technical support, with clean energy cooperation taking a prominent position.[40] All these programs were strong demonstrations impelling China to perfect its energy policies, improve energy efficiency, and promote the use of renewable energy sources. It's worth noting that clean energy cooperation between China and Germany was further fortified. The countries signed the *Joint Statement Between the Government of the People's Republic of China and the Government of the Federal Republic of Germany on Environmental Protection – Action Agenda* in 2000 to step up cooperation in the development and utilization of renewable energy. In 2003, they signed the *Memorandum of Cooperation in the New Applications in the Renewable Transport Energy Sector* to jointly promote the application of renewable energy in the transport sector. In 2004, their joint statement on a *Partnership of Global Responsibility* once again highlighted renewable energy as a key area of bilateral cooperation.

Chinese and American leaders visited each other in 1997 and 1998 respectively. This stage featured the positive influences exerted by bilateral political amiability on clean energy cooperation, which went deeper in the 21st century for three reasons: the need to ensure international energy security in a post-9/11 world, the positive effects of China's accession to WTO, and the need for both countries to change their structure of energy consumption. In 2000, China and the US signed the *Energy Efficiency and Renewable Energy Protocol Agreement*. In January 2004, they signed the *Protocol for Cooperation in Clean Energy Technologies for the 2008 Summer Olympic Games in Beijing* and formed a joint working group for a green Olympics; in May that year, they signed the *MOU on the Launch of Energy Policy*

Dialogue. All of these paved the way for the signing of the significant *Ten Year Framework for Energy and Environment Cooperation* in 2008.

IV. Stage of rapid and diversified development (2005–2012)

The fourth stage was one of rapid and diversified development. On the domestic level, the *Renewable Energy Law* enacted in 2005 created a favorable policy environment for the rapid development of clean energy by simulating Germany's FIT system, and in less than ten years, China had the world's largest clean energy capacity. On the international level, diplomatic cooperation between China and Europe, China and the US developed quickly, and clean energy became a key subject in the EU-China Partnership on Climate Change, China-US Energy Policy Dialogue (EPD), and China-US Strategic and Economic Dialogue (SED) in 2005.

(I) Domestically: from FIT to quota system

The year 2005 was a milestone in the development of China's clean energy policies. To realize the goal of building a resource-saving and environment-friendly society proposed by then Chinese premier Wen Jiabao, NDRC kicked off ten key energy conservation programs nationwide that year, the same year that the *Kyoto Protocol* took effect. Against such a background, the Chinese government began to mobilize international resources through CDM programs and consequently reinforce its capability of clean energy development. The Renewable Energy Law was adopted by the Standing Committee of the NPC in February 2005 and came into effect on January 1, 2006. The enactment of this law marked the establishment of a relatively sound policy system for renewable energy – the dispersive supportive policy measures were integrated into an organic system.[41]

The focus in this stage was on introducing the German-style FIT system. Also called a policy of on-grid tariff subsidy, the tariff-based FIT was widely implemented in the early stage of global renewable energy development. It provided renewables developers with a long-term selling price for renewable electricity that guaranteed a certain margin and obligated the power utilities to purchase renewable electricity over a relatively long period of time (e.g., 20 years).[42] Besides, FIT usually included an inherent "degressive subsidy" mechanism, which meant that with the progress of renewable technology, the on-grid tariff would come down over time, and the degressive subsidy could pressure developers to reduce their production costs.[43] The main purpose of reducing the subsidy was to track and encourage technological innovation and make renewables more competitive.[44] The *Renewable Energy Law* of 2005 stipulated three key principles regarding the implementation of FIT.

(1) Guaranteed grid connection and wholesale purchase. This policy required grid companies to sign an agreement with clean energy power generators within their service areas on purchasing all of their renewable electricity and providing grid connection services. Article 13 and 14 of *Renewable Energy Law* stated:

The state shall encourage and support synchronization of power generated by using renewable energy,[45] and Article 29 emphasized that grid companies failing to purchase the full amount of renewable electricity and thus causing economic losses to the relevant power generator shall be liable for such losses.

(2) Different on-grid tariffs for electricity generated from different types of renewable energy sources. This policy provided extra subsidy for renewable electricity that was more expensive than coal-fired electricity. The cost of generating electricity differed in different regions and for different types of renewables. Article 19 of *Renewable Energy Law* provided that the on-grid tariff of renewable electricity shall be determined by the administrative department of the price of the State Council on the principle of helping promote the development and utilization of renewable energy as well as the principle of economy and rationality, and be adjusted in a timely manner in light of the development of renewables technology.

(3) Apportionment of expenses and economic incentives. If the FIT paid by grid companies to purchase renewable electricity was higher than the average on-grid tariff of electricity generated from conventional energy sources, they could add the difference to their selling price. In other words, the excess could be accounted for as the power transmission cost of grid companies and be recovered from their power sales. Article 24 of *Renewable Energy Law* stated that the financial authorities of the state shall set up a special fund to support scientific and technological research, formulation of standards, and demonstration projects for the development and utilization of renewable energy. Article 25 provided that a financial institution may offer a subsidized loan for a renewable energy project that is listed in the national catalog guiding the development of the renewable energy industry and that meets the relevant requirements for loan application.[46]

However, the *Renewable Energy Law* was just a framework law that didn't lay down detailed, operable rules and procedures to facilitate the implementation of the three key principles. For instance, it didn't provide the specific on-grid tariff of wind, solar, and biomass electricity, or the concrete penalties for grid companies if they failed to purchase the full amount of renewable electricity. Therefore, several administrative regulations were enacted later as supplements to this law. For instance, NDRC released the *Trial Measures for the Management of Prices and Allocation of Costs for Electricity Generated from Renewable Energy* in 2006, the State Electricity Regulatory Commission issued the *Regulatory Measures for Grid Enterprises' Full Purchase of Renewable Energy Electricity* in 2007, and NDRC issued the *Provisional Methods for the Allocation of Additional Income on the Price of Renewable Energy Electricity* in 2007. In September that year, the State Council issued the *Medium- and Long-term Development Plan for Renewable Energy*, which set the medium- and long-term targets to meet the goal that nonfossil energy will account for 15% of primary energy consumption by 2020, with a special emphasis on boosting hydro, wind, solar, and biomass energies. The 11th Five-Year Plan incorporated the plan for renewables development to guide and propel the actions of governments of all levels and all social sectors. Although these administrative regulations fast-tracked the development of renewables, they didn't specify the FIT for different types of renewable electricity.

The three key principles (FIT, on-grid tariff, and cost apportionment) in *Renewable Energy Law* are related to each other. The FIT ensures profits for renewable power generators, but law must be in place to mandate grid companies to purchase renewable electricity and synchronize it to the grid. The cost apportionment mechanism makes sure the part of the cost of purchasing renewable electricity that's higher than the average power tariff of traditional energy sources is apportioned through the selling price to general users. In this stage, the development of renewables still faced two difficulties.

First of all, the tariff for renewable electricity differed from region to region. From January 2006 to June 2010, the FIT for biomass electricity was only RMB 0.25/kWh higher than the on-grid tariff of coal-fired electricity, which was not enough to push biomass energy forward. From 2005 to 2009, large-scale wind power projects were mainly supported with the franchised bidding policy without a national FIT for wind-based electricity (although auxiliary policies were in place in some wind-rich provinces). It wasn't until 2011 that a FIT for PV electricity was settled, which was the primary reason for the slow progress of the sector.

Second, grid connection was a key factor that impeded the development of renewable power generation. By 2009, wind capacity accounted for 1.85% of all power capacity, yet wind electricity accounted for only 0.75% of total power use. The difficulty in grid connection caused the unbalanced development of renewables. Still, take wind power for example. Thanks to subsidies, upstream businesses such as wind turbine manufacturing and wind farm construction prospered. In comparison, downstream businesses such as power transmission were inadequately bolstered, especially as state-owned grid companies were unwilling to purchase the "unstable, low-quality" renewable electricity.

In sum, the *Renewable Energy Law* enacted in 2005 marked the formation of a relatively complete policy system for renewables. Within this framework, FIT was the official policy to boost the development of renewable energy, along with two other key mechanisms: full-amount purchase of renewable electricity and apportionment of cost. This legislative framework powered the rapid development of renewables and made China a world leader in terms of wind capacity, solar panel manufacturing, and renewable energy investment. But the exceptional achievements came with some problems, such as grid connection for renewable electricity, which captured more attention in the society. Policy flaws in *Renewable Energy Law* were to be corrected and improved, to facilitate the implementation of FIT and ensure the healthy and orderly development of renewables, hence the rising call for revising the law.

At that time, the international community was full of expectations for the Copenhagen Conference to be held at the end of 2009, hoping it would generate a new legal framework comprising all contracting parties to address climate change in the post-Kyoto era. Facing unprecedented international pressure, China, before the Copenhagen Conference, proposed a voluntary pledge of emission reduction and the development of nonfossil energies – it will cut CO_2 emission per unit GDP by 40%–45% in 2020 from the 2005 levels and increase the percentage of nonfossil energy in total energy consumption to 15% by that time. However, what with its negotiating strategy and what with the skewed report by international media, China's voluntary pledge was still criticized internationally for not being ambitious enough, even though some scholars, based on deep-going studies, said that the 40%–45% reduction in carbon intensity was by no means an easy job. The *Copenhagen Accord* would have been a shell but for China's extra efforts, or rather the support from the Chinese leadership.[47] The pledge sent a strong signal at home, pushing, from outside in, the low-carbon transformation and the rapid development of renewables.

China surpassed the US to become the world's largest energy consumer in 2010, which exposed it to the dual pressure of rising energy dependence and the mounting task of carbon emission. As the development of traditional energy faced difficulties both at home and abroad, China attached more importance to emission reduction and stimulated the low-carbon shift of economic structure by developing renewables. At the thirteenth meeting of the Standing Committee of the eleventh NPC in 2010, NDRC released a report that officially listed carbon emission reduction and renewable energy development as important, imperative indicators in the 12th Five-Year Plan. The plan made it clear that China will strive to establish a competitive renewable energy industry and will slash energy intensity by 16% and carbon intensity by 17% in 2015 from the 2010 levels. NDRC also released the *12th Five-Year Plan for Renewable Energy Development*, which stipulated that the annual consumption of renewable energy in 2015 will reach 478 million TCE (ton of coal equivalent) – including 400 million TCE commercialized renewables – and it will account for 9.5% in total energy consumption.

China's pledge to bring down carbon intensity and its accentuation of low-carbon transformation further motivated the improvement of renewable energy policies, with significant progress in perfecting the *Renewable Energy Law* and implementing its three key principles. In this stage, the FIT for wind, solar, and biomass electricity was finally settled through vital administrative regulations. NDRC issued the *Notice on Raising the On-grid Tariff of Wind Electricity* in 2009, in which it officially set the tariff for wind electricity in four different regions – RMB 0.51/kWh, RMB 0.54/kWh, RMB 0.58/kWh, and RMB 0.61/kWh. The *Policy on Unifying the On-grid Tariff for Electricity Generated from Agricultural and Forest Biomass* issued in 2010 set the tariff at RMB 0.75/kWh, and the *Policy on On-grid Tariff for PV Electricity* issued in 2011 set the tariff at RMB 1/kWh and RMB 1.15/kWh in light of local solar resources.

Although the FIT for renewable electricity was settled, its implementation faced strong resistance from the traditional energy sector and the grid. To give teeth to the *Renewable Energy Law*, the NPC adopted the *Amendment to the Renewable Energy Law* in 2009 that came into effect in April the next year. The amendment made the following three improvements:

First, it introduced the quota system for renewables to better enforce the full-amount purchase and grid connection of renewable electricity. Article 14 of the *Amendment to the Renewable Energy Law* stipulated that the state will use the quota system to determine the percentage at which grid companies shall purchase renewable electricity, and the department of the State Council in charge of energy, along with the national electricity regulator, will supervise the implementation throughout the year. In the meantime, to guarantee grid stability, power generators are obligated to comply with the technical standards set by grid companies, create a priority dispatching system conducive to the transmission of renewable electricity, and work out the technical standards for grid connection. The amendment also provided that with the quota system, renewable targets will be designed in light of electricity output rather than installed capacity. This meant that the focus of renewable energy development had shifted from the quantity of green capacity to the quality of green electricity. However, the Amendment didn't specify the renewable quota for different stakeholders, such as grid companies.

Second, the state set up a fund for the medium- and long-term development of renewable energy sources. The fund, which consisted of additional income from the price of renewable electricity levied in accordance with law and the special funds allocated from national finance annually, was intended to facilitate the implementation of the cost-sharing system at provincial and lower local levels.

Third, the Amendment underlined the importance of perfecting the planning procedures and strengthening the integrity of national and local plans. During the years after the *Renewable Energy Law* was enacted, problems emerged regarding the overall planning for the development and utilization of renewables. For example, national and regional plans were not aligned, and so were the construction plans of power generators and grid companies. Therefore, better coordination of the plans among different levels became especially important. Besides, actions in violation of the law shall be subject to administrative punishment in accordance with law; those constituting crimes shall be subject to criminal liability in accordance with the law.

The most far-reaching achievement of the Amendment was the introduction of the quota system, which was combined with the existing FIT system. The renewable portfolio standard (RPS) or quota system is defined as a market-based renewable energy policy that usually enforces renewable quota upon power generators and grid companies by stipulating a fixed percentage of renewables in power production or consumption. The purpose of introducing this system was to address the abandonment of wind and solar electricity, designate mandatory renewable quota for state-owned grid companies and power generators, and coordinate the central and provincial plans for renewables development. After the *Amendment to the Renewable Energy Law* took effect in 2010, the State Council issued the *Decision on Accelerating the Cultivation and Development of Strategic Emerging Industries*, which underscored renewable energy as a crucial strategic industry and stressed promoting its grid connection and transmission by implementing the quota system. The government tried to guarantee grid connection for renewable electricity through a more detailed quota system.

(II) Internationally: proactive and institutional development of China's clean energy diplomacy

The *Renewable Energy Law* of 2005 escorted the rapid development of clean energy. China kept stepping up the R&D of core clean energy technologies and gradually moved to the forefront in several technological domains. With its growing strengths in technology and capital, China's mode of cooperation with Europe and the US began to change from passive acceptance to proactive and institutional development. It's worth noting that when the Ministry of Science and Technology issued the *Implementation Outline for the 11th Five-Year Plan for International Cooperation on Science and Technology* in 2006, the document required conducting international clean energy cooperation and proactively promoting relevant projects with China and its needs in the center. At the same time, Europe and the US wanted China to bear part of the financial risks for technology R&D, so they developed new models of sharing the capital, technology, and IP to jointly tackle technical bottlenecks. A key feature in this stage was that China, stepping away from the previous passive position in technological cooperation with Europe and the US, took the initiative to strengthen information sharing and experience exchange regarding the latest progress on clean energy technologies. It was also poised to carry out cooperation in the formulation of technical standards and sharing of IP, in hopes of creating the conditions for joint R&D and other pragmatic collaboration with European and American companies. It's safe to say that the diplomatic interactions on clean energy between China and Europe, China and the US entered the fast track now with a higher level of institutionalization.

To be specific, there are two principal institutional platforms for China-Europe cooperation – the China-EU Summit since 1998 and the China-EU Energy Cooperation Conference initiated in 1994. China-EU Summit is the highest-level mechanism for China-EU dialogue and cooperation on clean energy. At the eighth summit in 2005, the two sides forged the "Strategic Partnership on Climate Change" and explicitly set two long-term goals – carbon capture and storage (CCS) and renewable energy.[48] The China-EU Energy Cooperation Conference kicked off the "China-EU Energy Dialogue" in 2005, under which the two sides established the Europe-China Clean Energy Centre (EC2) in April 2010 and the EU-China Institute for Clean and Renewable Energy (ICARE) in 2012, pushing institutional clean energy cooperation to a new level. EC2 is a cooperative project initiated by the European Commission, China's National Energy Administration, and the Ministry of Commerce, with support from the Italian Ministry for the Environment, Land, and Sea. It aims to promote the use of clean energy in China and support the Chinese government in building a more sustainable, environment-friendly, and high-efficiency energy system as well as a green energy industry.[49] Officially coming into operation in March 2012, ICARE was established with the approval of the Ministry of Education at Huazhong University of Science & Technology. Supported by nine prestigious universities in six countries – China, France, Britain, Italy, Greece, and Spain – it was aimed at cultivating high-caliber talent specialized in clean energy and creating a long-term, institutional platform for the cooperation between Chinese and European academia.

There are also two principal platforms for China-US cooperation – the Energy Policy Dialogue (EPD) starting in 2005 and the Strategic Economic Dialogue (SED) starting in 2006. The center of bilateral discussions at the 4th EPD session was the development of clean energy. At the first SED in 2006, the two sides signed the

Energy Efficiency and Renewable Energy Protocol that made diplomatic cooperation on clean energy an important subject. At the 5th SED in 2008, they signed the *Ten Year Framework for Energy and Environment Cooperation – EcoPartnership*, aiming to get local governments, research institutes, universities, enterprises, and NGOs in both countries to engage in innovation and project cooperation. In April 2009, China and the US put forth the Strategic and Economic Dialogue (S&ED). Since then, strategic and economic issues were put under the same framework, and the first S&ED made clean energy development a key topic. The rising institutional level of bilateral cooperation was mainly reflected in two aspects.[50]

Table 5.6 Diplomatic cooperation on clean energy: China-EU vs China-US

	China-EU diplomatic cooperation on clean energy	*China-US diplomatic cooperation on clean energy*
Institutional platform	• Since 1994: China-EU Energy Cooperation Conference (ministerial level) • 1997: EU-China High Level Energy Working Group • 1998: China-EU Summit (head of state level) • Since 2012: China-EU High Level Energy Meeting (head of state level)	• Since 2005: China-US Energy Policy Dialogue (EPD) • Since 2006: China-US Strategic Economic Dialogue (SED) • Since 2009: Upgraded version of Strategic and Economic Dialogue (S&ED) (core mechanism now)
Milestones in different cooperation frameworks	In the framework of the China-EU Summit: • 8th Summit in 2005: China-EU Joint Declaration on Climate Change →2005: China-EU Strategic Partnership in Climate Change • 11th Summit in 2009: Joint Statement on Europe-China Clean Energy Center; EU-China Science and Technology Partnership Scheme • 12th Summit in 2009: Memorandum of Understanding Launching Phase II of the Near Zero Emission Coal Project	In the EPD framework: • 2004: MOU on China-US Energy Policy Dialogue laid the foundation for EPD • 2006: Clean energy was designated as an important area of bilateral cooperation • 2007: MOU Concerning Industrial Energy Efficiency Cooperation • 2009: U.S.-China Energy Cooperation Program
	• 14th Summit in 2012: Joint Declaration on the China-EU Partnership on Urbanization • 18th Summit in 2016: pragmatic cooperation project of urbanization partnership; 2016 China-EU Green & Smart City Awards	In the SED framework: • 2006: Energy Efficiency and Renewable Energy Protocol • 2008: Ten Year Framework for Energy and Environment Cooperation – EcoPartnership • 2008: Ten Year Energy & Environment Cooperation Framework • 2008: EcoPartnership Program

(*Continued*)

Table 5.6 (Continued)

	China-EU diplomatic cooperation on clean energy	*China-US diplomatic cooperation on clean energy*
	In the framework of the China-EU Energy Cooperation Conference: • Since 2003: China-EU Dialogue on Environment →China-EU Energy and Environment Program (2003–2009) →China-EU Environmental Governance Program (2008–2010) • 2005: Memorandum of Understanding on China-EU Dialogue on Energy and Transport Strategies • 2005: China-EU Energy Dialogue • 2010: Europe-China Clean Energy Centre (EC2) • 2010: Institute for Clean and Renewable Energy (ICARE) • China-EU High Level Energy Meeting • 2012: China-EU Joint Declaration on Energy Security • 2018: Leaders' Statement on Climate Change and Clean Energy	In the S&ED framework: • 2009: China-US Renewable Energy Partnership • 2009: China-US Clean Energy Research Center (CERC) • 2009: Memorandum of Understanding To Enhance Cooperation on Climate Change, Energy and the Environment • 2009: Joint Secretariat of EcoPartnership Program • 2013: Financing work group of CERC • 2015: Renewal of CERC for five years (2016–2020)

Source: Originally created by the author.

For one, during Barack Obama's China visit in November 2009, China and the US signed the *MoU on Establishing a US-China Renewable Energy Partnership* and forged the U.S.-China Renewable Energy Partnership (USCREP). The partnership operated in two ways. On the one hand, the two countries regularly held renewable energy forums to put in place a long-term cooperation mechanism. They also carried out sustained exchanges and cooperation in a variety of ways, including forming work groups, exchanging research findings regularly, and organizing technical training sessions. The first-ever US-China Renewable Energy Forum was held in 2010. Since the third forum in 2013, bilateral pragmatic cooperation has seen major achievements. (1) Cooperation on advanced technology has deepened, leading to the Concentrated Solar Power (CSP) demonstration project in Qinghai Province; (2) cooperation platform kept improving, represented by the China Variable-Generation Integration Group (CVIG); and (3) exchanges and joint research went deeper with the competition of case study reports on the synchronization of renewable electricity, distributed power generation, and micro grid.[51] On the other hand, USCREP was closely combined with the EcoPartnership under the *Ten Year Framework for Energy and Environment Cooperation* starting in 2008. The joint work group meeting was held regularly to pair up to research institutes, universities, enterprises, and NGOs on both sides and encourage investment and cooperation projects between the two countries. Five or six new pairs of eco-partners were added to the S&ED almost every year, indicating substantially enhanced flexibility and operability of bilateral cooperation.[52]

For another, the CERC is another important cooperation mechanism under S&ED. It is designed to promote joint research on clean energy technology between Chinese and American scientists and engineers, inspire innovation in the field, and raise energy efficiency to expedite the transition toward a low-carbon economy. According to the protocol signed in November 2009, the two sides set up a cooperation guiding committee and a joint high-level advisory group to guide, supervise, and evaluate CERC's research activities and direction. They would co-invest USD 150 million over five years (2010–2015) to support collaborative R&D in three priority areas – energy conservation in construction, clean energy vehicles, and clean coal – by the industry-college-research institute alliance. Running with great success, the CERC was renewed in 2015 for another five years. Its scope of research covered advanced clean coal technology, clean vehicles, energy conservation in construction, and energy and water.

As soon as he came into office on January 20, 2017, US President Donald Trump called off the "Climate Action Plan" and the "Clean Power Plan" initiated by his predecessor Obama and rolled back subsidies for renewables. These actions threw a wet blanket on global clean energy cooperation, but the cooperation between America's sub-national entities (states/cities), think tanks, research institutes, and enterprises with China couldn't be fundamentally affected. For instance, the USCREP established in 2009 emphasized a "bottom-up" approach driven by the society and the market and took in multiple stakeholders engaged in clean energy.[53] Among them, JUCCCE, an NGO committed to clean energy development in China and the US, made sustained efforts to push forward bilateral cooperation in four areas – green urbanization, circular industry, low-carbon consumption, and enduring strategic cooperation.

V. Stage of substantial advances (2013-present)

The fifth stage was one of the substantial advances. Being comprehensively merged with all kinds of multilateral mechanisms and platforms, clean energy diplomacy was an essential guiding force in forging new-type major-country relations, innovating South-South cooperation, planning Belt and Road construction, and reinforcing home-court diplomacy, stabilizing the surrounding situation, and participating in global governance. In this stage, China's international status and discourse power were heightened in the process of establishing a new world energy and climate order.

(I) Domestically: the combination of quota system and green certification system

To detail the implementation plan for the quota system, the China National Renewable Energy Center (CNREC) put forth a draft *Methods of Quota Management for Renewable Electricity*, which set detailed quotas for large power generators, state-owned grid companies, and provincial-level energy authorities. For the first time, it specified the quota of renewable electricity that grid companies must take on in the grid-covered area. By 2015, renewable electricity must account for 5% of State Grid's power mix, Southern Grid 3.2%, Inner Mongolia Grid 15%, and Shaanxi Power Grid 10%. This meant a national mandatory renewable electricity quota system was burgeoning. The quota system in China was a supplement to FIT because FIT only subsidized renewable power generators but could do little about grid companies, so the quota system was launched to give teeth to *Renewable Energy Law*. Besides, it was also designed to effect a market-oriented switch in renewable energy policies.

Renewable electricity generates profits in two ways: power supply and environmental benefits from replacing fossil energy. Theoretically speaking, electricity output from renewable energy is still lower than the optimal level because only its social benefits (as in power supply) are recognized and paid, whereas its environmental benefits are hard to measure and impossible to be financially rewarded. Therefore, a subsidy is offered to partly make up for environmental benefits with public finance and consequently stimulate investors to invest in renewables. The quota system is in fact another way of recognizing the environmental benefits of renewable electricity, with which power generators produce two products – electricity and renewable electricity certificate, and the certificate measures environmental benefits. If the government enforces the quota system, there would be market demand for renewable electricity certificates. In theory, the final market price of the certificate must reflect the value of socially recognized environmental benefits (as reflected in quotas). The issuance of the Green Electricity Certificate is an important development of the quota system.

Although the NEA enacted the *Ordinances of Quota Management for Renewable Energy (for discussions)* in 2012, it wasn't really implemented or received much attention until 2015. The underpinning reason was that the quota system hurt the interests of some groups.

> The top five power generation groups are the main force of renewable energy development, but they are at the same time the largest thermal power generators. They, with great discourse power, wouldn't say yes to a revolution of conventional energy sources. Renewable energy faces strong resistance.

Besides, linking the local implementation of the quota system with the performance of provincial governments would exert immense impacts, especially on economically developed provinces in eastern China, so it was strongly rejected and obstructed by some local governments.

In November 2015, the General Office of the State Council officially released the *Energy Development Strategy Action Plan (2014–2020)* and listed the abandonment of wind power and the restriction of its synchronization as major issues to be resolved during the 13th Five-Year Plan period. NEA issued the *Guiding Opinions on Improving the Formulation of the 13th Five-Year Plan for Renewable Energy Development*, stressing again the consumption of renewable electricity as a key task. This signaled an apparent shift in the country's model of developing clean electricity – from focusing on installed capacity to paying more attention to actual output and use.

On the international level, the signing of the *Paris Agreement* in 2015 ushered global climate governance into a new era. In June that year, the Chinese government submitted to the UNFCCC Secretariat its intended nationally determined contributions (INDC), vowing to increase renewable energy to 20% of its primary energy supply by 2030. That was a positive signal on the international level. At the G20 Hangzhou Summit in 2016, China enhanced its institutional power through home court diplomacy. It included clean development on the agenda, reached a consensus with other countries to push the *Paris Agreement* into force at an early date, and strongly advocated green finance and carbon trading, laying the institutional foundation for the implementation of a renewable energy quota system. Even after Trump announced to exit from the *Paris Agreement* in 2017, China reaffirmed its commitment to it and injected a booster into global climate governance. The report at the 19th CPC National Congress stated that China "will get actively involved in global environmental governance, play a leading role in global climate governance, and fulfill our commitments on emissions reduction", ready to "contribute to global ecological security".

On the domestic level, since the 18th CPC National Congress in 2012, ecological progress has been incorporated in the Five-sphere Integrated Plan for a socialist cause with Chinese characteristics and officially enshrined in the *Revised Constitution of the Communist Party of China* as an action guide for building a beautiful China. Ever since the fifth plenary session of the 18th CPC Central Committee in October 2015, green development, as an inseparable part of the Five Concepts for Development, has been a key concept guiding economic and social development in the 13th Five-Year Plan period and beyond. Performance assessment was no longer GDP-focused but greener and low-carbon-oriented, and the focus of development shifted from quantity to quality. The *Measures for the Accountability of Party and Government Leaders for Damage to the Ecological Environment (for Trial Implementation)* issued in August 2015 reinforced accountability for the ecological environment, especially immediate punishment for apparent damages and lifelong accountability for covert damages. On the basis of the overall guiding thought on ecological civilization, the report of the 19th CPC National Congress put forward feasible measures. In terms of guiding thought, the report said, "In addition to creating more material and cultural wealth to meet people's ever-increasing needs for a better life, we need also to provide more quality ecological goods to meet people's ever-growing demands for a beautiful environment." In terms of specific measures, the report highlighted the implementation of environmental policies in the following areas: "We will enforce stricter pollutants discharge standards and see to it that polluters are held accountable. We will improve our systems for mandatory release of environmental information, and for imposing severe punishment for environmental violations." "We will step up efforts to establish a legal and policy framework that promotes green production and consumption." "We will complete work on drawing redlines for protecting the ecosystems, designating permanent basic cropland, and delineating boundaries for urban development."

Against such a background, NEA released the *Guiding Opinions on Establishing a Target System to Guide the Development and Utilization of Renewable Energy* in 2016. The new draft on the quota system released by NEA to solicit opinions conveyed the administration's resolve to systematically consume renewable electricity. On the other hand, it revealed how difficult it was to put the quota system into practice given the intense tug-of-war among different interest groups.

At the same time, considering the widening shortfall of renewable energy subsidies,[54] the NDRC, Ministry of Finance, and NEA issued the *Notice on Piloting the Issuance of, Voluntary Subscription for and Trade of Green Electricity Certificate for Renewable Energy* in February 2017, which explicitly stipulated the subscription for Green Electricity Certificate starting from July that year. The Green Electricity Certificate is an electronic certificate with only code issued to an eligible renewable power generator through NEA's renewable energy information management platform.[55] It can be used as an instrument to transfer the ownership of renewable energy's environmental benefits. Essentially, it is a tradable and cashable token that confirms the generation of renewable electricity.[56] When the Green Electricity Certificate trading system is established, coal-fired power generators will be asked to buy a certain ratio of the certificates based on their actual output of fire-based electricity, and that can in a way mitigate the shortfall of renewable subsidies. As a result, renewable power generation projects can be compensated in three ways – market price for renewable electricity, fixed subsidy from central finance, and income from the trading of the Green Electricity Certificate. With the certificate as a transition, the fixed subsidy can be phased out moving forward with technological progress and cost reduction.[57]

After the 19th CPC National Congress, the nation took energy transition as a key approach to improving the ecological environment, creating tremendous opportunities for the clean energy industry to take off. Data from China Electricity Council (CEC) showed that by the end of 2017, China had 650GW renewable capacity, which accounted for 36.6% of all installed capacity in the country, with hydro, wind, and PV capacity all topping the world. Among that, there was 130GW PV capacity, which maintained the largest increment for five consecutive years and the largest cumulative capacity for three. Yet the splendid performance couldn't hide the dilemma for PV development – the gap in subsidy remained huge and synchronization remained difficult. The scale-back of PV subsidy was accompanied by a widening deficiency. According to data from the Ministry of Finance, renewable energy subsidy was short by up to RMB 100 billion by the end of 2017, half of which were in the PV sector. At the same time, abandoning wind and solar electricity remained a serious problem despite an abating trend. In 2017, PV power output in China increased 78.6% year-on-year, and 6% was given up, down 4.3 percentage points year-on-year. Although the rate of abandonment dropped for the first time, the problem wasn't fundamentally solved as the grid system was not strong enough either in synchronization or in the transmission of renewable electricity. In November 2017, NDRC and NEA jointly issued the *Implementation Plan for Addressing the Abandonment of Hydro, Wind and Solar Electricity*, and took effective measures to use renewable energy sources in a more efficient way. They strove to solve the problem once and for all by 2020.

In March 2018, NEA issued the *Methods of Renewable Electricity Quota and Assessment (draft for opinions)*, showing some hope of implementing the quota system that had been advocated for nearly 10 years since the *Amendment to the Renewable Energy Law* was enacted in 2009. Compared with the 2016 version, the contents of the assessment changed dramatically this time around. The focus moved from the power generation side to reform on the grid and power use side (from the amount of power generation to that of power use), and the quota increased for most provinces while only decreasing for some in central and eastern China. The methods made the consumption of renewable electricity an indicator and the basis for annual monitoring, evaluation, and assessment. It reflected three important principles. The first was that the focus should be on the demand side. The methods made it clear that "market entities obligated to undertake a quota include provincial-level grid companies, other kinds of power distributors and sellers (including privately funded ones), industrial enterprises with captive power plants, and direct electricity buyers that trade in the power market". This meant that the nation shifted the focus from power generators (suppliers in the power market) to the demand side. The second principle was that renewable electricity certificates must be traded freely in the real sense. The methods stated, "Provincial-level grid companies should formulate plans for fulfilling their quota in the service area, and guide market entities to prioritize trade in renewable electricity." This was a big step toward market-based certificate trading.[58] The third principle was reflecting the different capabilities of provinces and municipalities, which were assigned vastly different quotas due to their disparity in energy endowments. Sichuan had the highest renewable quota of 91%; Qinghai and Ningxia had the highest non-hydro quota of 21%, while Guangdong, Guangxi, and Chongqing had the lowest non-hydro quota of 3%.

As far as actual effects are concerned, the policy is tested not only in its principles and concepts but also in how well-conceived the details are and how aligned and coordinated it is with other policies. From this perspective, the methods still leave two major issues unresolved. The first is a "repeated" subsidy. It provides that "the renewable electricity sold to various market entities are credited to the buyers, not the sellers", a move to avoid double acing. Yet it also states, "despite the transfer and trading of renewable electricity certificate, the corresponding amount of electricity generated by renewable power generators shall continue to be eligible for national subsidy". This means renewable electricity subsidy and renewable electricity certificate, both being means of rewarding environmental benefits, will coexist at least for some time to come, but the coexistence may lead to unwanted results. The most direct consequence in the market is that the generation cost of renewable electricity will be artificially lowered by the grant of subsidy, which will stimulate investment and consequently create more renewable capacity. In the meantime, as every unit of renewable electricity will be matched with a unit of the certificate, the supply of certificates will expand, and that will bring down its price. The more subsidy, the lower the price of certificates, till the whole system becomes meaningless. Therefore, the two kinds of "reward" – in the form of subsidy and tradable certificate – will very likely offset rather than reinforce

Table 5.7 Assessment of implementation of quota system

Subject of assessment	*Duty 1*	*Duty 2*	*Duty 3*
Provincial-level people's governments	Formulate policies and measures to guarantee the fulfillment of renewable electricity quota in the administrative region	Carry out daily supervision and management, plan and create restrictive indicators, manage power construction and operation as required by the quota	Specify the minimal amount of renewable electricity in cross-region transmission as part of the provincial power balance
Provincial-level grid companies	Formulate implementation plan for fulfilling the quota in the service area; guide market entities to prioritize trade in renewable electricity	When the market mechanism cannot guarantee the full use of renewable electricity, enforce the quota as per the implementation plan approved by the provincial people's government	Sell Green Electricity Certificate
Industrial enterprises with captive power plants	Consume the minimal required amount of renewable electricity (higher than the local quota)	Captive power plants synchronized with the public grid must accept unified dispatching	Prioritize the consumption of renewable electricity
Institutions trading in the power market	Guarantee equal chance of trading for renewable electricity and electricity generated from other energy sources; guide market entities to prioritize trade in renewable electricity	Organize special trading for the consumption of renewable electricity	Monitor and provide information on renewable electricity transmitted across provinces/regions; the agency of the national energy administrator shall step in and make a decision in case of disputes.
Power generators	Actively build renewable capacity and produce renewable electricity according to programs, plans, and production management requirements	Coordinate with power dispatching agencies to prioritize the grid connection of renewable electricity	–

Source: Originally created by the author.

each other. This is essentially attributed to the coordination of different policies and must be addressed during the reform. At the end of 2017, China launched the carbon emission trade system in the electric power sector, giving market value to emissions. If the generation of renewable electricity can be financially rewarded for its contribution to emission reduction, we should think about how to have the two markets interact in a way that is mutually supportive rather than mutually weakening.

The second issue is well-conceived details to ensure the policy was effective. (1) As there is no effective penalty mechanism, enterprises would shirk responsibilities rather than willingly fulfill the quota. The methods provides that "market entities that fail to fulfill the quota must buy certificates from the local grid company to make up the gap". This resembles a penalty mechanism that makes sure market entities meet the quota as required; only the mechanism is very ambiguous.[59] (2) Is existing renewable electricity eligible for a certificate? We should reward renewable investments made in the past, but a more important purpose of the policy is to encourage more investment in the future. Therefore, more studies are needed to determine whether current renewable electricity is "qualified for certificate". (3) How does the government's quota allocation reflect a preference for certain renewable energy sources over others? Wind and solar are primary renewable energies at the moment, but the latter is known for conspicuous overcapacity. If we, from the industrial and environmental perspective, want to give more support to solar electricity, a feasible way is to put a multiplier on solar electricity, which means issuing more certificates. As a whole, there is still a long way to go before the quota system can be fully and truly implemented.

The *13th Five-Year Plan for Energy Technology Innovation* issued by NEA on January 13, 2017, vowed to concentrate efforts on making breakthroughs in major and key technologies, key materials, and key equipment. The purpose was to significantly enhance the capability of independent energy innovation, improve the international competitiveness of the energy industry, and primarily establish an energy technology innovation system in the 13th Five-Year Plan period. Special emphasis will be placed on clean and high-efficiency fossil energy, new-energy power system, safe, and advanced nuclear power, strategic energy, and basic energy materials.

(II) Internationally: clean energy diplomacy in global clean energy governance – an innovative demonstration and a guide on rules-making

With its rising overall national strength and influence, China's diplomatic philosophy has gradually changed from "hide our capacities and bide our time" to "exert ourselves and make a difference", displaying a new style of "growing enthusiasm and initiative". General Secretary Xi Jinping said in his report to the 19th CPC National Congress that "unconventional security threats like climate change continue to spread. As human beings we have many common challenges to face"; "taking a driving seat in international cooperation to respond to climate change, China has become an important participant, contributor, and torchbearer in the global endeavor for ecological civilization"; and "we should cooperate to tackle climate change, and protect our planet for the sake of human survival". At the 2017 Bonn Climate Change Conference, China, in addition to standing by the BRICS Group and providing full support for Fiji and the G77, also contributed to Chinese plans by submitting five of the 83 motions. It also set up a "China Corner", hosted several side events, and tried to enhance its discourse power and leading role in international climate governance by telling a good China story, making its voice heard loud and clear, and sharing its experience. In the field of clean energy, China overtook Germany and the US to become the largest investor and wind capacity holder in 2010. The remarkably consolidated green power gave China more confidence and weight in international clean energy cooperation.

First, China took advantage of home-court diplomacy and leaders' diplomacy to play a more active role in clean energy cooperation. At the 11th APEC Energy Ministers' Meeting held in Beijing in 2014, China, as the host country, determined the theme of "Joining Hands Towards Sustainable Energy Development in the Asia Pacific Region" and underlined the importance of clean energy cooperation for achieving the dual goals of promoting energy sustainability and preserving energy security in the region. The China-initiated APEC Sustainable Energy Center (APSEC) was officially established, dedicated to policy exchange, information sharing, capability building, joint R&D, and technological cooperation in sustainable energy.[60] In November 2014, when President Xi Jinping met with his American counterpart Barack Obama in Beijing, China, leveraging the opportunity of leaders' diplomacy, proposed to build a new model of major-country relationship between the two countries and jointly tackle regional and global challenges such as climate and energy. During the eighth session of S&ED in June 2016, China, once again taking advantage of home-court diplomacy, led the setting of the agenda. For instance, considering the difficulty in synchronizing clean electricity, China initiated a new cooperation – Power Consumption, Demand and Competition Cooperation – in the climate change working group. The new cooperation was focused on testing smart grid devices, equipment, standards, and systems in a bid to fundamentally break the bottleneck on the synchronization of clean electricity.

Second, China had more initiative in technological cooperation. During Obama's term, the China-US cooperation in clean energy topped the world in terms of investment, installed capacity, and trade volume. Their model of cooperation – with its demonstration, rules-making, and standard-setting – exerted a growing influence on global clean energy governance. The CERC set up at the end of 2011 made marked achievements in the first five-year period (2011–2015). It expanded to include two new research areas in 2014–2015 – water and energy technology as well as fuel-saving truck technology – and was renewed for a second five-year term (2016–2020). CERC operated much differently from traditional cooperation programs. Traditionally, the cooperating institutions conducted their R&D independently based on respective strengths and only interacted through friendly mutual visits and academic exchanges – a model of "external sharing" of research findings. This model generated only academic benefits but few, if any, IP benefits to the research partner. However, at CERC, both sides jointly made the work plan for research projects, which was an "internal sharing" of interdependence. The participating institutes conducted joint R&D in the complementarity of strengths, produced findings together, and the benefits were credited to the partnership and materialized through commercialization. Intellectual property (IP) was a pressing issue between the Chinese and American partners, and the new model helped them develop and acquire IP by working side by side in the whole process from R&D

to industrialization.[61] The CERC model was exemplary in that the Chinese and American sides reached an agreement on the IP protection and sharing framework through consultation, which was innovative because it used the Technology Management Plans (TMPs) to specify the distribution, ownership, management, and use of IP during collaborative research. TMPs offered an effective way of sharing interests and dispelling divergences concerning IP management in the cooperation among industry, universities, and research institutes.

Third, China contributed its plans and wisdom through intensified interactions with international platforms. For example, it was officially admitted to IRENA in January 2014, securing important international resources for its development and utilization of renewables. A major part of IRENA's work is building a database and agency to provide all countries with accurate information and professional technical services in their development and utilization of renewables. As an intergovernmental organization with a broad base of membership, IRENA's database is more comprehensive and authoritative, and making full use of its data and technical services helps China develop and use the energy source at home and abroad. In the meantime, as a major clean energy developer, China can showcase its achievements in renewables development to the world, share experience, and strengthen cooperation with other countries. Its achievements over recent years are obvious to all. Statistics show that it is the world's largest energy producer and one of the top investors in renewable energy. Joining IRENA enables it to better present China's achievements and successful experience, seek more cooperation opportunities, and enhance its international influence in the field.

Another example is China's active role in driving clean energy cooperation within the G20. G20 leaders adopted the G20 Principles on Energy Collaboration in 2014, for which China was the main proponent playing an active part in the drafting and negotiations. In the principles, countries agreed to

> (1) support sustainable growth and development, consistent with our climate activities and commitments, including by promoting cost-effective energy efficiency, renewables, and clean energy; (2) encourage and facilitate the design, development, demonstration and widespread deployment of innovative energy technologies, including clean energy technologies; (3) rationalize and phase out inefficient fossil fuel subsidies that encourage wasteful consumption, over the medium term, while being conscious of the necessity to provide targeted support for the poor; (4) make international energy institutions more representative and inclusive of emerging and developing economies; and (5) enhance coordination between international energy institutions and minimize duplication where appropriate.

The principles also set common goals regarding access to energy for all, energy markets, energy data and analysis, energy security, phasing out of inefficient fossil fuel subsidies, sustainable growth and development, and innovative and clean energy technologies. In addition, G20 set up a number of nonbinding energy cooperation mechanisms.[62] For example, treaty-based international energy organizations (e.g., IEA) founded a new cooperation platform with nonmember emerging economies, in which China was an active driver.

In November 2015, the IEA Association was officially formed, with China, Indonesia, and Thailand being the first batch of Association countries, and they began to cooperate in energy security, energy statistics, energy policy analysis, and other aspects. Existing cooperation mechanisms also improved their coordination. IEA, IEF (International Energy Fund) and OPEC (Organization of the Petroleum Exporting Countries) formed a symposium mechanism on the working level to regularly discuss methods of making energy forecasts and better coordinate their work to reduce duplication.[63]

Fourth, China pushed forward clean energy diplomacy across the board, strengthening cooperation with other developing countries and innovating the mode of South-South cooperation. Take clean energy cooperation between China and Brazil for example. In 2015, the two countries released the *Joint Statement Between the Government of the People's Republic of China and the Government of the Federative Republic of Brazil on Climate Change*. With this, they agreed to further strengthen bilateral high-level dialogue on domestic climate policy and multilateral process and intensify pragmatic cooperation, particularly in such areas as renewable energy, forest carbon sink, energy conservation, energy efficiency, adaptation, and low-carbon urbanization. In 2015, Premier Li Keqiang and then Brazilian president Dilma Rousseff signed the *Joint Action Plan Between the Government of the Federative Republic of Brazil and the Government of the People's Republic of China 2015–2021*. The Joint Action Plan pinpointed areas of cooperative research that would help them respond to climate change, covering bioenergy and biofuels, agrarian sciences, climate change, and new energy technology innovation.[64] The two countries should also fortify their complementarity in clean energy and support each other in biomass and solar energy technologies. On the one hand, China could work more closely with Brazil in second-generation bioethanol technology and the use of ethanol gasoline for motor vehicles, a purpose well served by the Brazil-initiated Biofuture Platform, which China joined at the end of 2016.[65] On the other hand, with its quality PV capacity, China could assist Brazil in its industrialization and clean energy development and help achieve its ambitious PV goals.[66] While deepening the cooperation in the solar energy industry, they could also carry out exchange and training on policy, planning, technical standards, testing, and certification.

Section 3 Path and features of China's clean energy diplomacy

Against the background of the global low-carbon transition, clean energy diplomacy is an important way of preserving a nation's core interests, enhancing low-carbon competitiveness, and improving the international environment for low-carbon development. To better deal with all challenges and shift toward low-carbon, clean energies, countries need to set clear goals and strengthen international cooperation. Though it's not easy to transform the industrial civilization based on fossil fuels (especially coal), China has declared its resolve to push the low-carbon energy transition and promote global cooperation in that area. Its clean energy diplomacy, while becoming increasingly institutionalized, has kept evolving and expanding in terms of diplomatic dimensions, patterns, and actors. An analysis of the developing stages of China's clean energy diplomacy shows a clear shift of focus from economic development to green governance and green strengths. First, as far as diplomatic level and dimension is concerned, it has evolved from traditional bilateral cooperation to multilateral diplomacy and a multi-dimension architecture comprising the international, regional, national, and sub-national levels (including private level). Second, as far as diplomatic scope is concerned, South-South cooperation has grown alongside South-North cooperation, with new breakthroughs in the mode of cooperation. Third, as far as the diplomatic model is concerned, China is paying more attention to expanding global partnership networks and building international cooperation platforms. At last, as far as diplomatic actors are concerned, in addition to government departments and intergovernmental organizations that used to dominate clean energy diplomacy, a variety of new actors have now joined, including research institutes, NGOs, social groups, multinational policy networks, and clean energy industry associations.

I. Clean energy diplomacy: from "bilateral major-country diplomacy" to "multilateral, multi-track diplomacy"

China's clean energy diplomacy got the fast track in 2007 as the country issued the *Medium- and Long-term Development Plan for Renewable Energy* and listed clean energy as a strategic emerging industry. Especially after 2008, the global strategic landscape of energy and climate evolved more quickly and a new situation of international low-carbon cooperation centering on clean energy took shape, providing a historical opportunity for the all-around development of Chinese clean energy diplomacy. This marked a new stage for China, a stage when it paid more attention to multilateral and multi-track cooperation on the global and regional level in addition to bilateral cooperation with Europe and the US. For instance, it advanced flexible cooperation with G20, Asia-Pacific Economic Cooperation (APEC), and the Association of Southeast Asian Nations (ASEAN), laying a solid foundation for regional clean development and green energy security. In this process, China played a more proactive and constructive role, changing from a participant and recipient to a leader and builder of diplomatic cooperation mechanisms.

On the global level, G20 became more influential in global clean energy governance.[67] At the 3rd G20 Summit in 2009, all participants agreed that developing clean energy offered a package solution to energy security, climate change, and economic development.[68] The first G20 Energy Ministerial Meeting held in 2015 adopted the *G20 Energy Access Action Plan: Voluntary Collaboration on Energy Access*, which focused on renewable energy, energy efficiency, and energy investment. It particularly launched the "G20 Toolkit of Voluntary Options for Renewable Energy Deployment" to make better use of clean energies. As the 2016 rotating chair of G20, China hosted three G20 Energy Sustainability Working Group (ESWG) meetings – the first time in Xiamen, the second in Shenzhen, and the third in Beijing. Later the NEA hosted in Beijing the Energy Ministerial Meeting (EMM) themed "Building a Low-carbon, Intelligent and Shared Energy Future" on June 29–30, 2016. Officials from 27 countries and relevant international organizations participated in the meeting, committed to bolstering energy cooperation in a wider scope within the G20 framework to deal with energy security and environmental security challenges. The meeting generated four deliverables – the *G20 Energy Ministerial Meeting Beijing Communiqué*,[69] *Enhancing Energy Access in Asia and* the *Pacific: Key Challenges and G20 Voluntary Collaboration Action Plan*, *G20 Voluntary Action Plan on Renewable Energy*, and *G20 Energy Efficiency Leading Programme (EELP)*.

Among them, the *G20 Voluntary Action Plan on Renewable Energy* encouraged members to formulate clean energy action plans based on national contexts and conditions, especially medium- and long-term energy strategies, including renewable energy. This was to boost financing and investment in the production and utilization of renewables, and increase green energy to a much higher percentage in the global energy mix.[70] At the 11th G20 Hangzhou Summit in 2016, China launched the Green Finance and Climate Fund aimed at driving the development of clean energy and the access to green energy, which caught the spotlight at the summit and led to a new trend in clean energy diplomacy. The Hangzhou Summit was of great importance for implementing the *2030 Sustainable Development Agenda* and the *Paris Agreement* signed in 2015. It fully demonstrated China's concept of "innovative, coordinated, green, open and shared development" established during the 13th Five-Year Plan period. In particular, green development based on clean energy was considered a key path to achieving the 2030 Sustainable Development Goals (SDGs) and delivering the *Paris Agreement*. Despite their different development stages and levels, all G20 members had set targets for the common goal of significantly increasing the percentage of renewables in the global energy mix by 2030.

On the regional level, the APEC member economies, including four of the top five energy consumers (China, the US, Russia and Japan), accounted for about 60% of the world's energy demand. The APEC Energy Working Group formed in 1990 was one of the first working groups under the APEC framework. Clean energy appeared high on the political agenda of Asian-Pacific cooperation at the 8th APEC Energy Ministerial Meeting in 2007 with the passing of the *Darwin Declaration*. In recent years, China has actively pushed low-carbon initiatives related to clean energy through the APEC Energy Working Group (EWG). In 2010, it created a 10-million-dollar "APEC Cooperation Fund" that prioritized sci-tech cooperation in clean energy and environmental protection.[71] At the APEC Summit in 2010 and 2011, Chinese leaders put forth the Low-carbon Demonstration Town (LCDT) initiative, with Yujiapu (YJP) Financial District in Tianjin designated as the first LCDT. In 2012, NEA submitted the *APEC Low Carbon Model Town Project – China Development Report*, advocated promotion activities, established the project database, and pushed forward project cooperation. When hosting the 11th APEC Energy Ministerial Meeting in Beijing in 2014, China, exerting home-court diplomacy, highlighted the critical role of clean energy in meeting the dual target of promoting energy sustainability and preserving energy security in the region.

Besides, the China-initiated APEC Sustainable Energy Center (APSEC), led and operated by Tianjin University, was officially established. The center was committed to promoting policy exchange, information sharing, capacity building, joint R&D, and technical cooperation among the economies for sustainable development. For instance, since 2015, APSEC has focused on advancing Solar-Powered Emergency Shelter Solutions (SPESS) that improve energy resilience and sustainable construction in disaster-hit areas of APEC economies, as well as clean coal technology (CCT) cooperation projects.[72]

Table 5.8 China's foreign cooperation in clean energy on global, regional mechanisms/platforms

Global/regional platform	*When the topic first draws attention*	*Main mechanisms and milestones*	*Achievements*
G20	2009: 3rd G20 Summit	Main mechanism: G20 Energy Ministerial Meeting • 2015: *G20 Energy Access Action Plan: Voluntary Collaboration on Energy Access* and G20 Toolkit of Voluntary Options for Renewable Energy Deployment • 2016: *G20 Voluntary Action Plan on Renewable Energy* • 2016: G20 Energy Ministerial Meeting Beijing Communiqué • 2016: *Enhancing Energy Access in Asia and the Pacific: Key Challenges and G20 Voluntary Collaboration Action Plan* • 2016: *G20 Energy Efficiency Leading Programme*	• 2016: G20 Green Finance Study Group promoting green finance • 11th G20 Summit: more ways of international cooperation in clean energy

(Continued)

Table 5.8 (Continued)

Global/regional platform	*When the topic first draws attention*	*Main mechanisms and milestones*	*Achievements*
APEC	2007: 8th APEC Energy Ministerial Meeting	Main mechanism: APEC Energy Ministerial Meeting • 2007: Darwin Declaration • 2014: Beijing Declaration • 2015: Building sustainable and resilient communities	• China-led APEC Energy Working Group (EWG) • 2010: APEC Cooperation Fund • 2012: APEC Low Carbon Model Town Project – China Development Report • 2014: China-US Joint Statement on Climate Change • 2014: APEC Sustainable Energy Center (APSEC)
Association of Southeast Asian Nations (ASEAN)	2007: 2nd East Asia Summit	Main mechanism: East Asia Summit • 2007: Cebu Declaration on East Asian Energy Security • 2007: Singapore Declaration on Climate Change, Energy and the Environment	• 2011: China initiated the regular meeting of energy and environmental ministers • 2014: Annual East Asia Summit Clean Energy Forum • 2017: China-ASEAN Clean Energy Capacity Building Programme – "100 policy and technical experts within 10 years"
		Main mechanism: ASEAN Plus China, Japan, ROK ("10+3") • Asia Energy Cooperation Task Force (ECTF)	• 2012: China advocated green energy connectivity
		Main mechanism: ASEAN Plus China ("10+1") • 2009: ASEAN-China Environmental Protection Cooperation Strategy (2009–2015) • 2010: ASEAN-China Leaders Joint Statement on Sustainable Development • 2010: China-ASEAN Environmental Cooperation Center • 2015: China-ASEAN Clean Energy Capability Building Center • 2017: Vision and Actions on Energy Cooperation in Jointly Building Silk Road Economic Belt and 21st-Century Maritime Silk Road	

(Continued)

Table 5.8 (Continued)

Global/regional platform	*When the topic first draws attention*	*Main mechanisms and milestones*	*Achievements*
Shanghai Cooperation Organization (SCO)	2008: 8th SCO Summit	Main mechanism: SCO Summit • 2008: Dushanbe Declaration of Heads of SCO Member States	• 2012: clean energy diversification plan • 2014: China-SCO Environmental Cooperation Center

Source: Originally created by the author.

The exchange between China and ASEAN countries on clean energy capability building will bring out their complementarity, further deepen their cooperation, and promote clean energy development and energy transition, thus facilitating regional economic integration. The East Asia Summit (EAS), ASEAN Plus China, Japan and ROK meeting ("10+3") and ASEAN Plus China meeting ("10+1") are the three chariots driving the cooperation between China and Southeast Asia, and also important platforms for clean energy diplomacy. The *Cebu Declaration on East Asian Energy Security* adopted at the Second East Asia Summit in 2007 set out the goals of regional clean energy cooperation as well as concrete measures, including technology R&D, formulation of standards, and innovation of financing schemes. The *Singapore Declaration on Climate Change, Energy and the Environment* signed at the third summit in November that year further underscored the pivotal role of clean energy in addressing climate change, energy security, and environmental protection.

After 2011, China succeeded in settling the regular meeting of energy and environmental ministers under the EAS framework and formed the energy cooperation task force focused on low-carbon development. China and ASEAN Energy Center co-initiated the EAS Clean Energy Forum, which, intended to deepen pragmatic cooperation and boost mutual benefits, has become a key platform for regional clean energy cooperation. It aims to tackle clean energy challenges facing the region, tighten energy cooperation, and strengthen exchanges on clean energy technology. The first forum was held in Chengdu, China, in August 2014, at which themed seminars on PV, biomass energy, and smart energy city were carried out within the "Maritime Silk Road" framework to promote the region's green transformation. The second forum was held in Haikou, China in November 2015, covering such topics as nuclear energy, solar PV, biomass energy, electricity, clean coal, and smart energy city. The third one in 2017 launched the China-ASEAN Clean Energy Capacity Building Programme, striving to cultivate 100 policy and technical experts for ASEAN countries within ten years. The program is co-implemented by China Renewable Energy Engineering Institute and ASEAN Energy Center.[73]

An Energy Cooperation Task Force (ECTF) was also set up in the ASEAN "10+3" framework to reinforce regional investment in and development of clean energy technology. On September 7, 2016, Chinese Premier Li Keqiang attended the 19th China-ASEAN (10+3) Summit in Vientiane, Laos, which released the *Chairman's Statement of the 19th ASEAN-China Summit* that "welcomed the program proposed by China to enhance capacity building on clean energy with the ASEAN Member States". In the ASEAN "10+1" framework, bilateral clean energy cooperation was based on established regional platforms for environmental cooperation. For instance, the *China-ASEAN Environmental Protection Cooperation Strategy (2009–2015)* highlighted clean production and environmental administration capability building as priority areas of cooperation. The China-ASEAN Environmental Cooperation Center was formed in 2010 to intensify scientific research and technological cooperation in clean energy and environmental cooperation and to push for the creation of policy dialogue platforms such as the China-ASEAN Green Envoys Program. In 2015, China General Nuclear Power Group (CGN) and ASEAN Energy Center decided to sign a cooperation agreement on nuclear construction capability to jointly advance the establishment of the China-ASEAN Clean Energy Capability Building Center.

With the *Dushanbe Declaration of Heads of SCO Member States* signed at the 8th SCO Summit in 2008, countries in the region reached a common stance on tackling climate change and developing clean energy sources. At the 10th SCO Summit in 2012, China called for promoting the use of clean energy to provide diversified energy solutions for member states to boost their economy. To intensify regional dialogue and coordination on that, Chinese Premier Li Keqiang said at the 2013 summit that all parties should work together to build an information-sharing platform and push forward the SCO strategy of environmental protection and sustainable energy cooperation. His call led to the creation of the SCO Energy Club,[74] in which clean energy development was listed on the agenda for cooperation among members. China, as a global leader in clean energy, could further explore how to carry out South-South cooperation in a green way, to help other members improve technologies for energy conservation and environmental protection and enhance their capability of clean energy development. Against such a background, clean energy holds the greatest potential for future energy cooperation among SCO members. In 2014, the China-SCO Environmental Cooperation Center was officially inaugurated, demonstrating China's efforts to actively expand multilateral, multi-track clean energy diplomacy. At the 15th SCO Summit in 2016, Li Keqiang advised the members, leveraging the organization as a platform for energy cooperation and environmental information sharing, to learn from each other and share successful experience in protecting the environment and developing clean energy.

In June 2018, the 18th SCO Summit was held in Qingdao, Shandong Province, at which China, exerting the advantage of home-court diplomacy, highlighted the strategic goal of preserving ecological balance and achieving green and sustainable development. The summit also started a new situation of regional clean energy cooperation, with a view to integrating the various energy cooperation regimes on the SCO platform to underpin and power Belt and Road construction. China's leading edge in renewable energy will be helpful for the green energy cooperation among SCO members and will stimulate sustainable, win-win development among other members. Regarding joint development of clean energy projects, for instance, the China-Kyrgyzstan hydropower project, China-Kazakhstan PV project, and China-Russia nuclear project will be highlights of bilateral energy cooperation.

II. Clean energy: a key innovation for South-South cooperation and foreign aid

"South-South cooperation" refers to the diplomatic cooperation regime whereby developing countries share their development plans, including knowledge, experience, policy, technology, and resources. In the narrow sense, it refers to the assistance offered by emerging major developing countries to medium- and small-sized ones, especially underdeveloped countries in Africa and Latin America; in the broad sense, it also includes the diplomatic cooperation between emerging major developing countries, such as clean energy diplomacy within the BRICS group. With its rapid development of clean energies and innovation of relevant technologies, China began to underline its contributions to South-South cooperation while continuing to promote South-North cooperation. Acting as a bellwether in international trade and technology cooperation, construction of green projects, and personnel training, it brought great opportunities for other "southern countries" to change course to green energy.[75]

First of all, clean energy took a more important position in "South-South Aid" in a growing number of forms, ranging from technology transfer, financial aid, and project construction to supply of materials, personnel training, and debt relief. China has established a sound technology system in areas such as energy efficiency, development, and utilization of renewable energy, forest management, and disaster prevention and mitigation. It has many low-cost, easy-to-learn, and quick-to-take-effect technologies that can apply to developing countries extensively.[76] African countries, for example, have neither the capital nor the technology to develop new energies, but they are structurally complementary to China in terms of capital, technology, resources, and market, thus creating vast space for new energy cooperation. The fourth Forum on China-Africa Cooperation (FOCAC) in 2009 decided that China will help build 100 clean energy projects in Africa, including solar, biogas, and small hydro; the fifth FOCAC in 2012 released the *FOCAC Beijing Action Plan (2013–2015)*, which said, "The two sides will actively advance cooperation in clean energy and renewable resources projects in keeping with the principles of mutual benefit and sustainable development." China and Africa cooperated extensively in clean energy, including wind, solar, biogas, and small hydro.[77] In June 2012, then premier of the State Council Wen Jiabao announced at the UN Conference on Sustainable Development that China will provide RMB 200 million in the next three years to support South-South cooperation in response to climate change. The white paper, *China's Foreign Aid*, issued by the State Council in 2014 showed that China had signed MoU on the provision of supplies with more than 20 countries and regions, cumulatively arranged RMB 720 million of special funds for that, and presented huge amounts of energy-saving products to developing countries. From 2010 to 2012, it undertook 64 renewable energy projects in 58 developing countries, including solar streetlamps and solar power generators. In addition to that, it provided 16 batches of clean energy equipment and supplies, including wind, solar, and biogas equipment, to 13 developing countries such as Cambodia, Myanmar, and Ethiopia. In this period, China hosted 150 training sessions on tackling climate change, developing low-carbon industries, and using clean energy, training more than 4,000 officials and technical personnel from over 120 developing countries.

At the same time, China worked closer with regional financial institutions such as Asian Development Bank, African Development Bank, West African Development Bank, and Caribbean Development Bank to channel more capital into clean development. In September 2014, Vice Premier Zhang Gaoli, special envoy of President Xi Jinping, announced at the UN Climate Summit that China would increase the funds for "South-South Cooperation on Climate Change" and set up the South-South Climate Cooperation Fund. In September 2015, the China-US Joint Presidential Statement on Climate Change was released, announcing the size of China's South-South Climate Cooperation Fund to be RMB 20 billion. In December of that year, President Xi Jinping, at the Paris Climate Change Conference, proposed the "10–100–1000" plan under the "South-South Climate Cooperation" framework, in a bid to improve developing countries' ability of low-carbon transformation by advancing clean energy and climate adaptation. The "10–100–1000" plan meant that from 2016, China would fund 10 low-carbon demonstration zones, 100 climate adaptation and mitigation projects, and 1,000 training opportunities in response to climate change.[78] When President Xi attended the FOCAC in December 2015, he proposed to elevate the China-Africa new-type strategic partnership to a comprehensive strategic partnership, which came with a USD 60-billion fund, with clean energy being the center of the aid. Under this arrangement, China would train 200,000 African technical personnel, some engaged in clean energy development, and support 100 clean energy projects in Africa.

During this period, clean energy diplomacy among emerging developing countries gained ground. After the financial crisis, these countries became more important in global governance, and China intensified diplomatic cooperation with other emerging countries such as India, Brazil, and South Africa. As a result, BRICS countries were not only a vital engine powering world economic growth, but also a powerful force driving the development of green energy. When BRICS' energy ministers met at the Clean Energy Ministerial in Beijing, they issued a joint statement pledging to support each other and promote renewables development. BRICS countries were making up a rising share in global renewables. According to data from IRENA, the group had 39.4% of the world's renewable capacity in 2016, more than their percentage in global GDP (22.5% in 2015). China was dominant in the picture with 2/3 of BRICS' total renewable capacity, while Brazil and India displayed robust momentum with about 5% each. In comparison, Russia and South Africa took a much smaller share, but their capacity kept increasing. They as a group are expected to play a much bigger role in global renewable energy development over the next few years.[79] Statistics show that according to their respective renewable targets, their total capacity will reach 1,252GW in 2020–2030, an increase of 498GW that, in itself, accounts for about 25% of the current capacity worldwide.[80] The first-ever BRICS Summit in 2009 vowed to diversify the supply of energy resources and carry out climate change dialogue, hence the solidarity of the BASIC (China, Brazil, India, and South Africa) at the Copenhagen Climate Change Conference. The 3rd BRICS Summit in 2011 released the *Sanya Declaration*, in which members agreed to step up cooperation and information exchange in the field of clean energy. The 4th Summit in 2012 made it clear that clean energy should be seen as an important opportunity to rocket the collective rise of emerging countries in the post-financial crisis era. The first BRICS Financial Forum that year, also initiated by China, tried to combine clean energy with financial governance on the existing platform, to power the green energy transition with financial leverage. This mechanism led to the establishment of the New Development Bank (NDB) in 2015, which was tasked with supporting infrastructure construction and promoting sustainable development. The NDB announced in 2016 its first batch of loans worth RMB 811 million, which were granted to support four renewable energy projects respectively in Brazil, China, India, and South Africa. This was a powerful channel of green finance for clean energy cooperation within the BRICS.

In the meantime, energy efficiency, a topic related to clean development, was also chosen as an entry point for energy cooperation. The first BRICS meeting on energy efficiency was held in May 2015; six months later, the first BRICS Energy Ministers Meeting was held in Moscow, at which the Memorandum of Mutual Understanding in Energy Saving and Energy Efficiency was signed and a corresponding task force was formed. On September 4, 2017, leaders of BRICS countries signed the *BRICS Leaders Xiamen Declaration* in Xiamen, East China's Fujian Province. The Declaration called upon all countries to fully implement the *Paris Agreement* under the principles of common but differentiated responsibilities and respective capabilities, and promote most effective use of fossil fuels and wider use of gas, hydro, and nuclear power, which will contribute to the transformation toward a low emissions economy, better energy access, and sustainable development. The leaders also encouraged continued dialogue on the establishment of a BRICS Energy Research Cooperation Platform and urged relevant entities to continue to promote joint research on energy cooperation and energy efficiency.

III. Clean energy diplomacy: more emphasis on global partnership networks

In recent years, clean energy diplomacy is getting increasingly networked, and building global partnership networks is an important part of diplomatic practices. Representative networks include International Renewable Energy Agency (IRENA), Renewable Energy Policy Network for the 21st Century (REN21), Renewable Energy and Energy Efficiency Partnership (REEEP), and Global Network on Energy for Sustainable Development (GNESD).[81] In terms of participants, these partnership networks involve a broader scope of actors, including intergovernmental organizations, government organs, and local governments, as well as NGOs, cross-national policy networks, universities, research institutes, think tanks, and the clean energy industry associations. On a functional note, these networked organizations can provide a platform for the flow of information, experts, and capital; on the other hand, they can coordinate the work of most international organizations and experts, as well as provide consulting services, promote technology, and set the framework for coordinating international law.[82] Therefore, for China to lead clean energy diplomacy, it must continuously build all kinds of partnership networks and enhance its agenda-setting power, rules-making power, and institutional discourse power in multi-dimension cooperation. Actively blending into the multi-dimensioned, networked international clean energy governance system can amplify China's institutional capability in forming the order of new energy sources.

In the past, China attached more importance to bilateral and multilateral cooperation on the state level, but had few interactions (with a weak discourse power as well) with non-intergovernmental organizations and policy/information networks. However, it has made active attempts to merge into global partnership networks and forums in recent years and played a leading part in such organizations as REEEP, REN21, IRENA, Clean Energy Ministerial (CEM), and Global Green Growth Forum (3GF).

For example, China joined REEEP rather early. With its East Asia Regional Secretariat based in China, REEEP is aimed at perfecting clean energy policies and accelerating the tapping of the global renewables and energy efficiency market (including clearing market obstacles, increasing financing channels, and raising public awareness).[83] Soon after REN21 was established in 2005, it co-hosted the Beijing International Renewable Energy Conference (BIREC) with China.[84] The Chinese Renewable Energy Industries Association (CREIA) of the China Association of Circular Economy led by Li Junfeng joined the network as an industrial association. Since its founding in 2009, the CEM has been dedicated to promoting clean energy cooperation and innovation between the 23 members and the EU. The Chinese Ministry of Science and Technology (MOST), NEA, and NDRC all joined the cooperation. In the CEM framework, China took the lead in pushing the advanced electric vehicle initiative and participated in the smart city program and smart grid program. At the 6th CEM in 2015, the energy ministers announced to kick off the second phase – the "CEM2.0" with China being a member of the steering committee. When hosting the 8th CEM in 2017, China proposed to integrate the Second Mission Innovation Ministerial (MI-2) with CEM into CEM&MI, to further prompt green energy development and achieve the INDC goals. China was pragmatic in its cooperation with IRENA, participating in all its preparatory meetings and being an observer at the first through the third IRENA Assembly. It applied to officially join the agency at the 4th Assembly in 2013, was admitted on January 2, 2014, and is now the main contributor; China was elected a council member at the 5th Assembly in 2015. The two sides carried out a lot of activities together within a short period after China's admission. They held the China Day event in Abu Dhabi on January 20, 2014; IRENA and China National Renewable Energy Center (CNREC) jointly issued the *Renewable Energy Prospects 2030: China* at the end of that year; and NEA, IRENA, and the Jiangsu Provincial People's Government co-hosted the International Forum on Energy Transitions in Suzhou, China, in November 2015.

The *Suzhou Declaration* adopted at the forum proposed to establish a global coalition for energy transition and set up an "IRENA-China Research and Co-operation Centre for Energy Transition" to support its activities.[85] The 3GF was co-founded by the governments of Denmark, ROK, and Mexico in 2011; China, Kenya, and Qatar joined the next year, and Ethiopia became the seventh partner in 2014. These governments, together with numerous public and private partners, launched global public-private partnerships for inclusive and green growth in the long run. As one of the seven government partners, China has been an active participant in the forum with many Chinese enterprises and associations taking part. The forum also concerns itself with other issues in relation to inclusive and green growth.

IV. Private sector: a new driver of multi-party clean energy governance

According to IEA's forecast, the global low-carbon transformation will need USD 13.5 trillion by 2030 for the development of low-carbon and energy-saving technologies, but judging from the current situation, the public sector can only contribute to about 15% of the global investment.[86] The coming into force of the *Paris Agreement* sent a strong signal to both public and private sectors worldwide – we should establish an effective green finance system and introduce a raft of measures, including green credit, green securities and funds, green bonds, green insurance, and carbon finance represented by the carbon market. With that, we can steer green financing and investment around the globe and perfect the climate finance regime to uplift the position of the private sector in clean energy governance.[87] At the moment, a mode of partnership – Public Private Partnership (PPP) – has emerged between the private sector and the government-dominated public sector. Based on the franchising agreement, PPP is a mode of cooperation for building clean-energy-related infrastructure and providing green public goods and services, in which the public sector and private sector share responsibilities and financing risks. As more large banks and international investment companies engage in clean energy, and as green investment instruments such as green bonds, crowdfunding, and futures gain traction, China began to pay attention to the important role of green finance and PPP[88] in developing global partnership networks.[89] The People's Bank of China and the United Nations Environment Programme (UNEP) formed a joint task force in 2014 and a green finance committee in 2015. By the end of 2016, China had issued RMB 220 billion in green bonds, more than 40% of the global issuance, and the country replaced the US to be the largest green bonds issuer.[90]

It must be noted that the PPP model is spreading across borders and driving the multi-entity governance network. For instance, before the Paris Conference convened in 2015, Bill Gates initiated to form Breakthrough Energy Coalition that brought together 28 business leaders from world-leading tech companies, industrial conglomerates, and investment groups. They pledged to pull the strengths of governments and enterprises to invest more resources in the next five years to address climate change and clean energy, provided the participating countries must promise to double their budget for the R&D of clean energy technology. In December 2016, Breakthrough Energy Coalition announced to create Breakthrough Energy Ventures worth more than USD 1 billion, which will invest in startups and growth enterprises and provide the world with reliable, affordable, zero-emission energy, food, and products of the next generation. This coalition is a perfect illustration of international PPP co-founded by governments, research institutes, and investors. Chinese entrepreneurs such as Ma Yun and Wang Shi took an active part in it. Wang even founded the C Team – the first private organization in China in response to climate change – during the Paris Conference, and it launched the Low-carbon Initiative on behalf of 450,000 Chinese enterprises during the Bonn Conference in 2017. In this period, China enacted the *Charity Law of the People's Republic of China* and clarified relevant institutional arrangements. As a result, new progress was made in Internet-based donations, charity trusts, and corporate social responsibility (CSR). As these latest practices were applied in climate governance, Chinese philanthropists began to cut a figure on the international stage. On January 11, 2018, for example, Chinese female entrepreneur He Qiao'nyu signed an agreement with United Nations Office for South-South cooperation at the East-West Philanthropists Summit, kicking off the "Qiao program" with RMB 85 million. The program, based on the UN network, solicited pragmatic cooperation projects and climate priorities of developing countries from around the world and boosted energy transition and clean development. It was the world's first private fund focused on climate change and sustainable development after the *Paris Agreement* took effect.

Even in bilateral cooperation, the participation of a growing diversity of stakeholders is a conspicuous trend in clean energy diplomacy. Take China-US clean energy cooperation during Obama's term for example. In the framework of bilateral strategic and economic dialogue (S&ED), the Clean Energy Research Center (CERC) and US-China Renewable Energy Partnership (USCREP) formed in 2009 were both typical examples of multi-party cooperation. When Obama visited China in November 2009, the two countries signed the *Memorandum of Cooperation on Establishing US-China Renewable Energy Partnership* and formed the USCREP, which underlined the diversification of participants and expanded official bilateral cooperation to more dimensions. In other words, it not only involved the Chinese and American governments but also boosted the cooperation between a wide range of actors on both sides, from local governments, universities, and think tanks to enterprises and NGOs. With the China-US Renewable Energy Forum as an opportunity, USCREP provided an inclusive platform for a broad scope of actors to work together, including government agencies, renewable energy equipment manufacturers and developers, investment and financing institutes, research institutes, and industrial associations.

Another example is the three industry-university-research-institute alliances under CERC. The alliance on construction energy efficiency, led by Lawrence Berkeley National Laboratory (LBNL) on the American side and the Promotion Center for Science and Technology Development (MOHURD) on the Chinese side, consists of 66 partners, including the Oak Ridge National Laboratory (ORNL), Massachusetts Institute of Technology (MIT), Natural Resources Defense Council, Energy Foundation, DOW, GE-Guangdong Provincial Academy of Building Research, China Architecture Design & Research Group, and China Institute of Building Standards Design & Research. The alliance on clean coal, led by West Virginia University on the American side and Huazhong University of Science and

Technology on the Chinese side, consists of 30 partners; and the alliance on clean energy vehicle (NEV), led by the University of Michigan on the American side and Tsinghua University on the Chinese side, consists of 36 partners. Even though Trump was opposed to the clean energy program, many sub-state-level relations under USCREP have been sustained.

Table 5.9 Various entities participating in China-US clean energy cooperation

	US	*China*
Government agencies	• Department of Energy (DOE) • Office of Energy Efficiency and Renewable Energy (EERE)	• National Energy Administration (NEA) – China National Renewable Energy Center (CNREC) • Energy Research Institute (ERI)
Research and academic institutions	• National Renewable Energy Laboratory (NREL) • Lawrence Berkeley National Laboratory (LBNL) • Los Alamos National Laboratory (LANL) • MIT • West Virginia University • University of Michigan	• State Grid Energy Research Institute (SGERI) • Chinese Academy of Sciences (CAS) • China Renewable Energy Engineering Institute (CREEI) • Peking University • Tsinghua University • North China Electric Power University
Government-private cooperation organizations	US-China Energy Cooperation Program (ECP)	
Private organizations	• American Council on Renewable Energy (ACORE) • Energy Council • Environmental Defense Fund (EDF) • World Resources Institute (WRI) • Energy Foundation	• Chinese Renewable Energy Industries Association (CREIA) • Global Environmental Institute (GEI) • Wind Power Professional Committee of Chinese Renewable Energy Society • China Renewable Energy Society
Corporate stakeholders	• Energy producers • Enterprises of grid operation, power transmission, and distribution • Enterprises engaged in the energy system, energy/power equipment, and service • Certification institutions and independent engineering institutions • Material and construction enterprises • Transportation and aviation enterprises	

Sources: Based on information about USCREP, with additions. www.nrel.gov/uscrep.

Section 4 Driving mechanisms of China's clean energy diplomacy

With significant changes in the global strategic landscape of climate and energy, both international climate diplomacy and energy diplomacy are obviously turning low-carbon, with the rise of clean energy being the absolute highlight. As clean energy plays a vital role in building the new international energy order and pushing pragmatic climate diplomacy, clean energy diplomacy is taking form as a new type of diplomatic pattern. While participating in global climate and energy governance and cooperation, China makes a special point of integrating the domestic and international situations. Its awareness of its responsibilities as a major country and the proactive diplomatic strategy also offers a precious opportunity for deploying clean energy diplomacy, the rapid advancement of which is powered by several mechanisms.

I. Rise of the clean energy industry and policy innovation: foundation for clean energy diplomacy

China is a latecomer in the field of clean energy, but in the 21st century, it took only ten years to come to the front of the pack in renewable energy, during which time its hydropower doubled, wind power increased by 60 times, and PV 280 times. China beat Germany and the US in 2010 to be the world's largest holder of clean energy capacity while also leading the world in the growth of wind and PV capacity. Pew Charitable Trusts pointed out in its report *Who's Winning the Clean Energy Race? Growth, Competition and Opportunity in the World's Largest Economies* that China is leading the global investment in clean energy.[91] In 2013, China's new clean energy capacity surpassed its same-period new fossil and nuclear capacity for the first time. By 2014, it had 24% of the world's renewable capacity and the increment was 42% of the global increase. In 2015, China's investment in the new energy industry exceeded the combined investment of the US and Europe. REN21's latest global report 2018 showed China had 334GW clean energy capacity, more than the total 320GW of the 28 EU members, accounting for 1/3 in the world and 77.9% within BRICS. Of the top six clean energy countries, the capacity in China was more than twice that in the US, nearly three times in Germany, more than five times in India and Japan, and nearly nine times in Britain.

To promote the development of renewable energy, NDRC issued the *Medium- and Long-term Plan for Renewable Energy Development (2020)*, *11th Five-Year Plan for Renewable Energy Development (2006–2010)*, *12th Five-Year Plan for Renewable Energy Development (2011–2015)*, and *13th Five-Year Plan for Renewable Energy Development (2016–2020)* in 2007, 2008, 2012, and 2016 respectively. They set China's near-, medium- and long-term objectives for renewables.

The *11th Five-Year Plan for Renewable Energy Development (2006–2010)* set out to have renewable energy account for 10% of energy consumption and to use 300-million-ton standard coal of renewables by 2010. Except for ethanol fuel and biogas, other types of renewables all passed the targets at the end of the 11th Five-Year Plan period. The *12th Five-Year Plan for Renewable Energy Development*

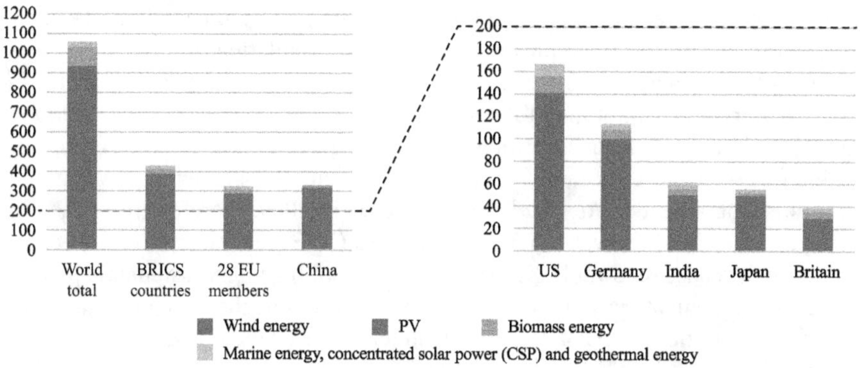

Figure 5.2 Capability of clean energy development in different countries (2017)

Source: REN21 Global Report 2018.

(2011–2015) proposed to have renewable energy account for more than 9.5% of energy consumption by 2015, which was equivalent to reducing about 1-billion-ton CO_2 emissions annually. In 2015, China used 436-million-ton standard coal of commercialized renewable energy, which was 10.1% of the total consumption of primary energies. The number would be 500-million-ton standard coal if non-commercialized renewables such as solar thermal energy were counted in, and the percentage of all nonfossil energy in primary energy consumption was 12% factoring in the contributions from nuclear power, up 2.6 percentage points from 2010. To reach the goal that nonfossil energy would make up 15% of primary energy consumption in 2020 and 20% in 2030, the *13th Five-Year Plan for Renewable Energy Development (2016–2020)* set clearer goals: By 2020, the annual use of renewables would reach 730-million-ton standard coal, including 580-million-ton standard coal of commercialized renewables; renewable capacity would reach 680GW with 1,900TWh power output, accounting for 27% of total power generation; wind power could compete with local coal-fired power in tariff; and PV power tariff was roughly on a par with the grid's selling price.

The rapid development of clean energy in China is partly attributed to its continuous policy innovations. The country has emulated and drawn on the innovative policies of green energy pioneers. Since NDRC's Energy Bureau set up a research institute on renewable energy policy in 2001, China expedited the three-phase process of studying and innovating clean energy policies, to provide a favorable policy, technical and social environment for clean energy development.[92] The first phase featured learning from the "British model". To have a clear idea of the cost of renewable energy production, China, drawing on the British model, launched a competitive franchised bidding system for wind power in 2000. In 2002, NDRC's Energy Bureau officially kicked off the bidding process, and it was promoted nationwide in 2004, leading to the 100MW franchised wind power project at Huitengxile wind farm Phase I in Inner Mongolia. The second phase featured learning from the "German model". In reference to the

German experience, China enacted the *Renewable Energy Law* in 2005 to guarantee profitability for green power generators by stipulating the FIT policy and the full-amount purchase of renewable electricity. The third phase, starting in 2009, featured the exploration to blend the "American model" with the "German model". Although FIT gave a strong boost to renewable capacity, the synchronization of green power became a new challenge with 30% of wind power going to waste. The amended *Renewable Energy Law* in 2009, therefore, proposed to bring in America's renewable portfolio standard (RPS) regime to force grid companies to purchase renewable electricity, in hopes of blazing a sustainable path of energy development truly suitable for China's conditions through policy innovation and integration. In 2014, the State Council released the *Energy Development Strategy Action Plan (2014–2020)*, which drew a blueprint for the medium- and long-term development of clean energy. It especially highlighted the coordinated planning of power sources and grid, the ability of frequency regulation and energy storage, as well as scientific peak shaving and the synchronization of all wind and solar electricity generated. However, the RPS, or quota system, aimed to address the abandonment of wind and solar electricity has been hard to carry out, which reflected how difficult it was to redistribute interests in the energy sector. Moreover, to make up for the subsidy deficit, market forces were mobilized to boost clean energy development too. A series of policy reforms, including the carbon market, Green Electricity Certificate, energy tax, and green finance, injected powerful impetus toward that goal. For instance, the national carbon trade market launched in 2017 provided a key guarantee for the effective implementation of RPS.[93] These efforts essentially augmented China's green strengths and confidence in clean energy diplomacy.

As shown in Table 5.11, China was a major country of clean energy development at the end of 2017, with the largest hydropower capacity, bioenergy output, wind power capacity, PV and solar-thermal capacity, and geothermal capacity. Its advantages in the field lie on the back end of the innovation industry chain – applying existing low-carbon technologies on a large scale and gradually improving them, such as the massive development of PV and wind power generation. China made tremendous contributions to the global low-carbon innovation by quickly lowering the cost of renewable energy production. As an emerging economy, it can participate in global energy innovation in the following two areas in the short term. First, it can continue to benefit from the transfer of high-quality energy technology from other countries. If developed countries transfer clean and high-efficiency energy technologies to China and other developing and emerging countries, the world will have a better chance of coping with climate change and realizing sustainable development. Besides, technology transfer only succeeds when intellectual property is well protected. Second, it can shift to the front end of the innovation industry chain regarding energy technology. To develop an innovative and sustainable economy, China needs to double up efforts in the first two stages of innovation, namely, basic research, application research and development of low-carbon technologies, and the piloting, demonstration, and early-stage application of existing technologies.[94]

Table 5.10 Main indicators of renewable energy development at the end of the 12th Five-Year Plan period

Content	*2010*	*Targets for the 12th Five-Year Plan period*	*2015*	*Average annual growth (%)*
I. Power generation				
1. Hydro (10MW)	21606	29000	31954	8.1
2. Synchronized wind power (10MW)	3100	10000	12900	33.0
3. PV (10MW)	80	2100	4318	122.0
4. Various bioenergies (10MW)	550	1300	1030	13.4
II. Gas supply				
Biogas (100 million m³)	140	220	190	6.3
III. Heating				
1. Solar water heater (10,000m²)	16800	40000	44000	21.2
2. Geothermal and others (10,000t standard coal/year)	460	1500	460	0.0
IV. Fuels				
1. Finished biofuels (10,000t)	0	1000	800	3.1
2. Ethanol fuels (10,000t)	180	400	210	9.9
3. Biodiesel (10,000t)	50	100	80	
Total use (10,000t standard coal/year)	28600	47800	51248	12.4

Source: 13th Five-Year Plan for Renewable Energy Development (2016–2020).

II. Power shift in the international system: a structural booster of clean energy diplomacy

In recent years, the international power shift between developed countries and developing ones has sped up as the global strategic landscape of climate and energy evolves. There is no denying that the power shift is a structural factor driving the rise of clean energy diplomacy. Let's first take a look at the world energy map. On the one hand, with the rise of emerging countries after the 2008 financial crisis, the gravity of global energy demand began to move eastward, and developing countries became more important in global energy governance. BP's statistics show that from 2011 to 2030, 93% of the increase in global energy consumption will come from non-OECD countries, and Asia-Pacific in particular is now the center of the growth, having more initiative in the current buyers' market. In comparison, the whole Western bloc is holding less sway in the energy system. Data from IEA show that the total energy consumption of Organization for Economic Co-operation and Development (OECD) countries began to shrink after peaking in 2007, and will account for only 30% of global consumption by 2040. On the other hand, developing countries represented by China have grown collectively in clean energy development amid the global switch toward low-carbon energy. As far as the development of clean energy technology is

Table 5.11 Top five countries in renewable energy capacity, 2017

Ranking	*1*	*2*	*3*	*4*	*5*
Electric power					
Renewable capacity (inc. hydro)	China	US	Brazil	Germany	India
Renewable capacity (exc. hydro)	China	US	Germany	India	Japan
Per capita renewable capacity (exc. hydro)	Iceland	Denmark	Germany/ Sweden		Finland
Bioenergy output	China	US	Brazil	Germany	Japan
Biomass capacity	US	Brazil	China	India	Germany
Geothermal capacity	US	The Philippines	Indonesia	Turkey	New Zealand
Hydropower capacity	China	Brazil	Canada	US	Russia
Hydropower output	China	Brazil	Canada	US	Russia
PV capacity	China	US	Japan	Germany	Italy
Per capita PV capacity	Germany	Japan	Belgium	Italy	Australia
CSP capacity	Spain	US	South Africa	India	Morocco
Wind power capacity	China	US	Germany	India	Spain
Per capita wind power capacity	Denmark	Ireland	Sweden	Germany	Portugal
Thermal energy					
Solar thermal capacity	China	US	Turkey	Germany	Brazil
Per capita solar thermal capacity	Barbados	Austria	Cyprus	Israel	Greece
Geothermal capacity	China	Turkey	Iceland		

Source: REN 21 Global Report 2018.

concerned, while Europe remains an important market and innovation center, developing regions are showing more vigor and vitality. Even when the international petroleum market was in a continued depression, clean energy investment from emerging countries kept increasing quickly, amounting to USD 167 billion in 2015, surpassing the USD 145 billion in developed countries for the first time.[95] The total investment from developing countries, including China, India, and Brazil, was up 19% year-on-year to reach USD 156 billion, with China contributing the dominant USD 102.9 billion (a year-on-year increase of 17%), which was 36% of the global total. Renewable investments in India, Mexico, South Africa, and Chile also increased markedly.[96]

The international climate governance landscape is closely linked with the strategic energy landscape. For one thing, the center of energy consumption moving eastward accelerated the division and regrouping of various forces in climate negotiations. The sharp increase in carbon emissions in developing countries put them at the center of global emission-cutting efforts. In this process, the main contradiction during the negotiations changed from the "South-North confrontation" between developing countries and developed ones to the "confrontation" between big and small emitters. Especially after the Durban Platform for Enhanced Action was set up in 2011, the EU strongly pushed for a legally binding agreement encompassing all contracting parties, and that became the general trend in international climate negotiations. After the *Paris Agreement* came into effect in 2016, carbon emission right became a rare strategic resource, and carbon constraints were tightening worldwide. For another, the world map of climate negotiations was in the middle of significant change. With the EU losing its leadership and the Obama administration facing more challenges outside the UNFCCC framework, global climate governance became increasingly fragmented without a pivot.[97] It was against such a background that the China-led BASIC Group was gaining weight and injecting new vitality into global climate governance. However, after Trump was elected US president in 2017, he seriously undermined and challenged global climate governance. On the one hand, the US was retrogressing across the board on clean energy and climate policies, be it legislative, administrative, or judicial, and that posed climate governance in the post-Paris era to a more complex and grave reality. On the other hand, major developing countries, primarily China, had more space to lead the establishment of a new order of climate governance and clean energy. In sum, the changing landscape of energy and climate provided more opportunities for emerging developing countries to form a new order of global energy and climate governance.

To be specific, developing clean energy has become a strategic consensus among BRICS countries. In recent years, Russia has made attempts at energy technology innovation to shed its heavy reliance on energy export and has made some breakthroughs in that and clean energy development. The *Energy Strategy to 2035* released by the Russian Ministry of Energy in February 2014 put forth a series of measures including reducing the reliance on the energy economy, adjusting the energy mix, and strengthening energy technology innovation. Committed to energy independence and diversification, Brazil has made clean energy the strategic focus of its energy development, with leading advantages in biomass and hydro energies. The country has put forth its energy development plan for 2030, with special efforts on the development of wind and solar energies. India is highly dependent on energy imports and its rural poor suffer from extremely low energy accessibility (India will have to import 90% of its oil and natural gas in 2030), so the Modi administration encourages scaling up the development and use of such renewables as solar, wind, and hydro to strive for energy security and meet rural power demand. As one of the most solar-abundant countries in the world, India founded the International Solar Alliance (ISA) in 2015, which gave it more initiative in clean energy diplomacy. With a rather developed power industry, South Africa produces 2/3 of Africa's electricity, 92% of which is thermal power. It is also one of the most solar-rich countries, with onshore solar and offshore wind resources promising enormous potential and values. The country also leads the world in clean coal technology.[98]

The BRICS group is attaching great importance to clean energy, as reflected in the fact that the first batch of loans granted by the New Development Bank were all dedicated to clean energy projects. As shown in Figure 5.3, IRENA's 2017 statistics showed that the total renewable capacity of BRICS countries accounted for more than 40% of the world (China 27.1%, Brazil 6.1%, India 4.5%, Russia 2.6%, and South Africa 0.2%), exerting a major influence on the global development of clean energy. Among that, China was the leader of BRICS with nearly 3/4 of the group's total capacity. Its clean energy diplomacy has structural advantages in the international system.

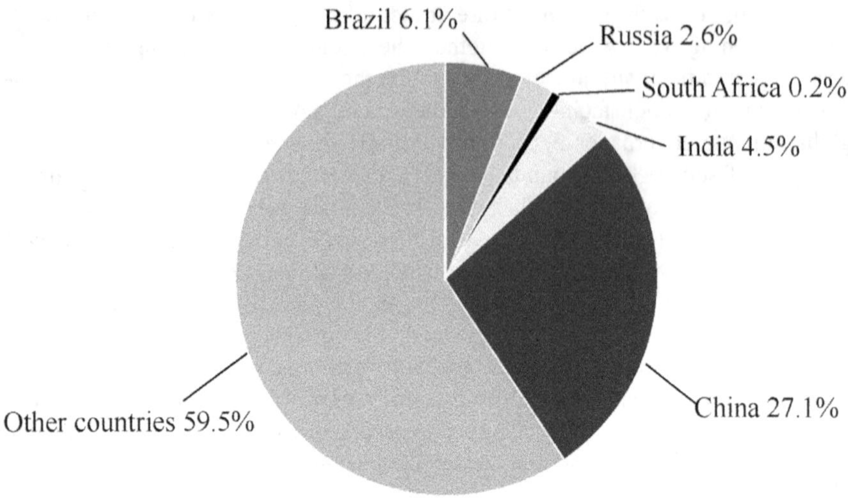

Figure 5.3 Global percentage of renewable capacity in BRICS countries

Source: IRENA Renewable Energy Statistics 2017.

III. Demand for a new energy governance order and dual governance deficit: an opportunity for China

The momentous development of clean energy in recent years entails building a new order of international energy governance that shifts from traditional energy to clean energy and exploring a new type of diplomacy. Take the reform of the International Energy Agency (IEA) for example. Closely related to the global energy transition, its reform involves important adjustments in two directions. One is stepping away from IEA's oil and gas background and placing more emphasis on the innovation of renewable energy technology and the development of clean energy in the backdrop of global climate and energy transformation.[99] The other is that its reform to keep in step with the times must fully reflect the collective wishes and political representation of developing countries. When IEA was founded, its member states – mostly developed countries – consumed a lion's share of the world's energy, but that percentage has shrunk to about 40% today. As emerging developing countries represented by China are taking a larger share in energy governance, the gravity of energy consumption is obviously moving eastward. In the meantime, developing countries are growing as a whole in clean energy development, with ever stronger structural influence over energy transition. Ensuring the effective participation of developing countries is imperative for IEA to enhance the legitimacy and authority of its governance in the future.

It must also be noted that the global order of energy governance is undergoing substantial changes with G20's participation. G20, which represents major energy producers and consumers, both developed and developing, is incorporating energy governance in its global dialogue system and is seen as a key coordinator and leader in the fragmented energy governance. Because it is geographically irrelevant, clean energy has advantages in promoting multi-lateral, win-win, long-term cooperation, and energy sustainability has become a handle in G20's energy governance landscape.[100] Therefore, clean energy development can pave the way for G20 to enhance interactions and cooperation with other organizations such as IEA, OPEC, and Energy Charter. In sum, the need to build a new order of international energy governance is an important driving force for China's clean energy diplomacy.

At present, international clean energy diplomacy is still nascent, and the global system of clean energy governance suffers from the lack of an authoritative organization and fragmentation. The pluralist networks of governance mean multiple centers and multiple regimes – an institutional complex that easily leads to fragmentation. Sebastian Obertur and others pointed out that the institutional fragmentation of the global governance complex doesn't necessarily mean a malfunction of governance. Of the three types of fragmentation – coordinated, cooperative, and conflicting – the first two types can enhance governance if correctly steered, but potential factors prone to a conflict should be prevented.

As pluralist networks of clean energy governance prosper, we cannot ignore the conflict of interests among the diverse actors and the complex interplay of various regimes. Poor coordination of basic rules and standards would lead to disorder and failure of global clean energy governance. First of all, the multiple actors on multiple levels are forming networks of multiple centers. The complexity of such a pluralist system and the conflict of interests among the actors have aggravated the disorder and failure of governance, resulting in divergences on a range of topics, including the governance rules, industrial standards, and project procedures. As a result, it's hard to provide a well-rounded solution to clean energy diplomacy and cooperation or meet the rising demand for energy transition and clean energy governance. Besides, the international organizations, actions, and conferences related to clean energy as well as their outcomes and plans have a weak legal binding force. The energy issue concerns the fundamental interests of all countries, which, coupled with economic, geographical, and political differences, makes it improbable to reach a universally acceptable international treaty or pact.

Second, greater efforts must be made to green traditional energy organizations and integrate them with clean energy organizations. Clean energy is marginalized in traditional energy organizations today.[101] It is necessary to intensify the coordination, exchange, and cooperation between renewable energy organizations and traditional ones to push clean energy to the center stage of global energy governance in the real sense. All these provide an opportunity for China to develop clean energy diplomacy. For the moment, China has set up energy groups in several multilateral organizations, including SCO, APEC, and G20, and carried out diplomatic cooperation on clean energy through these groups. It has played an especially positive role in prompting G20 to grow into the coordinating center of global clean energy governance and making the governance more inclusive. However, G20 doesn't have the corporate capacity yet – it's just an unofficial dialogue regime without even a permanent secretariat, so it has neither the organizational basis nor the operational network to execute the various commitments. With only an annual summit and several ministerial meetings, it is unable to timely respond to new issues, doesn't have enough enforcing power, and can hardly guarantee effective energy coordination worldwide.[102] Therefore, China should continuously search for innovative models of global clean energy governance.

IV. China's diplomatic strategy based on major-country responsibilities: essential engine powering its clean energy diplomacy

In recent years, China, as a major energy consumer and carbon emitter, is facing mounting diplomatic pressure. On the one hand, being relatively obscure in traditional energy diplomacy, China doesn't have enough say in traditional energy organizations, not to mention rules-making power and discourse power. On the other hand, emitting almost 1/3 (29%) of the world's GHG emissions, China easily falls into a passive spot in climate negotiations. To break this diplomatic dilemma, China has changed its diplomatic thinking at a faster pace and gradually moved from "passive response" to "proactive diplomacy". This self-motivated diversion of diplomatic strategy based on major countries' responsibilities is an essential engine powering China's clean energy diplomacy. The fifth session of the 18th CPC Central Committee adopted the *Suggestions of the CPC Central Committee on Formulating the 13th Five-Year Plan for Economic and Social Development.* Taking into account the new situations and tasks in the final stage of building a moderately prosperous society in all respects, the plan called for firmly upholding the concept of innovative, coordinated, green, open, and shared development. It particularly made "green" one of the five development concepts and emphasized the basic state policy of saving resources and protecting the environment. China is bringing itself to engage in international energy and climate cooperation with a "major-country mindset" and "proactive internationalism". It also calls for all major countries to share global responsibilities and integrate the domestic and international situations.[103] The central foreign work meeting in June 2018 clarified the Xi Jinping Thought on Socialist Diplomacy with Chinese Characteristics for a New Era – by actively participating in and leading the reform of the global governance system, we will forge better partnership networks to drive the building of a community with a shared future for mankind and eventually open a new horizon in Chinese-style major-country diplomacy.

As China transforms and upgrades its diplomatic strategy, the fast development of clean energy is considered a tool to smash the shackles imposed on its strategic development by excessive carbon reliance so that the energy industry chain could be quickly upgraded. Moreover, the practice of clean energy diplomacy can give China more diplomatic initiative in the changing energy and climate landscape. These are changing the position of clean energy from being an end in itself (clean energy development) to being a means (clean energy diplomacy) to the end. Therefore, driving the fast rise of clean energy diplomacy is an inevitable choice for China to play a vital role in the new diplomatic situation leveraged on its advantages in clean, low-carbon energy. It is also a green public good delivered by China to push forward the global governance process.

For starters, the fast rise of clean energy diplomacy gives China more rules-making power and discourse power to reshape its role in global climate governance and demonstrates how it as a major country is willingly sharing the global burden of carbon emission reduction and strongly promoting pragmatic climate diplomacy. Thanks to its flexible and pragmatic approach, China has evolved from an important participant in the Copenhagen Conference to a key leader at the Paris Conference. When negotiating a series of challenging topics, such as the principle of "common but differentiated responsibilities", financial and technical support, and legal force of the agreement, it has acted as an important navigator breaking stalemate and pushing the negotiations forward. Strongly developing clean energy is regarded as valuable leverage for seizing the initiative in climate negotiations. China set ambitious low-carbon goals in its INDCs (e.g., peaking CO_2 emissions around 2030), the realization of which depends largely on the development of clean energy and significant improvement of energy efficiency. By advancing clean energy governance, it can contribute more Chinese strategies and wisdom to innovating the model of global climate governance.

Second, regarding the participation in global energy governance, the geographically irrelevant diplomatic cooperation in clean energy can in a way mitigate the "China energy threat theory" and empower China to forge a new order of energy governance. For instance, G20 is now seen as a key cooperation platform for integrating and coordinating the fragmented global energy governance. Seizing the opportunity of being the rotating chair of G20 in 2016, China energetically carried out home-court diplomacy on clean energy and green finance, and prompted the creation of the G20 Green Finance Study Group (GFSG), aiming to propel green energy investment based on public-private partnership in the next 15 years. To achieve sustainable energy development and climate goals, the 2016 G20 Summit adopted the *G20 Voluntary Action Plan on Renewable Energy*, providing more green public goods to enhance other developing countries' capability of clean energy governance. These efforts, being part of clean energy diplomacy, have largely pushed forward international energy governance with green institutions.

At last, as China presses ahead with the Belt and Road Initiative (BRI), building a global energy network pivoted on clean energy has become a strategic fulcrum in its efforts to bring about energy transition in Belt and Road countries through grid connectivity.[104] At the UN Sustainable Development Summit in September 2015, President Xi Jinping proposed to build a global energy network, which will facilitate the creation of a better mechanism to share energy and climate dividends. The global energy network is a robust, universally connected smart grid with a UHV grid as the mainstay that mainly transmits clean electricity. Thanks to coordinated green resources through the diplomatic channel and the provision of public goods for the region on the principle of shared interests, the network acts as a platform that gathers common human interests and inspires the awareness of the community with a shared future for mankind. Building on that, it advances the fundamental reform of international energy order and climate governance, changes the global geopolitical landscape, and eventually powers clean energy diplomacy forward across the board.

Notes

1 Kai Fang, Yunheng Zhou, Shuang Wang, Ruike Ye, Sujian Guo, "Assessing National Renewable Energy Competitiveness of the G20: A Revised Porter's Diamond Model", *Renewable and Sustainable Energy Reviews*, No. 93, 2018, pp. 719–731.
2 Hongtu Zhao, *The Economics and Politics of China's Energy Security Transition*, New York: Academic Press, 2019, pp. 121–149.
3 J. I. Lewis, "China's Strategic Priorities in International Climate Change Negotiations", *Washington Quarterly*, Vol. 31, No. 1, 2008, pp. 155–174; J. I. Lewis, "Climate Change and Security: Examining China' Challenges in a Warming World", *International Affairs*, Vol. 85, No. 6, 2009, pp. 1195–1213; P. G. Harris, ed., *China and Global Climate Change*, Hongkong: Proceedings of the conference held at Lingnan University, June 2009, pp. 18–19.
4 Zhang Haibin, "China's Stance During International Climate Negotiations: Continuity, Changes and Reasons", *World Economics and Politics*, No. 10, 2006.
5 China has become more flexible and pragmatic. It began to pay more attention to the mutually beneficial cooperation in technology between developed and developing countries and established a technology transfer mechanism for mitigating climate change based on the principles of market economy. It also supports climate funds and explores new ways to scale up carbon financing.
6 Bali Conference is a watershed event because developing countries are willing to discuss their emission reduction commitments for the first time.
7 A. Hodgson, *Climate of Change: A Foreign Policy Analysis of China's Participation in International Environmental Agreements*, Master Thesis of the University of Kansas, 2011.
8 Fan Gang, *China and the World Toward Low-carbon Development – Suggestions from Chinese Economists*, Beijing: China Economic Publishing House, 2010.
9 G. Heggelund, "China's Climate Change Policy: Domestic and International Developments", *Asian Perspective*, Vol. 31, No. 2, 2007, pp. 155–191.
10 The Clean Development Mechanism (CDM) allows the governments and enterprises of developed Western countries to carry out emission reduction projects (mostly clean energy), either through investment or technological cooperation, in developing countries to help improve the latter's emission-cutting and climate-resilient capability. It also allows developing countries to sell certified emission reductions (CERS) to offset part of the emissions by developed countries and make high profits to improve their own capability of sustainable development.
11 W. Liang, "Changing Climate? China's New Interest in Global Climate Change Negotiations", in J. J. Kassiola and S. Guo, eds., *China's Environmental Crisis: Domestic and Global Political Impacts and Responses*, Basingstoke and New York: Palgrave Macmillan, 2010, pp. 61–84.
12 A. Hodgson, *Climate of Change: A Foreign Policy Analysis of China's Participation in International Environmental Agreements*, Master Thesis of the University of Kansas, 2011.
13 At this conference, China, instead of the US, was for the first time accused of encumbering the international climate negotiations and causing the "disappointing outcomes".
14 Pan Jiahua, "Carbon Budget Meeting Basic Needs and Its Significance for International Equity and Sustainability", *World Economics and Politics*, No. 1, 2008; Pan Jiahua, Chen Ying, "Budgeting Carbon for Equity and Sustainability", *Social Science in China Press*, No. 5, 2009; Pan Jiahua, Zhang Ying, *Budgeting Carbon for Equity and Sustainability*, Beijing: Social Sciences Academic Press, 2011.
15 O. Boyd, "China's Energy Reform and Climate Policy: The Ideas Motivating Change", *CCEP Working Paper, Centre for Climate Economics & Policy' Crawford School of Public Policy*, The Australian National University, 2012.
16 O. Boyd, *The Motivations for China's New Energy and Climate Policies*, 2012, www.eastasiaforum.org/2012/08/14/the-motivations-for-chinas-new-energy-and-climate-policies.

17 Hong-Yuan Yu, Song-Li Zhu, "Toward Paris: China and Climate Change Negotiations", *Advances in Climate Change Research*, No. 6, 2015, pp. 56–66.
18 Wang Binbin, Zhang Haibin, "Dual Transition in Global Climate Governance and China's Strategic Choice", *Journal of China University of Geosciences* (Social Sciences Edition), No. 3, 2017.
19 On the eve of the 2009 Copenhagen Conference, four major developing countries – China, India, Brazil, and South Africa – discussed what basic stance they should adopt at the upcoming conference and formed a united front – the BASIC – to defend the collective interests of developing countries in international climate negotiations. The BASIC Group had a ministers' meeting and an expert meeting. In April 2010, the 3rd BASIC ministers' meeting was held in South Africa, which, in the "BASIC PLUS" approach, invited representatives from the "G77 + China" Group, the Group of Small Island Countries, that year's host country of climate change conference, and some Latin American countries. After 2014, the election of a new administration in India, political turmoil in Brazil, and divergences of interests among the countries led to an obviously lower frequency of BASIC ministers' meeting and a virtual stagnation of the expert meeting. The group's influence was notably impaired.
20 Leaders' Statement on Climate Change and Clean Energy, *People's Daily*, July 17, 2018.
21 The electricity output from PV is not included here because it is too small compared with hydro, wind, and nuclear power. As wind and solar energy is sometimes given up due to issues with synchronization, the percentage of annual power output from clean energy is less than the percentage of its installed capacity.
22 China National Renewable Energy Center and Center for Renewable Energy Development of NDRC Energy Research Institute, *China Renewable Energy Outlook 2017*, Beijing: China Economic Publishing House, 2017, pp. 23–27.
23 REN21, *Renewables 2015 Global Status Report*, 2015, www.ren21.net/wp-content/uploads/2019/05/GSR2015_Full-Report_English.pdf.
24 Zhou Fengqi, Liu Xinyu, Chen Ning, *China's Renewable Energy Strategy and Institutions of Renewable Energy Industries*, Shanghai: Shanghai Academy of Social Sciences Press, 2016.
25 Yu Hongyuan, "Energy Chain in the Context of Power Shift and Its Challenges", *World Economy Studies*, No. 2, 2008.
26 Y. Li and W. Cao, "Framework of Laws and Policies on Renewable Energy and Relevant Systems in China under the Background of Climate Change", *Vemont Journal* of *Environmental Law*, Vol. 13, 2012, pp. 823–863.
27 REN21, *Background Paper: Chinese Renewables Status Report* 2009, Report of Renewable Energy Network for the 21st Century.
28 IUCN, UNEP, WWF, FAO, UNESCO, eds., *The World Conservation Strategy: Living Resource Conservation for Sustainable Development*, Gland: IUCN, 1980.
29 World Commission on Environment and Development (WCED), *Our Common Future*, Oxford: Oxford Paperbacks, 1987, p. 52.
30 D. B. Brooks, "The Challenge of Sustainability: Is Environment and Economics Enough?", *Policy Sciences*, Vol. 26, 1992, pp. 401–408.
31 Guo Guanyu, Dai Xiudian, "Renewable Energy Cooperation Between China and Germany: Foundation, Mechanism and Problems", *Journal of China University of Geosciences* (Social Sciences Edition), No. 4, 2012.
32 Li Yang, "China-US Clean Energy Cooperation: Foundation, Mechanism and Problems", *Contemporary International Relations*, No. 1, 2011.
33 Y. Li, W. Cao, "Framework of Laws and Policies on Renewable Energy and Relevant Systems in China under the Background of Climate Change", *Vermont Journal of Environmental Law*, Vol. 13, 2012, pp. 823–863.
34 Li Xinlei, "New Developments of China's Clean Energy Diplomacy Amid the Evolving Global Climate and Energy Landscape", *Pacific Journal*, No. 12, 2017.
35 Previously it was the China Meteorological Administration and China Environmental Administration that participated in climate negotiations on behalf of China. The National

Development and Planning Commission was the decision-making authority over national economic planning and energy use. The institutional change reflected the rising importance attached by China to climate negotiations.

36 A. Lema, K. Ruby, "Between Fragmented Authoritarianism and Policy Coordination: Creating a Chinese Market for Wind Energy", *Energy Policy*, Vol. 35, No. 7, 2007, pp. 3879–3890.

37 IPCC, *Renewable Energy Sources and Climate Change* Special Report of the Intergovernmental Panel on Climate Change, published by Cambridge University Press, 2009, p. 913.

38 G. Heggelund, "China's Climate Change Policy: Domestic and International Developments", *Asian Perspective*, Vol. 31, No. 2, 2007, pp. 155–191.

39 The EURO crisis cast a wet blanket on Europe's industrial production, which resulted in less energy consumption and consequently less demand for carbon emission right. Not only did the sluggish EU carbon trade market after 2011 affect CDM projects, but EU also imposed more restrictions on them and barely accepted applications from emerging countries like China and India after 2013.

40 The program lasted five years and had a total investment of EUR 42.9 million, including an EUR 20 million grant from the EU and EUR 22.9 million from the Chinese side in cash or kind. The program consisted of two stages. The first stage involved ten large-scale bidding projects, including offshore wind energy and biomass resources. The second stage focused on sponsoring, with EU grant, the feasibility study and demonstration projects for some key areas in China and sub-projects related with clean-energy-covered energy policy, energy efficiency, and renewable energy.

41 Li Yanfang, "Chinese Law on Renewable Energy in the Context of Climate Change", *Political Science and Law*, No. 3, 2010.

42 M. Mendonga, D. Jacobs, "Feed – in Tariffs Go Global: Policy in Practice", *Renewable Energy World*, Vol. 12, No. 4, 2009, pp. 1–6.

43 M. Mendonga, D. Jacobs, B. K. Sovacool, *Powering the Green Economy: The Feed-in Tariff Handbook*, London and Sterling: VA Earthscan/James & James, 2010.

44 T. Couture, Y. Gagnon, "An Analysis of Feed – in Tariff Remuneration Models: Implications for Renewable Energy Investment", *Energy Policy*, Vol. 38, No. 2, 2010, pp. 955–965.

45 The relevant grid enterprise shall, through entering into a synchronization agreement with renewable power generators that have obtained an administrative license or have reported for archival purposes, purchase the full amount of the renewable electricity, as covered by its grid, and provide synchronization services.

46 S. Schuman, A. Lin, "China's Renewable Energy Law and Its Impact on Renewable Power in China: Progress, Challenges and Recommendations for Improving Implementation", *Energy Policy*, Vol. 51, 2012, pp. 89–109.

47 C. Carraro, M. Tavoni, "Looking Ahead from Copenhagen: How Challenging is the Chinese Carbon Intensity Target?", 2010, www.voxeu.org/article/china-s-copenhagen-commitment-business-usual-or-climate-leadership.

48 Carbon capture and storage (CCS) is a technology that captures CO_2 emitted from large power plants, steel mills, and chemical plants and stores it in various ways to keep it from entering the atmosphere. This technology can cut carbon emission per unit power output by 85%–90%.

49 EC2 is focused on energy policy and technology transfer in the following five areas: clean coal (e.g., CCS for higher efficiency), sustainable biofuels, renewable energy, energy efficiency (in construction, product, and industrial production), and sustainable and effective energy allocation system.

50 Huiming Zhang, Dequn Zhou, Jie Cao, "A Quantitative Assessment of Energy Strategy Evolution in China and US", *Renewable and Sustainable Energy Reviews*, No. 15, 2011, pp. 886–890.

51 NEA, "Fourth China-US Renewable Energy Forum held in Washington", June 8, 2015, www.cpnn.com.cn/zdyw/201506/t20150608_805436.html.

52 Aimei Yang, Rong Wang, Jian (Jay) Wang, "Green Public Diplomacy and Global Governance: The Evolution of the U.S – China Climate Collaboration Network, 2008–2014", *Public Relations Review*, No. 43, 2017, pp. 1048–1061.
53 Aimei Yang, Rong Wang, Jian (Jay) Wang, "Green Public Diplomacy and Global Governance: The Evolution of the US-China Climate Collaboration Network, 2008–2014", *Public Relations Review*, No. 43, 2017, pp. 1048–1061.
54 The surcharge on renewable electricity went from 0.1 cent/kWh to 1.9 cents/kWh after 2006, but that still lagged behind the needs for renewable energy development. The shortfall of renewable subsidy amounted to more than RMB 40 billion at the end of 2015.
55 Projects eligible for the certificate include onshore wind power and PV but don't include distributed PV, biomass, and offshore wind power. The assessment of renewable quota and mandatory trade of green electricity certificate would be launched in due time after 2018 based on market subscription.
56 More than 20 countries, including the US, Japan, Germany, Britain, France, the Netherlands, Sweden, Denmark, Finland, Canada, and Australia, have adopted the green electricity certificate trading system. This market-based approach makes necessary economic compensation for clean electricity producers.
57 Qin Haiyan, "Why Establish the Green Electricity Certificate Trading Mechanism?" *China Energy News*, April 27, 2016.
58 Yin Haitao, "How to Achieve a Sound Renewable Energy Quota System?", *Energy Review*, June 1, 2018.
59 The usual practice in the American renewable energy quota market is selling the renewable electricity certificate at twice or thrice the price. The result is that no enterprise is willing to buy such certificate and therefore no enterprise sells it either in the short term. Such a provision makes the penalty flexible and ensures the implementation of the system.
60 Introduction to APSEC, www.apsec.org.cn/.
61 CERC, *Overview by U. S. & China CERC Directors*, 7th Steering Committee Meeting, Washington, DC, June 1, 2015.
62 A new trend in the past few decades is to build smaller, more flexible, and nonbinding mechanisms, partnerships, or political forums. The International Partnership for Energy Efficiency Cooperation (IPEEC), Global Green Growth Forum (3GF), and Sustainable Energy for All (SE4All), as well as other similar mechanisms or secretariats are small or open to the world.
63 Zhu Xuantong, "China's Engagement in Global Energy Governance", *IEA Annual Report 2016*, 2016, pp. 25–26, https://theasiadialogue.com/wp-content/uploads/2018/03/Partner-CountrySeries_ChinasEngagementinGlobalEnergyGovernance_Englishversion.pdf.
64 The China-Brazil Earth Resource Satellite (CBERS) project, reputed as a paragon of "South-South High-tech Cooperation", contributes most to Brazil's response to climate change. After Brazil used CBERS to monitor logging in the Amazon real-time and worked with relevant enforcement departments, forest logging has decreased yearly.
65 In September 2017, 15 ministries and commissions, including NDRC, NEA, and the Ministry of Finance, jointly issued the *Implementation Plan for Scaling up the Production of Biofuel Ethanol and Promoting the Use of Ethanol Gasoline for Motor Vehicles*.
66 The Brazilian government plans to increase its PV capacity to 7GW by 2024, making it about 3.3% of total power generation, and to 18% by 2050.
67 According to IRENA's analysis, G20 accounts for 80% of the global renewable capacity and 75% of the renewable potential in 2010–2030. G20 members take a dominant position in world renewables development and have the wish to intensify cooperation and further advance the cause.
68 Kai Fang, Yunheng Zhou, Shuang Wang, Ruike Ye, Sujian Guo, "Assessing National Renewable Energy Competitiveness of the G20: A Revised Porter's Diamond Model", *Renewable and Sustainable Energy Reviews*, No. 93, 2018, pp. 719–731.
69 The Beijing Communiqué pointed out that G20 members will endeavor to carry out "in-depth cooperation on knowledge sharing, capacity building, technology transfer,

financial innovation and pilot projects. We note the important role of government in supporting power sector evolution and energy system integration, and we promote technical development and deployment of energy storage, electric vehicles and modern bioenergy, including second generation and other advanced biofuels, and renewable heating. . . . We encourage cooperation on standards to accelerate smart grid deployment and interoperability."

70 China developed the EELP to exert G20's leading role in enhancing global energy efficiency and impel countries to make joint efforts to achieve one of UN's three sustainable development goals – double the global rate of improvement in energy efficiency. It urged all countries to set G20's medium- and long-term goal of energy efficiency toward 2030 and encouraged them to put forth targets matching their 2030 INDCs. Zhang Jianguo, Bai Quan, "G20 Energy Ministers' Meeting: Countries' Priorities for Improved Energy Efficiency", *Energy of China*, No. 11, 2016.

71 APEC Cooperation Fund sponsors APEC exchange and cooperation projects that are organized by domestic agencies or that they participate in. Yan Shigang, "China's International Cooperation on New Energy from the Perspective of Low-carbon Economy", *Foreign Affairs Review*, No. 5, 2012.

72 APEC Sustainable Energy Center, "About us and Activities", *APSEC*, www.apsec.org.cn/apsecen/, last accessed on October 30, 2014.

73 The program targets policy makers, research personnel, technical professionals, and operation and management personnel engaged in such areas as hydropower, pumped storage, wind, solar, and nuclear energies. Ways of implementation include classes by experts, exchanges and discussions, field visits, and more. Li Dandan, "China-ASEAN Clean Energy Capacity Building Programme Kicks Off", *Energy News*, July 5, 2017, www.in-en.com/article/html/energy-2262036.shtml.

74 The SCO Energy Club founded in December 2013 is an open, multilateral platform under the SCO framework to develop and expand energy cooperation. Current Club members include China, Russia, Kazakhstan, Tajikistan, India, Pakistan, Mongolia, Afghanistan, Iran, Belarus, Turkey, and Sri Lanka.

75 Rapid development of renewables in China has brought down global cost by 50%. Cooperation between China and other developing countries holds enormous potential. Africa, for instance, offers a market worth roughly RMB 1.5 trillion.

76 Qi Yue, Fan Yichun, "BASIC Group's South-South Cooperation on Climate Change: Policies, Actions and Lessons", *World Environment*, No. 1, 2017.

77 Zhang Yonghong, Liang Yijian, Wang Tao, et al., "New Energy Cooperation Between China and Africa: Prospects, Challenges and Policies", *Journal of International Economic Cooperation*, No. 2, 2013.

78 Department of Climate Change, Chinese Ministry of Ecology and Environment, "President Xi Jinping Announces '10–100–1000' Plan of South-South Climate Cooperation", January 29, 2016, www.ccchina.gov.cn/Detail.aspx?newsld=58712.

79 Jing Gu, Neil Renwick, Lan Xue, "The BRICS and Africa's Search for Green Growth, Clean Energy and Sustainable Development", *Energy Policy*, No. 120, 2018, pp. 675–683.

80 Zhou Dan, "BRICS Countries Strengthen Energy Cooperation", *Sino-Global Energy*, No. 3, 2018.

81 Paul H. Suding, Philippe Lempp, "The Multifaceted Institutional Landscape and Processes of International Renewable Energy Policy", *International Association for Energy Economics*, Second Quarter, 2007, pp. 4–10.

82 Achim Steiner et al., "International Institutional Arrangements in Support of Renewable Energy", in Dirk Assmann, et al., eds., *Renewable Energy, A Global Review of Technologies, Policies and Markets*, London: Sterling VA, 2006, p. 152.

83 REEEP was officially established in Vienna, 2004. It has forged partnerships with 270 entities worldwide, including governments, enterprises, development banks, and NGOs.

84 Founded in 2005, REN21 is an important global network of renewable energy policies. It collects comprehensive and up-to-date information on renewable energy and promotes knowledge exchange and policy spread. It is characterized by multiple stakeholders, multiple sectors (the participants are from environmental, energy, and development consortiums), and global presence (participants are from around the globe).

85 IRENA, *China, IRENA to Co-Host International Forum on Energy Transitions*, www.irena.org/News/Description.aspx?NType=A&mnu=cat&PriMenuID=16&CatID=84&News_ID-429, last accessed on November 2, 2015.

86 IEA, *Tracking Clean Energy Progress 2016: Energy Technology Perspectives*, 2016, pp. 6–17, https://iea.blob.core.windows.net/assets/6871b404-bcff-4c5d-b53e-d33a6ef347b9/TrackingCleanEnergyProgress2016.pdf.

87 REN21, *Renewables 2016 Global Status Report*, 2016, pp. 4–6, https://www.ren21.net/wp-content/uploads/2019/05/REN21_GSR2016_FullReport_en_11.pdf.

88 PPP is a kind of cooperation model in which the public sector and private sector, based on a franchising agreement, share responsibilities and financing risks on urban infrastructure construction or the provision of certain public goods or services.

89 Charles F. Sabel, David G. Victor, "Governing Global Problems Under Uncertainty: Making Bottom-up Climate Policy Work", *Climatic Chanye*, No. 144, 2017, pp. 15–27.

90 Shi Bowen, "Green Finance in China: The Next Grand Opportunity for Development", February 7, 2017, http://opinion.caixin.com/2017-02-07/101050831.html.

91 The Pew Charitable Trusts, *Who is Winning the Clean Energy Race? 2012 Edition,* April 17, 2013, https://www.pewtrusts.org/en/research-and-analysis/articles/2013/04/who-is-winning-the-clean-energy-race-2012-edition.

92 Li Xinlei, "National Learning Mechanism and Discourse Building in International Politics: Greening of China's Outlook on Energy Security and Its Effects on Energy and Climate Diplomacy", *Fudan International Studies Review*, No. 12, 2013.

93 China proposed at the Paris Conference that building on the seven carbon trade pilot projects in 2011, it will launch a national carbon market in 2017. By then, clean energy quota can be directly converted into certified emission reductions (CER) in the domestic carbon market, thus boosting the synchronization of clean electricity and promoting the quota system nationwide.

94 IEA, "China's Engagement in Global Energy Governance," *IEA Annual Report 2015*, pp.34–47,https://www.iea.org/reports/partner-country-series-chinas-engagement-in-global-energy-governance.

95 REN21, *Renewables 2016 Global Status Report*, 2016, https://www.ren21.net/wp-content/uploads/2019/05/REN21_GSR2016_FullReport_en_11.pdf.

96 In 2015, other developing countries investing more than USD 500 million in renewable energy were Morocco, the Philippines, Pakistan, Uruguay, and Honduras. Posing a sharp contrast was the fact that developed countries' overall investment in renewables fell 8% (at only USD 130 billion) that year.

97 Yu Hongyuan, Wang Wentao, "Institutional Fragmentation and Lack of Leadership: Dual Deficit in Global Environmental Governance", *The Journal of International Studies*, No. 3, 2013.

98 Zhou Dan, "Development of Energy Technology in BRICS Countries", *Sino-Global Energy*, No. 3, 2018.

99 The promotion of clean energy technology and sharing of experience and policies will play as important a part as energy trade and investment. How to function as a facilitator of technology exchange and information sharing is a major issue facing IEA.

100 Yang Yifang, "Energy Trend: Exploring Global Energy Governance in the G20 Framework", May 10, 2016, http://news.cnpc.com.cn/system/2016/05/10/001591752.shtml.

101 Bruce D. Jones, David Steven, *The Risk Pivot: Great Powers, International Security, and the Energy Revolution*, Washington, DC: Brookings Institution Press, 2015.

102 Zhao Qingsi, "China's Strategy of Engaging in Global Energy Governance through G20", *Contemporary World and Socialism*, No. 6, 2015.
103 Jing Gu, Neil Renwick, Lan Xue, "The BRICS and Africa's Search for Green Growth, Clean Energy and Sustainable Development", *Energy Policy*, No. 120, 2018, pp. 675–683.
104 Liu Zhenya, "Global Energy Internet Across Nations and Continents and Its Prospects", *Proceedings of the CSEE*, No. 19, 2016.

6 Clean energy diplomacy of China

Multiple challenges and all-round capacity building

Developing clean energy has become a global consensus since the end of the 1990s. Especially in the 21st century, clean energy has grown to be an important, competitive option in many countries. An array of factors have contributed to the fast development of clean energy worldwide, including new supportive policies by governments, higher technical and cost competitiveness, better financing channels, enhanced awareness of energy security and environmental protection, ever-rising energy demand in developing countries and emerging economies, and the demand for modern energy sources in underdeveloped regions. Against the background of an evolving global strategic landscape of climate and energy, a new round of global competition centered on energy revolution and low-carbon transition is on, bringing important opportunities as well as multiple challenges for China. To shift from a passive to a proactive position as it tries to better cope with the crises and challenges and turn disadvantages into advantages, China needs to strengthen its capabilities in all aspects of clean energy diplomacy.

Section 1 Multiple challenges faced by China's clean energy diplomacy amid changing international strategic landscape of climate and energy

As clean energy is not geographically dependent, countries can carry out more flexible cooperation in the field of clean energy governance and share interests in the long haul. However, they also compete for economic interests and power, a tendency that makes clean energy diplomacy geographically dependent again. If developing countries cannot break through their development bottlenecks as soon as possible and upgrade their energy industry chain, they won't be able to grasp the core technologies and have the rule-making power for clean energy and will consequently fall into a passive position. As the global system of clean energy governance is increasingly divided into the southern and the northern blocs, competition in this field may further widen the gap between developing and developed countries. Amid the decarbonizing trend in global economic and industrial structure, countries that take a preemptive step in transitioning to clean development will stand at an advantage in the international political and economic system. As a major developing country, China is faced with various difficulties as it strives to

DOI: 10.4324/9781003433903-9

change from a big producer to a strong developer of clean energy. That, in turn, has posed many challenges to its development of clean energy diplomacy.

I. Technical and managerial constraints on clean energy development in China

Clean energy accounts for a very small percentage of China's energy consumption mix today, a far cry from the 2020 target of having nonfossil energy account for 15%. For one thing, clean energy development in China faces many technical and managerial constraints. The immense pressure of carbon emission reduction at home in a way undercuts the potential of clean energy diplomacy. On the technical front, greater efforts must be made to stimulate industrial innovation for substantial progress in high-end equipment and key technologies. China's relative inferiority in the patent application isn't commensurate with its strategic goal of becoming an innovative country or its position as the world's second largest economy. The World Bank's low-carbon development report says China still needs more than 60 core technologies to meet its goal of lowering carbon intensity in main industrial sectors such as electricity, construction, iron and steel, transportation, and chemistry. Yet 70% of those technologies are inaccessible to China due to technical barriers to trade set up by Europe and the US. Therefore, China's clean energy technologies suffer from a systematic shortage saving the leading edge in EVs.[1]

While China must systematically enhance its innovation capability in clean energy technology, it also needs to perfect the regimes of IP protection and interactions among industry, university, and research institutes. Going forward, sectors of transport, heating, and refrigeration will continue to lag behind the electric power sector. As the heating and refrigeration markets are inherently independent and dispersive, the development of renewable energy technologies in these sectors is challenged. At the same time, decarbonization of the transport sector using renewables isn't taken seriously or given priority yet. Apart from the marked increase in EV sales, which is primarily credited to the falling cost of cell technology, more actions must be taken to ensure a sufficient amount of renewable-powered infrastructure. But the biggest challenge comes from transport and aerospace because supportive policies or disruptive commercial innovations haven't adequately inspired solutions in these sectors yet.

On the policy coordination front, clean energy policies must be improved, especially the subsidy scheme. The central government allocated RMB 43 billion in fiscal funds to subsidize the Golden Sun Programme implemented between 2003 and 2013, covering 50% of the total investment. But this approach – with upfront subsidy – encouraged fraudulent practices and led to substandard projects despite stimulating PV investment. Therefore, the implementation of policy and the supervision thereof must be bettered; eventually, technical innovation should be the key to bringing down the cost of clean power generation and accelerating the process toward its grid parity. The government must deploy the layout, scale, and speed of renewables development from a macro perspective, taking into account a slew of factors, including natural conditions, economic demand, and grid conditions, to avoid the waste of human resources, materials, and land resources.[2]

Besides the lagging reform of the power market, unmatching grid facilities, inadequate adaptation of the power system, and difficult absorption of renewable electricity have hampered the synchronization of renewable electricity, which is now the greatest barrier to its industrialization. This trend is exacerbated by the fierce competition among different power generation assets, including coal-fired power, nuclear power, and renewable power, because the power supply is in excess as the petroleum price is falling and the Chinese economy entering the new normal.[3] As the abandonment of wind, solar, and hydro energy resources becomes increasingly serious in the new energy industry, more needs to be done to make better use of renewables. The curtailment of renewable power generation first appeared in 2010, and the curtailment of wind power generation was most serious in 2012, when 17% of the energy was abandoned on national average, equivalent to about 20TWh electricity. The problem caught so much attention in society that it was mitigated later, yet an average 10% of wind energy was still abandoned in 2014. The situation worsened in 2015, when an average 15% of wind energy, equivalent to 33.9TWh electricity, was abandoned, a year-on-year increase of 21.3TWh. By the end of 2016, 126.8TWh electricity generated from hydro, wind, and solar energy was abandoned nationwide (49.7TWh wind, 7.1TWh solar, and over 70TWh hydro), causing RMB 52 billion worth of economic losses and wasting RMB 88 billion in investment. Throughout 2016, 17% of wind energy and 10% of solar energy were abandoned on average. The situation got better in 2017, but the grid's absorption of renewable electricity still wasn't effectively addressed. That year, 12% of wind energy was abandoned, equivalent to 41.9TWh electricity, down by five percentage points year-on-year or 7.8TWh; 6% of solar energy was abandoned, a year-on-year reduction of four percentage points and equivalent to 7.3TWh electricity.[4]

The poor stability of renewable power generation, caused by natural conditions, hinders its large-scale synchronization. Peak shaving and power quality are the key technical issues that urgently need to be addressed for sending renewable electricity to the grid. Authorities must work out detailed rules to prioritize the generation of clean electricity. They should improve the management of peak-shaving power sources through better dispatching, renovate coal-fired units for higher flexibility, and enhance the peak-shaving capability of the power system as a whole.

Environmental issues are another hurdle to the development of clean energy in China. The country remains in a stage of extensive development when development and manufacturing aren't well supervised, causing environmental pollution and ecological damages. Take the production of PV cells, which may cause serious poisoning, for instance. Monocrystalline silicon and polycrystalline silicon (raw material for the former) used to make PV cells come from an energy-guzzling, high-pollution industry. The production of 1kg polycrystalline silicon generates 4kg toxic substances. Examples are plenty. The emission of silicon tetrachloride and hydrogen chloride from the polycrystalline silicon plant in Shizuishan, Ningxia Hui Autonomous Region, has rendered barren the surrounding land. The Ningjin County of Hebei Province is the largest production area of monocrystalline silicon PV cells in the world, which turned out 3GW cells in 2016. On April 29, 2017, toxic gas leaked from a local chemical plant – mainly because of lax regulation and poor environmental technology – and triggered a mass protest involving nearly 10,000 residents. As to hydropower development, that in the southwest, resembling the "great leap forward" style, has also caused grave ecological and environmental damages. The southwestern region of China (including Sichuan, Chongqing, Yunnan, Guizhou, and Tibet) is home to clustered hydropower stations that feature a high density and large scale rarely seen in world history. The hydropower capacity there shot up from 5GW in 2005 to 153.13GW in 2016, making up 51% of the national total. The tens of thousands of hydropower stations scattered across the region have taken a heavy toll on local ecology and resulted in frequent geological disasters. On August 30, 2012, a geological catastrophe happened in the construction area of Jinping hydropower station in Liangshan, Sichuan Province, causing landslide and debris flow at more than 100 locations, killing ten people. The unbridled hydropower development has also made imminent the threat of drought and the extinction of fish varieties in the Yangtze River.

II. Strategic mismatch: lack of pricing power on resources and China-dominated platforms

With its remarkable achievements in clean energy, China is indisputably a global leader both in terms of installed capacity and investment. Yet posing a sharp contrast to this leading position is the fact that it doesn't have the international pricing power over vital mineral resources (e.g., rare earth) or a China-dominated platform for clean energy development. This creates a strategic mismatch – or a wide gap – between the current status of China's clean energy diplomacy and the country's international standing in the clean energy arena. While it plays a bigger role in global energy governance than other emerging or developing countries, such a position doesn't match the important part it plays regarding global energy issues. China's deeper engagement in the global energy governance system must proceed alongside necessary changes and reform of the system, and China must play a bigger part in it in the future.

Let's look at the international tussle in the export of rare earth, an important mineral resource for the production of clean energy. With abundant rare earth resources, China is nevertheless doing a poor job in managing them. Domestically, because of the absence of overall planning, local stakeholders excessively exploit and smuggle this vital strategic resource or export it as a primary raw material at an extremely low price with little value added. Moreover, the blind exploitation has caused serious environmental pollution and threatened to deplete rare earth resources at home. Such a pandemonium in the rare earth industry must be stopped. The Association of China Rare Earth Industry was formed in April 2012, but China, being inexperienced, stood at a disadvantage when handling international trade lawsuits. Internationally, China, with 23% of the world's rare earth resources, has provided over 90% of the global supply at a very low price,[5] but the high reliance of European and American clean energy markets on Chinese supply hasn't given China the pricing power in the international market.

The export control and tariff adopted by China to prevent the fast depletion of rare earth resources and mitigate environmental degradation were objected to by Europe and the US.[6] In 2009, the US, EU, and Mexico filed a suit to the WTO against China's control over the export of such raw materials as bauxite, charcoal, and rare earth; in January 2012, the WTO ruled China as violating world trade rules. In March 2012, the US, EU, and Japan filed another suit to the WTO against China's control over the export of certain raw materials including rare earth. When China increased the export tariff on some rare earth products to 25% in 2013,[7] developed countries toughened up against it regarding the international supply of this strategic resource. In March 2014, the WTO ruled China's export control measures concerning the products in question as violating trade rules; in August of the same year, it ruled against China again on the "rare earth case" and capped the tariff at 10%.[8] To comply with the WTO's ruling, on December 31, 2014, the Ministry of Commerce and the General Administration of Customs had to announce the decision to officially cancel the quota system on rare earth export. It's clear that not only did China lack the international pricing power, but its domestic policies were so susceptible to international influence that they couldn't guarantee the healthy and sustainable development of the clean energy industry that was closely linked with rare earth.

Considering the trade disputes and the lack of pricing power over rare earth and other strategic raw materials, we must adjust the current policies, raise the price of resources, and improve trade conditions without violating the WTO rules. For the moment, we can begin with more effective management of rare earth resources within the country. From the perspective of resources and environmental protection, rare earth and some other minerals are non-renewable. The mining, smelting, and processing of them cause serious pollution to surface water and groundwater, not to mention the pollution caused by the pile-up of tailings. As the damaged environment is extremely difficult or expensive to recover, it's natural and reasonable to impose resource and environmental taxes on the exploitation and production of rare earth and other raw materials. We can raise the export price of rare earth by heightening the cost of environmental protection, and regulate and control the allocation of resources through green, market means. Thus, we can replace the export quota and tariff with resource tax, which avoids trade disputes while achieving the same effects.[9] However, China needs to formulate a long-term strategy for resource development concerning clean energy as soon as possible to coordinate domestic policies with clean energy diplomacy, to protect its development rights and interests to the largest extent.

When the new order of energy and climate governance is being established, a China-dominated, institutional platform is also needed. There is much more China can do for global clean energy governance, and engaging itself more proactively and constructively will bring more profound effects to the country. As far as its current engagement in energy governance is concerned, China's lack of experience has impaired its influence on formulating international energy policies. It has joined many international energy governance organizations and paid huge amounts of membership fees, but to little avail. It has little discourse power in key areas such as energy price and emergency response; it is treated unfairly in international energy investment; it is unable to protect itself with international law at times of energy trade disputes; and its contributions to the international energy market, such as overseas oil and gas investment and trade in new energy goods, are often questioned and criticized rather than recognized.[10] Well, things are getting better in these areas, as China and other regions of the world have come to agree that they share extensive interests with each other in energy security, economic development, and sustainable growth. Yet the country still doesn't have adequate initiative or lead in the shaping of a new order of clean energy governance. It should play a bigger part especially in potential blind zones. For instance, in the current system of global energy governance, major developing countries are underrepresented; a financial regulatory system for the energy market is lacking; there isn't a mechanism that can protect energy IP and promote the spread of energy technology in parallel; the issue of energy poverty is neither fully recognized nor well tackled; international governance of climate change and low-carbon policies is non-existing; a mechanism is wanted to solve the disputes over the governance of energy transmission channels.

Two most pressing reforms are needed in global energy governance. One is expanding the participation of emerging economies and developing countries. As emerging economies have grown in the past two decades, global energy governance has changed as well, but at a lower speed than world economic growth. Therefore, large emerging economies are calling for a more equitable and democratic energy governance system. Without the participation of major countries, including emerging ones, all the efforts on energy governance would go down the drain. The other is expanding the scope of governance to go beyond energy security. For example, with the mounting pressure of climate response, countries need to consider the environmental cost of producing different types of energy sources when making a choice, and this should be one of the key points in future energy governance. There is also a better chance to produce energy at home, even to the point of energy self-sufficiency, as the world is shifting to low-carbon energy sources. That entails changing the traditional concept of energy governance to make sure future energies are cost-effective and sustainable. About 2/3 of global GHG emissions come from the energy sector, and coping with climate change is a grave challenge, so the environmental cost must be considered when we choose and use energy. The whole world working together to promote innovations and increase investment in energy technology is essential for economic growth and universal energy access. A few new initiatives were proposed at the Paris Climate Change Conference in December 2015, such as Mission Innovation. Developing clean energy technology is now a priority on the agenda for both developed and developing countries.

III. The "South-North" division in the global system of clean energy governance

In spite of the rising status of developing countries in clean energy governance, developed countries remain dominant in clean energy technology, with absolute superiority in the patent of low-carbon technologies (roughly 80%). This reveals a serious divide between the "South" and the "North" in the global system of clean energy governance. The gap between developed and developing countries, be it technology, capital, or governance capability, remains unbridgeable.

To be specific, there are more than 60 core and key technologies for energy conservation and emission reduction, covering the production, supply, and use of energy, but Chinese enterprises have grasped less than 1/3. Regarding the application of key clean energy technology, developed countries have such firm control over the international market and the formulation of industrial standards that their domination is hard to shake.[11] At the same time, South-North cooperation in clean energy, mainly in the form of financial aid and technology transfer, remains an important way of tackling climate change, ensuring energy security and promoting global clean energy governance. However, a technology divide lingers between developed and developing countries. The former usually set all kinds of barriers when transferring core technologies to the latter, with IP being a typical example.

The European Patent Office (EPO), United Nations Environment Programme (UNEP), and International Centre for Trade and Sustainable Development (ICTSD) jointly issued a report titled *Patents and Clean Energy: Bridging the Gap Between Evidence and Policy* in 2009. Based on in-depth research on how patent affects the transfer of clean energy technology, the report identified three lessons learned that could help bridge the gap between practice and policy making. (1) Accurate and publicly available information on existing and emerging clean energy technology, including patent application and licensing, is urgently needed; (2) policy making and policy signals can have a positive effect on technology development; (3) consider all possibilities to facilitate the licensing of clean energy technologies to developing countries. In light of the unfavorable factors impeding technology transfer between the South and the North, the report took IP protection as a potential incentive because, if implemented to an appropriate degree, it guarantees sustained innovation to provide climate mitigation technologies, whereas excessive IP protection impedes the South-North technology transfer with high cost.

That developed countries often excuse themselves on the ground that IP is controlled by businesses, not governments, has made it harder for developing countries to obtain low-carbon technologies and consequently enhance their climate responsiveness. According to IEA's forecast, up to 60% of energy demand and emission growth through 2030 will take place in non-OECD developing countries, which will face the trilemma of environmental security, energy security, and climate security. If the world needs a global, comprehensive revolution of energy technology to cope with the challenges of energy security and climate change, it must put an end to the non-discriminate IP principles. Or to put it another way, it must prevent the Western-style IP protection from further widening the "South-North" gap. For that purpose, a new mode of governance must be sought for IP cooperation and sharing to speed up the spread of low-carbon technologies to developing countries.

Both UNFCCC and the *Kyoto Protocol* underscored technology transfer from developed countries as a key means to helping developing ones participate in the global efforts of GHG emission reduction. However, developed countries often shirk their international obligation in this area by claiming that the IPs of climatically sound technologies belong to private businesses where government interference is impossible. Europe and the US have raised the bar for technology transfer to developing countries by making all kinds of laws cumbering that process.[12] In particular, turning a blind eye to developing countries' pressing needs to respond to climate change, they, through existing international platforms, have jointly established an international network of standards based on IP protection to intentionally obstruct technology transfer. For example, WTO has formed a global IP protection system through the Trade-Related Aspects of Intellectual Property Rights (TRIPS). With absolute control in the making of rules, developed countries are sparing no efforts to maximize their IP-related benefits and keep their green industries competitive.

Ever since the financial crisis in 2008, developed countries, especially EU members, have become increasingly tougher on the IP issue. At the 2015 Paris Conference, the EU and the US unanimously objected to any topics related to trade or IP in the climate agreement negotiations, and IP-related issues are still not listed as formal topics for climate negotiations to the present day. This has hindered international clean energy cooperation and aid.[13] If talks with patentees about bringing down to a reasonable level the price of their patented and expensive climate-friendly technologies come to nothing, compulsory licensing is an important option for developing countries to obtain the technology they need. The only way to promote the diffusion of technology in strategic emerging industries worldwide is creating a globally coordinated IP system. The current global system of clean energy governance, being more pluralist and networked as it is, remains covertly hierarchical. Given the divergences in IP policies in certain areas between developed and developing countries, it's extremely difficult to bridge the "South-North divide" or "gap" in clean energy technology and capital. Against such a background, major developing countries represented by China must carry out flexible and pragmatic clean energy diplomacy and advance the South-South cooperation, making the best efforts to clear away the obstacles to technology transfer and make low-cost clean energy technology available.

IV. The trend toward "geographical dependence" in global clean energy diplomacy

Being more reliant on tech innovation, clean energy, to some extent, is above the geographical competition of traditional fossil energies. As emerging developing countries make fast progress in this area, southern and northern countries have come to find themselves in a cooperative/competitive relationship. The escalated competition may make global clean energy diplomacy "geographically dependent" again. Developing countries are rising collectively in clean energy investment and development, as typified by the rapid tech innovations in emerging developing countries such as China, India, and Brazil, and the technologies are strongly promoted among developing countries through the South-South cooperation. Boasting advantages in the market, human cost, and other aspects, emerging countries will hopefully acquire competitive edges that will enable them to compete with developed countries at certain links or on certain products along the clean energy industry chain.[14] Competition in green industries is closely linked with every country's economic interests, space of industrial development, and strategic power layout. As a result, the "geographically independent" clean energy governance may inevitably become "geographically dependent" – countries will compete in the formulation of industrial standards and IP application, and trade protectionism in clean energy will be on the rise.

At the moment, companies in all countries try to secure a spot on the high end of the clean energy innovation chain by internationalizing domestic industrial standards and applying for patents. Not seeing eye to eye on many issues – rules of clean energy governance, industrial standards, and project procedures, they can hardly come up with a comprehensive solution and are therefore unable to meet the rising demand for energy transition and clean energy governance in the international community. Moreover, when the energy issue, which directly concerns their fundamental interests, is compounded by economic, political, and security factors, a universal international treaty or agreement is hard to come through. This explains why international actions, agreements, and conference outcomes in relation to clean energy have little legal binding force. At the same time, more efforts must be made to turn traditional energy organizations green and integrate them with their clean energy counterparts. Still marginalized in traditional organizations, clean energy will only come to the center stage when those organizations are better coordinated with renewable energy organizations through closer exchanges and cooperation.

China both cooperates and competes with Europe and the US in clean energy, and it is regarded as a major competitor because they feel pressured and anxious about its high-speed progress in the field.[15] As international competition gets fiercer, Western countries increasingly resort to green trade protectionism, such as taking advantage of WTO rules, adopting anti-dumping and countervailing measures, and setting green trade barriers. Their anti-dumping and countervailing investigations into Chinese PV and wind power products and the China-US trade war typically reflect the trend toward "geographical dependence". In May 2012, the US announced a levy of 31.14%–249.96% anti-dumping tariff on Chinese solar cell products and 20.85%–72.69% on wind power companies. Following in its step, EUProSun, an alliance of European PV manufacturers, filed in November 2012 for an anti-dumping and countervailing investigation into Chinese solar cells/panels exported to the EU. From June to August 2013, the EU imposed an 11.8% provisional anti-dumping tariff on Chinese goods, which later shot up to 47.6%. Though of much smaller scope and amount than the US tariff, the move had more far-reaching impacts on China as 90% of Chinese PV export went to Europe.

Besides, although developing members account for a certain percentage at the International Organization for Standardization (ISO), developed ones still dominate the process of standard making. Vicious competition such as "patent enclosure" has appeared in the application for tech patents, whereby developed countries apply for massive amounts of patents for PV, geothermal, wind, and carbon capture technologies to create an enclosed circle that keeps competitors out and obstructs follow-up

R&D and patent application.[16] Apart from the anti-dumping and countervailing probe, the US imposes even more stringent control over high-tech export to China, and its firm grip on the export of clean energy technology has directly affected bilateral cooperation in the field. Its trade protectionism has also hindered Chinese businesses from entering the American market due to, to give one example, difficult financing. The "articles for non-market economy countries" expose Chinese enterprises to the constant threat of anti-dumping measures and export restrictions.

Trump, with a clean energy outlook purely driven by market competition, made clean energy part of the China-US trade war after he stepped into office. On June 15, 2018, he slapped a 25% tariff on USD 50 billion worth of Chinese goods, including products involving major industrial technologies. The tariff initially affected 818 items – worth about USD 34 billion – that were concentrated in such high-tech areas as new energy, information technology, aviation and aerospace, automaking, and medical apparatus. Those related to energy included nuclear reactors, steam boilers, electric equipment, electric motors, power generator sets, and some batteries. In the broad sense, much equipment could be categorized as energy and power-related, including wind turbines, and PV products might be subject to a 55% superposed tariff. On July 10, 2018, the US took a step further to impose an additional 10% tariff on another USD 200 billion worth of Chinese goods, including PV inverters and AC components (solar panels with micro inverters) this time, in retaliation to China's imposing tariff on USD 50 billion worth of American exports. The new move further hindered the overseas expansion of the Chinese PV industry.

Section 2 China builds all-round capacities of clean energy diplomacy

Clean energy technology is an important engine to power sustainable economic development and prosperity in the future. It also holds the key to meeting the diverse needs for energy security and tackling climate change. Clean energy technology will guarantee the world the ability of innovative development, the ability to manufacture clean energy facilities will make a country more competitive, and the clean energy market will give a country the opportunity for continuous upgrade and transformation. Therefore, developing clean energy diplomacy is not only an important way of preserving national competitiveness in clean energy but also a vital factor that affects the power balance and strategic competition internationally. In the long term, clean energy diplomacy holds great prospects as countries attach more importance to the development of and cooperation in clean energy. Compared with Europe and the US, China needs more professional platforms and financing schemes for its clean energy diplomacy, and the coordination, cooperation, and aid mechanisms also require improvement. How effective a diplomatic strategy can be essentially depends on the country's strategic diplomatic capacities, which include diplomatic strengths, resource-coordinating capability, system-building capability, and discourse power. In light of the aforementioned challenges facing China's clean energy diplomacy, we need to fundamentally enhance our strategic diplomatic capacities in the following five ways.

I. Strengthening the capacity of clean energy diplomacy: improving domestic governance system and coordinating interdepartmental response

Clean energy diplomacy wouldn't succeed if not bolstered by the robust green capabilities at home. To fundamentally consolidate the long-term strategic advantages of Chinese clean energy diplomacy, the only way is to continuously innovate clean energy policies and consequently improve the low-carbon governance system as a whole. The biggest problem with the Chinese clean energy industry now is this: while upstream industries develop with a sweeping momentum, with equipment manufacturing and total installed capacity increasing at a high speed, downstream auxiliary industries are lagging behind, with much to be desired in synchronization and convenience for users. Besides, there is much room for improvement in technological innovation as well. The *Amendment to Renewable Energy Law* of 2009 proposed the renewable portfolio standard (RPS) system to make up for the shortcomings of the FIT system established by the *Renewable Energy Law* enacted in 2005, as an innovation of the Chinese clean energy policy system. But this system hasn't been put into practice effectively all these years because it involves too many stakeholders and concerns the distribution of their interests. At present, as international petroleum price drops and the Chinese economy enters the new normal, "abandoning wind and solar energy" becomes more serious, with up to 33.9TWh wind electricity and an average 15% of wind energy given up in 2015. Even though the situation got better after 2017, synchronization of clean electricity remained a prominent problem, as well proven by the difficulty in implementing RPS. To make China stronger in clean energy, efforts can be made in three areas – conducting innovative R&D, expanding the domestic market, and establishing market-oriented mechanisms.

First, China must reinforce its independent R&D capability in the clean energy industry and enhance its core competence in the global industry chain. By perfecting domestic energy laws, setting standards for industrial access or promoting industrial self-discipline, China can guide the clean energy industry to develop more rationally to avoid overcapacity.[17] When making macro policies for renewables, the Chinese government should actively adjust the industrial structure and direction, and seize the opportunity through scientific macro control. For one thing, we should reinforce research capability and the development of related facilities. China's reliance on the import of inverters, the device needed for large-scale synchronization of solar electricity, has seriously limited the scale-up of PV power generation. For another, we should make renewable energy products more tech-intensive, avoid blind scale-up, and strive for coordinated, balanced, and comprehensive development industry-wide. Take wind power equipment, for example. Breakthroughs are urgently needed in the overall design of wind turbine, their life span, and the design and manufacturing of key parts and components, while blind scale-up will only lead to low-level repetition and redundancy. Last but not least, we should tap the niche markets for renewables equipment. Tidal energy, geothermal, and bioenergy are non-mainstream in China but have broad market prospects. We should make tentative plans for developing corresponding industry chains to avoid overreliance on imports.

Second, China must pay close attention to the grid connection of clean electricity and keep tapping the domestic market. Strong support policies such as green assessment and distributed synchronization systems must be rolled out to enforce the RPS. A mixture of the "American approach" (RPS) and the "German approach" (FIT), the Chinese RPS system was intended to explore a clean energy development strategy suitable for China's national conditions. In particular, it sets a target percentage of renewables for grid companies, power generators, and local governments alike to make sure renewable electricity can be synchronized smoothly. Considering how difficult it is to implement the system nationwide, we can, in reference to foreign experience, launch pilot projects first and try the RPS assessment.[18] That means a specific quota will be distributed to each grid company, power generator, and local government, and how they fulfill the quota will be taken as a key indicator to assess the performance of the company head or local leader, prompting them to implement the system.[19] In April 2016, the National Energy Administration (NEA) issued a *Notice Soliciting Opinions on Implementing RPS Assessment (Non-hydro Renewables) on Coal-fired Power Units*. The notice demanded that renewable electricity generated by coal-fired power generators must make up 15% of their thermal electricity by 2020, otherwise they'd be delicensed. The *Law of the People's Republic of China on Climate Change* and the *Environmental Protection Tax Law (for opinions)* were also enacted to tax air, water, and land pollution.

Third, China must intensify the market mechanism and push clean energy into the power market and carbon market through the trading of green certificates and carbon-emitting rights. By aligning those two trading regimes, we can come to a relatively reasonable on-grid tariff in the power market[20] with renewables as an integral part of it. With the trading of green certificates, coal-fired power generators can implement RPS either by building renewable power projects or by buying green certificates from the market; thus they will not only meet the requirements for RPS assessment but also help include renewables in the power market. In this scenario, earnings from renewable electricity will consist of three parts – on-grid tariff, fixed subsidy, and gains from trading green certificates, with which less government subsidy will be required.[21] At the moment, the fiscal subsidy for clean energy is in a widening deficit. To address that, the technological upgrade must be advanced to lower the cost of renewable energy. On the other hand, a more mature green certificate trading regime can increase the earnings of clean energy and eventually realize its grid parity at a reduced subsidy, thus enabling it to fully participate in the power market.

Meanwhile, reform of the carbon market can also stimulate the implementation of RPS because RPS can directly translate into certified emission reduction (CER). China lifted the curtain on carbon trade in 2011 by launching pilot projects in seven provinces and cities, the first emerging developing country to ever do that. At the Paris Conference, it vowed to launch a national carbon market in 2017 with a long-term view to becoming the world's largest. In the long run, China can expand the communication and cooperation with countries and regions, such as ROK, EU, and the US, that have already established and run national or regional carbon markets and jointly explore the possibility of connecting the markets between regions and worldwide.

Furthermore, China must be more crisis-responsive and resilient at times of trade frictions. It should make the clean energy governance system more orderly and policy making more scientific through organizational innovation, such as by promoting the development of think tanks in relevant fields. In 2012, the Center of Clean Energy Research under the Energy Research Institute (ERI) of the National Development and Reform Commission (NDRC) was elevated to be the China National Renewable Energy Centre (CNREC), which was tasked with assisting the energy authority of the State Council in studying renewable energy policies and organizing their implementation. Being a high-level think tank, CNREC is directly accountable to state leaders and provides professional technical and policy support for coordinating the administration of the clean energy industry.[22]

When Europe and the US launch anti-dumping and countervailing attacks and trade sanctions, the Chinese clean energy industry must be more responsive and resilient, while Chinese clean energy diplomacy should have a better emergency mechanism – the two should reinforce each other. To begin with, in the middle of a crisis, China must seek key areas that can serve as a breach point and push for practical cooperation there. With NEV as an example, although America has mature technologies in certain areas, it isn't that advanced in such frontier domains as thin-film solar cells. Therefore, as two major auto producers and sellers, China and the US can build a cooperation demonstration zone together where they may explore a viable business model as soon as possible. In fact, many American investors have seen opportunities for clean energy projects in China's green capital, and some new technologies that cannot secure funds from the American financial system can instead be supported with long-term loans from Chinese banks. Secondly, China must take the initiative to use WTO rules to protect its interests at times of trade frictions. It must work to gain a louder voice and more rules-making power within the WTO and link WTO with other global governance mechanisms concerning finance, investment, and the environment. Meanwhile, Chinese government departments must make new laws and regulations that consist with international norms and avoid any incompatibility with WTO rules. Thirdly, direct government subsidies should be replaced with indirect subsidies, and subsidies should not be limited to the production stage either. Rather, preferential policies on tax and loans can be offered, or more flexible indirect subsidies can be provided by funding the use of clean energy in families or communities, as is the practice in the US.[23]

II. Strengthening institutional capacity: intensifying major-country coordination and capacity of building platforms

The strengthening of China's institutional capacity of clean energy diplomacy is mainly reflected in its enhanced power of agenda-setting, rules-making, and narrative-leading in clean energy governance. It should not only make a point of coordinating with major countries to forge a new type of major-country relationship but also further integrate the green resources on existing cooperation platforms, especially seizing opportunities and mobilizing resources to create a new institutional platform for cooperation.

First and foremost, what's most essential for major-country coordination in clean energy diplomacy is, on the principle of benefit sharing, promoting the construction of flexible and variable "new-type major-country relationships" in a "green and win-win" spirit. China should take concrete diplomatic actions to define what "a community with a shared future for mankind" means, and enhance its power over green resources as part of its diplomatic deployment by supplying public clean energy goods to the region. It should leverage its advantages in clean energy development and build sustainable new-type relationships with major energy countries. Efforts must be made in the following directions.

The first is establishing institutional mechanisms for strategic coordination and communication among major countries. Although China and other regional powers have fundamentally different strategic objectives, there is still room for coordination and cooperation. They can put in place an institutionalized and normalized communication and coordination mechanism on a specific topic of clean energy cooperation. Or they may try to "positively interrelate" clean energy topics with other regional political and economic issues so that other bilateral or multilateral platforms can be utilized as a stage for their consultation and coordination.

The second is building demonstration zones for clean energy cooperation with major European and American countries. We can create regional dialogue regimes for Belt and Road countries, cooperate with other regional powers in the development and utilization of clean energy, and build demonstration zones for that. This will enlarge the space for win-win cooperation and give those countries more strategic trust in China and the China-proposed Belt and Road Initiative (BRI).[24]

The third is emphasizing clean energy cooperation and coordinated action among major developing countries. China played a key role in enhancing the BASIC mechanism at the 2017 Bonn Conference. At the 26th BASIC Ministerial Meeting on Climate Change in 2018, China advocated comprehensively intensifying the BASIC mechanism and continuing the regular ministerial consultations. It insisted on having full discussions under the BASIC framework before proposing its coordination plan at international climate negotiations. It especially called for resuming the "BASIC PLUS" mode as needed, whereby the experts' meeting and the ministerial meeting could interact, and experts in the four countries could carry out joint research and provide suggestions and plans on topics that interested the ministerial meeting. In the BRICS mechanism, China, leveraged by its structural advantages in clean energy development, has intensified its clean energy cooperation and heightened its collective voice in the new global landscape of climate and energy governance.

Besides, in comparison with other countries, China is in want of more professional, mainstream platforms and institutional financing guarantees for international clean energy cooperation, and its cooperation and coordination mechanisms are in urgent need of improvement. By dominating multilateral cooperation systems with their structural advantages in the low-carbon economy and clean energy technology, Europe, and the US aim to build a new order of clean energy governance in their favor. China needs to actively lead the establishment of new regional and global platforms for clean energy cooperation and be more proactive in the cooperation. It should also move beyond bilateral cooperation, further tap international platforms, and guide the green narrative and rules-making, to seize the opportunity to build and lead the new global order of clean energy governance.

There are currently two ways for China to enhance its institutional capacity – through the agenda-setting power and the rules-making power. One is forming clean energy cooperation agencies on existing multilateral platforms. While utilizing and connecting the existing platforms, China, backed by its advantages in clean energy development, can push for topics and rules in relation to clean energy governance. For example, it can strive to lead clean energy governance on such platforms as SCO, APEC, G20, China-ASEAN (10+1), Conference on Interaction and Confidence Building Measures in Asia (CICA), Asia-Europe Meeting (ASEM), Asia Cooperation Dialogue (ACD), Great Mekong Subregion Cooperation (GMS), and Central Asia Regional Economic Cooperation (CAREC).

China can also propose new cooperation initiatives within existing international platforms to augment its agenda-setting power and create a new situation of international clean energy development. In September 2014, the 11th APEC Energy Ministerial Meeting was held in Beijing under the theme of "Joining Hands Toward Sustainable Energy Development in the Asia-Pacific Region". Being the host, China took the opportunity to announce the official inauguration of the APEC Sustainable Energy Center (APSEC) initiated by NEA and built under the lead of Tianjin University. Serving as a stable and mature information sharing platform and efficient coordination mechanism, the center will strengthen the exchange on energy policy and tech research in the Asia-Pacific, promote energy sustainability in the region, and meet the dual objectives of sound economic development and environmental protection.[25] Four East Asia Summit Clean Energy Forums have been held with China's support since 2014, which consisted of themed seminars on electric power, smart energy and city, nuclear energy, PV, bioenergy, and clean coal. They were aimed at boosting the clean energy cooperation and development in East Asia, especially between China and ASEAN.

The biggest achievement in this period was how China promoted and led clean energy development at G20. The G20 Energy Sustainability Working Group is a platform for sustained discussions on energy efficiency, a core topic ever since G20 began to talk about energy in 2011. In recent years, China has been actively sharing its experience in raising energy efficiency under the G20 framework. Thanks to its strong support, G20 leaders announced the G20 Energy Efficiency Action Plan (EEAP) at the Brisbane Summit in November 2014. A practical plan to strengthen voluntary energy efficiency collaboration in a flexible way, EEAP allows countries to share knowledge, experience, and resources by choosing, on an opt-in basis, the activities that best reflect their domestic priorities and interests. G20 members agreed to cooperate in three key areas – finance (for large energy efficiency projects), energy conservation for Internet devices (with embedded Internet access), and transportation (heavy-duty vehicles), and China has joined all three working groups. When it was the rotating chair of G20 in 2016, China demonstrated its ability of making rules and systems. The G20 Energy Ministers Meeting held in June that year adopted the *G20 Energy Ministerial Meeting Beijing Communique*, which listed clean energy, energy efficiency, energy sustainability, and energy availability in backward regions as the breakthrough areas for reshaping the global order of energy governance. Considering the Trump administration's passive attitude toward climate change and clean energy, when Germany assumed the rotating presidency of G20 in 2017, China could tighten the coordination with it and other European countries to further enhance its own institutional power in climate and clean energy governance.[26]

The other way to enhance China's institutional capacity is to join with global clean energy governance agencies to build new cooperation platforms. China has interacted more closely with IRENA, an international organization founded in 2011 to promote the universal and sustainable use of renewable energy across the globe.[27] It joined the agency in January 2013, has actively taken part in its activities, and kept improving its abilities of clean energy governance through the interactions. In 2015, China participated in the study of IRENA's Renewable Energy Roadmap 2030 (REmap 2030) and released the primary findings of the study of its own Renewable Energy Roadmap 2030 with IRENA's help. In November that year, China and IRENA co-hosted the International Forum on Energy Transitions in Suzhou, China's Jiangsu Province. They advocated creating a global coalition of partner countries undertaking energy transition to further advance the global energy transition process and set up an "IRENA-China Research and Co-operation Centre for Energy Transition" to support the coalition's activities and set the stage for global energy transformation. While working with IRENA, China has learnt how it stays attractive in innovative ways. For one, for developed countries that are capable of innovating global governance, their domestic political system must have a lasting demand for international cooperation – that's the push. For another, IRENA provides net benefits for every country and participant, especially developing countries, to make itself an appealing option that other organizations would emulate – that's the pull.

Since 2010, China has been a member of the Steering Committee at every Clean Energy Ministerial (CEM). It co-initiated the "Target Indicator" working group and raised an array of clean energy initiatives, including carbon capture, utilization and storage (CCUS), electric vehicle initiative (EVI), Global Sustainable Cities Network (GSCN), and International Smart Grid Action Network (ISGAN). In June 2017, the Eighth Clean Energy Ministerial (CEM8) and the Second Mission Innovation Ministerial (MI-2) were held in Beijing. Taking such a great opportunity of home-court diplomacy, China, in the form of themed speech or fireside chitchat, released the clean energy projects it had accomplished, determined new objectives for the future, and prodded the global energy transition further down the clean path. It also staged an exhibition of innovative clean energy technologies on the sidelines, attracting industrial leaders from more than 20 CEM and MI member states as well as the EU to present their innovative technologies and products. The exhibits covered six major areas – renewable energy, high-efficiency energy conservation technology and equipment, technology and equipment for energy storage, digital energy and smart grid, EV and related technologies, and financial and business innovations, in addition to the clean utilization of traditional fossil energies.

Feeling some pressure from IRENA, the International Energy Agency (IEA) worked more closely with China in renewables. Not only did China participate in its variable renewable energy synchronization program, but CNREC and IEA jointly issued the *China Wind Energy Development Roadmap 2050*. In July 2015, IEA and China's State Grid formed a joint working group to study the global energy network, including the synchronization of renewable electricity. At the IEA Ministerial meeting in November that year, China, Indonesia, and Thailand became the first association countries of the agency,[28] which enabled China to access IEA's expertise and international best practices much more easily than before. China is now equipped with the conditions to make up for its deficiencies, and the nearly ten Chinese experts based at IEA for work or exchange can help the two sides better understand each other. IEA is the only international agency with the charter and means to organize a collective emergency response in the event of a disruption of global oil supply, and one that encompasses all types of fuels and energy technologies. China can well rely on it to share resources and uplift its position and role in global clean energy governance. As a big developing country, it isn't likely for China to independently create an international organization dedicated to clean energy governance – like Germany with IRENA. Therefore, it should make full use of existing platforms and make institutional innovation, policy coordination, and governance contribution on that basis, to enhance its own institutional power.

III. Strengthening the capacity of building diplomatic networks: forging a global network of partnerships for better clean energy governance

The international system of clean energy governance has basically taken shape, which involves six dimensions: (1) intergovernmental organizations incorporating clean energy development as an important item on its agenda, such as the UN Commission on Sustainable Development (UNCSD), UNEP, and IEA; (2) international associations and clubs focused on renewables research, such as IRENA, World Council for Renewable Energy (WCRE), and European Renewable Energy Council (EREC); (3) bilateral or multilateral clean energy partnerships, such as Asia Pacific Partnership on Clean Development and Climate (APP), Johannesburg Renewable Energy Coalition (JREC), Renewable Energy and Energy Efficiency Partnership (REEEP), and IEA's Networks of Expertise in Energy Technology (NEET); (4) global networks of clean energy policies, such as REN21, International Science Panel on Renewable Energies (ISPRE), and Global Network on Energy for Sustainable Development (GNESD); (5) organizations for the exchange of clean energy information, such as Commission on Sustainable Development Matrix (CSD Matrix); and (6) international programs of voluntary public commitments, such as International Action Program (IAP) on renewable energy.[29]

The clean energy governance mechanisms on those six dimensions overlap in function and membership, thus forming a global network. While expanding clean energy diplomacy in bilateral and multilateral interactions, China must also merge into the international system comprehensively and forge an all-round network of partnerships. It should also seize the opportunity to establish and lead new international clean energy platforms (like the Germany-led IRENA) on which it can enhance its institutional capacity, namely, the agenda-setting power, rules-making power, and system-leading power. With these, China will be able to create a sound diplomatic environment for forging a "green, global network of partnerships" and for exercising its structural power over green resources. With these, it will evolve from an onlooker and a follower in the international system to a rules-maker and a norm-setter.

The REEEP is one of the first multilateral clean energy organizations that China joined.[30] Highlighting developing countries and their emerging green markets, it is aimed to improve clean energy policies and management measures and accelerate and expand the global market for renewables and energy efficiency mechanisms, ranging from removing market barriers to increasing financial channels to raising public awareness. By working with development agencies, REEEP encourages the promotion of business operations and financing modes in developing and emerging countries to channel more capital into this burgeoning market. In 2004, the REEEP East Asia Regional Secretariat was set at the Chinese Renewable Energy Industries Association (CREIA). Knowing that promoting modern energy services is essential for the economic and social development in East Asia, the Regional Secretariat supports REEEP's work by enlarging its network, conducting preliminary screening in bidding projects, and running and managing the projects. It also forms a steering committee comprising influential leaders and experts on renewables and energy efficiency to supervise and guide its own work.

In 2008, the G8, China, India, and ROK jointly put forth the vision of raising energy efficiency, based on which they founded the International Partnership for Energy Efficiency Cooperation (IPEEC). As a founding member, China signed the Terms of Reference (TOR) and made voluntary donations to expedite the application of clean energy technologies worldwide. It has served as vice chair of the IPEEC Policy Committee starting from 2012 and vice chair of the Executive Committee from 2013, engaged in several working groups either as a participant or observer, and hosted relevant meetings and seminars several times. In 2013, China proposed to set up the Top Ten Energy Efficiency Best Practices and Best Available Technologies Task Group (TOP TENs); in 2014, IPEEC China Secretariat was formed.

As a global renewable energy policy multi-stakeholder network that connects a wide range of key actors, the Renewable Energy Policy Network for the 21st Century (REN21)[31] aims to facilitate the comprehensive and timely collection of renewables information, knowledge exchange, policy development, and joint actions towards a rapid global transition to renewable energy. It achieves its goals in six ways: Renewables Global Status Report (GSR), Renewables Regional Status Reports, Renewables Interactive Map, Renewables Global Futures Report (GFR), Renewables Academy, and International Renewable Energy Conferences (IRECs). To help and facilitate policy and decision-making, REN21 provides high-quality information, promotes discussions, organizes debates, and supports the development of themed networks.[32] Soon after its foundation in 2005, REN21 co-hosted the Beijing International Renewable Energy Conference (BIREC) with China. The Chinese Renewable Energy Industries Association (CREIA) of China

Association of Circular Economy led by Li Junfeng joined the network as an industrial association, but the Chinese government hasn't assigned a resident representative to the network yet.

Besides, as clean energy diplomacy involves many actors, its smooth implementation depends on effective coordination among domestic sectors. In order to prevent fragmented decision-making and inefficient governance, it is necessary to perfect the top-level decision-making system. A national mechanism of coordinating for clean energy diplomacy should be put in place to better the communication and collaboration among different departments and between them and local governments. Clean energy industry associations should also join hands so that enterprises no longer have to "go global" on their own, and the country will do a better job at coordinating domestic resources.[33] During the Belt and Road construction, for instance, the China Overseas Development Association, CREIA, and other organizations jointly founded the China New Energy International Alliance in 2016. The new alliance is expected to boost regional capacity cooperation and facilitate exchange, communication, and coordination in driving the overseas development of the clean energy industry.

IV. Strengthening the capacity of guiding green finance: steering investment and expanding finance through PPP

In order to fulfill its international commitment to carbon peaking by 2030 or earlier and meet the goals of domestic environmental governance, China expects to need RMB 3–4 trillion green investment every year down the road, only 15% of which can be covered by fiscal funds, whereas more than 80% will have to come from the private sector.[34] Without the joining of more investors, the need for clean energy investment and environmental protection funding will put immense financial pressure on the government in the medium and long term, which might drain the momentum of the green transition. Therefore, when China is providing green public goods, it must not only stimulate the initiative of government departments on all levels but also mobilize private investors to pool more funds for clean energy projects overseas, thus fundamentally enhancing the structural influence of our clean energy diplomacy. International practices prove that private funding will not automatically flow into clean energy without policy guidance. That means we must create an effective green finance system to channel funds and investments to clean energy through a spate of measures, including green credit, green funds and bonds, green insurance, and carbon finance represented by the carbon market.

During the preparations for the 2016 G20 Hangzhou Summit, China and the UK specifically established the G20 Green Finance Study Group (GFSG) that presented the *G20 Green Finance Synthesis Report*; later they successfully incorporated topics such as expanding green investment and finance, and issuing green bonds in the *G20 Leaders' Communique*. China is now the largest issuer of green bonds in the world.[35] The ability to guide green finance is also reflected in institutionalizing and internationalizing its market norms, financial regulations, and other principles that standardize the financial market. Other than the New Development Bank (NDB), more commonly known as the BRICS Bank, whose first batch of USD 811 million loans in 2016 went to four clean energy projects, none of the other outward development institutions (e.g., AIIB and Silk Road Fund) has made special requirements on green investment. Therefore, as China implements clean energy diplomacy, it should first urge the acceptance of the Equator Principles, so as to create a high-standard environmental risk management system and fully disclose environmental information. It should especially stress such principles as "sustainable infrastructure" and "green procurement" when investing in projects, promote our clean energy products in surrounding countries, and build up China's international image as a responsible major country.[36] Under the current new circumstances, only by enhancing China's ability to steer green finance can we fundamentally reinforce its structural influence and leadership in the regional supply of public goods, can we provide an inexhaustible source of strength for establishing a new order of climate and energy governance through more scientific investment.

The growing presence of public-private partnership (PPP) in international clean energy cooperation can invigorate international capital and private capital to engage in green industries. Based on the franchising agreement, PPP is a mode of cooperation in which the public sector and private sector share responsibilities and financing risks for providing certain public goods for infrastructure construction.[37] In recent years, clean energy development in China has been troubled by difficult and expensive financing. In April 2016, NEA released the *Notice on Actively Promoting Public-Private Partnership in Energy Sector*, a signal on the national level to encourage and guide private capital toward clean energy. This could mitigate the state's fiscal burden, effectively improve public services in the clean energy sector, and lure more stakeholders to help perfect the industry chain. With the help of PPP, we can also reform the way public services are provided in the clean energy sector, broaden channels of investment and financing, and fully stimulate private capital to join the construction of energy projects. Improved public services can better meet people's demand for safe, reliable, and clean energy sources. Electric power and clean energy projects were dominant in NEA's Notice,[38] including renovation and upgrade of the rural grid, construction, and operation of charging infrastructure, distributed power generation, micro grid construction and renovation, energy storage, PV projects for poverty alleviation, hydropower station, and electric alternatives.

On the international level, as international organizations are more open to private capital, international PPP comprising governments, research institutes, and investors have come to the fore. For example, Bill Gates led the formation of the Breakthrough Energy Coalition, which involved 28 top business leaders from some of the world's most influential tech companies, industrial complexes, and investment groups, right before the Paris Conference. Integrating the resources of governments and the private sector (research institutes and investors), the coalition planned to invest more in the next five years to address climate change and clean energy issues through technological innovation and diffusion. The participating governments pledged to double their budget for the research and development of clean energy technologies. To be more specific, Breakthrough Energy Coalition, by pooling together public and private forces, aims to find more technical methods to stop the earth from getting warmer, especially those ideas and technologies that have the potential of changing the current way of energy production and consumption. The key technologies it is interested in include power generation and storage, industrial use, transportation, agriculture, and energy efficiency, with the ultimate goal of "near zero emission".[39]

At the same time, PPP is also a good way of weaving multi-track networks of clean energy partnerships that are open to all actors. Cooperation between China and Europe, China and the US is progressing fast in this area, as represented by the Joint US-China Collaboration on Clean Energy (JUCCCE) program advanced during Barack Obama's term, the China-US Clean Energy Forum, Asia Society (AS), and the Initiative for US-China Cooperation on Energy and Climate.[40] When pushing forward the construction of partnership networks using existing PPP platforms, China should exert greater initiative and leadership by building cooperation platforms dominated by itself.

In the meantime, as cities are getting more important in international clean energy cooperation, partnership networks with cities as primary actors should be strongly promoted.[41] In September 2015, the first ever China-US Climate-Smart/Low-Carbon Cities Summit was held in Los Angeles, attended by representatives from 29 provinces or states, cities, or counties of both countries; in June 2016, representatives from 66 provinces or states, cities, or counties attended the second summit in Beijing. The summits laid a solid foundation for weaving and enlarging the clean energy partnership network. Low-carbon and clean energy cooperation between the two countries on the sub-national level continued even despite Trump's passive climate policies. In June 2018, governor of California Edmund Brown visited China. He not only signed a memorandum of cooperation on green technology research and development with the Chinese minister of science and technology, but also saw remarkable achievements in sub-national cooperation. For one thing, he affirmed the further implementation of the green technology cooperation agreements signed with Sichuan and Jiangsu provinces, pledging to deepen their collaboration in renewable energy, energy storage, zero-emission vehicles, grid modernization, and low-carbon city. For another, the state of California and Tsinghua University jointly established the China-US Climate Change Institute to provide intellectual support for coping with climate change and speeding up breakthroughs in clean energy technology.

As to sub-national collaboration between China and the EU, the two sides kicked off the Europe-China Eco Cities Link (EC-LINK) in November 2013, which, by generating an eco-city toolkit, launching pilot eco-cities and intensifying capacity building, was expected to act as an all-round platform to promote eco-city cooperation and share technology and experience among cities. The platform provides training, technical support, and package solution for people engaged in relevant domains.[42] It has already launched two overall pilot cities – Zhuhai and Luoyang – and specific pilot projects in eight cities – Zhuzhou, Liuzhou, Guilin, Changzhou, Hefei, Qingdao, Weihai, and Fengxi New City of Xixian New Area. In 2018, the EU approved the plan to renew EC-LINK, originally designed for four years, for another two years till September 2020. For the next steps, the two sides will tighten cooperation in the joint research on and the introduction and application of clean energy technology.

V. Strengthening the capacity of diplomatic narrative: fostering normative power and expanding public clean energy diplomacy

Clean energy diplomacy manifests the moral and normative power of Chinese diplomatic thoughts. Strengthening the narrative capacity means we must demonstrate and interpret China's diplomatic thoughts and innovative concepts in a logical and powerful way, backing them with a scientific basis, rational analysis, and moral principles. That's how we rephrase our advanced concepts into an international mainstream narrative that can be widely accepted. When carrying out clean energy cooperation with neighboring countries or providing climate aid to them, China has interpreted its concept of "greater good and shared interests" and the "community with a shared future for mankind" with concrete diplomatic actions. It has also endeavored to build a "new type of major-country relationship" in the spirit of "green, win-win" development. All these efforts go a long way for comprehensively uplifting China's discourse power as part of its master diplomatic strategy.

It must be noted that China's clean energy diplomacy, which is gaining importance and influence, is implemented in a "top-down" approach. In other words, the Chinese government is the main actor in foreign exchanges and the provision of public goods, and more attention is paid to the country's role in major-country diplomacy (the forging of a new type of major-country relationship), home-court diplomacy, South-South cooperation, and the establishment of international mechanisms. Indeed, enhancing China's institutional capacity will undoubtedly give the country more discourse power and initiative when carrying out clean energy diplomacy on the national level. However, when it comes to fostering national image and forming an international narrative (e.g., responding to the theory of "China's clean energy export and threat"), public diplomacy has unique advantages. This is because its mainstay non-state actors, including NGOs, think tanks, research institutes, media, social groups, and businesses, are more flexible and approachable when presenting to foreign public China's national conditions and explaining its policies. More importantly, they can better answer foreign citizens' questions and clear their misunderstandings about Chinese policies and better understand their views and positions in the process, thus deepening mutual understanding.[43] Supported by the authoritative research and transparent information from private organizations, non-state actors can be informative and enlightening to foreign audiences in a subtle and unobtrusive way and minimize misperceptions arising from the lack of communication and exchanges between Chinese and foreign people.

Clean energy diplomacy on the public level is "second-track" diplomacy. Being more flexible than official diplomacy, it is able to convey messages that cannot be conveyed on the first track in a way more acceptable to the local people. The government should encourage more NGOs, media, think tanks, academic organizations, industrial associations, and enterprises to participate in public clean energy diplomacy. They have not only improved the way how China's propositions and stance on clean energy are presented but also employed new approaches to clean energy diplomacy. Other than conducting cultural exchange programs, holding press conferences, and using international press and the Internet for publicity, we can also urge non-state actors to take part in international conferences, partnership dialogues, and relevant side events, and to release clean energy study reports. China can sponsor domestic NGOs and industrial associations to join the activities of international clean energy networks, fund academic exchanges and programs, promote international cooperation and PPP, and boost green finance.[44]

The China Institute of Strategy & Management (CISM),[45] for instance, held the high-level forum titled "US-China Strategic Forum on Clean Energy Practical Cooperation with America's Brookings Institution" in October 2009. The forum discussed clean energy topics both on the strategic, intergovernmental level and the specific project level, paving the way for bilateral clean energy cooperation to be confirmed during Obama's China visit in November. At the China-US clean energy roundtable, Chinese and American leaders held in-depth talks about three major areas – renewable energy, energy efficiency, and tech cooperation – and signed relevant cooperation agreements, which were largely based on and driven by the policy suggestions proposed at the October forum.[46]

The China-based Global Environmental Institute (GEI)[47] has played a positive role in international clean energy cooperation, particularly projects concerning energy and climate change, investment, trade and environment, and capacity building. It hopes to build an open platform of environmental studies in China that will work alongside the government, enterprises, and farmers to try the most advanced ideas, models, and policies toward sustainable development. Being a neutral institute, GEI encourages cross-agency and international cooperation, especially South-South cooperation, and provides a whole set of solutions, ranging from market surveys, technical support to financing schemes and business plans, to the implementation of pilot projects. The most renowned projects undertaken by GEI are the Sri Lanka biogas training program in the South-South cooperation framework and the China-US "second-track" dialogue on climate change in the South-North cooperation framework.[48] Through the first project, GEI brought Chinese clean energy production technology to Sri Lanka, which not only enabled the locals to tackle climate change and obtain modern energy but also left them and the local government a good impression of China, reinforcing China's international image and discourse power. With the second project, GEI and American Center for Climate Strategies (CCS) teamed up to localize the methodologies and modeling tools of America's state-level climate action plans (CAPs) and developed a set of tools for making low-carbon plans suitable for China. The tools could help local governments conduct quantitative analysis of the cost and benefits of various policies, evaluate how the policies and plans will affect the local economy, and eventually achieve economic development, energy conservation, and emission reduction in parallel.[49]

Founded in 2004 in Chaoyang District of Beijing, GEI has moved beyond Chinese borders and carried out projects in Southeast Asia and South Asia, covering biodiversity protection, energy and climate change, investment, trade and environment, and capacity building. By bringing expertise to and working with local communities, GEI has helped improve the local environment and gained the local government and public's recognition of China as a "climate-responsible country". In 2017, GEI, Guangzhou Institute of Energy Conversion (GIEC) of the Chinese Academy of Sciences, and the Department of Research and Innovation (DRI) of Myanmar's Ministry of Education signed a cooperation agreement on pushing the renewable energy planning in Myanmar. Following up on the Workshop, GEI and DRI would submit to the Myanmar government a proposal on furthering the capacity-building training, and the three parties would continue technical discussions and cooperation in renewables. As a result, the "Workshop on Promoting Renewable Energy and Sustainable Development in Myanmar" was jointly held in 2018, a meaningful attempt to improve local governance practices in response to climate change and innovate the patterns of South-South cooperation.[50] In view of China's BRI and the climate change projects under South-South cooperation, Xie Zhenhua, China's special envoy for climate change affairs, and experts from the UN Global Alliance for Clean Cookstoves (GACC) visited the GEI-launched pilot community in Myanmar in March 2017. They commented highly on GEI's work at the China-Myanmar climate aid handover ceremony.

Notes

1 Jiang Shu, Li Qingsi, "The China-US Cooperation/Competition in New Energy – from PV to Wind", *International Forum*, No. 2, 2013.
2 Fan Liuyan, Qu Delin, Wang Haibo et al., "Japan's New Energy Situation in the Post-Fukushima Era: Changes and Lessons", *Renewable Energy Resources*, No. 5, 2011.
3 Another reason for this situation is the unbalanced distribution of renewable energy sources. On the one hand, renewables in China are concentrated in western provinces and autonomous regions and along the eastern coast. For example, Tibet abounds in solar and geothermal energy, Qinghai in hydro and solar, and Inner Mongolia in solar and wind. They therefore need to develop the renewable industry in such a way as to have all kinds of renewables flourish in complementarity. On the other hand, where renewable energy is produced is far from where it is used. Renewables in China are concentrated in economically less developed provinces and autonomous regions, such as Tibet and Qinghai, whereas most electricity is consumed in economically developed regions in the central and eastern part of the country. This requires the transmission of electricity over long distances, something our grid system cannot handle right now given its weak network structure.
4 Currently, wind abandonment is concentrated in Xinjiang and Gansu, where a high rate of wind energy is abandoned that's equivalent to a large amount of electricity. The abandonment rate in Inner Mongolia has fallen by a large margin, but the amount of abandoned electricity remains large given the huge installed capacity.
5 Statistics of global mineral resources show China has a rare earth reserve of 55 million tons and an output of 100,000 tons, accounting for 39% and 91% in the world each.
6 China began to tariff rare earth export in 2006 and raised the rate to 15% in 2007. At the same time, its export quota was slashed by nearly 40% in 2009–2010, was on a par in 2010–2011, and slightly increased by 2.7% in 2011–2012. China continued the quota system in 2014 even though it was to lose the case at WTO.
7 Xu Bin, "Multiple Options of Rare Earth Policies in China: Reflection and Response", *Intertrade*, May 2015.

8 Pursuant to the *Protocol on the Accession of the People's Republic of China*, China should eliminate all taxes and charges applied to exports unless otherwise specified. The appendix lists 84 types of products with a designated tax rate, 10% for rare earth, which must be the highest tariff for rare earth except under exceptional circumstances.
9 Du Fenglian, Wang Yuan, "Study of Alternative Policies for Tariff on Strategic Resources – With the Export of Rare Earth as an Example", *Economic Science*, No. 3, 2015.
10 Zhu Xuantong, "China's Engagement in Global Energy Governance", *IEA Annual Report 2016*, 2016, pp. 14–15, https://theasiadialogue.com/wp-content/uploads/2018/03/Partner-CountrySeries_ChinasEngagementinGlobalEnergyGovernance_Englishversion.pdf.
11 UNEP, EPO, ICTSD, *Patents and Clean Energy, Bridging the Gap between Policy and Evidence*, Geneva, Munich, 2010, p. 9.
12 For instance, the US House of Representatives in 2009 passed the *Clean Energy and Security Act of 2009, Foreign Operations, and Related Programs Appropriations Act of 2010*, and *Foreign Relation Authorization Act for the Fiscal Year of 2010 and 2011*. These acts contained preconditions on which the US could participate in international climate change affairs. They also set the conditions for providing financial aid for foreign countries to cope with climate change and required rigorous compliance with existing international laws on IP.
13 UNFCCC, *Streamlined and Consolidated Text*, Ad Hoc Working Group on the Durban Platform for Enhanced Action, Second Session, Part Nine, June 11, 2015.
14 Jiang Jiani, Wang Can, "IP Issue in Global Climate Negotiations – Progress, Trend and China's Response", *World Outlook*, No. 2, 2016.
15 Peter V. Marsters, Jennifer L. Turner, "Cooperative Competitors: Potential of U. S. – China Clean Energy Cooperation", *China Environmental Forum Brief*, Woodrow Wilson International Center for Scholars, 2012.
16 Jiang Jiani, Wang Can, "IP Issue in Global Climate Negotiations – Progress, Trend and China's Response", *World Outlook*, No. 2, 2016.
17 CNREC, renewable energy development center of Energy Research Institute (ERI) of NDRC, ed., *China Renewable Energy Industry Development Report 2017*, Beijing: Economic Press China, 2017.
18 The Inner Mongolia Autonomous Region released the *Guiding Opinions on Creating a Long-term Mechanism to Guarantee the Procurement of Renewable Electricity* in April 2015, the first local area in China to pilot the RPS. It vowed to increase on-grid renewable electricity to 15% of total electricity consumption across the region by 2015 and 20% by 2020.
19 "Inner Mongolia pilots RPS", April 3, 2015, www.cspplaza.com/article-4976-1.html.
20 Tan Zhongfu, Liu Wenyan, Liu Pingkuo, "Effects of Green Certificate Trade and Carbon Emission Right Trade on Chinese Power Market", *Technology Economics*, No. 9, 2014.
21 Shi Jingli, "RPS and Green Certificate Trade A Policy Pathway for Renewable Energy Development", *China Energy News*, May 19, 2016.
22 CNREC has the following tasks: studying and formulating national strategies, plans, and policies on renewable energy development; organizing the implementation of national demonstration projects; coordinating the formulation of industrial standards and norms; collecting, monitoring, and evaluating industrial data; and managing international cooperation projects.
23 Li Dong, Wei Xiaosha, "Trade Frictions Between China and US on Clean Energy: Trend, Reasons and Countermeasures", *Seeker*, No. 11, 2012.
24 Gao Shixian, Yang Jing, "Deepening International Energy Cooperation Through Belt and Road Initiative", *Macroeconomic Management*, No. 3, 2016.
25 The APEC Sustainable Energy Center (APSEC) is affiliated to NEA and operated and managed by Tianjin University. It makes contributions to the sustainable development of Asia-Pacific by promoting policy exchange, information sharing, capacity building, joint R&D, and tech cooperation among regional economies.

26 Kai Fang, Yunheng Zhou, Shuang Wang, Ruike Ye, Sujian Guo, "Assessing National Renewable Energy Competitiveness of the G20: A Revised Porter's Diamond Model", *Renewable and Sustainable Energy Reviews*, No. 93, 2018, pp. 719–731.
27 Johannes Urpelainen, Thijs Van de Graaf, Lin Xuefei, "The International Renewable Energy Agency: A Successful Institutional Innovation?", *Foreign Theoretical Trends*, No. 2, 2017.
28 Zhu Xuantong, "China's Engagement in Global Energy Governance", *IEA Annual Report 2016*, 2016, pp. 6–7, https://theasiadialogue.com/wp-content/uploads/2018/03/Partner-CountrySeries_ChinasEngagementinGlobalEnergyGovernance_Englishversion.pdf.
29 Paul H. Suding and Philippe Lempp, "The Multifaceted Institutional Landscape and Processes of International Renewable Energy Policy", *International Association for Energy Economics*, Second Quarter 2007, pp. 4–10.
30 Founded in Vienna in 2004, REEEP's main sponsors include Australia, Austria, Canada, EU, Germany, Ireland, Italy, the Netherlands, New Zealand, Norway, Spain, the US, and the UK. It conducts cooperation projects directly with countries that have legal or regulatory needs or development-oriented financing institutions in need of support in financing and business operation.
31 Founded in 2005, REN21 is not an organization but a policy network that is characterized by multiple stakeholders from a variety of sectors around the globe. The stakeholders include national or local governments, multilateral organizations, NGOs, industrial associations, financial institutions, and other groups, and are from environmental, energy, or development communities worldwide.
32 REN21, *Renewables 2015 Global Status Report*, 2015, www.ren21.net/wp-content/uploads/2019/05/GSR2015_Full-Report_English.pdf.
33 Xu Hui, "Chinese Clean Energy Industry Going Global – Founding Conference of China New Energy International Alliance and Asia Solar Energy Forum Successfully Held", *China Electrical Equipment Industry*, No. 4, 2016.
34 Ma Jun, "Building a Green Financial System in China", *Finance Forum*, No. 5, 2015.
35 Sean Kidney, Beate Sonerud, *Green Bonds Can Help Plug the Climate Finance Gap*, April 12, 2015, www.chinadialogue.net-article/show/single/en/8398-Green-bonds-can-help-plug-the-climate-finance-gap.
36 According to Equator Principles, when a financial institution invests in a project, it should conduct a comprehensive evaluation of the project's environmental and social impacts and use financial leverage to make sure it plays a positive role in sustainable development and social and environmental responsibility.
37 Emi Minghui Gui, Iain Mac Gill, "Typology of Future Clean Energy Communities: An Exploratory Structure, Opportunities, and Challenges", *Energy Research & Social Science*, No. 35, 2018, pp. 94–107.
38 For a long time, China faces huge pressure in synchronizing clean electricity, and it is common to see wind and solar energy abandoned. The construction of cross-regional UHV grid, which covers extensive areas and requires enormous capital, calls for a multi-actor and multilayer investment system. Domestic and foreign experience shows that the PPP model is beneficial for integrating advantageous resources and can match the long schedule of large grid projects. It is a rather ideal investment model for new energy projects for strengthening the cooperation between government and private capital and effectively spreading and defusing investment risks.
39 Breakthrough Energy Coalition website, www.b-t.energy/.
40 Joanna I. Lewis, "Managing Intellectual Property Rights in Cross-border Clean Energy Collaboration: The Case of the U.S.-China Clean Energy Research Center", *Energy Policy*, No. 69, 2014, pp. 546–554.
41 Qingchan Yu, et al., "China-U.S. Cooperation on China's Subnational Low Carbon Planning Toolkit Development and Application", *Journal of Renewable & Sustainable Energy*, Vol. 7, No. 4, 2015, pp. 71–77.

42 The Europe-China Eco Cities Link (EC-Link) Project is funded by the European Union in cooperation with the Ministry of Housing and Urban-Rural Development (MOHURD) and technically supported by Deutsche Gesellschaft für Internationale Zusammenarbeit (GIZ). The project office is set at Chinese Society for Urban Studies (CSUS). The four-year project entered the implementation stage in June 2014, with EUR 9.3 million funds from the EU.
43 Actors of public diplomacy include governments, private organizations, social groups, social elites, and the general public. The government is the leading actor, the public is the basis, and the rest is mainstay.
44 Zhang Lijun, "Chinese NGOs Engaged in Climate Change Actions", *Public Diplomacy Quarterly*, No. 1, 2016.
45 China Institute of Strategy & Management (CISM), also known as Chinese Commission of Strategic Studies, is a national comprehensive institute of strategic research. Reputed as a "strategic think tank for China" in the international community, CISM provides decision-making consulting and policy suggestions for the country, forges sound co-operative relations with government bodies, academic groups, and NGOs at home and abroad, and plays an important role in public diplomacy.
46 Wang Lili, "Functions and Roles of American Think Tanks in Public Diplomacy", *Contemporary International Relations*, No. 1, 2012.
47 Founded in 2004, Global Environmental Institute (GEI) is a Chinese nongovernment, nonprofit organization aimed to address environmental issues by comprehensively evaluating economic, environmental, and social factors. Its projects focus on biodiversity protection, sustainable rural development, capacity building for Chinese government and public, energy sources, energy efficiency and global warming, and its own capacity building for working with international organizations.
48 For information on GEI projects: www.geichina.org/?controller=Articles&action=View&aid-121.
49 GEI and CCS have been working to promote cooperation and dialogue on climate change between American states and Chinese provinces since 2009. In May 2011, they successfully joined the "Green Partnership Program" under the U.S.-China Ten Year Framework for Cooperation on Energy and the Environment co-initiated by China's NDRC and US Department of State, the only pair of NGO partners among the six pairs of successful candidates.
50 GEI, "GEI and DRI co-host the Workshop on Promoting Renewable Energy and Sustainable Development in Myanmar", 2018, www.geichina.org/workshop_in_myanmar/.

7 Clean energy diplomacy of China

Strategic options in the BRI context

Under the Belt and Road Initiative (BRI), China's efforts to participate in global green governance and enhance its leadership are concentrated on three areas – responding to climate change, protecting the environment and ecology, and pursuing energy utilization and transformation. Climate change is the centerline, eco-environmental protection is the basis for responding to it, while a key factor that affects both climate and environment is energy use – the three areas are closely interrelated and complement each other. In the era after the financial crisis, the collective rise of emerging developing countries has caused structural changes in the world power system – the East is rising while the West is falling. The BRI comes exactly at a time when developed countries are experiencing a weakening economy and influence. While fully acknowledging the economic development needs of China and other developing countries, the initiative puts China, the initiator of the ancient Silk Road, at the helm again of the modern-day Silk Road. According to the *Vision and Actions on Jointly Building Silk Road Economic Belt and 21st-Century Maritime Silk Road* issued in 2015, China, leveraging its advantages in clean energy development, must strongly promote green energy cooperation of all forms with countries along the Belt and Road. On May 12, 2017, the National Energy Administration (NEA) issued the *Vision and Actions on Energy Cooperation in Jointly Building Silk Road Economic Belt and 21st-Century Maritime Silk Road.* The document set out six principles – open and inclusive, mutually beneficial, market-oriented, safe and secure, green, and harmonious development – demonstrating China's firm resolve to carry out friendly energy cooperation with Belt and Road countries and jointly drive global energy development.

The BRI-based regional cooperation mode integrates the current economic cooperation mechanisms, which are dispersive and involve complex factors, among developing countries, thus largely reducing the cooperation cost. In the meantime, it highlights China's role as a responsible major country in providing international public goods for regional cooperation. Close attention must be paid to some basic realities. To start with, along the Belt and Road are mostly developing countries, who face the common challenges of disorderly resource exploitation and environmental pollution arising from global industrial transfer, industrialization, and urbanization. Meanwhile, due to economic, capital, technological, and other limitations, these countries are usually not capable enough to respond to climate change

DOI: 10.4324/9781003433903-10

and environmental crises. Therefore, green development should be an intrinsic theme of the Belt and Road construction. The flourishing of the clean energy industry along the Belt and Road has created favorable conditions for the full-blown development of China's clean energy diplomacy. It is also an indispensable part of China's efforts to implement its diplomatic strategy as a responsible major country. Advancing clean energy diplomacy step by step will help upgrade the clean energy industry chain in China, reform the regional energy supply system, and amplify China's discourse power and international influence when a new regional order of energy governance is being established. This will also pave the way for effecting a green energy transition and building a community of green energy in the Belt and Road region.

Section 1 Belt and road construction provides important opportunities for clean energy diplomacy

In the backdrop of China's economic new normal, Belt and Road construction is at the core of its expanded foreign cooperation and diplomatic strategy. It has not only improved the external development environment for China but also given a strong impetus to building a regional community with a shared future through joint contribution and shared benefits. In the BRI vision and actions issued by the Chinese government, the Green Silk Road, which focuses on eco-environmental protection and green energy development in Belt and Road countries, is receiving more attention. International clean energy cooperation and "South-South Aid" innovations in the BRI framework have provided valuable opportunities for China to exercise clean energy diplomacy.

I. Rich resources and huge cooperation potential along Belt and Road give a head start to clean energy diplomacy

Belt and Road countries abound in mineral resources and clean energy sources. Countries in Central Asia, for example, boast varied clean energy endowments with tremendous potential. Located on the wind belt in the northern hemisphere, they are among the best places in the world for wind energy development, especially Kazakhstan, Uzbekistan, and Turkmenistan.[1] The three countries also boast rich solar energy sources, especially in southeast Uzbekistan where the sun shines for around 10 hours per day 2/3 of the year.[2] As shown in Table 7.1, Africa, Asia, and Europe all have their own strengths in clean energy development. The combined volume of main clean energy sources in Asia, home to most Belt and Road countries, and Africa, home to immense cooperation potential, is well over 50% of the global total. Most Belt and Road countries still follow the energy-extensive growth pattern and sit on the production or supply side of the global energy system. In terms of the percentage of energy consumption, per capita energy consumption in those countries, though slowly growing, is still a far cry from the world average. In Central Asia and Africa, the shortage of capital, tech support, and capacity training encumbers clean energy development. China, in comparison, has proven experience, tech reserve,

Table 7.1 Distribution of main clean energy sources in Belt and Road

Region	*Hydro*		*Wind*		*Solar*	
	Theoretical reserve (1,000TWh/a)	*Ratio (%)*	*Theoretical reserve (1,000TWh/a)*	*Ratio (%)*	*Theoretical reserve (1,000TWh/a)*	*Ratio (%)*
Africa	173	7.7	14	7.6	318	3.6
Asia	56	2.5	15	8.2	2884	32.4
Europe	198	8.8	57	30.6	3105	34.8

Source: IRENA, Renewable Capacity Statistics 2017.

and ample capital in the development and utilization of PV, wind, and other clean energies. By cooperating with Belt and Road countries, China can combine its technical and equipment strengths and their rich resources, and consequently drive clean energy development and use as well as green economic transformation across the entire region.

Regarding infrastructure construction: Other than transportation/transmission facilities, the grid is also vital for guaranteed energy supply. The populous Asia-Pacific has a huge power demand, but uneven distribution of resources has caused a power imbalance – the power-rich areas have more electricity than they can consume, whereas power-poor areas don't have enough. An improved grid can better balance power demand and supply. When China helps upgrade and renovate the seriously outdated power grids in countries and regions that cannot meet their public power demand, it can export its electric power standards, integrate cross-border power trade, and strengthen grid connectivity. Starting with surrounding countries and regions, China can then improve the connectivity facilities with South Asia and Southeast Asia, and the DC connectivity with Russia. Moreover, the UHV power transmission network between Xinjiang and the five Central Asian countries, and the big grid construction in Northeast Asia are also priorities for future grid connectivity.

Regarding energy use and transition: Raising the efficiency of energy production, conversion, and use, and transforming the energy and economic sectors to be green, efficient, clean, and low-carbon are the key elements of green energy cooperation on the Belt and Road. Take a look at the export standards for coal-fired power generation units included in OECD's *Arrangement on Officially Supported Export Credits* and the current caps on the emission of air pollutants set by major coal-power countries, we'd see that China's coal-fired power generation technology and environmental standards are both among the best in the world. High-efficiency and clean coal power and energy-saving technologies are more suitable for economically backward countries with a low rate of electrification. As renewable energies such as hydro, wind, and solar are distributed rather evenly around the world, boosting renewables development can effectively help countries short of fossil energies mitigate their electricity shortage. In light of resource endowments in different regions and their future energy plans, Table 7.2 summarizes the types of renewables where China can work with other regions and lists their

Table 7.2 Types of renewables and planned installed capacity for 2015

Countries/regions	*Types of renewables*	*Planned installed capacity for 2015 (MW)*
South Asia, Southeast Asia	PV, wind, hydro, biomass	148,513
Central Asia	Wind, hydro, PV	12,401
Central and East Europe	PV, wind, hydro	54,096
West Asia, Middle East	PV, hydro, wind, nuclear	65,212

Source: IRENA, Renewable Energy Statistics 2016, www.irena.org/publications/2016/Jul/Renewable-Energy-Statistics-2016.

planned installed capacity for 2015. Moreover, China should intensify the energy technology cooperation with developed European countries, create joint development and sponsoring mechanisms, and work together on new-generation nuclear power technology, new energy storage technology, smart grid, and high-efficiency renewable energy technology.

Regarding energy service and equipment: Energy services, covering think tank services, product certification, project design, and evaluation, upgrade and renovation, training, and finance and investment, can make energy development, conversion, and utilization much more efficient. Boasting an energy service industry with specialized technologies and services, China can provide capital, products, and intelligent support for Belt and Road countries to reform their energy-gobbling enterprises, prospect and exploit resources, and build power sources and grids. With regards to equipment manufacturing, Chinese ultra-supercritical (USC) coal-fired power generation units have better technical parameters than foreign standards; its wind turbine towers, hydro turbines, solar panels, and third-generation nuclear energy equipment are internationally competitive in performance and cost. These services and equipment can go a long way in promoting energy development in Belt and Road countries and immensely supporting the progress of BRI.

II. "Flourishing green industry" amid Belt and Road construction injects internal drive for clean energy diplomacy

In recent years, the rapid development of clean energy in China has laid a firm foundation for promoting green industry along the Belt and Road, an intrinsic part of the BRI. In the *Vision and Actions on Jointly Building Silk Road Economic Belt and 21st-Century Maritime Silk Road* jointly issued by NDRC, Ministry of Foreign Affairs (MFA), and Ministry of Commerce (MOFCOM), clean energy was pinpointed as a crucial carrier for creating the Green Silk Road. According to this document, China, on the principle of complementarity and mutual benefits, will advance and intensify the in-depth cooperation with Belt and Road countries in clean energy technology and industry. It will also use its advantages in this field to drive the regional transformation toward green energy and the realization of 2030 sustainable development goals (SDGs). Offering a "three-in-one" package solution to climate change, energy security, and energy accessibility for the poor, clean energy development has gained traction across the globe. At the moment, the global clean energy industry is thriving with great appeal to international investors, and Belt and Road countries are giving it ever more attention and investment. As shown in Table 7.3, renewables investment in America and Belt and Road region was soaring in 2004–2015. IEA's 2016 report showed nearly 60% of the world's new installed capacity will come from clean energy sources by 2040, most of which is competitive even without subsidy.[3]

China has gathered rich experience in technology R&D and product upgrades in clean energy over recent years while also catching up with developed countries in key technologies.[4] Its experience and expertise in transforming and upgrading the energy industry and in using energy efficiently are of great value for developing countries along the Belt and Road that are suffering from economic bottlenecks. In addition to the exploitation and transportation of traditional fossil energies, Belt and Road energy cooperation also encompasses some key areas such as grid and other infrastructure construction, use of and shift to green energies, clean energy services and equipment, and energy governance platforms. As the Chinese economy enters the new normal, the Chinese clean energy industry has become more competitive with advantages in products, technologies, and cost of equipment, and it is embracing rare historical opportunities of going global thanks to the BRI. Since energy security and sustainability is the cornerstone for guaranteeing a nation's sound economic development and strategic energy security, clean energy can be a key area in the construction of the "Belt and Road".

China should make full use of the domestic and foreign markets and resources to continuously integrate clean energies in the region. It should carry out green cooperation with Belt and Road countries to upgrade its own clean energy industry chain and ensure energy supply and sustainability in the region. It should also raise its position in the global clean energy supply chain. In 2015, China General Nuclear Power Group (CGN) led a group of Chinese clean energy and electric power companies, including Goldwind, Dongfang Electric Corporation, and Shanghai Electric Group, to present and promote Chinese nuclear and clean energy technologies and projects in Kazakhstan. After learning about how advanced and competitive China is in clean energy, Kazatomprom signed an MOU with CGN on clean energy cooperation. In March 2016, China Overseas Development Association undertook the Asia Solar Energy Forum. More than 200 representatives from over 100 organizations, including the Department of Asian Affairs of the Chinese Ministry of Foreign Affairs, Office of the Leading Group of BRI Work, NDRC's Department of Foreign Capital and Overseas Investment, clean energy industry associations, and foreign embassies in China, attended the forum. The event gave a strong boost to building the platform for clean energy diplomacy and to the discussions of practices thereof, which was conducive to the complementarity and cooperation among Belt and Road countries in energy security. In this process, Chinese businesses need to actively fulfill their social responsibilities and respect local customs and religious beliefs. They must engage with local communities as much as possible, provide jobs to help develop the local economy and society, and make due contributions to protecting the environment, building harmonious and stable communities, and increasing public welfare in the host countries.[5]

Table 7.3 Renewable energy investment in America and Belt and Road region (2004–2015)

Unit: USD 1 billion

Year		*2004*	*2005*	*2006*	*2007*	*2008*	*2009*	*2010*	*2011*	*2012*	*2013*	*2014*	*2015*	*2015 total*
America	US	5.6	11.9	29.1	33.2	35.5	23.9	34.7	49.1	40.6	35.3	37.0	44.1	64
	Brazil	0.8	3.1	5.2	11.4	11.8	7.9	7.2	10.2	7.7	4.4	8.0	7.1	
	Other American countries	1.7	3.3	3.7	5.0	6.1	5.5	12.0	9.3	10.1	12.0	13.3	12.8	
Belt and Road region	Europe	24.8	33.3	46.9	66.8	81.8	82.7	113.4	122.9	89.0	60.0	62.0	48.8	222
	Middle East, Africa	0.6	0.8	1.1	1.8	2.3	1.6	4.1	3.0	10.2	9.3	7.9	12.5	
	China	3.0	8.3	11.2	16.7	25.6	38.8	39.6	47.4	61.7	62.0	87.8	102.9	
	India	2.7	3.0	4.9	6.7	5.6	4.3	8.8	12.8	7.8	6.6	8.3	10.2	
	Asian countries other than China, India	7.3	9.0	10.0	12.4	13.6	13.9	19.3	23.8	30.2	44.4	48.8	47.6	

Source: FS-UNEP, *Global Trends in Renewable Energy Investment* 2016, FS-UNEP Collaborating Centre for Climate & Sustainable Energy Finance, 2016.

III. Belt and Road countries' demand for green energy development provides external thrust for clean energy diplomacy

Located across Asia, Europe, and Africa, the more than 70 countries involved in BRI include some of the most promising emerging economies, oil exporters in the Middle East, small island countries, and some least developed countries. Combined, they make up 65% of the global population and 32% of GDP, consume 53.9% of energy (57.9% petroleum, 54.2% natural gas, and 70.5% coal), and emit 60.6% of CO_2. From 2000 to 2015, Belt and Road countries' CO_2 emissions increased 95.2%, twice as fast as the world average. In the meantime, most of them are climate- and environment-fragile, with an annual per capita GDP of only USD 5,000 or so, which makes them incapable of responding and adapting to climate change. In 2015, 73 Belt and Road countries signed the *Paris Agreement*, and 70 (except Uzbekistan, Syria, and Palestine) have developed and submitted their Nationally Determined Contributions (NDCs). Moreover, over 3/4 of them have set goals for GHG emission reduction, though with conditions for more than 40% of the goals. Such a robust demand for green development and low-carbon switch lays the ground for developing clean energy diplomacy.

Along the Belt and Road are mostly developing countries that are in the initial or accelerating stage of urbanization or industrialization. For example, countries like Pakistan, Myanmar, and Nepal are on the low end of economic development, with small domestic markets, backward grid and other infrastructure, and a per capita energy consumption that is 82.7% of the world average. They are caught in a dilemma of industrial and energy development: On the one hand, the rapid industrialization creates a sharp rise in energy demand; on the other hand, the lack of capital, technology, and experience has led to low availability of energy and inadequate development of their clean energy sources. At the moment, there are still 1.2 billion people on the planet who don't have reliable access to electricity, and most of them live in developing Asian and African countries along the Belt and Road, where the per capita electricity available is only 2,621KWh, 83.4% of the world average. Therefore, these countries have an urgent need to improve their capability of developing clean energy to systematically cope with environmental constraints, address energy security threats, and achieve sustainable development goals. Most of them have put forth their clean energy targets and supportive policies, which not only offer a great opportunity for international cooperation in clean energy, but also give a strong thrust to China's clean energy diplomacy.

At the 6th International New Energy Expo held in Jiuquan, China, in August 2015, energy officials from 36 Belt and Road countries introduced the status of clean energy development in their countries and expressed a strong wish to cooperate with China in this field. Belt and Road countries are facing many common challenges, such as energy shortage, deteriorating environment, and low level of industrialization. For instance, the power shortage is threatening Thailand's energy security so much that the Thai government is putting clean energy on top of its energy strategy, hoping to increase its percentage from the current 13% to 25% in 2020 through cooperation with China. Pakistan also expects to quicken its steps of green development and energy transition with technical and capital aid from China.

Table 7.4 NDCs of Belt and Road countries (by sector)

Sector	*Emission-cutting policies and actions*	*Countries*
Electricity	Developing renewable or clean energy	Most Belt and Road countries
	Raising energy efficiency	
Transport	Improving road network and management	Mongolia, UAE, Jordan, Thailand, Macedonia
	Promoting NEV (hybrid or EV, bio-fueled)	Mongolia, UAE, India, Nepal, Vietnam, Brunei, Azerbaijan
	Improving public transit, developing sustainable urban transport	Israel, Turkey, Sri Lanka, Thailand, Vietnam, Azerbaijan, Macedonia
	Raising fuel economy, promoting the use of clean fuels with economic incentives	Mongolia, UAE, Thailand, Brunei, EU members
	Raising energy efficiency	Tajikistan, Yemen, Bahrain, Turkey
Agriculture	Strengthening land administration	Yemen, Tajikistan
	Stepping up emission reduction in agriculture and animal husbandry	Mongolia, Azerbaijan, New Zealand
Forestry	Increasing forestry carbon sink	Jordan, India, Nepal, Sri Lanka, Laos, Azerbaijan, Belarus, China
	Participating in REDD+ programs (REDD+: Reducing Emissions from Deforestation and forest Degradation, plus the sustainable management of forests, and the conservation and enhancement of forest carbon stocks)	Myanmar, Thailand, Vietnam
Industry	Promoting energy conservation in industrial sectors	Mongolia, Turkey, India, Sri Lanka
	Promoting industrial modernization	Tajikistan, Sri Lanka
Wastes	Strengthening waste management	UAE, Thailand, Brunei, Indonesia, Azerbaijan
	Recycling wastes (e.g., generating electricity from landfill gas)	Jordan, Yemen, India, Nepal, Thailand, Vietnam, Indonesia
Market mechanism	Carbon trade market	China, ROK, Kazakhstan, New Zealand, EU members

Source: Originally created by the author.

In February 2015, the loan agreement for the Sachal wind power project in Pakistan undertaken by Power China was signed in Beijing, the first green finance project under the China-Pakistan Economic Corridor program, which is a significant part of BRI. The China-Pakistan 300MW PV Industrial Park located in Bahawalpur, Punjab, was completed in December 2015. As professional technicians are needed to operate and maintain clean energy facilities and equipment, China organized 16 intensive training sessions for Pakistan workers who never worked on PV power before to familiarize them with relevant technologies and maintenance skills.[6]

Table 7.5 Supportive policies for clean energy in some Belt and Road countries (2016)

Countries in different regions of the Belt and Road		*Clean energy targets*	*Clean energy regulations*							*Financial incentives and public financing for clean energy*				
			FIT	*RPS*	*Net metering/ net billing*	*Green transport regulations*	*Green thermal power regulations*	*Tradeable REC*	*Bidding for clean energy projects*	*Subsidy/ loan/ refund*	*Tax break for investment/ production*	*Tax break for VAT and other taxes on energy sales and energy consumption*	*Energy production*	*Preferential loans or special funds for public investment*
	China	R	R	•		•	•		•	•	•	•	•	•
Central Asia	Kazakhstan	•	•					•		•				
	Tajikistan	•	•									•		•
	Uzbekistan								•					
Northeast Asia	Russia	•	•					R	•					
	Mongolia	R	•						•			•		
	Japan	R	R					•	•	•		R		•
	ROK	•		•	•	R	•	•	•	•	•	•		•
Southeast Asia	Singapore	R			•				•					•
	Malaysia	•	R	•		R						•		•
	Thailand	R	R			R						•	•	•
	Indonesia	R	•	•		R			•	•	•	•		•
	Myanmar	R										•		
	The Philippines	•	R	•	•	•			•	•	•	•	•	•
	Sri Lanka	•	•	•	•	•						•	•	•
South Asia	India	R	•	•	R	R	•	•	•	•	•	R	•	•
	Bangladesh	R							•	•		•		•
	Pakistan	•	R		•	•		•		•		R		•
Middle East	Iran	•	•								•		•	•
	Jordan	R	•		•		•		•			•		•
	Lebanon	R			•							•		•
Africa	Ghana	R	•	•	•	•		•		•		•		•
	Algeria	R	•						•	•			•	•
	Angola					•								•
	South Africa	•		•		R	•		•	•		•		•
	Kenya	•	•		•		•		•			•	•	•

Note: • means the policies are both national and local; R means one or more policies have been revised.

Source: Based on REN21 report. REN21, *Renewables 2017 Global Status Report*, 2017, pp. 199–201.

It's worth noting that some important oil exporters on the Belt and Road are also paying attention to the energy transition. They've realized how important it is to develop the clean energy industry in the "post-petroleum era" and have shown greater interest in working with China. According to Iran's clean energy development plan made in 2014, the country planned to install 5GW new PV and wind capacity by 2018 and expressed welcome to Chinese investors, pledging to subsidize a 20-year-long cooperation agreement. In January 2016, President Xi Jinping and King Salman of Saudi Arabia signed the *Memorandum of Understanding Between National Energy Administration of China and King Abdullah City for Atomic and Renewable Energy for Cooperation on Renewable Energy*. They vowed to jointly promote the mutually beneficial China-Saudi cooperation on the development and utilization of clean energy and to transform the energy production and consumption system to be cleaner and more sustainable.[7]

IV. BRI supports clean energy diplomacy with a platform of resource complementarity, capacity optimization, and green finance

Accentuating inclusive and open cooperation, the BRI supports clean energy diplomacy by providing a cooperation platform to realize resource complementary, optimize production capacity, and increase green finance. To begin with, Belt and Road countries, with abundant clean energy sources, can promote joint clean energy development in light of national conditions. According to MOFCOM's 2016 statistics, in China's overseas investment, 65% of the projects worth over USD 30 million are related to clean energy and grid upgrades. With its advantages in PV, wind, and hydropower technologies and products, China is well-positioned to drive the green industries in Belt and Road countries. Examples are many. China has worked with Southeast Asian countries to jointly develop cross-border rivers and make overall use of PV power; it has launched biogas, bioethanol, and biomass power generation in South Asia; it has promoted PV in Central Asia (e.g., Uzbekistan, Kazakhstan, and Turkmenistan) and South Asia; it has pushed large-scale wind power projects in wind-rich countries such as Kazakhstan, Uzbekistan, and Mongolia; and it has carried out small-scale hydropower projects with and in hydro-rich regions, including the Far East and Siberia of Russia, Tajikistan, and Kyrgyzstan. Meanwhile, South-South cooperation in clean energy should be strengthened, for which China can assist in the construction of PV, solar-thermal, distributed wind power, and geothermal projects, and promote teaching buildings, museums, and other public facilities that use zero or little energy.[8] Being strong in UHV grid technology, it can also push for the upgrade of regional grids to make them more adaptive to renewable electricity and enhance grid connectivity with Southeast Asia, Northeast Asia, and South Asia. This will help guarantee a secure energy supply for Belt and Road countries and better coordinate economic growth with environmental protection in the region.

Next, Belt and Road construction can ameliorate the production capacity structure between China and countries along the routes. While upgrading the clean energy industry chain in China, it also boosts the construction of clean energy infrastructure in less developed areas. Apart from high-speed railway and satellite, the clean energy industry represented by PV, wind, and hydro is regarded as the most competitive one to "go global", which, with its features, level of advancement, and intensive factors, can meet the needs of Belt and Road countries with satisfaction. The *Guiding Opinions on Promoting International Cooperation in Production Capacity and Equipment Manufacturing* issued by the State Council in 2015 specifically called for enhancing new energy capacity cooperation along the Belt and Road. A typical example is that of all the power projects undertaken by China in Africa from 2010 to 2020, clean energy contributed to 56% of the total installed capacity, mostly hydropower, but the percentage of PV and wind power was rising (more than 7%).[9]

Most Belt and Road countries are developing ones, whose industrialization process needs electric power. Yet their shortage of capital and technology makes them unable to upgrade their grid system or manufacture electric equipment, seriously impairs the translation of clean energy advantages into economic strengths, and eventually hinders the overall industrialization process and the improvement of local people's living standards. This creates a vast space where China and these countries can work together to build grids and plan clean energy facilities. Moreover, BRI also brings new green financing mechanisms to fund clean energy cooperation and aid projects in those countries. We must be fully aware though that building clean energy infrastructure and green grids requires an astronomical amount of money, has a long payback period, and involves numerous risks. To smooth the implementation of BRI, China has initiated to form the Asian Infrastructure Investment Bank (AIIB), a financial institution, and the Silk Road Fund, a financing mechanism, both in operation now, while the SCO Development Bank is in the pipeline. These institutions will all be able to provide financial support for clean energy diplomacy.[10]

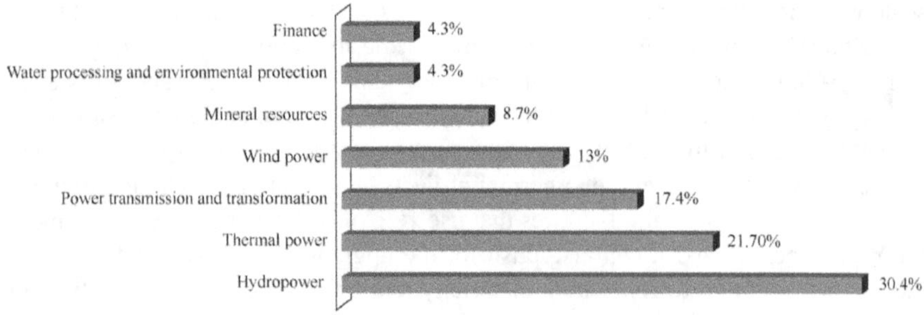

Figure 7.1 Portfolio of China-invested projects overseas worth more than USD 30 million in 2015

Note: PV projects worth less than USD 30 million are not counted.

Source: MOFCOM: Report on Development of China's Outward Investment and Economic Cooperation 2016, p. 105.

Section 2 Risk control for China's clean energy diplomacy in BRI framework

Although the "Belt and Road" construction provides a historical opportunity for China to vigorously carry out clean energy diplomacy, various headwinds are unavoidable on the way forward. In addition to what we talk about in Chapter 5 of this book – technological and policy restrictions on clean energy development, strategic mismatch, South-North division, and a return to geographical dependence – China's clean energy diplomacy in the BRI context faces some special risks and challenges. The BRI covers an expansive reach of areas and a large number of entities; cross-border investment spans a variety of domains; the countries are generally ecologically fragile; medium- and low-income countries are troubled by extremely outdated infrastructure; infrastructure construction is crippled by insufficient capital and impeded financing; major countries in the region are in geopolitical contention; the industrial policies and standards vary from one country to another. All these are challenging China's implementation of clean energy diplomacy.[11]

I. Political, economic, and security risks within Belt and Road countries threaten the security of Chinese clean energy assets overseas

The Belt and Road crosses the Middle East, West Asia, Central Asia, and South Asia, where the complicated security situation poses challenges to clean energy cooperation. Such projects usually require huge investment upfront, and the investment in and operation and management of wind turbines, hydro facilities, and electricity transmission networks need a stable environment. Risks facing these projects along the Belt and Road fall in the political, social, and economic categories.

Political risks refer to political turmoil within countries and interest disputes and armed conflicts across borders. Therefore, we need to conduct a thorough investigation of the political system in the target country and the political security in the region. For example, Pakistan, a strategic pivot of BRI, has been consistently supportive of the construction of Gwadar Port and China-Pakistan Economic Corridor, but we cannot neglect its political instability and the military's takeover of state power, as a new administration is inclined to overturn projects approved by its predecessor. The same happens in Thailand too, where the constant alternation between the military regime and publicly elected administration has mystified its political future.

Social risks refer to ethnic and religious conflicts and the proliferation of terrorism. The inter-state relations in the Belt and Road region are complex and volatile because of their distinctive political systems and unsolved historical issues. Adding to this are the religious and ethnic entanglements between countries, further compounded by such security threats as extreme nationalism, religious extremism, international terrorism, and cross-border trafficking of drugs and weapons. A case in point is Afghanistan, the hub of Belt and Road. After US and NATO troops pulled back in October 2014, local terrorist forces have strengthened and caused frequent violent riots on the border with Pakistan, which impeded the construction of the

China-Pakistan Economic Corridor.[12] Aiming at regional prosperity through joint contribution and shared benefits, the Belt and Road construction is an existential threat to the three forces of violent terrorism, religious extremism, and ethnic separatism. Naturally, they will try hard to sabotage and obstruct the BRI through all kinds of violent activities, including poisoning, arson, terrorist activities, and rioting. At present, the situation in Central Asia, Africa, and Southeast Asia is getting more similar to that in the Middle East, and the number of extremists in countries along the routes is rising. The extremist organizations are aimed at overthrowing existing regimes and taking state power into their own hands, and that is against the objectives of BRI in every way, prompting China and regional countries to beef up cooperation on nontraditional security.

Economic risks refer to the unstable and fragile financial and economic systems in the target country, including a low level of forex reserve, high debt ratio, sustained depreciation of the home currency, and poor resistance to external economic risks. For example, Pakistan has a limited reserve of US dollars, and its debt ratio is sometimes higher than the 20% international warning line. As a result, it may ask for an exchange premium far higher than the market level during transactions, exposing clean energy projects to great losses. In view of this, China must take a composite approach – combining investment with imparting of experience – to reduce investment risks.[13] In the meantime, we need to fend against the superposition of sovereign debts and local debts, as advancing Belt and Road construction, namely, increasing the investment in infrastructure construction, while local government debts are already on a high level would push the debt ratio higher. We should also be cautious about and prevent investment and financing risks, improve the mechanisms (e.g., exchange and cooperation) to cope with risks and crises, and create a regional pre-warning system against financial risks. As China continues to carry out clean energy diplomacy, it needs to fully investigate and evaluate the development environment in target countries and its own crisis-response capability. It may perfect the BRI risk control system by, say, establishing an investment insurance bank to protect its overseas assets.

II. Major-country geopolitics along Belt and Road restrict diplomatic deployments

Eurasia, the key region of BRI, is where major-country geopolitics are concentrated in the region. The disintegration of the Soviet Union has left a vacuum of power, and countries along the routes (e.g., in Central Asia) boast resource advantages and significant strategic positions. These make the Eurasian region a target that out-of-region major countries contend for and try to impose influence on. The US, though a declining hegemon, still has important geographical interests throughout the Belt and Road; India and Russia, as key players in BRI, carry heavy weight in regional affairs – such major-country struggles tend to complicate the overall environment. While clean energy development is somewhat "geographically independent", competition and even conflicts have been on the rise among major countries as they vie to maintain their competitive edge in the new energy industry chain and enhance their regional influence. While engaging in international activities, the small neighbors around China would invite foreign forces in to strike a balance among different major countries and consequently maximize their own interests. This kind of "balance diplomacy", which is being practiced by Central Asian and ASEAN countries, will probably erode the pragmatism of the China-initiated BRI amid the rivalry among out-of-region countries.[14]

To get into more details, when the US rolled out the "Asia-Pacific rebalancing" strategy during Obama's term, it was trying to set barriers to various cooperation projects, including those on clean energy, conducted by China by taking advantage of certain neighbors' concerns and doubts about the country. Take trans-national hydropower cooperation for instance. Through a series of institutional cooperation with China's neighbors, the US has accelerated its strategic deployments in the region and marginalized China in the process. The international situation became highly uncertain after Trump came into power, sending shock waves to the China-led BRI in both overt and covert ways. On the overt side, Trump's Asian-Pacific policy is driven by an aggressive, utilitarian mindset that emphasizes strengths and interests in diplomatic engagement. Being more targeted at China, the policy has influenced the security situation across the entire Asia-Pacific and further complicated relevant geopolitical issues. On the covert side, Trump's conservative moves in the economic and trade sector have reinforced the undercurrent against globalization and posed a grave challenge to global governance and regional integration. It would be no surprise that these moves will sabotage the diverse and inclusive cooperation on clean energy.[15]

India, as a regional power, has been striving for greater dominance and discourse power in international affairs. China and India are competitors in traditional energy and both view Central Asia as an important source of energy; now China's promotion of clean energy diplomacy also meets competition from India, whose clean energy industry has seen high-speed growth in recent years. By the end of 2015, India was a close competitor against China with its hydro, wind, and PV capacity all ranking top five in the world; regarding hydropower, they are at constant odds on the development of the Yarlung Zangbo-Brahmaputra River due to border disputes.

The closer cooperation between China and Central Asia in clean energy has also made Russia worried and suspicious. This, if not properly handled, might trigger an economic and diplomatic rivalry in the region, cause a rift in China-Russia strategic partnership, and add instabilities to our clean energy diplomacy. The BRI has to both compete and align with the Eurasian Economic Union (EEU) initiative proposed by Russia. Moscow is concerned that China, through clean energy diplomacy, may strengthen the economic and trade cooperation with Central Asian countries in more areas, thus gaining more dominance in the region and hindering the progress of the EEU. Therefore, China must well manage the conflicts of interests and prevent vicious competition with other powers along the Belt and Road and try to expand as much as possible the consensus on and space for coordinated and mutual interests.

III. Belt and Road countries: fragile ecology and serious environmental and social risks

Belt and Road countries, usually ecologically fragile, are barely able to respond to environmental crises due to backward infrastructure, outdated industries, and a low level of social development. Specifically, the Maritime Silk Road is prone to volatile weather and a growing number of extreme weather conditions, whereas the land Silk Road, which passes through the inland Eurasian region, is usually subject to the arid climate, scarce water resources, and dire desertification. The water shortage in certain countries has even triggered a series of chain effects concerning energy security and food security. Any environmental damage would be highly destructive, wide-ranging, and improbable to recover.

Take Central Asia, the traditionally resource-reliant pivot of the Silk Road Economic Belt. Rampant exploitation of coal, oil, gas, and mineral resources and unclean use of them have polluted the local water sources and consequently undermined sustainable security. Still imitating the economic development pattern of the former Soviet Union, Uzbekistan, a country chronically suffering from water shortage, lists cotton planting and textile, two industries that consume a lot of water, in the national development strategy, resulting in a vicious cycle between eco-environmental condition and economic development. The development of water conservancy projects by Tajikistan and Kyrgyzstan, which are located upstream, has worsened their scramble for resources with downstream counterparts. It's clear that the extremely fragile ecological environment has caused tremendous negative effects on the economic development and political coordination in Belt and Road countries, not only deteriorating neighborly relations, but also impeding regional integration. Unfortunately, these countries, including those in Central Asia, are not paying enough attention to ecological issues, not to mention establishing a regional mechanism to share information on environmental resources or a platform for ecological conservation.

Against such a background, there are two things that China must attach great importance to. For one thing, when building infrastructure along the Belt and Road, it will face natural risks (e.g., mudslides, landslides, and floods) arising from the harsh and varied natural conditions and landforms on the Eurasian continent. Poor operation and management would expose the projects to losses both in revenues and reputation due to security risks caused by force majeure. For another, many infrastructure facilities in the region come with environmental hazards themselves, as extensive mineral exploitation may harm local soil and water sources, and cause pollution with wastewater, dust, and residual wastes. If sustainable development is not taken seriously or pollutants not handled carefully, negative environmental and social impacts would ensue, sometimes so serious that they may escalate into political and security risks between countries. In that case, not only would local residents boycott or vandalize Chinese projects, but certain international forces would jump at the opportunity to clamor "environmental pollution caused by China-funded projects". There are some NGOs backed by Western countries that are active in Belt and Road countries. Tasked with finding fault with Chinese resource enterprises and China-funded infrastructure projects, they are bent on mobilizing the locals against these enterprises and projects, portraying them as China's attempt to plunder local resources and destroy the ecological environment. These NGOs have severely endangered the security of China's overseas assets and harmed our national image. Based on past experience in outward investment and cooperation, China did sometimes find itself in frictions due to poor fulfillment of environmental responsibilities, which could evolve into a sensitive political issue. Especially in areas of political intricacies and social turmoil, political manipulation in the disguise of environmental issues has been an old trick played by the West to contain China's overseas investment.[16]

As Belt and Road construction moves forward, China is investing more in the resources of those countries. While the investments have driven the local economy and brought material public goods, we should pay more attention to environmental preservation, and provide more green public goods for sustainable development, environmental remediation, and energy transition. Throughout the process, we must underscore ecological fragility survey and evaluation upfront, push enterprises to perform their environmental and social responsibilities, and turn investors' attention to clean energy projects. What we must especially keep in mind is that even clean energy projects may be questioned on their environmental impacts. For instance, the large-scale water conservancy facilities built by China overseas have been subject to intense criticism because no environmental survey or risk evaluation has been done. It is high time that we put in place a list of ecological and environmental risks and a risk evaluation mechanism for Belt and Road countries and regions.[17] Moreover, we must bring public diplomacy into play alongside official diplomacy, and create more opportunities for Chinese civil groups and NGOs to play a part.

IV. Supportive policies, legal systems, and industrial standards for clean energy vary among Belt and Road countries

Given its higher production cost than traditional electricity, clean energy, especially the development and operation of wind and PV projects, couldn't succeed without government support. However, Belt and Road countries differ from China wildly in the legal regulations, subsidies, industrial standards, management system, policy environment, and social acceptance of clean energy. Neglect of these differences during project survey and operation would exert adverse effects on the smooth implementation of clean energy diplomacy. These adverse effects come from the following three areas.

Changes in legal and policy environment

Clean energy projects represented by wind, PV, and hydro usually involve a lot of steps and a long period, which means more risks as the legal environment in the emerging market isn't well established yet. Major adjustments in the clean energy policies of the target country can bring substantial consequences to China's investment projects. When working with Belt and Road countries, we should pay special attention to the risks deriving from their different legal systems. These include legal risks from investment (a foreign majority shareholder is not allowed in certain sectors), from labor issues (percentage of layoffs, compensation for laid-off employees, etc.), from environmental issues (compliance with local environmental standards and CSR requirements), from business malpractices (unfamiliarity with foreign laws, business corruption, tax, etc.), and from the imperfections in their legal systems. Anytime the laws or policies in the host country change, be it the equity ratio, scope of investment, or degree of market openness, Chinese enterprises will be exposed to many unpredictable legal risks.[18]

Unaligned standards

There are no uniform standards for the clean energy industry among Belt and Road countries. China implements a different subsidy policy from them, and that, in the absence of an effective and smooth coordination mechanism or strategic mutual trust, can sometimes be a fuse to an anti-dumping case on clean energy, even escalating into diplomatic frictions and disputes. A case in point happens with the EU. China and the EU employ different subsidy standards, and the latter suffered from an economic decline after the EURO crisis. These led to EUProSun, an alliance of European PV manufacturers, filing in November 2012 for an anti-dumping and countervailing investigation into Chinese solar cells/panels exported to the union, which caused RMB 350 billion worth of losses to the Chinese PV industry. Therefore, apart from policy discussions, we should work harder to align industrial standards, especially promoting the development of commonly used clean energy standards. While adopting existing international standards, China must also take an active part in formulating standards in new domains such as renewable energy and smart grid. As relevant technical standards haven't been formulated yet, it should seize the opportunity to propose standards that are favorable for the development of the clean energy industry in developing countries.

Less-than-perfect project management

Many clean energy projects are very demanding on follow-up management and services because the equipment has to be maintained and checked regularly. Overseas biogas and PV projects usually face difficulties in maintenance, for example. This reminds us that while designing and building the project, we must consider problems that may pop up during operation and try to prevent them as much as possible. Meanwhile, the skill and technical training of foreign personnel must be intensified, so they are qualified to independently operate and maintain the equipment later. In sum, when the Chinese clean energy industry "goes global", it's not just a matter of capital but a whole system involving the alignment of standards, promotion of technology, implementation of policy, and after-services.

Section 3 Clean energy diplomacy in China's master diplomatic blueprint: strategic position and tactical choice

The Chinese clean energy diplomacy is evolving from an economic focus to a governance focus centered on green strengths, and China is enjoying a rising position and influence in the construction of the new order of global climate and energy governance. In advancing clean energy diplomacy in the BRI framework, we need to analyze China's role and function from a systematic and holistic perspective. With three challenges hanging over our heads – global economic slump, sustainable energy security, and climate change, a low-carbon economic and industrial revolution centered on clean energy is sweeping the world. In this process, a new diplomatic model also characterized by clean energy has become an indispensable part of national diplomatic strategy. As a major power of clean energy development, China, leveraging on its superiority and experience in green development, can drive clean energy diplomacy in the BRI framework to gain more recognition among surrounding countries and better illustrate what a green community with a shared future means. The Belt and Road construction has offered a great opportunity to do that, but challenges remain, especially Trump's negative stance on globalization and environmental protection. Under such circumstances, China must have clear priorities and work for breakthroughs when practicing clean energy diplomacy, with a special emphasis on fostering strategic diplomatic capacities across the board.

I. Promoting practices of state governance overseas to meet Belt and Road countries' demand for clean development

The provision of clean energy public goods in the region is essentially the international spillover of China's public goods provided at home, including the best practices concerning products, systems, and technologies. It has gathered a myriad of successful experience in the development of such clean energies as wind, PV, and bioenergy and in electricity storage and transmission represented by UHV, blazing out a unique path featuring "urbanization, industrialization, and low-carbon development" in parallel. China's excellent practices at home lay the groundwork for it to promote these practices overseas and meet the demand of Belt and Road countries for clean development. When providing institutional public goods for the region, we must think beyond financial aid and pay more attention to the specific wishes and detailed demands of those countries.

Except for economic cooperation, China doesn't have strong clout in some Belt and Road countries, with little means to sway the regional situation, to say nothing of infrastructure shortcomings and weak financial and cultural influence. Therefore, when promoting our practices overseas and building a regional system of public goods, China should take into full consideration the relevant countries' real appeals for ecology, development, and fairness, and optimize the distribution of green resources among different countries as it advances clean energy diplomacy. While working on interconnectivity along the Belt and Road, it should, more importantly, spur the countries to seize the opportunity of green development and realize energy transition and industrial upgrade, change the energy mix by developing the clean energy industry, and push for a revolution in the way of energy consumption and economic structure. Thus, the countries will be fundamentally more capable of handling the trilemma of climate change, energy security, and energy accessibility for the poor.

Take the establishment of a global energy network for example. Chinese President Xi Jinping made this proposal at the UN Sustainable Development Summit in September 2015, which reflected the concept of green, open, innovative, and sustainable development. An energy network achieves electric connectivity through clean energy development, with UHV grid and smart grid as the backbone frame, and pushes towards the vision for "sustainable energy for all" and an innovative and upgraded energy industry. Building such a network will help Belt and Road countries achieve the goal of sustainable energy security. With an optimized energy mix, they will be able to cope with the climate crisis and environmental pollution, reduce the overreliance on fossil energy, and make a low-carbon shift on the regional economy – an all-win outcome for environmental protection, energy security, and economic development. Especially, the region's unfair position in the global economic system will be changed, lifting regional resources up the value chain and raising the level of industrialization.

Currently, China's State Grid, with advanced and proven UHV power transmission technology, has built and operated seven UHV projects (three AC, four DC) at home cumulatively with another ten underway (four AC, six DC). Its successful track record provides a firm guarantee for cross-border grid connectivity.[19] In the early stage of undertaking the Belt and Road network of clean electricity, China and the countries concerned can carry out renewable energy demonstration projects in light of local conditions. Their cooperation can span across solar, wind, hydro, geothermal, biofuel, and technologies for the clean use of traditional energy like coal. It can also take a variety of forms, including investment, project contracting, labor service, technology R&D, formulation of energy standards, personnel training, and coordination of energy policies.[20] For instance, on-grid PV, wind, and Ground Source Heat Pump (GSHP) projects based on the UHV network should be promoted in populous areas; small-scale wind, hydro, and distributed PV projects can be built in remote areas that the grid cannot reach in the short term, so as to increase the availability of modern energy for poor population in the shortest time.

When dovetailing the needs for developing the power network, we must pay special attention to coordinating the multiple stakeholders and fully engage the governments, research institutes, and private sectors. In August 2017, the general assembly of the China Energy Internet Alliance (CEIA)[21] and the Internet of Energy Conference China 2017 were held in Beijing, attracting more than 400 participants from governments, universities, research institutes, and enterprises. The establishment of the alliance pooled together various forces to foster a systematic industry chain and support the Belt and Road energy development on multiple dimensions. At the Energy Internet Research Institute of Tsinghua University, the Center of Energy Management and Control developed the Integrated Energy Management System (IEMS), and the Center of Energy Internet Security Control and Efficient Use developed the CloudPSS. These innovations will help bring out the immense economic, social, and environmental benefits of energy Internet as an interconnected network of energy, transport, and communication information. These, together with the multistakeholder platforms, provide essential support for meeting Belt and Road countries' demand for clean development. In March 2016, China's State Grid, Japan's

SoftBank Group, Russian Grids (ROSSETI), and Korea Electric Power Corporation (KEPCO) signed the *Memorandum of Understanding to Cooperate on Research and Planning for Interconnected Power Grid Spanning Northeast Asia*. They also formed the Global Energy Interconnection Development and Cooperation Organization, the first of its kind initiated by China, which could help promote and apply China's excellent practices and advanced concepts in international governance.

II. Building new BRI platforms to lead a global network of clean energy partnerships

To fortify China's institutional capacities as it pushes forward clean energy diplomacy along the Belt and Road, it has to reinforce the power of setting the agenda, making rules, and leading the narrative in clean energy governance. To that end, we must not only broaden and deepen the cooperation with existing international organizations in that field but also conduct energy cooperation in new modes for multi-win results and promote the Belt and Road green energy strategy. What's more, we should integrate the "green elements" of existing cooperation platforms and forge new ones for clean energy governance, which usually come in three forms: Belt and Road cooperation platform, international financial system, and multi-party dialogue and coordination mechanism based on project cooperation. Based on these platforms, we can establish a global partnership network and lead the global clean energy governance.

First, for current clean energy governance on the Belt and Road, China fully relies on the existing multilateral mechanisms while making institutional innovations with clean energy development in the center. Some progress has been made in institutionalizing clean energy diplomacy in the Asia-Pacific and ASEAN. At the 2014 APEC Energy Ministerial Meeting, China announced its decision to form the "APEC Sustainable Energy Center (APSEC)", which was expected to become a stable and mature platform for sharing research information and a high-efficiency mechanism of policy coordination. Four East Asia Summit Clean Energy Forums have been held with China's support since 2014 to boost the clean energy cooperation and development in East Asia, especially between China and ASEAN. The forum, known for strengthening pragmatic cooperation and promoting win-win outcomes, has become an important platform for discussing regional cooperation on clean energy. The first forum was held in Chengdu, Sichuan Province, in August 2014, at which themed seminars on PV, bioenergy, and smart energy/smart city were carried out in the framework of the "Maritime Silk Road" to drive the region's green transformation. The second forum was held in Haikou, Hainan Province, in November 2015, which covered a broad range of topics, including nuclear energy, PV, bioenergy, electric power, clean coal, and smart energy/smart city. The third forum in 2017 gave a boost to the China-ASEAN Clean Energy Capacity Building Programme jointly carried out by China Renewable Energy Engineering Institute and ASEAN Center for Energy. The Programme could further spur the clean energy cooperation between the two sides, who will jointly enable energy transition through clean energy development and push for regional economic integration.

Second, while trying to create a distinctive clean energy governance mechanism by innovating regional cooperation platforms, China focuses on forging the regional partnership network and enhancing the region's capacity for clean energy development. In May 2017, it released the *Vision and Actions on Energy Cooperation in Jointly Building Silk Road Economic Belt and 21st-Century Maritime Silk Road*, which vowed to actively implement the China-ASEAN Clean Energy Capacity Building Programme and carry out exchange activities on a specific clean energy topic each year. On the basis of the East Asia Summit (EAS) and its Clean Energy Forum, and the ASEAN "10+3" and "10+1" mechanisms, China and ASEAN countries have jointly implemented this program.[22]

The first phase of the program carried out in Hangzhou in 2017 was themed "Technology and Development of Pumped Storage Power Stations". Energy think tanks on both sides conducted in-depth research together and released the ASEAN Power Cooperation reports and other quality findings, which were widely acclaimed in the industry. The second phase was carried out in Xi'an, Shaanxi Province in 2018. More than 20 energy officials, experts, and scholars from China and the ten ASEAN countries participated in the seminar on the Effective Utilization of Diverse Energy Resources. The effective utilization of multiple energy sources can lower carbon emissions, promote clean energy use, raise energy efficiency, and reduce cost by means of system integration, mutual complementarity, and structural improvement. The integration of multiple energy sources, primarily clean ones, and the supply of a portfolio of products enables a sound interaction between the supply side and the demand side.[23]

Apart from interacting with regional multilateral platforms by innovating the mechanisms of clean energy cooperation, China must also work to create a comprehensive, innovative platform for clean energy and environment cooperation for the entire Belt and Road region. In December 2016, UNEP and the Chinese Ministry of Environmental Protection signed a memorandum on the green development of the Belt and Road. They planned to build the first platform of information sharing and green finance that would concern itself with the environmental status in China and Belt and Road countries, evaluate relevant projects and their impacts on local development and the environment, and bring more capital to clean energy projects. In September of that year, the BRI Environmental Big Data Platform came up online. With the help of information technologies such as big data and satellite remote sensing, the platform assorted information on the ecological and environmental conditions of relevant countries and their environmental policies, laws and regulations, standards, technologies, and industries. It provides basic environmental information to support decisions on investment by enterprises and clean energy diplomacy by governments.[24]

Third, as far as the new type of international financial system for clean energy development is concerned, Belt and Road financial regimes represented by Asian Infrastructure Investment Bank (AIIB) and Silk Road Fund lay the economic foundation for clean energy diplomacy. One sign of the ability to attract green finance is institutionalizing and internationalizing the principles regulating the financial market, including market standards and financial regulations. At the moment, other than the New Development Bank (NDB), more commonly known as the BRICS Bank, whose first batch of USD 811 million loans in 2016 went to four clean energy projects, none of the other outward development institutions (e.g., AIIB and Silk Road Fund) has made special requirements on green investment. Therefore, as China promotes clean energy diplomacy along the Belt and Road, it should first urge the acceptance of the Equator Principles to create a high-standard environmental risk management system and fully disclose environmental information. It should especially stress such principles as "green procurement" and "sustainable infrastructure" in project investment, which will not only increase the consumption of Chinese clean energy products in surrounding countries but also preserve our international image as a responsible major country.

The Belt and Road construction should proceed in parallel with such policies as green procurement and green finance. The first thing to do is to conduct a deep study of the capacity of and needs for green investment and financing of countries along the routes, to come up with a targeted, practicable guidebook for each different region in consideration of its industrial features. Work should be done, step by step, toward establishing a BRI Green Development Fund to drive clean energy diplomacy. On that basis, and with caution and clear priorities, we can support different countries in fostering their clean energy capacities, building ecological and environmental infrastructure, developing green industries and projects, and training relevant personnel. In this process, the private sector must particularly be mobilized, green financing instruments such as green bonds should be used to raise funds, and PPP or other cooperation modes can be employed to advise decisions on green investment. Infrastructure should be built, operated, and managed in a green and low-carbon way, ecological and environmental requirements earnestly implemented, and standards and practices for green transport, green buildings, and green energy promoted. We should facilitate trade in environmental products and services and strengthen the management of the green supply chain. Under the new circumstances, only by enhancing China's ability to lure green finance can we fundamentally reinforce our structural influence and leading power in the supply of regional public goods. Enlarging the global network of partnerships and perfecting global investment and financing governance is our way of providing an inexhaustible source of strength for establishing a new order of global climate and energy governance.

III. Forging a new type of green relations and coordinating standards for clean energy governance among major countries

The core and kernel of clean energy diplomacy, which essentially means diplomatic coordination, is the principle of interest sharing. China strives to forge "a new type of major-country relations" in various forms with the concept of "win-win green development". Providing public clean energy goods for the region gives it more green power in its overall diplomatic deployments, a tangible diplomatic action that elucidates what "a community with a shared future" means. Leveraged on its advantages in clean energy development, China should work in the following areas to build sustainable, new-type major-country relations. One is making institutional arrangements for strategic coordination and communication between major countries. Despite their different strategic goals, China and other regional major countries have much room for coordination and cooperation. They can put in place an institutionalized and normalized communication and coordination mechanism on a specific topic of clean energy cooperation. Or they may try to "positively interrelate" clean energy topics with other regional political and economic issues so that other bilateral or multilateral platforms can be utilized as a stage for major countries to consult and coordinate. The other is building demonstration zones for clean energy cooperation. We can create regional dialogue regimes among major countries along the Belt and Road, cooperate with them in clean energy projects, and build demonstration zones for that. This will enlarge the space for win-win cooperation and give those countries more strategic trust in China's intention of carrying out the BRI.

Interactions between major countries are particularly active when they try to reach an agreement on the standards for clean energy governance along Belt and Road. When we promote clean energy diplomacy with Belt and Road countries, we must attach great importance to aligning Chinese practices with international standards and mechanisms, and promote "Chinese standards" through clean energy cooperation and by presenting best practices. China is a global leader in nuclear power, clean and efficient coal power, large-scale renewable energy, and UHV power transmission, with equipment costs falling year by year. Internationalizing "Chinese standards" will make it much easier for Chinese enterprises to go global and realize energy interconnectivity across the region. Coordination and cooperation based on a new type of green major-country relations are especially important for developing the system of standards for clean energy governance. During Obama's term, for example, with their rapid development of clean energy technology and massive deployment of clean energy projects, both countries and their industrial standards had to press ahead with the times to adapt to the evolving needs. During this period, the two countries could partner up to lead the standard-setting, testing, and certification for clean energy development.

When the US-China Renewable Energy Partnership (USCREP) was first established, the two countries explicitly stated in their memorandum of cooperation that the standards, testing, and certification for clean energy (especially wind and solar) were one of the five key areas for cooperation. The fast development of clean energy technology and market has created the opportunity for them to erect new standards in the field, including consistency of testing results, unified standards and certifying process, and mutual acceptance of each other's testing and certification results. As the leading organization under USCREP for each side, the National Renewable Energy Laboratory (NREL) and China General Certification Center (CGC) have been working more closely together in the technical standards, testing, and certification for PV and wind power. A priority of USCREP is to internationalize the new clean energy standards developed by China and the US by participating in the plan-making of international standard organizations, such as the International Electrotechnical Commission (IEC).[25] For example, the standards for wind turbine blades jointly developed by the two countries were recognized by IEC (IEC TC88

PT5) as the new norms in the wind power domain, covering technical parameters, manufacturing, and maintenance requirements for blades.[26] Clearly, cooperation in making standards between the two clean energy leaders can pave the way for the sound development of global clean energy governance.

Regarding the supply of green public goods for the region, China can interact and coordinate with other major countries in a complementary way.[27] It should make special efforts to coordinate policies and forge consensus with the US, European countries, Russia, and Japan, which have a stake in the Belt and Road region, dovetail BRI with their strategies, and make clean energy development and cooperation the engine and bond of multilateral cooperation. There are several examples. The China-Central Asia Energy Internet based on clean energy is a prime example of China's interactions with other major countries or regions, including Russia, the US, and Europe. The EU began to carry out the Sustainable Energy Program for Central Asia: Energy Efficiency and Renewable Energy Sources (CASEP) in 2013. The US' New Silk Road Strategy included the "CASA-1000" 500kV AC grid project that, officially coming into operation in 2014, was intended to connect Kyrgyzstan, Tajikistan, Azerbaijan, and Pakistan into a "Central Asia-South Asia common power market".[28] These projects all compete with China-Central Asia Energy Internet in technical indicators and network standards, making major-country coordination necessary. As Russia has gained more presence and influence in Central Asia while America is losing luster, the situation is in China's favor. Whether it can play an active part in building the energy Internet depends on whether the Silk Road Economic Belt initiative can gear with Russia's Eurasian Economic Union (EEU) strategically.

China should always maintain strategic dialogue and communication with Russia, highlight the staggered and symbiotic relation of BRI and EEU, and reduce their strategic misunderstanding.[29] The good news is that economic and trade ties between the two countries have upgraded at a faster pace and with better quality in recent years, injecting a strong impetus into the overall bilateral relations. The Eastern Economic Forum they co-initiated in September 2015 created a new opportunity for China and Russia to work on clean energy together along the Belt and Road.[30] At the fourth forum in 2018, titled "The Russian Far East: Expanding the Range of Possibilities", China's MOFCOM and the Ministry for the Development of the Russian Far East signed the *Development Plan of China-Russia Cooperation in the Russian Far East (2018–2024)*. An *MOU on Forming a Council of Business for Northeast China and the Russian Far East and Baikal Region* was also signed to help enterprises on both sides align their projects, provide information and consulting services for them, and solve their problems during collaboration. Such cooperation between China and Russia is of special importance at a time of mounting trade protectionism. Their cooperation used to focus on political and military domains but has been strengthening in economy, trade, and energy in recent years. This fourth forum, for example, discussed global economic governance under the WTO framework. It also witnessed the signing of several cooperation agreements between local governments and enterprises from both sides, ranging from energy and resources, agriculture and forestry, machine-making to transportation and logistics, pharmaceutical, and finance. More importantly, both countries are willing to go beyond traditional energy to cleaner and more environment-friendly energy cooperation. As mentioned earlier, they can jointly tap into the rich energy sources in Russia's Far East region (e.g., wind, solar, and gas), and transmit electricity to China and other regions in Northeast Asia using China's UHV technology, which could amount to 40TWh per year.[31]

IV. Innovative South-South cooperation and upgraded BRICS in the BRI framework

Belt and Road countries, mostly developing ones and emerging economies, have shown keen enthusiasm for and strong confidence in BRI as a cooperation platform for shared development. In May 2017, high-level representatives from more than 100 countries and regions attended the Belt and Road Forum for International Cooperation (BRF), including heads of state and government who were mostly from developing countries. BRI upholds the Silk Road Spirit of openness and inclusiveness – all countries are equal, be they big or small, strong or weak, rich or poor; and it promotes "five-pronged connections" – policy coordination, facilities connectivity, unimpeded trade, financial integration, and people-to-people bonds. BRI provides a golden opportunity for developing countries to achieve tangible benefits and solid development through cooperation. As the country that advances, innovates, and leads the South-South cooperation, China also provides a new chance and motivation to further institutionalize that initiative and carry it out in more ways through the BRI platform. By developing the clean energy industry that can "kill three birds" (climate change, energy security, energy availability for the poor) all at once, countries along the routes can take a free ride on China's green express train powered by economic and technological development and enhance their capacity for low-carbon industrialization and boost energy transition at the same time.[32] Thus, when carrying out clean energy diplomacy on the Belt and Road, we get to constantly upgrade and innovate South-South cooperation in the clean energy domain, and putting that in a more strategic position will add to China's moral lead and its rules-making power and discourse power in this emerging industry.

For example, in BRICS, a group of emerging developing countries, all members but Brazil are located along the Belt and Road. With regard to renewable energy, Brazil is most interested in bioenergy, hydro, and electricity generation; Russia focuses on raising energy efficiency and developing hydropower technology; India places more emphasis on the R&D of wind, solar, and bioenergy; China's priority is solar, wind, and key energy-saving technology; and South Africa gives preference to solar, bioenergy, and energy efficiency. It is expected that BRICS members along the Belt and Road will soon play a significantly larger role in the world's renewables development. In Russia, large hydropower stations take a lion's share of its renewable electricity. According to the *Energy Strategy of Russia to 2030*, the country plans to increase the percentage of renewable electricity (excluding large hydropower stations) to 4.5% by 2020, which means an additional capacity of

22GW. At the end of 2015, renewable power (excluding large hydropower stations) accounted for roughly 15% of India's total installed capacity; at the end of 2016, the country released its thirteenth draft plan for national power development, planning to increase renewable capacity to 175GW in 2022 and 275GW in 2027. South Africa's renewables industry has also seen rapid development despite the country's heavy reliance on fossil fuels. Its renewable capacity (including large hydropower station) stood at 4GW at the end of 2016, and it plans to increase that to 17.8GW by 2030 according to its *Integrated Resource Plan 2010*.[33]

The New Development Bank (NDB), the official bank of BRICS, has made clean energy projects the key recipients of support, and the group's existing financial cooperation regimes are fully brought into play. For instance, NDB has worked with the central banks or leading commercial banks of BRICS members to allocate more funds for renewables development. At the same time, BRICS should seek to work in concert with China's national initiatives such as Shanghai Pilot Free Trade Zone (FTZ), BRI, and AIIB. In the foreseeable future, the Fortaleza BRICS monetary system and NDB will exert themselves in a broader scope, which will hit three targets in parallel – the country bearing loan risks, enterprises exporting excess capacity, and the RMB becoming more internationalized. BRICS members must engage in extensive monetary and financial cooperation on energy and carbon trade. That will de-peg their currencies from the US dollar, and free their financial systems, including monetary policies, from the USD-pivoted international monetary system.

BRICS collaboration to address climate change and green development creates another strategic opportunity for China to export capital and production capacity. This includes oil and gas transportation, railway, road, power grid, communication and port, solar, wind, and nuclear equipment, and other low-carbon energy technologies. Apart from European and American markets, China can find new export destinations for its low-carbon products and capacity in emerging markets, and one way to do that is expressing the willingness to grant national loans to developing countries such as India (Asia), South Africa (Africa), and Brazil (Latin America) to build low-carbon infrastructure. Furthermore, emerging major countries can further intensify their clean energy cooperation through the ministers' consultation mechanism under Fortaleza Action Plan.[34] The *Fortaleza Declaration* was reached at the 6th BRICS Summit in 2014, in which the five members ratified the *Fortaleza Action Plan*. With that, they increased the number of ministers participating in the regular ministerial meeting from seven (national security advisors, foreign ministers, finance ministers and central bank governors, trade ministers, technology ministers, health ministers, and ministers of agriculture and agrarian development) to ten (with the addition of officials and experts on population matters, anti-drug experts, and anti-corruption experts). Going forward, they should consider incorporating climate change, clean energy, and green development in the framework of a closer BRICS economic partnership and the Strategy for BRICS Economic Partnership.[35] The group should also step up international cooperation in clean energy through carbon trade, trade in low-carbon products, and transfer of low-carbon technologies.

At present, trade among BRICS members is concentrated on primary and intermediate goods and hasn't reached a large scale across their vast consumer markets, leaving numerous opportunities for cooperation in both bilateral and multilateral markets. In terms of their trade and industrial structure, the five members are complementary in many ways – some have resources and some manufacturing, some focus on trade in goods and some trade in services – this promises a larger scope of economic partnership. Chinese exports to the other four members are mostly finished industrial goods where we have a leading edge, while our imports from them are basically raw materials and energy sources. Because of China's dominance in electromechanical products and equipment manufacturing regarding PV, wind power, and high-speed railway, the import and export of low-carbon technologies and products will take a growing share in its trade with the other four members. They can jointly develop key renewables technologies to make emerging economies more technically strong in that area; they can carry out joint research on policies and business models to share development experience and information; they can also conduct pilot or demonstrative renewable energy projects together and garner highly operable and imitable experience. All in all, BRICS countries should merge with the BRI more deeply either as countries located along the routes or as partners. China is committed to a green Belt and Road, and the BRICS Spirit of openness, inclusiveness, and win-win cooperation echoes the BRI concept of "extensive consultation, joint contribution, and shared benefits" perfectly. There lies a great opportunity for the seamless connection of the "BRICS Plus" model with BRI in the field of renewable energy.[36]

V. Encouraging private participation in Belt and Road construction; enhancing public clean energy diplomacy

According to data from the World Bank, the public sector is only able to provide less than 20% of the upfront capital needed to achieve the 2030 sustainable development goals and intended nationally determined contributions (INDCs), while about 80% has to be financed by the private sector and social forces. Without a large variety of investors, the clean energy investment and environmental funds needed for Belt and Road construction will put tremendous financial pressure on the governments. Therefore, when providing green public goods,[37] China must not only stimulate the initiative of governments of all levels within the country but also actively engage the domestic and foreign private sectors. Effective and practical policies should be launched to attract more investment and financing for clean energy projects overseas, thus fundamentally enhancing the structural influence of China through clean energy diplomacy.

It must be noted that private capital will not automatically flow into the clean energy sector without policy guidance, so we need to create an effective green finance system to channel private investment and finance to clean energy through a spate of measures, including green credit, green bonds, green insurance, and carbon finance represented by the carbon market. During the 2016 G20 Hangzhou Summit, for instance, China and the UK issued the *G20 Green Finance Synthesis*

Report, successfully incorporating green finance and clean development in the *G20 Leaders' Communique*. In 2018, China became the largest green bond issuer in the world. Meanwhile, after it kicked off the national carbon trade market in the power sector in 2017, China has been trying to engage the private sector more deeply in green development and energy transition to pump ceaseless and powerful momentum into clean energy diplomacy along the Belt and Road.

In the process of engaging the private sector through PPP, smooth diplomatic interactions depend on effective coordination among different departments at home as clean energy diplomacy involves a large number of actors. For that matter, we should, on the one hand, carefully design the top-level diplomatic architecture and create a national-level coordination mechanism to facilitate the communication and collaboration between different departments and between them and local governments. On the other hand, we should actively foster BRI cooperation blocs and networked partnerships. Clean energy industry associations should join hands to better coordinate domestic resources so that enterprises don't have to "go global" all on their own but can take joint actions through mutual help for common development. In this process, for example, the China Overseas Development Association, Chinese Renewable Energy Industries Association (CREIA), and other organizations jointly founded the China New Energy International Alliance in 2016. The new alliance is expected to boost regional capacity cooperation and facilitate exchange, communication, and coordination in driving the overseas development of clean energy. Enterprises coming together can enhance their collective competitiveness in the international market. They should choose cooperation strategies and the approach and scale of investment more prudently to spread risks and take full advantage of their preemptive position to avoid disorderly and vicious competition. They should comply with local policies, laws and regulations, make their projects truly beneficial for local communities, and bear social and environmental responsibilities. In this process, China should improve the green finance mechanism for BRI, adhere to the principle of "enterprises being the backbone, market-oriented operation, and mutual benefits", and keep a sustainable flow of capital. It should also guide governments, financial institutions, enterprises, and public groups to participate in public governance, avoid conflicts and enforcement in communities, and diversify the way of governance based on extensive consultation.[38]

As clean energy diplomacy proceeds along the Belt and Road, public diplomacy driven by non-state and sub-state actors (e.g., NGOs, social organizations, think tanks, enterprises, and cities) provides important strategic assistance and functional supplement. For it makes up for the inflexibility of official diplomacy and gathers more normative forces during collaboration. As a grand initiative that will exert far-reaching effects on global development and the new international economic order, BRI is a highly complicated and integrated system that involves policies on the national, regional, and international levels, in which NGOs can be a valuable asset for policy coordination and promotion. The government should encourage various actors to engage in clean energy diplomacy for they will bring more means and approaches for its execution and deliver China's stances on clean energy development in a better way so that positive messages will be driven home more accurately among people living in Belt and Road countries. Other than conducting cultural exchange programs, holding press conferences, and using international press and Internet for publicity, we can also urge non-state actors to take part in international conferences, partnership dialogues, and relevant side events and to release clean energy study reports. China can sponsor domestic NGOs and industrial associations to join the activities of international clean energy networks, fund academic programs on clean energy governance, boost green finance, and advance cooperation in many other forms.[39]

With China's rising influence in the world, Chinese NGOs with an international vision specializing in clean development, environmental protection, and energy transition are growing both in quantity and quality, as typically shown in the foundation of the Global Environmental Institute (GEI) in 2004. Working closely with governments, businesses, academia, highly respected locals, and local communities, GEI is committed to promoting dialogues and innovative solutions to environmental protection and economic development in China, Southeast Asia, and Africa. Carrying out international cooperation projects on energy and climate change, investment and trade, and environmental capacity building, it has the potential to be a strong driving force of public clean energy diplomacy along the Belt and Road. With the primary purpose of preserving resources, the organization mainly works in three areas – guiding the formulation of policies, facilitating high-level cooperation, and promoting community development.

In 2015, China donated 5,000 sets of 100W household solar power systems and 10,000 clean bio-fueled ovens to Myanmar to help improve the living conditions and increase energy supply in its rural areas, reduce deforestation and carbon emission, and boost China-Myanmar cooperation in response to climate change. GEI was present at the signing ceremony of the supplementary agreement to the China-Myanmar MOU on the presenting of supplies under South-South cooperation on climate change. Earlier on, when it carried out the "Myanmar Forest Protection Demonstration Project based on Clean Energy Technology", GEI donated 180 sets of household solar power systems, 193 clean bio-fueled ovens, and one solar-powered water pump to the village of Thanbayarkhon, which were warmly welcomed and acclaimed by the recipients. In addition to these donations, the Myanmar Ministry of Environmental Conservation and Forestry made other material requests to the Chinese side.[40] GEI provided many suggestions to local organizations on how to join BRI for clean energy development and environmental conservation. (1) They should act as think tanks – precisely analyzing needs and comprehensively considering all factors, including economic benefits. (2) They should act as leverage. On the premise of not affecting normal market activities, they can enhance publicity and influence with small-sum funds or subsidies to stimulate sustained demand and supply. (3) They should act as complement – filling spaces where governments and businesses haven't reached and caring more about the vulnerable and susceptible groups for fair and equitable allocation of resources.

To sum up, China must support multiple stakeholders to join the Belt and Road construction to enhance public clean energy diplomacy. We should encourage them to participate in various international public welfare projects and community governance innovations, which bring direct benefits to people living in countries and regions along the Belt and Road, as part of the efforts to build a social community and a community with a shared future for mankind. At the same time, positively affecting the behaviors of market entities engaged in BRI goes a long way in promoting environmental and ecological progress and corporate social responsibilities. In addition to urging more Chinese social organizations to play a part in clean energy diplomacy, we should also provide better services for overseas NGOs to join the Belt and Road construction and, particularly, communicate and coordinate more closely with their competent departments to give them more support in the form of policy guidance, consulting, and guarantee.[41] The 2018 BRF in Beijing was an intergovernmental event. It is necessary, therefore, with the support of competent authorities, to try and launch a BRI NGO forum, through which social organizations can actively take part in and push forward policy coordination and promotion concerning them. Through such exchange and cooperation, overseas NGOs can help Chinese social organizations go global in the joint endeavor to drive BRI forward.

Notes

1 Li Xinlei, Yao Shifan, Su Jianjun, "Strategic Options Towards Sustainable Energy Security on the Belt and Road: An Analysis of Public Goods Supply in Building China-Central Asia Energy Network", *Qinghai Social Sciences*, No. 4, 2018.
2 Qiao Gang, Yang Cuiping, Sun Wenting, "Clean Energy in the Five Central Asian Countries: Status & Suggestions on Development", *Journal of Xinjiang University* (Chinese Edition on Philosophy, Humanities, and Social Sciences), No. 6, 2013.
3 IEA, *World Energy Outlook Executive Summary*, 2016, p. 3, https://iea.blob.core.windows.net/assets/680c05c8-1d6e-42ae-b953-68e0420d46d5/WEO2016.pdf.
4 IEA, *Energy Technology Perspectives 2015: Mobilising Innovation to Accelerate Climate Action, Executive Summary*, 2015, p. 6, https://iea.blob.core.windows.net/assets/3f901e93-c083-4649-a9e6-c591e28a7b70/ETP2015.pdf.
5 Li Xinlei, "China's Clean Energy Diplomacy in BRI Framework – Opportunities, Challenges, and Fostering of Strategic Capacities", *World Outlook*, No. 3, 2017.
6 Mao Hongtao, "An Exemplary Project Lighting Up BRI – A Record of PV Power Generation Project in Bahawalpur, Punjab of Pakistan", *International Project Contracting & Labour Service*, No. 3, 2016.
7 NEA, "China, Saudi Arabia Sign MOU on Cooperation in Renewable Energy", March 27, 2016, www.chinapower.com.cn/focus/20160203/13903.html.
8 Gao Shixian, Yang Jing, "Deepening International Energy Cooperation Based on BRI", *Macroeconomic Management*, No. 3, 2016.
9 IEA, *Boosting the Power Sector in Sub-Saharan Africa: China's Involvement*, Paris: IEA, 2016.
10 Wang Yuesheng, "World Economy: 'Dual Circulation', New 'South-South Cooperation', and 'Belt and Road' Construction", *Expanding Horizons*, No. 12, 2015.
11 Li Xinlei, "China's Clean Energy Diplomacy in BRI Framework – Opportunities, Challenges, and Fostering of Strategic Capacities", *World Outlook*, No. 3, 2017.
12 Wang Yu, "Energy Cooperation in the Context of BRI: Opportunities and Challenges", *People's Tribune*, No. 7, 2015.
13 Zhang Shixiang, Zhang Xiaoling, "China Builds Grids Around the World – A Strategy and Its Implementation", *Journal of Shanghai University of Electric Power*, No. 3, 2016.
14 Wang Yiwei, *The BRI: Opportunities and Challenges*, Beijing: People's Publishing House, 2015.

15 "Counter-Globalization and New Opportunities for Globalization under Trumpism", *China Economic Times*, February 16, 2017, http://finance.sina.com.cn/roll/2017-02-16/doc-ifyamvns5632567.shtml.
16 WWF, *Environmental and Social Safeguards Framework of Regional Development Agencies*, Switzerland: World Wildlife Fund, 2015.
17 Yan Xiaodong, Cheng Cuiyun, "Strategic Framework for Green Development on Belt and Road", *Chinese Journal of Environmental Management*, No. 2, 2016.
18 Wang Yiwei, *The BRI: Opportunities and Challenges*, Beijing: People's Publishing House, 2015, pp. 144–145.
19 Liang Xuming, "Grid Connectivity Across Countries and Continents: Technologies and Prospects", *Global Energy Interconnection Development and Cooperation Organization*, February 2017, pp. 5–9.
20 Zhang Ning, "Working for an Upgraded Version of China-Central Asia Energy Cooperation", *People's Tribune*, No. 36, 2016.
21 China Energy Internet Alliance (CEIA) is a national, nonprofit, social organization formed on the principle of "voluntariness, equality and cooperation", under the support and guidance of NEA Leading Group of Energy Internet Action. Its members include enterprises, universities, research institutes, testing and certifying organizations, service agencies, and related societies that are of a certain scale and influence and that are engaged in the technological innovation, industrial development, and application and promotion of energy internet.
22 ASEAN Center for Energy is an intergovernmental organization affiliated to ASEAN (Association of Southeast Asian Nations). It holds an annual exchange program with China Renewable Energy Engineering Institute that focuses on the policy and technical aspects of a specific topic, such as pumped storage, wind power, solar power, nuclear power, and traditional hydropower. The policy aspect includes policy framework, overall planning, and approaches of industrial management; technical aspect includes requirements on resources, use of equipment, development, operation and maintenance, synchronization management, risk control, and environmental and social impacts.
23 ASEAN members abound in renewable energy sources and have a lot of islands. Those scarcely populated and remotely located islands have an urgent need to increase electricity access and availability and realize long-distance transmission of electricity. The effective utilization of multiple energy sources offers a good solution to achieving cost-effective, safe, green, low-carbon, and efficient energy development all at once. "A Perspective on China-ASEAN Clean Energy Capacity Building Programme", May 25, 2018, http://ex.bjx.com.cn/html/20180525/27190.shtml.
24 Its first major achievement – *Blue Book on Greening the Belt and Road Initiative: The Countries' Environment State Report (2015)* – provides scientific basis for evaluating the environmental risks and inclusive environmental/social governance in Belt and Road countries.
25 Joanna I. Lewis, "Managing Intellectual Property Rights in Cross-border Clean Energy Collaboration: The Case of the U.S.-China Clean Energy Research Center", *Energy Policy*, No. 69, 2014, pp. 546–554.
26 William Wallace, Sarah Kurtz, Xie Bingxin, "China-US Collaboration on Renewable Energy Standards, Testing, and Certification", *China Renewable Energy*, Vol. 2, No. 2, July 2013, pp. 1–5.
27 Huang He, "BRI from the Perspective of Public Goods", *World Economics and Politics*, No. 6, 2015.
28 He Maochun, Zhang Jibing, "Analysis of National Strategy for New Silk Road Economic Belt – China's Historical Opportunities, Potential Challenges, and Responses", *People's Tribune.Frontiers*, No. 23, 2013.
29 Zhan Yannan, "Differences and Connection Between Silk Road Economic Belt and Eurasian Economic Union", *International Economic Review*, No. 4, 2017.

30 Eastern Economic Forum is established with the approval of Russian President Putin and held annually in Vladivostok, Russia. It has been held three times so far. While committed to promoting economic development in Russia's Far East region, the forum also provides an international political and economic platform for cooperation dialogue for the development of the Asian Pacific region.
31 Peng Hui, "4th Eastern Economic Forum Brings New Opportunities for China-Russia Economic and Trade Ties", September 16, 2018, www.bbtnews.com.cn/2018/0916/266302.shtml.
32 Xu Liping, "BRI Injects New Impetus into South-South Cooperation", *PLA Daily*, April 23, 2017.
33 Zhou Dan, "Targets of Renewable Energy Development in the Five BRICS Countries", *Sino-Global Energy*, No. 3, 2018.
34 Chai Qimin, Tian Chuan, Gao Xiang, et al., "Cooperation Mechanism among the Four BASIC Countries and A Comparative Study of Their Low-carbon Development Model", *Comparative Economic & Social Systems*, No. 3, 2015.
35 Jing Gu, Neil Renwick, Lan Xue, "The BRICS and Africa's Search for Green Growth, Clean Energy and Sustainable Development", *Energy Policy*, No. 120, 2018, pp. 675–683.
36 Su Xing, Pang Jinfu, "Prospects of Renewable Energy in BRICS Countries and Application of 'BRICS Plus' Model", *Sino-Global Energy*, No. 3, 2018.
37 Ma Jun, "Establishing a Green Finance System in China", *Finance Forum*, No. 5, 2015.
38 Charles F. Sabel, David G. Victor, "Governing Global Problems Under Uncertainty: Making Bottom-up Climate Policy Work", *Climatic Change*, No. 144, 2017, pp. 15–27.
39 Zhang Lijun, "Chinese NGOs Engaged in Climate Change Actions", *Public Diplomacy Quarterly*, No. 1, 2016.
40 GEI, "China, Myanmar Sign Supplementary Agreement to MOU on the Presenting of Supplies Under South-South Cooperation on Climate Change", November 6, 2015, http://new.geichina.org/china-and-myanmar-sign-south-south-cooperation-donation-on-clean-energy/.
41 Since the *Law on the Administration of Activities of Overseas Non-Governmental Organizations within the Territory of China* came into force on January 1, 2018, 82 overseas NGOs have been successfully registered, another more than 180 in the process. Public security organs of provincial level should provide convenient services for overseas NGOs that come to China for BRI cooperation and be more efficient in registering them for temporary activities. Cui Jia, "Overseas NGOs to Play Irreplaceable Role in BRI Cooperation", May 10, 2017, http://cn.chinadaily.com.cn/201705/10/content_29291234.htm.

8 Closing remarks

Energy supply is regarded as the indispensable "vitamin" for national development. To achieve sustainable energy development marked by cleanness, security, and high efficiency, we need to strongly develop clean energies represented by wind, solar, hydro, biomass, clean energy vehicle, and technologies for the clean use of fossil energies. As shown in Figure 8.1, the global energy sector has been moving faster on the "decarbonization" track, especially after the 2008 financial crisis sent shock waves across the current energy governance order.[1] Human use of energy is undergoing the third transition from oil and gas to new energy sources, with the latter taking a fast-growing share alongside oil, natural gas, and coal.[2] Unlike oil and gas, clean energy can be developed and used at home, driving domestic energy transition and economic development directly. Whoever masters the technology of manufacturing clean energy equipment gets a head start in development and can also get a grip on foreign countries' energy development by investing overseas. That's why all countries are now turning their eyes to this new domain that encompasses wind, solar, biomass, smart grid, EV, and energy storage, from technological R&D to industrialization to commercialization. Adopting a narrow-sense definition of clean energy, this book focuses on analyzing how the development of renewable energies, including wind, solar, and biomass, affects the international power shift.

As far as the global industry chain is concerned, when developed countries in Europe and America and emerging countries like China are adjusting their industrial structure, they focus on burgeoning industries represented by new energy, new materials, modern biotechnology, data processing and information technology, and aerospace and marine development, to gain competitive advantages in the future. The international industrial restructuring used to be driven by the global transfer of industries dominated by developed countries, but now it is driven by the competition/cooperation between developing and emerging countries on burgeoning industries – this switch has brought about a new balance in global division of labor. In face of the trilemma of economic crisis, energy security, and climate change, the world is going through a low-carbon economic and industrial revolution spearheaded by clean energy. Whether it's the US whose hegemony is declining, the EU priding itself on its normative power, or emerging countries on the rise, they all uplift clean energy development as a national strategy. China's rapid progress

DOI: 10.4324/9781003433903-11

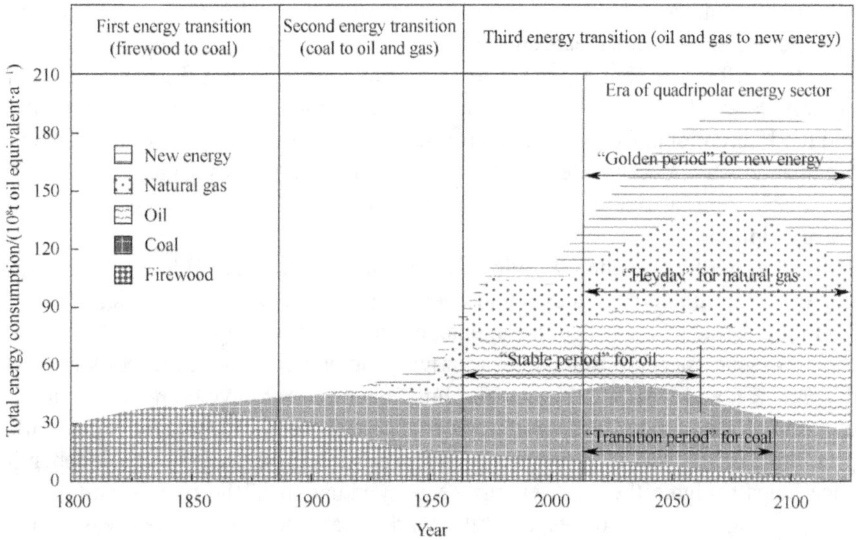

Figure 8.1 Trend and forecast of global energy consumption

Source: Zou Caineng, Zhao Qun, Zhang Guosheng, et al., "Energy Revolution: from Fossil Energy to New Energy", Natural Gas Industry, No. 1, 2016.

in that area has caught global attention.[3] Against such a background, clean energy diplomacy is a pivotal point on which a country works to optimize its international development environment, ensure low-carbon competitiveness, and push for the establishment of a new order of global climate and energy governance.[4] This book discusses how China, amid the changing strategic landscape of climate and energy governance, has become more competitive in the global clean energy arena through clean energy diplomacy, enhanced its discourse power and rule-making power in global energy and climate governance, and elevated its international image. The book is of great realistic importance and reference value for making our green diplomatic strategy more progressive and effective.

Clean energy diplomacy can be defined as the process of formulating the lines, principles, and strategies of foreign interactions and carrying out concrete diplomatic activities with clean energy at the core. This includes making mutual visits between governments, signing bilateral or multilateral cooperation agreements, handling trade frictions and conflicts endangering national interests, setting up dialogue and coordination mechanisms and institutional cooperation platforms, and exploring pathways of providing foreign aid. The main purpose is to guarantee green energy security, advance all-round energy transition, achieve good regional governance of clean energy, and forge a new international order of energy governance. Unlike traditional energy diplomacy that concentrates on resource-rich regions (e.g., the Middle East), clean energy diplomacy is chiefly concerned with cooperation and competition regarding industrial standards, future lifestyle, and market rules. With traditional energy diplomacy, major countries are the main actors, and major-country struggle and even military rivalry are common in energy politics. But with clean energy diplomacy, international organizations and non-state actors play an important role alongside great powers. The International Solar Alliance (ISA) co-initiated by India and International Energy Agency (IEA), and the International Renewable Energy Agency (IRENA), a pioneer clean energy organization founded by Germany with developing countries, bypassing the US and Japan, demonstrate the revolutionary changes of actors playing out the clean energy diplomacy.

The study of clean energy diplomacy expands the theoretical horizon of traditional energy diplomacy studies and deepens and enriches the theoretical dimensions of existing studies of environmental diplomacy. This book generalizes several traits of clean energy diplomacy – relative geographical independence, technical dependence, and strong linkage with climate and energy development. Clean energy diplomacy can tighten a country's friendly relations with its neighbors while promoting the sharing of green energy interests. Its relative geographical independence helps mitigate the stern energy security situation in the region, and showcases a country's sense of responsibility and moral leadership while breaking the dilemma of climate and energy diplomacy. It also helps reinforce a country's low-carbon influence and green competitiveness and fundamentally cements its vantage position in the future strategic landscape amid the decarbonizing trend.

Part I of this book – "International Situation and Theories" – puts creating a new global order of clean energy governance and geographical energy struggle between major countries together. It analyzes the general trend of clean energy diplomacy on two dimensions: the governance-driven dimension (rules-based institutional governance) and the competition-driven dimension (market competition based on the scramble for interests). On the first dimension, clean energy diplomacy displays the following features: major countries are an important driver in the early stage of clean energy governance and make it more institutionalized; the governance becomes increasingly networked; plural actors, including governments, market entities, and social groups, play a bigger part; and developing countries make up a larger percentage in clean energy governance. On the second dimension, the features are geographical competition for raw materials to develop clean energy, competition in green technology and investment amid the low-carbon transformation, competition in clean energy markets and industrial standards, and constraints from carbon tariffs and frictions from clean energy trade. However, it must be noted that the clean energy diplomacy of any country is complex and comprehensive, with the two dimensions coexisting with or even interdependent on each other. In a way, competition is one of the key factors that drive the fast rise of clean energy. To prevent vicious competition and better regulate clean energy development, the governance-driven dimension becomes more important and imperative.

On these two dimensions, which may be high or low in degree, clean energy diplomacy can be categorized into four strategic positions. They are respectively characterized by standard governance (high governance, low competition), green hegemony (high governance, high competition), market competition (low governance, high competition), and green economy (low governance, low competition).

Based on this categorization, the book analyzes the strategic positioning of the clean energy diplomacy adopted by Germany, the US, Japan, India, and Brazil, and draws references from them. Clean energy diplomacy in Germany is typically governance-driven. That of the Obama administration features green hegemony, while that of the Trump administration is typically competition-driven – both, however, are high on the competition-driven dimension despite different policies. That in Japan is competition-driven for energy security, while that in India and Brazil is basically driven by green development. However, India has shown signs of turning to the governance drive. For instance, it was a key founder of ISA with a view to enhancing its international influence in clean energy development.

Based on a systematic analysis of the connotations and strategic positioning of clean energy diplomacy, Part II – "China's Practices and Policies" – conducts a thorough study of the evolution, phased features, and basic approaches of China's clean energy diplomacy. On that basis, it discusses in depth how to foster China's capacities for clean energy diplomacy and how to fit it into the broader diplomatic strategy, to come up with targeted opinions and foresightful suggestions on its positioning, guidelines, and strategic choices.

When the global strategic landscape of climate and energy is going through massive adjustments and changes, China needs to significantly deepen its perception and understanding of clean energy diplomacy. (1) It involves a growing diversity of actors, with sub-state actors, international organizations, and enterprises playing a more important role. (2) The existing global clean energy mechanisms, which are rather fragmented, aren't capable enough to achieve their goals, and well-organized agencies with strong action power such as the Organization of the Petroleum Exporting Countries (OPEC) and IEA are lacked. (3) Global clean energy governance conflicts with major countries' interest demand given America's "relative gains" philosophy. The about-face of the American climate stance has directly affected the ongoing process of establishing clean energy governance for the whole world. The legislative, administrative, and judicial retrogression within the US on clean energy and climate policies has exposed climate governance to a more severe and complicated reality in the post-Paris era. Furthermore, the current international rules on energy governance are unreasonable either in structure or power distribution, as major clean energy producers such as China and India don't have the discourse power and rules-making power to match their global position and importance. (4) To deal with these challenges, international organizations and regimes on clean energy, such as IEA, IRENA, and other sub-national organizations, must be reformed in the new era to be more constructive in energy governance. We need also to be clear that as the world energy and climate situation evolves, the appearance of a governance vacuum actually creates more space and opportunities for China and other developing countries to lead in the establishment of a new global order of climate and energy governance.

The report made at the 19th CPC National Congress made it clear that the principal contradiction facing Chinese society has evolved – what we now face is the contradiction between unbalanced and inadequate development and the people's ever-growing needs for a better life. Being able to breathe fresh air freely is undoubtedly an essential part of a better life, so we must speed up energy transition and the four energy revolutions. After China issued the *Renewable Energy Law* in 2005, the latecomer took only ten years to surpass Germany and the US to rank on top of the world in terms of renewable capacity and green investment. Clean energy has not only boosted China's low-carbon economic development and energy transition but has transformed from an "end" to a diplomatic "means". With its economic growth, China needs to go global not just economically but, more importantly, diplomatically. It should act more actively to merge into the current energy and resource governance regime and lead the establishment of new ones. It should also grasp more initiative while steering the global shift toward clean energy.

China is already a world leader in certain areas of clean energy technology, such as smart grid, EV, and integrated gasification combined cycle (IGCC). The application of these technologies lays the groundwork for the formulation of standards and rules for clean energy governance, and the international spillover of China's best practices further fortifies its institutional power. However, this process isn't without problems. (1) Clean energy development in China is still restricted by technological and managerial weaknesses; (2) there is a strategic mismatch in China's clean energy diplomacy – the country has no power over the pricing of resources or an institutional platform dominated by itself; (3) the global system of clean energy governance suffers from a "South-North divide"; and (4) global clean energy diplomacy is showing a tendency toward "geographical dependence" again.

From a problem-oriented perspective, this book underscores China's augmented competitiveness in clean energy as the bedrock for clean energy diplomacy and points out that it still needs to make strategic deployments flexibly in light of the new situation to enhance its capacities. The book especially proposes "five pillars" that prop up China's clean energy diplomacy, namely, reinforcing its green strengths, institutional power, the capacity of forging diplomatic networks, guiding green finance, and setting the pace for diplomatic narrative. Empowered by these capacities, China will be able to set the agenda, initiate processes, create systems, and lead the narrative in the new order of clean energy governance. Now that capacities are in place, China should also fully recognize that diplomatic strategies and tactics must be practical.

In view of the multiple challenges during the evolution of the international strategic landscape, this book makes it clear that China must keep a sober mind about establishing the new order of energy and climate governance. First of all, the advent of the new order will, to some extent, still be the outcome of political parry and thrust among major countries. As global competition in green energy intensifies, China must face up to the fact that the world worships strength and power. It should carry out clean energy diplomacy in a flexible, pragmatic, and rational manner, strive to forge a new type of green major-country relationship, and work for long-term development in the spirit of win-win cooperation. In the meantime, to plant itself in a dominant position in clean energy diplomacy, China should make good use of its economic, political, and moral resources, provide more green public goods, and consequently enhance its green influence among neighboring countries. It should also seize the initiative in forging new order and setting new agenda for regional governance, such as the Green BRICS and South-South cooperation. On the tactical level, it must set great store by pragmatic cooperation, and the chips and moves it employs should be able to tilt the negotiations in our favor.

Therefore, the key to successful clean energy diplomacy by China is to comprehensively blend it into China's master diplomatic strategy in the BRI framework and achieve green, open, shared, and inclusive development. Bearing in mind the special challenges under BRI, China should make overall strategic plans, give full play to the advantages of clean energy diplomacy in gaining power over green resources, structural power, and discourse power, and guarantee its leading position in building the new climate and energy order. With a huge forex reserve, growing overall economic strength, and new achievements in building a green Belt and Road, China is looking at bright prospects for energy conservation, emission reduction, and the development and utilization of clean energy technologies in Belt and Road construction. It can urge Belt and Road countries to jointly set up the architecture for clean energy cooperation. Regional connectivity in the resource market, natural gas, and renewable energy can be the short-term priority, whereas a BRI network of resource infrastructure is the medium- and long-term goal, to achieve clean development of fossil energies, multi-source supply of renewables, and multi-energy complementarity.

In the BRI context, China, supported by clean energy advantages at home and flexible and practical diplomatic actions abroad, can create an inclusive global energy governance mechanism and a new governance order that is green, pluralist, and networked. This means that the strategic positioning of China's clean energy diplomacy has shifted from a passive one – depending on international clean energy cooperation and assistance – to one driven by green economic development. Going forward, especially in the BRI framework, it will be more driven by green strengths and governance norms, meaning collaboration and coordination on clean energy will be the main way how China is going to carry more weight in the regional provision of public goods. Conducting clean energy diplomacy and innovative South-South cooperation in green capital and technology will also augment China's image and moral appeal among neighboring countries. However, it must be made clear that providing green public goods doesn't just mean capital input – it also means advancing international cooperation on clean energy on the basis of respecting local conditions and balancing ecology, development, security, fairness, and many other elements. Only when we identify and provide the clean energy public goods truly suitable for Belt and Road countries can we help them grow more capable of achieving sustainable development goals, developing modern energy sources, driving green economic development, and boosting low-carbon industrialization. At that time, a community of a shared future for mankind marked by ecological civilization will be built for all living along the Belt and Road.

At last, deeper studies have to be done on several issues as far as future research is concerned. First, not enough theories on clean energy diplomacy have been developed by the academia yet. Indeed, even the cross-disciplinary concept of clean energy is still being debated and must be further studied in reference to relevant subjects, including energy science and low-carbon economics. Second, a global clean energy governance system isn't fully developed yet, and the standards and rules in related domains are in the making. This book, a three-year project endorsed by the National Social Science Fund, has only a short research cycle and will need to be improved through long-term tracking and research. Third, clean energy diplomacy is a dynamic rather than static process, and all the factors at work are interrelated rather than independent with broad rather than local effects. Therefore, the clean energy diplomacy of each country must be followed in a sustained way. In particular, as America's clean energy policies and decisions are highly volatile, we need to pay close attention to how its domestic changes will affect its clean energy diplomacy after 2020. Fourth, global climate and energy governance is increasingly reflected with facts, figures, and indicators. Therefore, while getting a grip on the new development of clean energy diplomacy, we will need to put in place a set of systematic measurements to evaluate objectively and truthfully where China stands in the evolving international strategic landscape – the strengths and potential of its clean energy diplomacy. Thus, we can make sure our strategic evaluation and tactical planning are science-based and well-conceived.

Notes

1 Yu Hongyuan, "Climate Change, Energy Security and Evolution of World Order – Low-carbon Competition Between Developed and Emerging Market Countries", *People's Tribune Frontiers*, No. 22, 2015.
2 Zou Caineng, Zhao Qun, Zhang Guosheng, et al., "Energy Revolution: From Fossil Energy to New Energy", *Natural Gas Industry*, No. 1, 2016.
3 Bruce D. Jones, David Steven, *The Risk Pivot: Great Powers, International Security, and the Energy Revolution*, Washington, DC: Brookings Institution Press, 2015.
4 Mihaela Papa, Nancy W. Gleason, "Major Emerging Powers in Sustainable Development Diplomacy: Assessing their leadership Potential", *Global Environmental Change*, No. 22, 2012, pp. 915–924.

Bibliography

I. Chinese bibliography

(I) Books and reports

BASICS Expert Group, *Equitable Access to Sustainable Development: Contribution to the Body of Scientific Knowledge*, Beijing: Intellectual Property Publishing House, 2012.

Bo, Yan, Gao Xiang, *Evolution of Climate Governance Regime in China and the World*, Shanghai: Shanghai People's Publishing House, 2017.

Chen, Yue, Xu Qinhua (Eds.), *China International Energy Cooperation Report: Towards Low Carbon Era's Global and Regional Energy Governance*, Beijing: Current Affairs Press, 2012.

China Electricity Council, *Clean Development of Coal-Fired Power in China*, Beijing: China Electric Power Press, 2017.

China National Renewable Energy Center, *China Renewable Energy Industry Development Report 2016*, Beijing: China Economic Publishing House, 2016.

China National Renewable Energy Center, Center for Renewable Energy Development of NDRC Energy Research Institute, *China Renewable Energy Industry Development Report*, Beijing: China Economic Publishing House, 2017.

China National Renewable Energy Center and NDRC Energy Research Institute, *International Renewable Energy Development Report*, Beijing: China Environment Publishing Group, 2017.

Chinese Society for Urban Studies, *Development Report on Low-carbon, Ecological Cities in China*, Beijing: China Architecture & Building Press, 2017.

Compiling Group, *Energy Internet Boosts Energy Transition and Institutional Innovation in China*, Beijing: China Development Press, 2017.

Fan, Gang, *China and the World Toward Low-carbon Development – Suggestions from Chinese Economists*, Beijing: China Economic Publishing House, 2010.

Gao, Guowei, Ma Li, Xu Yang, *Study of Energy Cooperation Between China and Belt and Road Countries*, Beijing: People's Daily Press, 2017.

Gao, Shixian, Zhu Yuezhong, *Deepening International Energy Cooperation Through Belt and Road Initiative*, Beijing: China Economic Publishing House, 2016.

He, Jiankun (Ed.), *China's Low-carbon Development Strategy: Pathways and Policies*, Beijing: Science Press, 2018.

Huang Maoxing, *On the Green Development of Belt and Road Initiative – Opportunities, Challenges and Future*, Beijing: Economic Science Press, 2018.

IEA, *Boosting the Power Sector in Sub-Saharan Africa: China's Involvement*, 2016, https://www.iea.org/reports/partner-country-series-boosting-the-power-sector-in-sub-saharan-africa.

Jin, Zhengkun, *Introduction to Modern Science of Diplomacy*, Beijing: China Renmin University Press, 1999.

Li, Huiming, *Ecological Modernization and Climate Governance*, Beijing: Social Sciences Academic Press, 2017.

Lin, Boqiang, *New Energy System of the World*, Beijing: Science Press, 2016.

Lu, Xiaocheng, *An International Comparative Study of the Addressing of Urban Maladies (Reflections about the Low-carbon Development in Beijing, Tianjin and Hebei)*, Beijing: China Social Sciences Press, 2016.

Ma, Xiaozhe et al., *International Carbon Emission Governance*, Beijing: Science Press, 2018.

Pan, Jiahua, Zhang Ying, *Budgeting Carbon for Equity and Sustainability*, Beijing: Social Sciences Academic Press, 2011.

NCSC, *Progress Report of China's Low-carbon Pilot Provinces and Cities*, Beijing: China Planning Press, 2017.

SinoCarbon Innovation & Investment and China Environmental Exchange Alliance, *2014 China Carbon Market Report*, Beijing: Social Sciences Academic Press, 2015.

Smil, Vaclav, *Energy Transitions: History, Requirements, Prospects*, translated by Gao Feng, Jiang Aixin, Li Hongda, Beijing: Science Press, 2018.

State Grid Energy Research Institute, *World Energy Clean Development and Interconnection Evaluation Report (Europe)*, Beijing: Social Sciences Academic Press, 2018.

Su, Shuhui, *Annual Report on Development of Greenhouse Gas Emissions Control and Carbon Market (2016)*, Beijing: World Affairs Press, 2016.

Wang, Yiwei, *The BRI: Opportunities and Challenges*, Beijing: People's Publishing House, 2015.

Wang, Yiwei, *An Interconnected World Through BRI*, Beijing: The Commercial Press, 2016.

Wang, Zhongying, Ren Dongming, Qin Haiyan et al. (Eds. and Trans.), *The World Renewable Energy Policies and Regulations Compilation*, Beijing: China Economic Publishing House, 2013.

Wang, Zhongying, Kaare Sandholt, *China Renewable Energy Outlook 2016*, Beijing: Science Press, 2017.

Wu, Jing, Wang Zheng, Zhu Qianting, Zhu Yongbin et al., *A Study of Global Governance in Response to Climate Change*, Beijing: Science Press, 2016.

WWF, *Environmental and Social Safeguards Framework of Regional Development Agencies*, 2015, https://amurinfocenter.org/upload/iblock/5be/%E5%8C%BA%E5%9F%9F%E5%BC%80%E5%8F%91%E6%9C%BA%E6%9E%84%E7%8E%AF%E5%A2%83%E4%B8%8E%E7%A4%BE%E4%BC%9A%E7%AE%A1%E7%90%86%E6%A1%86%E6%9E%B6%E5%9B%BD%E9%99%85%E7%BB%8F%E9%AA%8C%E7%A0%94%E7%A9%B6(belt).pdf.

Xia, Yishan, Chen Dezhao, *China's Grand Vision of Energy, Environment and Climate Diplomacy*, Beijing: World Affairs Press, 2012.

Xu, Hongfeng, *China and the US: Clean Energy Cooperation in Response to Global Climate Change*, Beijing: Social Sciences Academic Press, 2017.

Xu, Qinhua, *China Energy International Cooperation Report: "The Belt and Road" Energy Investment (2015/2016)*, Beijing: China Renmin University Press, 2016.

Xu, Qinhua et al., *International Comparative Study on Clean Energy Development in the Low Carbon Era*, Guangzhou: Guangdong World Publishing Corporation, 2013

Xue, Jinjun, Zhao Zhongxiu, *Annual Report on China's Low-carbon Economic Development 2017*, Beijing: Social Sciences Academic Press, 2017.

Yang, Yanqiang, *Energy Security for China in Low-carbon Economy*, Beijing: Guangming Daily Press, 2014.

Yang, Yimin, *How to Dispose of Domestic Wastes Amid Climate Change*, Beijing: Science Press, 2018.

Yang, Yufeng, Neil Hirst, *Global Energy Governance Reform and China's Participation*, Beijing: Tsinghua University Press, 2017.

Yu, Hongyuan, *Environmental Change and Power Shift: Institutions, Negotiations and Policies*, Shanghai: Shanghai People's Publishing House, 2011.

Yu, Hongyuan, *Global Environmental Governance: Connotations and Trends*, Shanghai: Shanghai People's Publishing House, 2018.

Yu, Hongyuan, *International Climate and Environmental Diplomacy: China's Actions*, Shanghai: Orient Publishing Center, 2013.

Zhang, Xiliang, Qi Ye, *Annual Review of Low-carbon Development in China (2017)*, Beijing: Social Sciences Academic Press, 2017.

Zhao, Qingsi, *International Cooperation and China's Energy Diplomacy: Concept, Mechanism and Path*, Beijing: Law Press China, 2012.

Zhou, Fengqi, Chen Ning, Liu Zhaofeng et al., *Low Carbon City and Carbon Governance Innovation – Case Study of Shanghai*, Shanghai: Shanghai Academy of Social Sciences Press, 2016.

Zhou, Fengqi, Liu Xinyu, Chen Ning, *China's Renewable Energy Strategy and Institutions of Renewable Energy Industries*, Shanghai: Shanghai Academy of Social Sciences Press, 2016.

Zhou, Jie et al., *Annual Report on Development of International Clean Energy (2014)*, Beijing: Social Sciences Academic Press, 2014.

Zhou, Yueyun, Liang Benfan, *Smart Low-Carbon Development of Cities in China (2017)*, Changsha: Hunan People's Publishing House, 2017.

Zhu, Tong, *National Energy Transition*, Hangzhou: Zhejiang University Press, 2016.

Zhu, Tong, Wang Lei, *National Energy Transition*, Hangzhou: Zhejiang University Press, 2015.

Zhu, Xuantong, "China's Engagement in Global Energy Governance", *IEA Annual Report 2016*, 2016, https://theasiadialogue.com/wp-content/uploads/2018/03/PartnerCountrySeries_ChinasEngagementinGlobalEnergyGovernance_Englishversion.pdf.

Zhu, Yuezhong, Liu Jianguo, Liang Qi, *Energy Cooperation under BRI*, Xi'an: Xi'an Jiaotong University Press, 2018.

Zhuang, Guiyang, *A Blueprint for Low-carbon Development for Chinese Cities*, Beijing: Social Sciences Academic Press, 2015.

(II) Papers

Bai, Ding, "Rare Earth – Essential Resource for Green Energy", *Rare Earth Information*, No. 9, 2014.

Bi, Yantao, Wang Dan, Li Chunxin et al., "Renewable Energy Development by International Petroleum Companies – Current Status and Lessons", *International Petroleum Economics*, No. 4, 2017.

Chai, Qimin, Tian Chuan, Gao Xiang et al., "Cooperation Mechanism Among the Four BASIC Countries and A Comparative Study of Their Low-carbon Development Model", *Comparative Economic & Social Systems*, No. 3, 2015.

Chen, Fengying, "New Changes in International Energy Security", *Contemporary International Relations*, No. 6, 2006.

Chen, Xiaoding, "Regional Public Goods and Strategic Connotations of China's New Concept of Neighborhood Diplomacy", *World Economics and Politics*, No. 8, 2016.

Chen, Ying, "New Changes in International Climate Governance at Bonn Conference and China's Response", *Environmental Protection*, No. 1, 2018.

Development Research Center of the State Council, "Global GHG Emission Reduction: Theoretical Framework and Solution", *Economic Research Journal*, No. 3, 2009.

Development Research Center of the State Council, "National Account for CO_2 Emission: Governance Framework for Tackling Climate Change and Achieving Green Growth", *Economic Research Journal*, No. 12, 2011.

Ding, Zhongli, Duan Xiaonan, Ge Quansheng, Zhang Zhiqiang, "Atmospheric CO_2 Intensity in 2050: Emission Rights by Country", *Science in China (Series D): Earth Sciences*, No. 8, 2009.

Ding, Zhongli, Duan Xiaonan, Ge Quansheng, Zhang Zhiqiang, "Evaluation of International GHG Emission Reduction Scheme and China's Long-term Emission Right", *Science in China (Series D): Earth Sciences*, No. 12, 2009.

Du, Fenglian, Wang Yuan, "Study of Alternative Policies for Tariff on Strategic Resources – With the Export of Rare Earth as an Example", *Economic Science*, No. 3, 2015.

Du, Qun, Liao Jiankai, "Comparative Study of New Energy Law in Germany and Britain and Lessons for China", *Law Review*, No. 6, 2011.

Fan, Gang, Su Ming, Cao Jing, "Economic Analysis of End Consumption and Carbon Emission Reduction Responsibilities", *Economic Research Journal*, No. 1, 2010.

Fan, Liuyan, Qu Delin, Wang Haibo et al., "Japan's New Energy Situation in the Post-Fukushima Era: Changes and Lessons", *Renewable Energy Resources*, No. 5, 2011.

Feng, Zhaokui, "International Energy Landscape in Early 21st Century and Its Medium- and Long-term Changes – Japan's Dilemma in Energy Security and Its Way Out", *Journal of International Security Studies*, No. 6, 2013.

Fu, Xueqian, Deng Guangchang, "Renewable Energy in India", *Power Demand Side Management*, No. 1, 2013.

Gao, Shixian, Yang Jing, "Deepening International Energy Cooperation Through Belt and Road Initiative", *Macroeconomic Management*, No. 3, 2016.

Gong, Na, "NEW JICA and Japan's Soft Power", *Japan Studies*, No. 4, 2012.

Guo, Guanyu, Dai Xiudian, "Renewable Energy Cooperation Between China and Germany: Foundation, Mechanism and Problems", *Journal of China University of Geosciences (Social Sciences Edition)*, No. 4, 2012.

Guo, Jiwei, Wang Xiaolu, "Energy Transition in Germany: Experience, Challenges, and Lessons", *Global Science, Technology and Economy Outlook*, No. 1, 2014.

He, Jiankun, Teng Fei, Liu Bin, "Advancing Global Response to Climate Change on the Principle of Equity", *Journal of Tsinghua University (Philosophy and Social Sciences)*, No. 6, 2009.

He, Maochun, Zhang Jibing, "Analysis of National Strategy for New Silk Road Economic Belt – China's Historical Opportunities, Potential Challenges, and Responses", *People's Tribune Frontiers*, No. 23, 2013.

He, Tingting, "India to Have 16% of Electric Power from Wind Energy in 2030", *Wind Energy*, No. 11, 2017.

Huang, He, "BRI from the Perspective of Public Goods", *World Economics and Politics*, No. 6, 2015.

Huang, Lijun, "Abe Promotes Energy Diplomacy by Haggling and Peddling", *China Business News*, May 6, 2013.

Jiang, He, "Brazil's Development and Utilization of Renewable Energy: Achievements and Lessons", *Journal of Jiangsu Normal University (Philosophy and Social Sciences Edition)*, No. 2, 2017.

Jiang, Jiani, Wang Can, "IP Issue in Global Climate Negotiations – Progress, Trend and China's Response", *World Outlook*, No. 2, 2016.

Jiang, Shu and Li Qingsi, "The China-US Cooperation/Competition in New Energy – from PV to Wind", *International Forum*, No. 2, 2013.

Jiang, Zemin, "Thoughts on the Energy Issue of China", *Journal of Shanghai Jiaotong University*, No. 3, 2008.

Kang, Xiao, "Paths and Problems for China's International Cooperation on Renewable Energy", *Contemporary International Relations*, No. 6, 2009.

Li, Dong, Wei Xiaosha, "Trade Frictions Between China and US on Clean Energy: Trend, Reasons and Countermeasures", *Seeker*, No. 11, 2012.

Li, Fan, Xu Xin, Dai Yongwei, "Comparative Study of Renewable Energy Policies in BRICS Countries", *Asia-pacific Economic Review*, No. 3, 2017.

Li, Huiming, "Age of Institutional Fragmentation for Global Climate Governance: International Leadership and China's Strategic Options", *Journal of Contemporary Asia-Pacific Studies*, No. 4, 2015.

Li, Huiming, "Global Climate Governance and Transition of International Order", *World Economics and Politics*, No. 3, 2017.

Li, Jin, "Analysis of World Competition for Rare Earth Resources", *World Nonferrous Metals*, No. 4, 2013.

Li, Jun, Wang Xuchun, Li Xiaozhao, "Energy Situation and Use of Renewable Energy in Japan", *Solar Energy*, No. 12, 2017.

Li, Meiyan, Feng Lianyong, "Impacts on and Lessons for Japan's Energy Strategy from Fukushima Nuclear Crisis", *Sino-Global Energy*, No. 3, 2013.

Li, Renfang, Shan Dan, "New Energy Policies in Brazil and Their Effects", *Journal of Southwest University of Science and Technology (Philosophy and Social Science Edition)*, No. 5, 2013.

Li, Xinlei, "China's Clean Energy Diplomacy in BRI Framework – Opportunities, Challenges, and Fostering of Strategic Capacities", *World Outlook*, No. 3, 2017.

Li, Xinlei, "Global Climate Governance: Shift of Leading Power and China's Strategic Options", *Journal of Shandong University (Philosophy and Social Sciences)*, No. 1, 2017.

Li, Xinlei, "Governance Nesting: Evolution of Global Climate Governance Complex", *Chinese Journal of European Studies*, No. 2, 2018.

Li, Xinlei, "National Learning Mechanism and Discourse Building in International Politics: Greening of China's Outlook on Energy Security and Its Effects on Energy and Climate Diplomacy", *Fudan International Studies Review*, No. 12, 2013.

Li, Xinlei, "New Developments of China's Clean Energy Diplomacy Amid the Evolving Global Climate and Energy Landscape", *Pacific Journal*, No. 12, 2017.

Li, Xinlei, "Non-state Actors Participate in Global Network of Climate Governance: Patterns, Motivations and Effects", *International Forum*, No. 2, 2018.

Li, Xinlei, "Transnational Clean Energy Governance – Characteristics, Motivations and Challenges of Multi-party Networking", *International Review*, No. 6, 2017.

Li, Xinlei, Yu Hongyuan, "Public Diplomacy's Assistant Role in Building National Soft Power and Innovation of Its Communication", *Contemporary World*, No. 9, 2017.

Li, Xinlei, Yao Shifan, Su Jianjun, "Strategic Options Towards Sustainable Energy Security on the Belt and Road: An Analysis of Public Goods Supply in Building China-Central Asia Energy Network", *Qinghai Social Sciences*, No. 4, 2018.

Li, Yang, "China-US Clean Energy Cooperation: Foundation, Mechanism and Problems", *Contemporary International Relations*, No. 1, 2011.

Li, Zhiguo, Du Xiu'e, "Empirical Study of Clean Energy Utilization and Energy Consumption Structure in BRICS Countries", *Asia-pacific Economic Review*, No. 3, 2012.

Lin, Lyu, Wu Yanan, Dong Zhanfeng et al., "Policy Innovation in Germany and America's Energy Transition and Lessons for China", *Environmental Protection*, No. 19, 2017.

Lin, Xuanchen, Li Yan, Li Changsheng, "California's Experience and Reference in Responding to Climate Change", *Macroeconomic Management*, No. 4, 2017.

Liu, Changsong, "International Energy Transition: Progress and Lessons for China", *Journal of Poyang Lake*, No. 3, 2016.

Liu, Jiangyong, "Sustainable Security Depends on Justice, Not Force – On Building Sustainable Security Strategy Again", *World Economics and Politics*, No. 8, 2011.

Liu, Jiangyong, "Sustainable Security from the Perspective of International Strategy", *International Review*, No. 6, 2014.

Liu, Mingde, Yang Yuhua, "Reference Value of Key Projects in Germany's Energy Transition for China's Energy Policy", *Journal of North China Electric Power University (Social Sciences)*, No. 6, 2015.

Liu, Qing, Liu Rongrong, "Clean Energy Cooperation Between China and the US", *International Studies*, No. 2, 2011.

Liu, Zhenya, "Global Energy Internet Across Nations and Continents and Its Prospects", *Proceedings of the CSEE*, No. 19, 2016.

Luo, Chengxian, "Supportive Policies for Renewable Energy: Changes and Trends", *Sino-Global Energy*, No. 9, 2016.

Ma, Jianying, "An Analysis of China-US Clean Energy Cooperation", *Contemporary International Relations*, No. 12, 2009.

Ma, Jun, "Building a Green Financial System in China", *Finance Forum*, No. 5, 2015.

Mao, Hongtao, "An Exemplary Project Lighting Up BRI – A Record of PV Power Generation Project in Bahawalpur, Punjab of Pakistan", *International Project Contracting & Labour Service*, No. 3, 2016.

Mao, Jinsheng, Cheng Wenting, "Intellectual Property Policy for Strategic Emerging Industries", *Intellectual Property*, No. 9, 2011.

Niu, Wenyuan, "Theory of Sustainable Development – At the 20th Anniversary of UN Conference on Environment and Development in Rio de Janeiro", *China Population, Resources and Environment*, No. 5, 2012.

Oberthür, Sebastian, Stephanie Pfahl, Dennis Tänzler, "Renewable Energy Needs International Cooperation", *World Economics and Politics*, No. 4, 2005.

Pan, Guang, "China's Energy Diplomacy Through 30 Years of Reform and Opening-up", *International Studies*, No. 6, 2008.

Pan, Jiahua, "Carbon Budget Meeting Basic Needs and Its Significance for International Equity and Sustainability", *World Economics and Politics*, No. 1, 2008.

Pan, Jiahua, Zheng Yan, "Carbon Emission Based on Interpersonal Equity and Its Theoretical Significance", *World Economics and Politics*, No. 10, 2009.

Pan, Jiahua, Chen Ying, "Budgeting Carbon for Equity and Sustainability", *Social Science in China Press*, No. 5, 2009.

Peng, Feng, "New Development of EU's Green Energy Policy and Inspirations from It", *Environmental Protection*, No. 9, 2016.

Qi, Yue, Fan Yichun, "BASIC Group's South-South Cooperation on Climate Change: Policies, Actions and Lessons", *World Environment*, No. 1, 2017.

Qiao, Gang, Yuan Tiejiang, Alimasibiekeo·Shakenbieke, "Development Situation of Electric Power Industry of Five Countries in Central Asian Countries and Analysis on Cooperation Chance", *Power Capacitors & Reactive Power Compensation*, No. 3, 2015.

Schreurs, Miranda, Wang Congcong, "The Competition for Leadership in Clean Energy and Environmental Technology", *Green Leaf*, No. 3, 2012.

Schreurs, Miranda, Li Qing, "International on Germany's Energy Transition and Demand for New Governance Modes", *Journal of Nanjing Tech University (Social Science Edition)*, No. 2, 2015.

Shen, Yongping, Wang Guoya, "Latest Scientific Points about Global Climate Change in the Fifth Assessment Report by IPCC Working Group I", *Journal of Glaciology and Geocryology*, No. 5, 2013.

Special Correspondent, "Bonn Political Declaration at the First International Conference for Renewable Energies", *Science, Technology & Intelligence*, No. 12, 2005.

Special Correspondent, "Climate Change and China's National Strategy – An Interview with Professor Wang Jisi", *The Journal of International Studies*, No. 4, 2009.

Special Correspondent, "Japan, India to Cooperate on Renewables, Clean Coal, Energy Efficiency", *China Energy News*, January 18, 2016, p. 6.

Special Correspondent, "Japan to Peak New PV Capacity This Year", *China Energy News*, February 29, 2016, p. 9.

Special Correspondent, "New Energy and Peaceful Diplomacy – CPPCC Standing Committee Member Liu Hanyuan's Proposal at Two Sessions", *Sun Energy*, No. 2, 2011.

Su, Xing, Pang Jinfu, "Prospects of Renewable Energy in BRICS Countries and Application of 'BRICS Plus' Model", *Sino-Global Energy*, No. 3, 2018

Tan, Zhongfu, Liu Wenyan, Liu Pingkuo, "Effects of Green Certificate Trade and Carbon Emission Right Trade on Chinese Power Market", *Technology Economics*, No. 9, 2014.

Urpelainen, Johannes, Thijs Van de Graaf, Lin Xuefei, "The International Renewable Energy Agency: A Successful Institutional Innovation?", *Foreign Theoretical Trends*, No. 2, 2017.

Wang, Binbin, Zhang Haibin, "Dual Transition in Global Climate Governance and China's Strategic Choice", *Journal of China University of Geosciences (Social Sciences Edition)*, No. 3, 2017.

Wang, Bo, Li Chaoqian, "Global Status and Trend of Renewable Energy Development", *China Prices*, No. 5, 2018.

Wang, Haibin, "The Changing World Energy Landscape and China's Response", *Ziguangge*, No. 3, 2018.

Wang, Lei, "Clean Energy Development in Brazil: Policies and Practices", *Global Science, Technology and Economy Outlook*, No. 10, 2017.

Wang, Lili, "Functions and Roles of American Think Tanks in Public Diplomacy", *Contemporary International Relations*, No. 1, 2012.

Wang, Qingsong, "Study of the Legal System of IRENA", *Social Sciences in Xinjiang*, No. 3, 2015.

Wang, Ruibin, "Shift in America's Climate and Energy Policy and Its Effects", *International Petroleum Economics*, No. 4, 2017.

Wang, Yu, "Energy Cooperation in the Context of BRI: Opportunities and Challenges", *People's Tribune*, No. 7, 2015.

Wang, Yuesheng, "World Economy: 'Dual Circulation', New 'South-South Cooperation', and 'Belt and Road' Construction", *Expanding Horizons*, No. 12, 2015.

Wen, Jing, "Renewable Energy Development in Germany: Policy Environment, Main Achievements, and Lessons", *Agriculture Engineering Technology: New Energy Industry*, No. 11, 2011.

Wu, Shaobo, Yin Haiqing, Zhang Kaihua et al., "Floating Wind Power Technology in Japan: Current Status and Future Development", *China Harbour Engineering*, No. 6, 2017.

Wu, Xinbo, "The New Normal of China-US Relationship", *Fudan Journal (Social Sciences Edition)*, No. 3, 2015.

Xie, Xuxuan, Wang Tian, Ren Dongming, "RPS in America: Latest Development and Lessons for China", *Energy of China*, No. 3, 2012.

Xu, Bin, "Multiple Options of Rare Earth Policies in China: Reflection and Response", *Intertrade*, May 2015.

Xu, Hui, "Chinese Clean Energy Industry Going Global – Founding Conference of China New Energy International Alliance and Asia Solar Energy Forum Successfully Held", *China Electrical Equipment Industry*, No. 4, 2016.

Xu, Qinhua, "China's Energy Diplomacy Strategy: An Analysis and Thoughts", *Teaching and Research*, No. 12, 2008.

Xu, Yao, "Age 3.0 for Renewable Energy – Germany Revises EEG", *China Electric Power News*, June 25, 2016.

Yan, Shigang, "China-EU New Energy Cooperation in the Low-carbon Era: Challenges and Solutions", *Economic Forum*, No. 3, 2011.

Yan, Shigang, "China's International Cooperation on New Energy from the Perspective of Low-carbon Economy", *Foreign Affairs Review*, No. 5, 2012.

Yan, Shigang, "China's New Energy Cooperation with the US and Europe: Problems and Prospects", *Practice in Foreign Economic Relations and Trade*, No. 5, 2012.

Yan, Shigang, Liu Shuguang, "China's Energy Diplomacy under the New Outlook on Energy Security", *International Studies*, No. 2, 2014.

Yan, Xiaodong, Cheng Cuiyun, "Strategic Framework for Green Development on Belt and Road", *Chinese Journal of Environmental Management*, No. 2, 2016.

Yang, Guang, "EU's Energy Security Strategy and Its Lessons", *Chinese Journal of European Studies*, No. 5, 2007.

Yang, Xiaoping, "Cross-border Water Resources Amid the Rise of China and India: Beyond the 'Scarcity-Conflict' Perspective", *International Forum*, No. 4, 2012.

Yang, Zewei, "China's Energy Security: Challenges and Responses", *World Economics and Politics*, No. 8, 2008.

Yu, Hongyuan, "Adjustment of Climate Policy During Trump Administration and Its Effects", *Pacific Journal*, No. 1, 2018.

Yu, Hongyuan, "China's Energy and Environmental Diplomacy Centered on Green, Win-win Development", *International Outlook*, No. 4, 2011.

Yu, Hongyuan, "Clean Energy and China's Environmental Diplomacy: China's Rise in International Energy System", *Green Leaf Special Issue: Scientific Outlook on Development and Environmental Diplomacy*, No. 4, 2008.

Yu, Hongyuan, "Climate Change, Energy Security and Evolution of World Order – Low-carbon Competition Between Developed and Emerging Market Countries", *People's Tribune Frontiers*, No. 22, 2015.

Yu, Hongyuan, "Energy Chain in the Context of Power Shift and Its Challenges", *World Economy Studies*, No. 2, 2008.

Yu, Hongyuan, "Institution and Capacity: Dual Determinants in America's Climate Diplomacy", *Journal of Contemporary Asia-Pacific Studies*, No. 4, 2012.

Yu, Hongyuan, "New Changes in Global Climate Negotiations", *Contemporary International Relations*, No. 6, 2012.

Yu, Hongyuan, "Obama's Plan for an Energy-powered Country and China-US Energy Relation", *International Review*, No. 5, 2014.

Yu, Hongyuan, "Utilitarianism and Globalism in Global Energy Governance", *Journal of International Security Studies*, No. 5, 2013.

Yu, Hongyuan, Wang Wentao, "Institutional Fragmentation and Lack of Leadership: Dual Deficit in Global Environmental Governance", *The Journal of International Studies*, No. 3, 2013.

Zha, Daojiong, "China-US Energy Cooperation – Challenges and Opportunities", *International Petroleum Economics*, No. 11, 2005.

Zha, Daojiong, "Strategic Commanding Height in Clean Energy and National Competitiveness", in Wang Jisi (Ed.), *China International Strategy Review*, Beijing: World Affairs Press, 2010.

Zhan, Yannan, "Differences and Connection Between Silk Road Economic Belt and Eurasian Economic Union", *International Economic Review*, No. 4, 2017.

Zhang, Haibin, "China's Stance During International Climate Negotiations: Continuity, Changes and Reasons", *World Economics and Politics*, No. 10, 2006.

Zhang, Jianguo, Bai Quan, "G20 Energy Ministers' Meeting: Countries' Priorities for Improved Energy Efficiency", *Energy of China*, No. 11, 2016.

Zhang, Jie, Guan Kejiang, Qu Song, "Energy Alliance Tests EU's Cohesion", *People's Daily*, April 7, 2015.

Zhang, Lifeng, Feng Hongxia, "Evolution of Germany's EEG and Lessons for China", *Hebei Law Science*, No. 10, 2017.

Zhang, Lijun, "Chinese NGOs Engaged in Climate Change Actions", *Public Diplomacy Quarterly*, No. 1, 2016.

Zhang, Ning, "Working for an Upgraded Version of China-Central Asia Energy Cooperation", *People's Tribune*, No. 36, 2016.

Zhang, Qian, "Japan Strongly Develops Renewable Energy; Solar Power and Offshore Wind Power Have Obvious Advantages", *China Environment News*, May 1, 2017.

Zhang, Shixiang, Zhang Xiaoling, "China Builds Grids Around the World – A Strategy and Its Implementation", *Journal of Shanghai University of Electric Power*, No. 3, 2016.

Zhang, Weichong, Meng Hao, Li Weibo, "Clean Energy Development in South Africa: Latest Progress and Lessons", *Global Science, Technology and Economy Outlook*, No. 11, 2016.

Zhang, Yonghong, Liang Yijian, Wang Tao et al., "New Energy Cooperation Between China and Africa: Prospects, Challenges and Policies", *Journal of International Economic Cooperation*, No. 2, 2013.

Zhao, Changqing, "Major-power Contention and Stance of Central Asian Countries", *Journal of Xinjiang Normal University (Philosophy and Social Sciences)*, No. 2, 2014.

Zhao, Hongtu, "International Energy Transition: Current Status and Prospects", *Contemporary International Relations*, No. 6, 2009.

Zhao, Qingsi, "China's Strategy of Engaging in Global Energy Governance through G20", *Contemporary World and Socialism*, No. 6, 2015.

Zhao, Yongqiang, "International Renewable Energy Development and Reform of Global Energy Governance", *Macroeconomics*, No. 4, 2017.

Zheng, Yanting, Xu Ligang, "How Developed Countries Promote Green Energy: Experiences and Lessons", *Resources Science*, No. 10, 2012.

Zhou, Dan, "BRICS Countries Strengthen Energy Cooperation", *Sino-Global Energy*, No. 3, 2018.

Zhou, Dan, "Targets of Renewable Energy Development in the Five BRICS Countries", *Sino-Global Energy*, No. 3, 2018.

Zhou, Qi, Fu Suixin, "America's Clean Power Plan and Its Effects on American Energy Industry", *International Petroleum Economics*, No. 10, 2015.

Zhou, Zhiwei, "Brazil's Participation in BRICS Cooperation: Strategic Considerations and Effects", *Journal of Latin American Studies*, No. 4, 2017.
Zhu, Tong, "Comparative Analysis of Energy Transition in Germany and the US", *International Petroleum Economics*, No. 5, 2016.
Zhuang, Guiyang, Zhou Weiduo, "Change of Global Climate Governance Mode and China's Contributions", *Contemporary World*, No. 1, 2016.
Zong, He, "Emerging Industries Become Object of Trade Protection", *China's Foreign Trade*, No. 9, 2013.
Zou, Caineng, Zhao Qun, Zhang Guosheng et al., "Energy Revolution: From Fossil Energy to New Energy", *Natural Gas Industry*, No. 1, 2016.
Zou, Zhiqiang, "G20 and Global Energy Governance: Results and Prospects", *Modern Economic Research*, No. 1, 2016.
Zuo, Anlei, "Patent Protection of Clean Energy Technology and Industry – World Development and China's Response", *Science, Technology and Law*, No. 1, 2012.

II. English bibliography

(I) Books and reports

Aklin, Michaël, Johannes Urpelainen, *Renewables*; *The Politics of a Global Energy Transition*, Cambridge, MA and London: The MIT Press, 2018.
Andrews-Speed, Philip, *The Governance of Energy in China*; *Transition to a Low-Carbon Economy*, London: Palgrave Macmillan, 2012.
Barbara, Weiss and M. Obi, *Climate Change Mitigation and Clean Energy Technology Policies. Environmental Risk Mitigation*, Berlin: Springer, 2016.
Bernice, Lee, Ilian Iliev, Felix Preston, *Who Owns Our Low Carbon Future? Intellectual Property and Energy Technologies, A Chantham House Report*, London: Royal Institute of International Affairs, September 2009.
Bloomberg Philanthropies, *America's Pledge, Phase 1 Report States, Cities, and Businesses in the United States Are Stepping Up on Climate Action*, November 2017, www.bbhub.io/dotorg/sites/28/2017/11/AmericasPledgePhaseOneReportWeb.pdf.
Bloomberg Philanthropies, *Fulfilling America's Pledge: How States, Cities, and Businesses Are Leading the United States to a Low-Carbon Future*, 2018, www.bbhub.io/dotorg/sites/28/2018/09/Fulfilling-Americas-Pledge-2018.pdf.
BNEF, *Global Renewable Energy Market Outlook: Executive Summary*, Report from Bloomberg New Energy Finance, 2011.
Boyle, Godfrey, *Renewable Energy: Power for a Sustainable Future*, Oxford: Oxford University Press, 2012.
British Petroleum, *BP World Energy Statistics Yearbook*, 2016, http://large.stanford.edu/courses/2016/ph240/stanchi2/docs/bp-2016.pdf.
British Petroleum, *BP World* Energy *Statistics Yearbook*, 2017, https://www.bp.com/content/dam/bp/business-sites/en/global/corporate/pdfs/news-and-insights/speeches/bp-statistical-review-of-world-energy-2017-lamar-mckay.pdf.
British Petroleum, *BP World Energy Statistics Yearbook*, 2018, https://www.bp.com/content/dam/bp/business-sites/en/global/corporate/pdfs/energy-economics/statistical-review/bp-stats-review-2018-full-report.pdf.
Bruckner, T., A. Jaegerwaldau, "Renewable Energy and Climate Change", *IPCC Special Report on Renewable Energy Sources and Climate Change Mitigation*, 2010, http://www.ipcc-wg3.de/report/IPCC_SRREN_Ch01.pdf.

Bulkeley, H., L. B. Andonova, M. M. Betsill, D. Compagnon, Th. Hale, M. J. Hoffmann, P. Newell, M. Paterson, Ch. Roger, S. VanDeveer, *Transnational Climate Change Governance*, New York: Cambridge University Press, 2014.

Busch, Per-Olof, Helge Jorgens, *Governance by Diffusion-International Environmental Policy Coordination in the Era of Globalization*, FFU Berlin PhD Dissertation, 2009.

Chasek, Pamela S., *Earth Negotiations*; *Analyzing Thirty Years of Environmental Diplomacy*, Tokyo: United Nations University Press, 2001.

The Cleantech Group-Heslin Rothenberg Farley & Mesiti P. C., *Clean Energy Patent Growth Index* (*CEPGI*), 2016, www.cleantechintellectualproperty.com; www.cepgi.com.

Dent, Christopher M., "Clean Energy Trade Governance: Reconciling Trade Liberalism and Climate Interventionism?", *New Political Economy*, Vol. 23, No. 2, 2017.

Edenhofer, O., et al., "IPCC Special Report on Renewable Energy Sources and Climate Change Mitigation Summary for Policymakers", *IPCC*, 2012, https://www.ipcc.ch/site/assets/uploads/2018/03/SRREN_Full_Report-1.pdf.

Eisen, Joel B., "New Energy Geopolitics: China, Renewable Energy, and the Greentech Race", *Chicago-Kent Law Review*, Vol. 86, 2011.

Eldridge, Janet H., *Global Clean Energy Cooperation*, New York: Nova Science Publishers, 2012.

Harris, Paul G. (Ed.), *China and Global Climate Change*, Hongkong: Proceedings of the Conference Held at Lingnan University, June 2009.

Harris, Paul G. (Ed.), *China's Responsibility for Climate Change*; *Ethics, Fairness and Environmental Policy*, Bristol: The Policy Press, 2011.

Hills, Jeremy Maxwell, E. Michalena, *Renewable Energy Governance*, Berlin: Springer, 2013.

Hoffmann, Matthew J., *Climate Governance at the Crossroads*: *Experimenting with a Global Response after Kyoto*, New York: Oxford University Press, 2011.

IEA, *Energy Technology Perspectives 2015*: *Mobilising Innovation to Accelerate Climate Action*, Executive Summary, 2015, https://iea.blob.core.windows.net/assets/3f901e93-c083-4649-a9e6-c591e28a7b70/ETP2015.pdf.

IEA, *Tracking Clean Energy Progress 2016: Energy Technology Perspectives*, 2016, https://iea.blob.core.windows.net/assets/6871b404-bcff-4c5d-b53e-d33a6ef347b9/TrackingCleanEnergyProgress2016.pdf.

IEA, *World Energy Outlook 2016*, Executive Summary, 2016, https://iea.blob.core.windows.net/assets/680c05c8-1d6e-42ae-b953-68e0420d46d5/WEO2016.pdf.

IEA, *World Energy Outlook 2017*, Executive Summary, 2017, https://iea.blob.core.windows.net/assets/4a50d774-5e8c-457e-bcc9-513357f9b2fb/World_Energy_Outlook_2017.pdf.

IEA, *World Energy Outlook 2018*, Executive Summary, 2018, https://iea.blob.core.windows.net/assets/77ecf96c-5f4b-4d0d-9d93-d81b938217cb/World_Energy_Outlook_2018.pdf.

IEA, *World Energy Outlook Special Report 2016: Energy and Air Pollution*, 2016, https://iea.blob.core.windows.net/assets/6b75c4ae-e633-4fa0-9569-b28e226e6103/WorldEnergyOutlookSpecialReport2016EnergyandAirPollution.pdf.

IPCC, *Renewable Energy Sources and Climate Change Mitigation*, Special Report of the Intergovernmental Panel on Climate Change, Cambridge: Cambridge University Press, 2009.

IRENA, *Renewable Capacity Statistics*, 2017, www.irena.org/publica-tions/2017/Mar/Renewable-Capacity-Statistics-2017.

IRENA, *Renewable Energy Statistics*, 2016, www.irena.org/publica-tions/2016/Jul/Renewable-Energy-Statistics-2016.

Jin, Jiaman, *Promoting China-US Subnational Cooperation on Clean Energy Development – Study of Policies on Energy Saving and Renewable Energy in Guangdong Province and California*, November 2009, http://www.geichina.org/_upload/file/climate_change/energy_policy_chn_en.pdf.

Jnicke, Martin, Klaus Jacob (Eds.), *Environmental Governance in Global Perspective New Approaches to Ecological Modernization*, Berlin: Fu Berlin Press, 2006.

Jones, Bruce, David Steven, *The Risk Pivot: Great Powers, International Security, and the Energy Revolution*, Washington, DC: Brookings Institution Press, 2015.

Kassiola, J. J., S. Guo (Eds.), *China's Environmental Crisis*: *Domestic and Global Political Impacts and Responses*, Basingstoke and New York: Palgrave Macmillan, 2010.

Kidney, Sean and Beate Sonerud, *Green Bonds Can Help Plug the Climate Finance Gap*, April 12, 2015, www.Chinadialogue.net/article/show/single/en/8398-Green-bonds-can-help-plug-the-climate-finance-gap.

Klare, Michael T., *The Race for What's Left*; *The Global Scramble for the World's Last Resources*, New York; Metropolitan Books, 2012.

Lesage, Dries, Thijs Van de Graaf (Eds.), *Rising Powers and Multilateral Institutions*, New York: Palgrave Macmillan, 2015.

Mendon, Ç. A. M., D. Jacobs, B. K. Sovacool, *Powering the Green Economy: The Feed-in Tariff Handbook*, London and Sterling, VA: Earth-Scan/James & James, 2010.

Nordhaus, William, *A Question of Balance*: *Weighing the Options on Global Warming Policies*, New Haven, CT: Yale University Press, 2008.

The Pew Charitable Trusts, *Who Is Winning the Clean Energy Race*? (2012 Edition), www.pewtrusts.org/en/research-and-analysis/reports/2013/04/17/whos-winning-the-clean-energy-race-2012-edition.

REN21, *Key Findings of Renewables of 2016 Global Status Report*, 2016. https://www.ren21.net/wp-content/uploads/2019/05/REN21_GSR2016_KeyFindings_en_10.pdf.

REN21, *Renewables 2010 Global Status Report*, 2010, www.ren21.net/wp-content/uploads/2019/05/GSR2010_Full-Report_English.pdf.

REN21, *Renewables 2013 Global Status Report*, 2013, www.ren21.net/wp-content/uploads/2019/05/GSR2013_Full-Report_English.pdf.

REN21, *Renewables 2014 Global Status Report*, 2014, www.ren21.net/wp-content/uploads/2019/05/GSR2014_Full-Report_English.pdf.

REN21, *Renewables 2015 Global Status Report*, 2015, www.ren21.net/wp-content/uploads/2019/05/GSR2015_Full-Report_English.pdf.

REN21, *Renewables 2016 Global Status Report*, 2016. www.ren21.net/wp-content/uploads/2019/05/REN21_GSR2016_FullReport_en_11.pdf.

REN21, *Renewables 2017 Global Status Report*, www.ren21.net/wp-content/uploads/2019/05/GSR2017_Full-Report_English.pdf.

REN21, *Renewables 2018 Global Status Report*, www.ren21.net/wp-content/uploads/2019/08/Full-Report-2018.pdf.

REN21, *Renewables 2019 Global Status Report*, www.ren21.net/wp-content/uploads/2019/05/gsr_2019_full_report_en.pdf.

Roehrkasten, Sybille, *Global Governance on Renewable Energy; Contrasting the Ideas of the German and the Brazilian Governments*, Wiesbaden: Springer Fachmedien Wiesbaden, 2015.

Stem, Nicholas, *The Economics of Climate Change*: *The Stern Review*, Cambridge: Cambridge University Press, 2007.

Swedish Environment Protection Agency/NatureVards Verkets, *The Top Runner Program in Japan*; *Its Effectiveness and Implication for the EU, Report 5515*, November 2005, http://sh1.ateles.se/epages/miljo.storefront/47960ca200054dde271d526316e40616/UserTemplate/46?Filename=620-5515-1.pdf.

Szyliowicz, Joseph S., Bard O'Neill (Eds.), *The Energy Crisis and U. S. Foreign Policy*, New York: Praeger, 1975.

UNEP, *Financing Renewable Energy in Developing Countries: Drivers and Barriers for Private Finance in sub-Saharan Africa*, United Nations [UN] Environment Programme Report, 2012.

UNEP, *South-South Trade in Renewable Energy – A Trade Flow Analysis of Selected Environmental Goods*, United Nations [UN] Environment Programme Report, 2014.

UNEP, EPO & ICTSD, *Patents and Clean Energy: Bridging the Gap Between Evidence and Policy*, Geneva, Munich, www.epo.org/news-is-sues/issues/clean-energy/study.html.

UNFCGC, *Adoption of the Paris Agreement Decision 1/CP. 21*, Paris, January 2016.

Veziroglu, Nejat (Ed.), *Alternative Energy Sources I–VIII*, Washington, DC: Hemisphere Pub. Corp., 1979–1989.

White House Press Office, *Press Background Briefing on White House Announcement on Auto Emission and Efficiency Standards*, May 18, 2009, https://obamawhitehouse.archives.gov/the-press-office/background-briefing-auto-emissions-and-efficiency-standards.

World Commission on Environment and Development (WCED), *Our Common Future*, Oxford: Oxford Paperbacks, 1987.

(II) Papers

Abraham, David S., "The Battle for New Resources; Minor Minerals in Green Technologies", *RIETI Policy Discussion Paper Series 12-P-005*, March 2012, https://www.rieti.go.jp/jp/publications/pdp/12p005.pdf.

Aden, Nathaniel, Jonathan Sinton, "Environmental Implications of Energy Policy in China", *Environmental Politics*, Vol. 15, No. 2, 2006.

Alicia, García-Herrero, Xu Jianwei, "China's Belt and Road Initiative; Can Europe Expect Trade Gains?", *China & World Economy*, Vol. 25, No. 6, 2017.

Bach, David, Abraham L. Newman, "Transgovernmental Networks and Domestic Policy Convergence; Evidence from Insider Trading Regulation", *International Organization*, Vol. 64, No. 3, 2010.

Benecke, Elisabeth, "Networking for Climate Change; Agency in the Context of Renewable Energy Governance in India", *International Environmental Agreements Politics Law & Economics*, Vol. 11, No. 1, 2011.

BJX, "The Distributed Grid Connection Power Promoted by Li Keqiang", 2013, http://news.bjx.com.cn/html/20130318/423160.shtml.

BJX, "The Operating Rate of PV Polysilicon Enterprises Less than 20% Due to the Dropping Price", *The Website of Polaris Power*, 2012, http://guang-fu.bjx.com.cn/news/20121010/393180.shtml.

Boyd, Olivia, "China's Energy Reform and Climate Policy; The Ideas Motivating Change", *CCEP Working Paper, Centre for Climate Economics & Policy*, Crawford School of Public Policy, the Australian National University, 2012.

Boyd, Olivia, "The Motivations for China's New Energy and Climate Policies", August 14, 2012, www.eastasiaforum.org/2012/08/14/the-motiva-tions-for-chinas-new-energy-and-climate-policies/.

Breyer, Christian et al., "On the Role of Solar Photovoltaics in Global Energy Transition Scenarios", *Progress in Photovoltaics Research & Applications*, Vol. 25, 2016.

Brooks, D. B., "The Challenge of Sustainability; Is Environment and Economics Enough?", *Policy Sciences*, Vol. 25, No. 4, 1992.

BUNR, "Indicative Target of the Federal Republic of Germany for the Consumption of Electricity Produced From Renewable Energy Source in 2010 and Measures to Achieve This Target", *2001, Report from the Federal Republic of Germany Pursuant to Article 3 Para. 2 of UN Directive*, 2001/77/EC.

Cama, Timothy, "Trump; Wind Power 'Kills All Your Birds'", *The Hill*, August 2, 2016, http://thehill.com/policy/energy-environment/290093-trump-wind-power-kills-all-your-birds.

Chan, Sander, Clara Brandi, Steffen Bauer, "Aligning Transnational Climate Actionwith International Climate Governance; The Road From Paris", *Review of European Comparative & International Environmental Law*, Vol. 25, No. 2, 2016.

Chan, Sewell, "U. S. Says, Chinese Fund Breaks Rules", *New York Times*, December 22, 2010.

Cory, Karlynn, Toby Couture, Claire Kreycik, "Feed-in Tariff Policy; Design, Implementation, and RPS Policy Interactions", *Technical Report*, www.nrel.gov/docs/fy09osti/45549.pdf, last accessed on January 26, 2011.

Couture, Toby, Yves Gagnon, "An Analysis of Feed-in Tariff Remuneration Models; Implications for Renewable Energy Investment", *Energy Policy*, Vol. 38, No. 2, 2010.

Cox, Sadie, Eliza Hotchkiss, Dan Bilello, Andrea Watson, Alison Holm, "Bridging Climate Change Resilience and Mitigation in the Electricity Sector Through Renewable Energy and Energy Efficiency", *Emerging Climate Change and Development Topics for Energy Sector Transformation*, November 2017, www.nrel.gov/docs/fyl8osti/67040.pdf.

Criekemans, David, "The Geopolitics of Renewable Energy; Different or Similar to the Geopolitics of Conventional Energy?", *ISA Annual Convention Paper*, 2011, https://exploringgeopolitics.org/wp-content/uploads/2019/01/Criekemans_David_Geopolitics_Renewable_Energy.pdf.

De Melo, Conrado Augustus, Gilberto de Martino Jannuzzi, Sergio Valdir Bajay, "Nonconventional Renewable Energy Governance in Brazil; Lessons to Learn from the German Experience", *Renewable & Sustainable Energy Reviews*, Vol. 61, 2016.

Dreyer, Lana, "Renewables; Do They Matter for Foreign Policy?", *Brief Issue of European Union Institute for Security Studies*, No. 3, 2013.

Drezner, Daniel W., "Globalization and Policy Convergence", *International Studies Review*, Vol. 3, No. 2, 2001.

Elkins, Zachary, Beth A. Simmons, "On Waves, Clusters, and Diffusion; A Conceptual Framework", *The Annals of the American Academy of Political and Social Science*, Vol. 598, March 2005.

European Commission, "Critical Raw Materials for the EU; Report of the Ad-Hoc Working Group on Defining Critical Raw Materials", Vol. 39, July 2010, https://www.euromines.org/files/what-we-do/sustainable-development-issues/2010-report-critical-raw-materials-eu.pdf.

Federal Ministry of Economics and Technology (BMWi) of Germany, "Energy Concept for an Environmentally Sound, Reliable and Affordable Energy Supply", 2010, https://cdn.climatepolicyradar.org/navigator/DEU/2010/energy-concept-for-an-environmentally-sound-reliable-and-affordable-energy-supply_ce0f139a23a921c29e1fdbdb92cdd36d.pdf.

Federal Ministry of Education and Research, "Federal Government to Open Lead Markets for the Environment", November 12, 2008.

Friberg, Lars, "Varieties of Carbon Governance; The Clean Development Mechanism in Brazil: A Success Story Challenged", *The Journal of Environment & Development*, Vol. 18, No. 4, 2009.

Gawel, Erik, S. Strunz, P. Lehmann, "Germany's Energy Transition Under Attack; Is There an Inscrutable German Sonderweg?", *Nature & Culture*, Vol. 8, No. 2, 2013.

Goodell, Jeff, "Obama's Climate Challenge", *Rolling Stone*, Vol. 1175, January 31, 2013.

Groen, L., A. Niemann, "The European Union at the Copenhagen Climate Negotiations; A Case of Contested EU Actorness and Effectiveness", *International Relations*, No. 27, 2013.

Guan, Ting, Joergen Delman, "Energy Policy Design and China's Local Climate Governance: Energy Efficiency and Renewable Energy Policies in Hangzhou", *Journal of Chinese Governance*, Vol. 2, No. 1, 2017.

Guerra, Flávia, "Mapping Offshore Renewable Energy Governance", *Marine Policy*, Vol. 89, 2018.

Hale, Thomas, "'All Hands on Deck'; The Paris Agreement and Non-state Climate Action", *Global Environmental Politics*, Vol. 16, No. 3, 2016.

Hatch, M. T., "Chinese Politics, Energy Policy, and the International Climate Change Negotiations", in P. G. Harris (Ed.), *Global Warming and East Asia: The Domestic and International Politics of Climate Change*, London and New York: Taylor & Francis Group, 2003.

Heggelund, Gørild, "China's Climate Change Policy; Domestic and International Developments", *Asian Perspective*, Vol. 31, No. 2, 2007.

Heuskel, Dieter, Philipp Gerbert, Stefan Schlotjunker, Patrick Herhold, Jens Burchardt, "Is Germany Pioneering a Global Transformation of the Energy Sector? Toward a New Balance of Power", March 13, 2013, www.bcg.com/publications/2013/energy-environment-toward-a-new-balance-of-power.aspx.

Hodgson, A., "Climate of Change; A Foreign Policy Analysis of China's Participation in International Environmental Agreements", Thesis of the University of Kansas, 2011, www.irena.org/menu/index.aspx?mnu=cat&PriMenuID=30&CatID=142.

IRENA, "China, IRENA to Co-Host International Forum on Energy Transitions", www.irena.org/News/Description.aspx?NType=A&mnu=cat&PriMenuID=16&CatID=84&News_ID=429, last accessed on November 2, 2015.

Jacob, Klaus et al., "Lead Market for Environmental Innovations", *Physica-Verlag HD*, Vol. 27, No. 1, 2005.

Jones, Bruce, David Steven, Emily O'Brien, "Fueling a New Disorder? The New Geopolitical and Security Consequences of Energy", *Project on International Order and Strategy*, Brookings, www.brookings.edu/~/media/Research/Files/Papers/2014/04/14%20geopolitical%20security%20consequences%20energy%20jones/14%20geopolitical%20security%20energy%20jones%20steven_fixed.pdf.

Jordan, Andrew J., Dave Huitema, Mikael Hildén, et al., "Emergence of Polycentric Climate Governance and Its Future Prospects", *Nature Climate Change*, Vol. 11, No. 5, 2015.

Jun, Aruma, "Top Runner Program; Japan", *Paper Presented at Workshop on Best Practices in Practices in Policies and Measures*, Copenhagen, April 11–13, 2000.

Karnrnen, Daniel, "Renewable Energy in United States Foreign Policy", *Golden Gate University Law Review*, Vol. 36, 2010.

Knill, Christoph, Andrea Lenschow, "Compliance, Communication and Competition; Patterns of EU Environmental Policy Making and Their Impact of Policy Convergence", *European Environment*, Vol. 15, No. 2, 2005.

Kooroshy, Jaakko, Rem Korteweg, Marjolein de Ridder, "Rare Earth Elements and Strategic Mineral Policy", *The Hague; The Hague Centre for Strategic Studies & TNO*, 2010, http://static.hcss.nl/files/uploads/33.pdf.

Kumar, A. A., K. Karthick, "Clean Energy Resources Available in India", *International Journal of Environmental Science & Development*, Vol. 2, No. 1, 2011.

Kumar, Sanjay, "Green Climate Fund Faces Slew of Criticism", *Nature*, Vol. 527, 2015.

Leal-Arcas, Rafael, Stephen Minas, "The Micro Level; Insights from Specific Policy Areas; Mapping the International and European Governance of Renewable Energy", *Yearbook of European Law*, Vol. 35, No. 1, December 2016.

Lema, Adrian, Kristian Ruby, "Between Fragmented Authoritarianism and Policy Coordination: Creating a Chinese Market for Wind Energy", *Energy Policy*, Vol. 35, No. 7, 2007.

Lewis, Joanna I., "China's Strategic Priorities in International Climate Change Negotiations", *Washington Quarterly*, Vol. 31, No. 1, 2008.

Lewis, Joanna I., "Climate Change and Security; Examining China's Challenges in a Warming World", *International Affairs*, Vol. 85, No. 6, 2009.

Li, Y., W. Cao, "Framework of Laws and Policies on Renewable Energy and Relevant Systems in China under the Background of Climate Change", *Vermont Journal of Environmental Law*, Vol. 13, 2012.

Liang, Wei, "Changing Climate? China's New Interest in Global Climate Change Negotiations", in J. J. Kassiola and S. Guo (Eds.), *China's Environmental Crisis; Domestic and Global Political Impacts and Responses*, Basingstoke and New York: Palgrave Macmillan, 2010.

Lieberthal, Kenneth G., "US-China Clean Energy Cooperation; The Road Ahead", *Energy Security Initiative at Brookings*, 2009, https://www.brookings.edu/wp-content/uploads/2016/06/09_us_china_energy_cooperation_lieberthal.pdf.

Marsters, Peter V., Jennifer L. Turner, "Cooperative Competitors: Potential of U. S. China Clean Energy Cooperation", *China Environmental Forum Brief*, Washington, DC: Woodrow Wilson International Center for Scholars, 2012.

McGarrity, John, "China Wind Boom to Continue in 2015, But Grid Reform Needed", *Chinadialogue*, January 4, 2015, www.chinadialogue.org.cn/article/show/single/en/7827-China-wind-boom-to-continue-in-2-15-but-grid-reform-needed-report.

Mendonçga, M., D. Jacobs, "Feed-in Tariffs Go Global; Policy in Practice", *Renewable Energy World*, Vol. 12, No. 4, 2009.

Messner, Dirk, Jennifer Morgan, "Germany Needs an Energy Transformation Foreign Policy", *German Development Institute Report*, 2013, https://www.idos-research.de/uploads/media/German-Development-Institute_Messner_Morgan_07.01.2013.pdf.

Moni, Monir Hossain, "Why Japan's Development Aid Matters Most for Dealing with Global Environmental Problems", *Asia-Pacific Review*, Vol. 16, No. 1, 2009.

Obama, Barack, "The Irreversible Momentum of Clean Energy", *Science*, Vol. 355, 2017.

Okano-Heijmans, Maaike, "Japan's 'Green' Economic Diplomacy: Environmental and Energy Technology and Foreign Relations", *Pacific Review*, Vol. 25, No. 3, 2012.

Orr, Franklin M., "Addressing Climate Change with Clean Energy Technology", *ACS Energy Letters*, 2016, https://pubs.acs.org/doi/pdf/10.1021/acsenergylett.6b00136.

Park, Sunjoo, "State Renewable Energy Governance; Policy Instruments, Markets, or Citizens", *Review of Policy Research*, Vol. 32, No. 3, 2015.

Pereira, Guillermo Ivan, Patrícia Pereira da Silva, "Energy Efficiency Governance in the EU-28; Analysis of Institutional, Human, Financial, and Political Dimensions", *Energy Efficiency*, Vol. 10, No. 5, 2017.

RalphLuken, Frank Van Rompaey, "Drivers for and Barriers to Environmentally Sound Technology Adoption by Manufacturing Plants in Nine Developing Countries", *Journal of Cleaner Production*, Vol. 16, No. 1, 2008.

Ridder, Marjoleinde, "The Geopolitics of Mineral Resources for Renewable Energy Technologies", *The Report of Hague Center for Strategic Studies*, 2011, https://hcss.nl/wp-content/uploads/2013/08/The_Geopolitics_of_Mineral_Resources_for_Renewable_Energy_Technologies.pdf.

Robins, Nick, "What Next for Green Finance?", January 16, 2017, www.huffingtonpost.com/nick-robins/2017-what-next-for-green_b_14203706.html.

Roehrkasten, Sybille, Kirsten Westphal, "IRENA and Germany's Foreign Renewable Energy Policy Aiming at Multilevel Governance", *SWP Working Papers*, 2013, https://www.swp-berlin.org/publications/products/arbeitspapiere/Rks_Wep_FG08WorkingPaper_2013.pdf.

Scarlat, Nicolae et al., "Renewable Energy Policy Framework and Bioenergy Contribution in the European Union: An Overview from National Renewable Energy Action Plans and Progress Reports", *Renewable and Sustainable Energy Reviews*, No. 51, 2015.

Schreurs, Miranda A., "Assessing Japan's Role as a Global Environmental Leader", *Policy & Society*, Vol. 23, No. 1, 2004.

Schuman, Sara, Alvin Lin, "China's Renewable Energy Law and Its Impact on Renewable Power in China; Progress, Challenges and Recommendations for Improving Implementation", *Energy Policy*, Vol. 51, 2012.

Seiwert, Martin, Matthias Hohensee, Matthias Kamp, "Hot Technology to Protect the Earth", *German News*, Vol. 27, No. 1, 2007.

Sovacool, Benjamin K., Vlado Vivoda. "A Comparison of Chinese, Indian, and Japanese Perceptions of Energy Security", *Asian Survey*, Vol. 52, No. 5, 2012.

Stahl, Anna, Claudio A. Schioppa, "The Renewable Energy Opportunity for EU-China Collaboration", *The Asia Papers of BICCS*, Vol. 7, 2013.

Steiner, Achim, et al., "International Institutional Arrangements in Support of Renewable Energy", in Dirk Assmann et al. (Eds.), *Renewable Energy, A global Review of Technologies, Policies and Markets*, London: Sterling VA, 2006.

Suding, Paul H., Philippe Lempp, "The Multifaceted Institutional Landscape and Processes of International Renewable Energy Policy", *International Association for Energy Economics*, 2007, https://www.researchgate.net/profile/Paul-Suding/publication/265045597_The_Multifaceted_Institutional_Landscape_and_Processes_of_International_Renewable_Energy_Policy_A_Renewable_Energy_Policy_Jungle/links/575fc97108ae414b8e54a352/The-Multifaceted-Institutional-Landscape-and-Processes-of-International-Renewable-Energy-Policy-A-Renewable-Energy-Policy-Jungle.pdf.

Tews, Kerstin, "The Diffusion of Environmental Policy Innovations; Cornerstones of an Analytical Framework", in Martin Jnicke and Klaus Jacob (Eds.), *Environmental Governance in Global Perspective New Approaches to Ecological Modernization*, Berlin: Fu Berlin, 2006.

Thiebaut, Renata, "The Green BRICS; How to Cooperate and Leverage Renewable Energy Strategies", *Conjuntura Internacional*, Vol. 10, 2013.

Tracy, Carty, "Righting Two Wrongs; Making a New Global Climate Fund Work for Poor People", *Oxfam Policy & Practice Climate Change & Resilience*, Vol. 6, 2010.

UNEP, "Global Green New Deal; Environmentally-Focused Investment Historic Opportunity for 21st Century Prosperity and Job Creation", *Press Release*, October 22, 2008.

UNFCCC, "Streamlined and Consolidated Text", *Ad Hoc Working Group on the Durban Platform for Enhanced Action*, Second Session, Part Nine, June 11, 2015.

United States Environmental Protection Agency, "EPA to Review the Clean Power Plan Under President Trump's Executive Order", www.epa.gov/newsreleases/epa-review-clean-power-plan-under-president-trumps-executive-order.

Wallace, William, Sarah Kurtz, Bingxin Xie, "China-US Collaboration on Renewable Energy Standards, Testing, and Certification", *China Renewable Energy*, Vol. 2, No. 2, July 2013.

Wang, Feng, H. Yin, S. Li, "China's Renewable Energy Policy: Commitments and Challenges", *Energy Policy*, Vol. 38, No. 4, 2010.

Wang, Yao, Zhi Qiang, "The Role of Green Finance in Environmental Protection: Two Aspects of Market Mechanism and Policies", *Energy Procedia*, Vol. 104, 2016.
World Resources Institute, "A Closer Look at Brazil's New Climate Plan (IN-DC)", September 30, 2015, www.wri.org.cn/en/node/41350.
World Resources Institute, "A Closer Look at China's New Climate Plan (IN-DC)", July 2, 2015, www.wri.org/print/43035.
Wright, Glen, "The International Renewable Energy Agency; A Global Voice for the Renewable Energy Era?", *Renewable Energy Law & Poly Review*, November 4, 2012.
Yergin, Daniel, "Energy Security in the 1990s", *Foreign Affairs*, Vol. 67, No. 1, 1988.
Zaman, Khalid, Alias bin Abdullah, Anwar Khan, et al., "Dynamic Linkages Among Energy Consumption, Environment, Health and Wealth in BRICS Countries: Green Growth Key to Sustainable Development", *Renewable & Sustainable Energy Reviews*, Vol. 56, 2016.
Zhang, Peidong et al., "Opportunities and Challenges for Renewable Energy Policy in China", *Renewable & Sustainable Energy Reviews*, Vol. 13, No. 2, 2009.

Index

Note: Page numbers in *italics* indicate a figure and page numbers in **bold** indicate a table on the corresponding page.

For Product Safety Concerns and Information please contact our EU
representative GPSR@taylorandfrancis.com
Taylor & Francis Verlag GmbH, Kaufingerstraße 24, 80331 München, Germany

www.ingramcontent.com/pod-product-compliance
Lightning Source LLC
LaVergne TN
LVHW020924061026
849535LV00011B/3709
* 9 7 8 1 0 3 2 5 6 1 0 5 9 *